ASTROLOGICAL PATTERNS

ASTROLOGICAL

Frances Sakoian
and Betty Caulfield

PATTERNS

The Key to Self-Discovery

PERENNIAL LIBRARY
Harper & Row, Publishers, New York
Cambridge, Philadelphia, San Francisco, London
Mexico City, São Paulo, Singapore, Sydney

A hardcover edition of this book is published by Harper & Row, Publishers, Inc.

 For information address Harper & Row, Publishers, Inc., 10 East 53rd Street, New York, N.Y. 10022. Published simultaneously in Canada by Fitzhenry & Whiteside Limited, Toronto.

First PERENNIAL LIBRARY edition published 1989

Designed by Sidney Feinberg

Library of Congress Cataloging-in-Publication Data

Sakoian, Frances.
Astrological patterns.

Bibliography: p.
Includes index.
1. Astrology. I. Caulfield, Betty. II. Title.
BF1708.1.S243 1989 133.5 88-24445
ISBN 0-06-091547-1 (pbk.)

89 90 91 92 93 FG 10 9 8 7 6 5 4 3 2 1

This book is dedicated to our
many students all over the world

Whatever is born, or done, in this moment of time,
has the qualities of this moment of time.

—C. G. Jung

Contents

PART III
SIGN, HOUSE, AND PLANETARY PATTERNS

Acknowledgments

Our thanks and gratitude to Caroline Rains for her loyalty and dedication and for the long hours that went into the preparation of this book.

Our special thanks to Fred Johnson for his time and assistance with the mathematical computations and in compiling the Ascendant and Midheaven Tables for this book.

We are also grateful to our husbands, Thomas Caulfield and Sark Sakoian, for their encouragement and support during the writing of this book.

Our thanks and appreciation to "Joan Stables" for allowing us to use her horoscope as an example chart for interpretation.

Our thanks also extend to Nahum J. Waxman, editor in charge of our book at Harper & Row, for his cooperation and support in getting this book to you.

Foreword

Long ago an Eastern sage told his apprentice about the journey through life that every illumined master must make.

"At first," began the sage, "this would-be master is only a seeker. He looks about and sees the mountains, trees, rivers and lakes, and even a vast ocean. He sees them as he has always seen them—they are there as they have always been there. All around him, everything seems just as it has always been, and now he seeks to look elsewhere, to go somewhere he has never been, experience something he has never experienced. In his mind, it is this 'something else' that will bring him knowledge, understanding, wisdom, and mastery of life.

"So he leaves home, seeking that which he has not yet experienced. As he travels, he sees many new things: new mountains, new trees, new lakes and rivers, and even vast new oceans. Everything appears to be different from what he knew before, and he is quite impressed with the splendor of Nature. These wonders do indeed bring about a change in his consciousness, for he is now seeing with new eyes. So he continues this journey, seeking evermore new experiences, new visions that will stimulate his thirsty mind, for as a seeker, he is no longer satisfied, not yet content, and yearns for more.

"After many long years of wandering, this seeker finally pauses and reflects upon his journey. Now that I have traveled far and wide, he thinks to himself, and have seen so many things of this world, I realize that everything is just so incredible. In fact, it is so incredible and amazing that nothing ceases to amaze me anymore. It all works! It is all so beautifully organized and arranged in perfect order. After seeking so much, I finally see that it is so simple, and it is truly the simplicity of it all that is amazing!

"And as this seeker looks about him, he suddenly becomes aware of what it was all about. To his wonderment, he sees once more that those mountains are indeed mountains, as all mountains are mountains. He sees that trees are indeed trees, and rivers and lakes are rivers and lakes, and even the oceans are really vast oceans.

"In that moment of vision, he sees that all of Nature is indeed what it is and always has been. At that moment, he understands, and becomes a master of what he is."

The field of astrology has changed so much since the mid-1960s that it bears only a superficial resemblance to what it was four thousand–plus years previously. The amount of data and new knowledge accumulated by our half brother astronomy, combined with the brilliant applications of modern-day geocosmic researchers, has expanded the field of astrology into what appears to be a totally new study. No longer does the image of a fortune-telling, crystal-ball-gazing, determinist-minded fatalist describe today's astrologer.

Instead we see the modern-day astrologer as a sophisticated counselor, a diligent researcher, possessed by an unending curiosity to know and apply anything dealing with celestial conditions to the human or world-life condition.

In the past fifteen years, this yearning for knowledge, combined with its availability, has resulted in a literal renaissance for the field of astrology. Relationships between psychology, business cycles, health, interpersonal relationships, and growing patterns in the plant kingdom are being correlated to movements in the heavens above. So rapid is the expansive growth of astrology that it can now offer an exciting challenge to the most intellectual, philosophically inclined minds of our modern age—without fear that the knowledge will ever be exhausted in a single lifetime of study!

During this renaissance, practitioners in the astrological community have been exposed to a wide variety of new applications of their art. The excitement of "this new technique" and "that new concept" generated a collective wave of enthusiasm to explore heretofore unknown or untried avenues. It seemed like everyone became a seeker of this "new energy"; everyone in the astrological field seemed "turned on" mentally.

The intensity of this enthusiasm has not died down, or passed away.

Innovative techniques and applications of astrology abound continually, and the beauty of it is that they all work.

But at some point in the astrologer's path of study, the question inevitably arises, "Now that I have looked into all of these fields and possible ways of application, which do I choose?" One must now commence the process of discernment, limitation, concentration, and refinement of tools. Otherwise the ever-expanding wealth of knowledge will surely overwhelm and confuse.

This is where Frances Sakoian and Betty Caulfield's *Astrological Patterns: The Key to Self-Discovery* fits in so beautifully. In this book they lucidly explain the basic principles of astrology, show with refinement effective uses of these principles, while at the same time introducing innovative new ideas. But please do not misunderstand one important feature of Sakoian and Caulfield's work: Though they introduce a generous amount of rich material, it all connects, it all relates, and hence they keep intact the simplicity of the structure while tastefully showing the reader exciting applications of this basic foundation.

As one reads the book, one instinctively gets the impression that years of study and application are transmitting their wisdom onto the pages. And it is true. The reader is probably already aware that he or she is dealing with two of the world's most astute and prolific astrological writers. Frances and Betty are indeed largely responsible for, and certainly two of the pioneers of, the modern-day astrological renaissance. Frances's numerous high-quality books have blazed the path for many of our present-day seekers, including this writer. It is particularly gratifying to look up now and see that Sakoian and Caulfield provide us with yet another significant work and message: that even though all of these new and exciting developments are occurring in our field, the beauty of the simplicity still remains. And the *real* art to our study, as the authors have realized through years of exploration and practice, is in the *application* of the foundations.

Frances Sakoian and Betty Caulfield understand the foundations of astrological practice. They have explored many of the new dimensions offered in our field—have in fact taught us many of these techniques. Once again, it is our privilege to experience yet another level of these brilliant authors' enlightenment. For whether they are aware of it or not, they have served as sages to a whole generation of apprentices—and they continue to do so through this book.

—RAYMOND A. MERRIMAN

Birmingham, Michigan
April 10, 1979

About This Book

This volume is the fourth of a series that analyzes the major areas of astrology. Although there are many approaches to astrology, this book deals with astrological patterns or techniques in a simple, step-by-step manner, enabling the individual to see at a glance the strong and weak points of the personality. This book will spotlight the way an individual functions and the way he or she deals with various human experiences. We feel that this book is a valuable tool in understanding the various modes of individual behavior.

The hemispheric patterns deal with an overall view of the individual's particular orientation and general approach to life. Patterns of Mental Chemistry deal with the way an individual receives impressions from outside stimuli and rationalizes experiences. The Natural Disposition patterns deal with the individual's psychological slanting, which can be very subtle. The temperament- type patterns give an overall view of the individual's basic drives. Dynamic Focus patterns indicate where he or she needs to accept the challenge of accomplishment or cooperation.

These patterns will help the individual to understand his or her own makeup and structure of being. It is our hope that they will be used to understand the life process and to bring a new attitude toward life fulfillment.

Included in this book are Ascendant and Midheaven Tables, which can be used in setting up a horoscope wheel, as well as a simple method for erecting a horoscope and interpolating the house cusps.

Included also is a professional delineation with rules and procedures that can be applied in reading any natal horoscope.

It is our hope that eventually this text will be used in universities and colleges throughout the world.

PART I

ABOUT ASTROLOGY

1

History of Astrology

When and where did astrology begin? There is no accurate recorded history of astrology. The subject is so vast that many believe that it was originally brought to Earth by great beings of superior intelligence who came to this planet to guide humanity.

According to Josephus, the celebrated Jewish historian, Adam was instructed in astrology by divine inspiration. Adam taught it to his sons, and Seth became very proficient in astrology. After Seth, the first positive proof that astrology had taken an important place in humanity's scheme of things is in the Chinese records. In these records it is told that the Emperor Yao divided the twelve signs of the Zodiac by the twenty-eight mansions of the Moon; this was done 2,317 years before the Christian era.

Before the dawn of recorded history, zodiacs were constructed by various ancient cultures, which would presuppose a previous knowledge of astrology. According to some of the most probable estimates, astrology goes back to twenty-six thousand years before the Christian era, indicating that its origin is lost in the dimness of antiquity.

Evidence of the influence of the stars upon human beings was recognized by the Egyptians many centuries before Christ. There was a tradition that the kings were astrologers as well as priests. Jean François Champollion, the great French pioneer in Egyptology, found in the tomb of Rameses V a papyrus left there to help the dead king on his journey to the other world. It gave the ascending stars and their influence for every day of a whole year.

According to Dr. H. J. Spendon of the Peabody Museum of Harvard, remarking on the amazing knowledge of the Mayans, their record of eclipses from the eighth to the fifteenth century was 70 percent accurate, which is astounding, considering that only 10 percent of the eclipses can be seen from Central America.

The Babylonians developed an extraordinary civilization in which the chief science was astrology; by the eighth century before Christ, the Chaldeans had become the ruling class in Babylonia, and their very name became a synonym for astrology.

Ptolemy, a native of Egypt who lived in Alexandria in the second century A.D., was the main authority on astronomy until the time of Copernicus, fourteen hundred years later. Ptolemy wrote a treatise on astrology, called *Tetrabiblos;* he also wrote one hundred aphorisms on astrology, called *Centiloquy*.

The Arabs obtained scientific and astrological books from the Byzantines. These books were translated into Latin.

The Druids were also great astrologers, but much of their learning was lost in the Dark Ages.

During the Middle Ages there was a revival of astrology. The knowledge of astrology seems to have come from the Byzantine Empire through the Arabic translations. As the Arabs grew in knowledge, they developed writers who wrote about astrology. Arabic textbooks were the standard textbooks down to the seventeenth century. Longfellow, when translating Dante into English verse, studied these textbooks in order to follow the astronomical and astrological references in the *Divine Comedy*. The basic structure of Dante's *Divine Comedy* is astrological.

Tycho Brahe was an astronomer-astrologer who wrote horoscopes for the king's family in 1577.

Johannes Kepler (1571–1630) was the first assistant astronomer to Tycho Brahe; he succeeded him as the principal mathematician to the emperor. He was a good astrologer and did some valuable work on progressions, directions, and aspects which is used in astrology today. Kepler chose his second wife by means of astrology.

Many of the greatest mathematical discoveries came as a result of a search for better techniques in making astrological calculations. John Napier (1550–1617), a Scottish mathematician, was interested in astrology. He invented logarithms in order to simplify some of the astrological calculations.

In India even to this day astrology is used in ascertaining the compatibility of suggested marriage partners, thus reducing undesirable friction to a minimum. Comparison charts are also widely used in this modern day.

In ancient times the words *astrology* and *astronomy* were used interchangeably. In our day there is a parting of the ways. The astronomers study the motions, magnitudes, distances, and physical constitutions of the heavenly bodies. The astrologers study the effects of the movements of the heavenly bodies upon the Earth and its inhabitants.

Copernicus rediscovered the fact that the Earth travels around the Sun instead of vice versa. This rediscovery did not upset astrologers because we live on the Earth, not on the Sun. The Sun is the center of our solar system, and we are affected by the planets and the signs as they relate to our earthly position.

Heliocentric astrology reduces the heliocentric position to geocentric terms; it is more or less experimental and used by very few astrologers today.

Astrology and the Bible

There are many astrological references in the Old and New Testaments in the Bible; however, most lay people do not recognize them because they are veiled in symbolism.

Perhaps the most famous example of biblical astrology is found in the blessing of the twelve tribes by Jacob (Genesis, 48, 49). There were twelve sons of Jacob and twelve sons of Ishmael (Genesis, 25). Jacob gathered his twelve sons to bless them, and it is quite evident that in describing the twelve sons each son or tribe corresponded to one of the twelve zodiacal signs.

Ezekiel described his new city of Jerusalem as having twelve gates. It was to be a square city with three gates on each side. The twelve gates represented the twelve zodiacal signs. The square city with the four sides represented the four signs belonging to each quadruplicity: Cardinal, Fixed, and Mutable. The three gates on each side represented the elements, or triplicities, in astrology.

Genesis 1:28 states: "and God blessed them, and God said unto them, be fruitful, multiply and replenish the earth, and subdue it, and have dominion over the fish of the sea, over the fowl of the air, and over every living thing that moveth upon the earth, and everything in between."

Astrologers ask the question: Do humans want to have dominion over the birds of the air, or the types of birds that are indigenous to any place on Earth? As a rule, humans do not occupy themselves with that kind of dominion. In astrological symbolism the birds of the air represent the intellectual Air signs of Gemini, Libra, and Aquarius. The birds of the air represent the thoughts that we allow to pass through the discriminating part of our minds, which in turn affect our health, work performance, and life itself. In astrology the individual is taught that it is a discipline to observe and eliminate the kinds of thoughts that are detrimental to the well-being of an individual. This kind of dominion is a real challenge because the thoughts allowed into the mind will mold the life expression. For instance, thoughts of resentment, anger, fear, or any kind of negative thinking interfere with the creative potential. If this is doubted, try a fast of the mind where negative thoughts of any kind are not permitted to enter the mind. True dominion of the mind will truly bring out man created in God's image.

The Bible states that man is to have dominion over the fish of the sea. In astrology the fish of the sea represent the various kinds of emotions. Emotional responses often get humanity into undesirable situations. When an individual does not have dominion or control over the emotions, he or she is at the mercy of forces that interfere with creative potential.

"Every living thing that moveth upon the earth" relates to the Earth signs: Taurus, Virgo, and Capricorn. These Earth signs represent the various resources of the planet that the Bible says are to be multiplied and replenished.

For example, inherent in a tiny apple seed are a whole apple orchard; apples for cider, applesauce, apple pies, bakeries, truck routes, and deep-freezes to store apple turnovers. The apples can be mixed with cranberries and called cranapple. The apple obeys the law of creation, which is the law of love in Nature. It gives to what is not itself. It says, "Take me, use me, multiply my uses, make me greater than I am." Humans alone do not observe this law of love—that we give of ourselves totally and completely to our relationships and our environment—because humans do not understand this principle of love. They withhold love. Humans stand on holy ground because of who they are and where they are; they are the only creatures able to give to their environment and relationships that which is needed at any given moment. Do they obey this law of love?

"Everything in between" represents the element of Fire and symbolizes the law of love which is the lesson of the Fire signs, which are the creative, inspirational signs of Aries, Leo, and Sagittarius. This law of love and creativity should permeate human thoughts and emotions and human use of the resources of this planet. For example, the creative inspiration to build a house must be intermingled with love for the resources represented by the tree that gives up its life to make the house possible.

All the emotions, attitudes, and skills that deal with this creative effort will determine the strength, beauty, and utility of the house.

This astrological symbology found in Genesis and other parts of the Bible gives deep insights into the laws of the universe and of humankind. When humans finally have true dominion over the elements, the promise of a new Heaven and Earth will become a reality.

To the astrologer the astrological symbology of the Bible renders the highest interpretation or means by which humans can understand themselves and their ultimate place in the universal scheme of things.

Suggested Reading:

The Bible and the Stars, by Corinne Helene
Beethoven's Nine Symphonies, by Corinne Helene
The Labours of Hercules, by Alice Bailey

Astrology in Literature

What causes humans to hate, love, aspire, or fall? All teachers try to discover new ways to express old truths in dealing with the roots of human conduct that are hidden from the eye. Why is the same scent sweet to one and not to another? Why is the same sound noise to one and music to another? Why is one individual practical and another flighty? Why is it that when the same Sun is shining down on three people, one is uncomfortably hot, another feels cool, and the third feels very comfortable?

In "The Wife of Bath" from *The Canterbury Tales,* the Wife attributed her amorous nature to her horoscope aspects. She had five husbands; she describes herself astrologically:

For certes, I am all Venerien
In feeling, and in my heart Marceen.
Venus gave me lust, my wantonness,
And Mars gave me my sturdy brazenness.
My ascendant was Taur, and Mars therein,
Alas, alas, that ever love was sin.

She describes her fifth husband as incompatible because of his scholarly ways and lack of concern with the flesh:

Mercurie loveth wisdom and science,
And Venus loveth riot and extravagance.
And thus, God woot, Mercurie is desolate
In Pisces, where Venus exalted.

She is describing her horoscope as having a Taurus ascendant, with Mars in Taurus, indicating a preoccupation with sex and sensuality. Mars rules the desire principle and is not happily placed in Taurus because it is in the sign of its detriment. Her husband had Mercury in Pisces. Chaucer said that Mercury is desolate in Pisces, where Venus is exalted. This is pure astrology, indicating Chaucer had a profound knowledge of the subject.

Many of the passages of the Old English poems are unintelligible without some knowledge of astrology. For example, Chaucer in "The Knight's Tale" says,

Fortune has given us this adversity
Some wicked aspect or disposition
of Saturn by some constellation
So stood the heavens when we were born.

Again:

The cruel Mars has slain this marriage,
Unfortunate ascendant tortuous
O Mars, O influence; as in this case
O feeble Moon, unhappy been thy pace.

Chaucer here once again speaks of the stress positions of the planets.

In the second part of *Faust,* Goethe has the emperor telling the people of his auspicious horoscope:

You meet beneath a fortunate star;
Welfare and luck are now the aspects royal.

Goethe also wrote an astrological description of his delayed birth, in which he added, "These auspicious Aspects which the Astrologers subsequently interpreted for me may have been the cause of my preservation."

Wordsworth observes in "Lubbock": "The sage has read the stars with skill so true."

In his writing, John Ruskin states: "The greatness or smallness of man is, in the most conclusive sense, determined for him at his birth."

Spenser in his *Faerie Queene* says: "What evil starre on you hath frowned?"

Coleridge writes: "And this was Jupiter my father's star."

Shakespeare's many references to astrology indicate a remarkable knowledge of the subject, as evidenced by the following verses:

In *Romeo and Juliet* (the star-crossed lovers):

> My mind misgives some consequence yet hanging in the stars.

Again:

> Shake the yoke of inauspicious stars from this wearied flesh.

In *Henry IV:*

> O malignant and ill boding Stars;
> Now art come unto a feast of death.

In *Richard III:*

> At their birth good stars were opposite.

In *The Tempest:*

> I find my zeneth doth depend upon a most auspicious star.

In *King Lear:*

> It is the stars, the stars above us govern our condition.

One of Shakespeare's characters states: "I was born sir, where the Crab was ascending: all my affairs go backwards."

In *All's Well That Ends Well,* a whole dialogue is based on astrology:

> "You were born under a charitable star."
> "Under Mars I."
> "I especially think under Mars."
> "Why under Mars?"
> "The Wars have kept you under that you must needs be born under Mars."

Another quote from Shakespeare:

> Why, man, he doth bestride the narrow world
> Like a Colossus; and we petty men
> Walk under his huge legs, and peep about
> To find ourselves dishonourable graves.
> Men at some time are masters of their fates:
> The fault, dear Brutus, is not in our stars,
> But in ourselves, that we are underlings.

Humans are at times masters of their fate. At this point, a little analogy will clarify this statement. Suppose the heavens are dark, the winds are blowing, and the snow is starting to fall. The weatherman states that there is a blizzard on its way, and John Doe has an important appointment in town. If he is determined to keep the appointment and if he is wise, he will make certain that he is dressed warmly and his car is equipped to operate in the storm; then, should it fail him, he will be warm enough to survive. Should John Doe go out in the storm ill-prepared and should his car fail, he is liable to get pneumonia or freeze to death. However, he has another choice. John Doe can decide that he does not want to battle the elements and can try to arrange the meeting for some other time.

John Doe can do nothing to stop the blizzard; he has jurisdiction only over what action, if any, he will take regarding it. In this way, at times man is master of his fate. In this way, a man has free will, but he cannot stop the blizzard.

This analogy can also be related to the use of astrology; knowing the potential of a horoscope is like offering the individual choices, the same as John Doe can use the weather report to make his decision.

PART II

BASICS OF ASTROLOGY

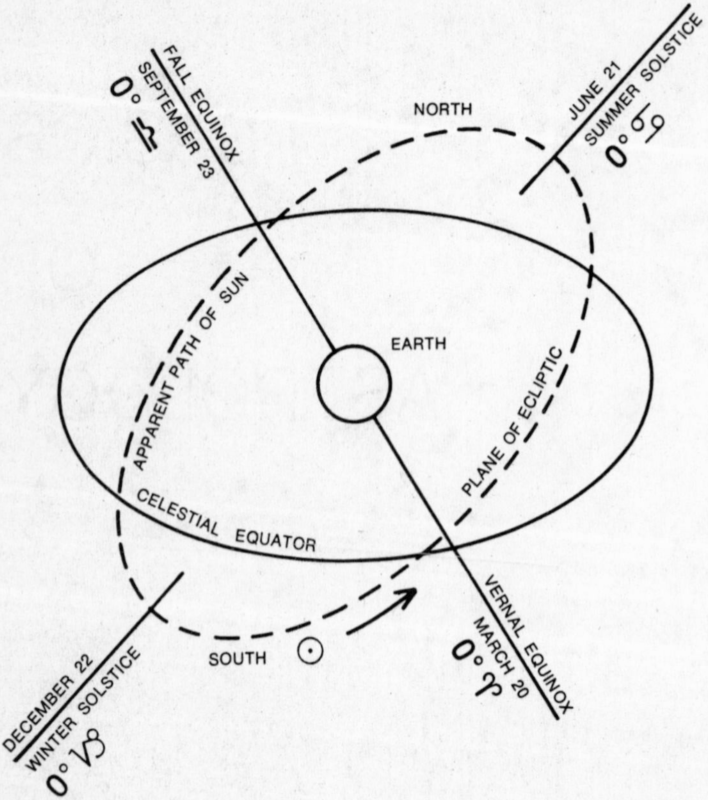

FALL EQUINOX
SEPTEMBER 23
0° ♎
NORTH
JUNE 21
SUMMER SOLSTICE
0° ♋
APPARENT PATH OF SUN
EARTH
PLANE OF ECLIPTIC
CELESTIAL EQUATOR
SOUTH
VERNAL EQUINOX
MARCH 20
0° ♈
DECEMBER 22
WINTER SOLSTICE
0° ♑

2

The Zodiac of the Astrologers Versus the Zodiac of the Astronomers

The signs of the Zodiac and the constellations of the Zodiac are not the same thing. A constellation is a group of stars, whereas a zodiacal sign is one-twelfth of a circle, or the volume of space included within an angle of 30 degrees.

The Zodiac used by most Western astrologers is determined by the Vernal Equinox. This is the position of the Sun about March 20 or 21 of each year when the days and nights are of equal length. The Vernal Equinox is defined as that point in space where the plane of the Earth's orbit around the Sun intersects the plane of the Earth's Equator extended into space. This occurs when the Sun moves from a position south of the Equator to a position north of the Equator in its apparent motion along the ecliptic as seen from the Earth. However, the Earth is actually revolving around the Sun.

In astrology this point is known as 0° Aries and marks the beginning of what astrologers call the Tropical Zodiac. The signs of the Zodiac are defined by the Earth's yearly revolution around the Sun. The houses are defined by the Earth's twenty-four-hour rotation on its axis. The time and location of an individual's birth will determine which of the twelve signs will be rising on the eastern horizon.

At one time the first point of the constellation Aries corresponded in space to the point of the Vernal Equinox of the sign Aries. Because of the precession of the equinoxes, the two points do not coincide in space today. The constellation Aries is no longer lined up with the sign Aries.

The Natural Zodiac is the Zodiac starting with 0° Aries, with Taurus, Gemini, Cancer, Leo, Virgo, Libra, Scorpio, Sagittarius, Capricorn, Aquarius, and Pisces following. The Zodiac in this order is known as the Natural Zodiac and never changes.

Each horoscope contains the whole Zodiac. This is why everyone relates in some manner to all signs. There are twelve signs of the Zodiac,

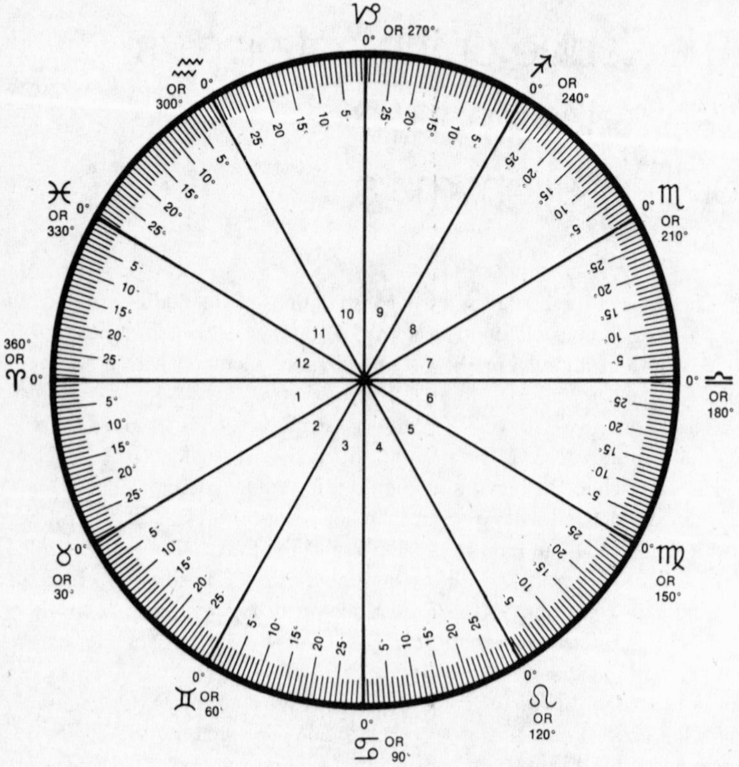

The Natural Zodiac

The wheel above is the Natural Zodiac, showing that each sign of the Zodiac covers a span of exactly 30 degrees of space. There are twelve signs, and $12 \times 30 = 360$ degrees. The Zodiac starts at 0 degrees of Aries at the cusp of the first house.

and one of these signs is found in each department of our life. In astrology these departments of life are called houses. The houses represent different areas of experience. The sign found on the cusp of a house is determined by the time of birth, and this in turn describes the way the affairs of that house will be handled by the individual. Thus all twelve signs are part of our life experience.

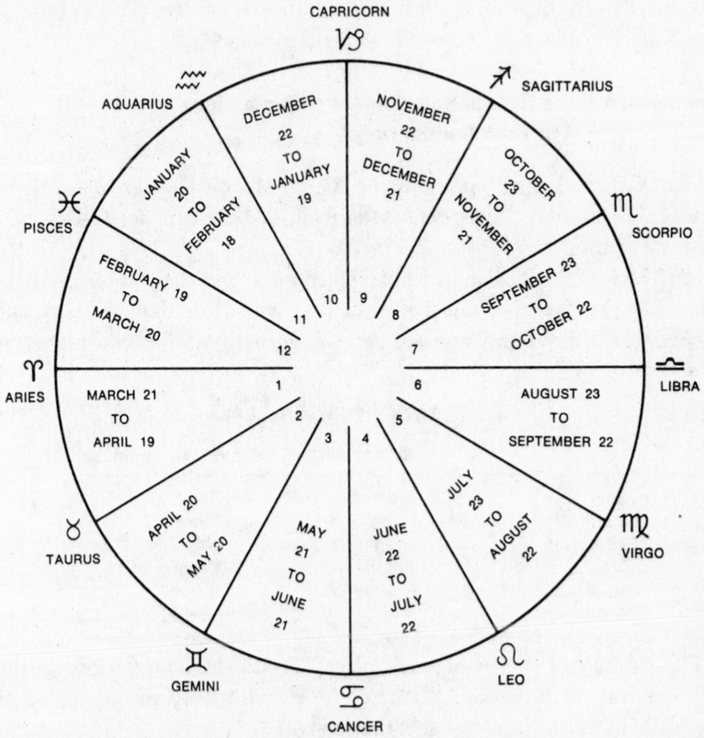

Sign Symbols and Approximate Dates of the Signs

The wheel above represents the Natural Zodiac with the symbols that represent the signs of the Zodiac. The signs are placed in their natural order. The dates given are approximate and include the beginning and end of each sign. These dates can vary because the months of the year are not divided equally, and because we have a leap year every four years in our calendar.

If an individual is born with the Sun at the end of a sign, it indicates that he or she is finishing up evolutionary lessons indicated by that sign. An individual born at the beginning of a sign is beginning a new cycle of experience indicated by that sign. An individual born at the beginning or end of a sign often says, "I was born on a cusp." This is a fallacy. An individual is born either in one sign or another, and is either beginning or ending a cycle of experience indicated by the birth sign or the Sun in the zodiacal sign in which he or she was born. When this condition exists, the Sun sign can be determined by an exact mathematical formula outlined in the chapter on how to cast a horoscope.

The Division of the Natural Horoscope Wheel into Signs, and Planets and Their Rulers in Their Natural Order

The Natural Zodiac represents the "Great Mandala" in astrology, from which the meaning of aspects is derived. (These are dealt with in a separate chapter.)

Each sign of the Zodiac has a planetary ruler, and these rulers must be memorized so that they can be recalled at will. Note that Mercury and Venus rule two signs. There are several signs that have two planetary rulers:

SIGNS WITH DOUBLE RULERS

SIGN	PLANETARY RULER	PLANETARY CO-RULER
Aries ♈	Mars ♂	Pluto ♇
Scorpio ♏	Pluto ♇	Mars ♂
Sagittarius ♐	Jupiter ♃	Neptune ♆
Capricorn ♑	Saturn ♄	Uranus ♅
Aquarius ♒	Uranus ♅	Saturn ♄
Pisces ♓	Neptune ♆	Jupiter ♃

The symbols of the planets are placed inside the houses close to the sign they rule. The symbols of the co-rulers are placed in the center of the wheel in the house of the sign they co-rule.

Cosmic Code—Symbols of Signs and Planets

Symbols are pictured expressions of a universal language, understandable by anyone. Astrological symbols were conceived and developed in the hieroglyphic era, and they are by far the most widely known and used in the world.

In astrology this code or shorthand must be memorized. For instance,

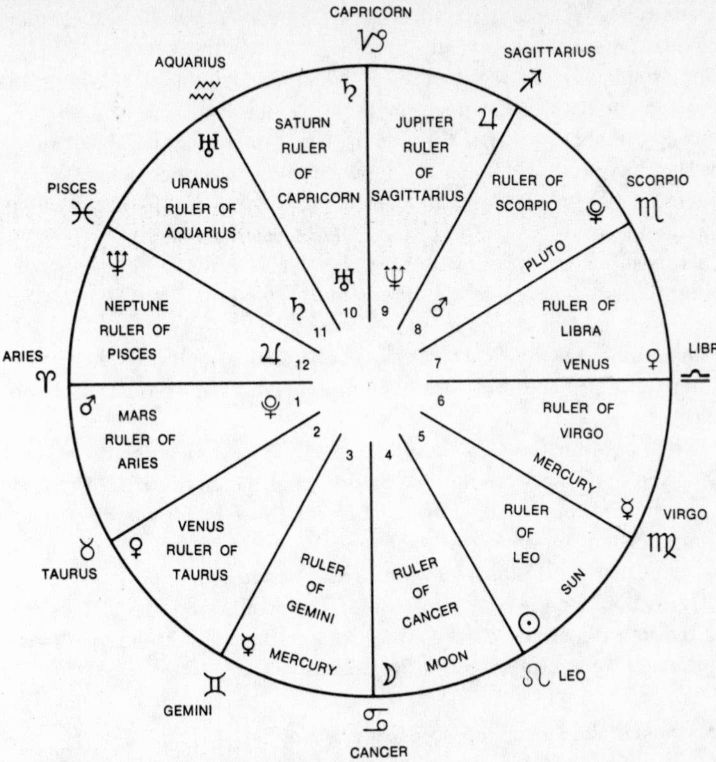

it is much easier and faster to write the symbol ♐ than it is to write the eleven-lettered word Sagittarius, although they signify exactly the same thing. However, the hidden implications that are conveyed by the symbols* and their construction are much more complex.

The symbol for the sign Aries is ♈. The symbols for the planets ruling the sign Aries are ♂ (Mars) and ⯓ (Pluto). Pluto is the co-ruler of the sign Aries. There are two different symbols for the planet Pluto in common use today, ⯓ and ♇.

The symbol for the sign Taurus is ♉. The symbol for the planet ruling the sign Taurus is ♀ (Venus).

The symbol for the sign Gemini is ♊. The symbol for the planet ruling the sign Gemini is ☿ (Mercury).

* For further study of the meanings of the symbols see Ellen McCaffery, *Graphic Astrology*. Richmond, Va.: Macoy Publishing Co., 1952.

The symbol for the sign Cancer is ♋. The symbol for the planet ruling the sign Cancer (in this case the lesser light) is ☽ (the Moon).

The symbol for the sign Leo is ♌. The symbol for the planet ruling the sign Leo (in this case the greater light) is ☉ (the Sun).

The symbol for the sign Virgo is ♍. The symbol for the planet ruling the sign Virgo is ☿ (Mercury). (Notice Mercury also rules Gemini.)

The symbol for the sign Libra is ♎. The symbol for the planet ruling the sign Libra is ♀ (Venus). (Notice Venus also rules Taurus.)

The symbol for the sign Scorpio is ♏. The symbols for the planets ruling the sign Scorpio are ♇ (Pluto) and the co-ruler ♂ (Mars). (Notice Pluto and Mars also co-rule Aries.)

The symbol for the sign Sagittarius is ♐. The symbols for the planets ruling the sign Sagittarius are ♃ (Jupiter) and the co-ruler ♆ (Neptune).

The symbol for the sign Capricorn is ♑. The symbols for the planets ruling the sign Capricorn are ♄ (Saturn) and the co-ruler ♅ (Uranus).

The symbol for the sign Aquarius is ♒. The symbols for the planets ruling the sign Aquarius are ♅ (Uranus) and the co-ruler ♄ (Saturn). (Notice Uranus and Saturn also co-rule Capricorn.)

The symbol for the sign Pisces is ♓. The symbols for the planets ruling the sign Pisces are ♆ (Neptune) and co-ruler ♃ (Jupiter). (Notice Jupiter and Neptune also co-rule Sagittarius.)

Placement of the Sun on the Horoscope Wheel

There is one way of being sure that the mathematics used in casting the horoscope has been done correctly, and that is to observe the placement of the Sun in the wheel. At 12:00 midnight, one twenty-four-hour period, or one whole day, is separated from the next. Every twenty-four hours, all the signs of the Zodiac travel through all the houses. The houses always stay in the same place, and so as the signs travel through the houses, the Sun, Moon, and planets travel through the houses also, because the planets are in the signs. It takes the signs approximately 4 minutes to travel 1 whole degree. There are 30 degrees in each sign. If 30 degrees is multiplied by 4 minutes, the answer is 120 minutes, which equals 2 hours (there are 60 minutes in one hour). Therefore, it takes the signs and the Sun approximately 2 hours to travel through one house.

The Sun rises in the east and travels in a clockwise direction around the houses, which are stationary. Therefore, if an individual is born at midnight, the Sun will be found in the area of the fourth house, depend-

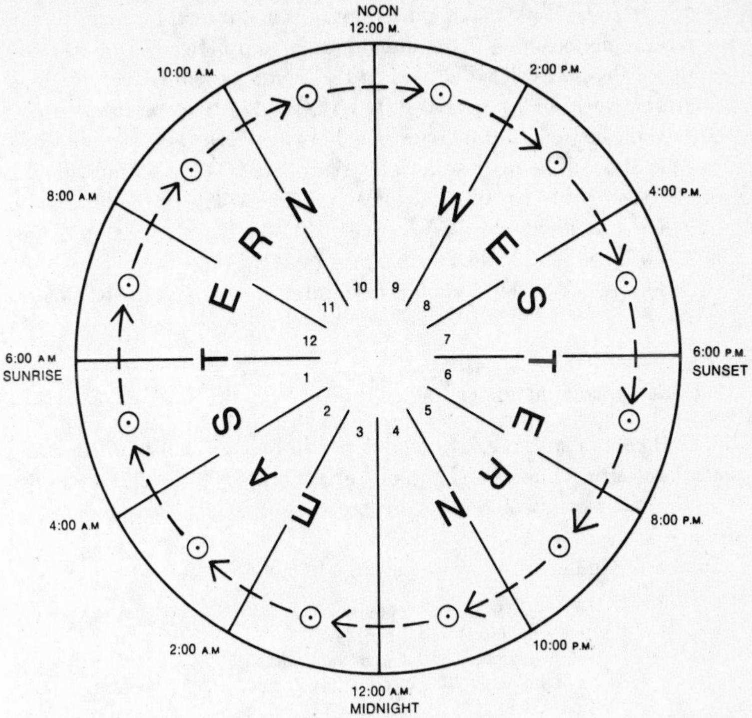

ing on the exact birth data and the location of the birth. If an individual is born between midnight and 2:00 A.M., the Sun will be found in the area of the third house; when an individual is born between 2:00 A.M. and 4:00 A.M., the Sun will be found in the second house. When the individual is born between 4:00 A.M. and 6:00 A.M., the Sun will be located in the first house and is said to be "rising." If the individual is born between 6:00 A.M. and 8:00 A.M., the Sun will be in and around the twelfth house. When one is born between 8:00 A.M. and 10:00 A.M., the Sun will be in or around the eleventh house, and when an individual is born between 10:00 A.M. and 12:00 noon, the Sun will be located in the tenth house.

Therefore, for all A.M. births the Sun is found on the eastern side of the horoscope, with few exceptions. In rare cases the Sun may be found in the western half of the chart.

Moving to the western side of the horoscope wheel, if an individual is born between 12:00 noon and 2:00 P.M., the Sun will be found in and around the ninth house; if the individual is born between 2:00 P.M. and 4:00 P.M., the Sun will be located in the eighth house. If the individual is born between 4:00 P.M. and 6:00 P.M., the Sun will be in or around the seventh house. If an individual is born between 6:00 P.M. and 8:00 P.M., the Sun will be in or around the sixth house. When an individual is born between 8:00 P.M. and 10:00 P.M., the Sun will be in the fifth house, and when an individual is born between 10:00 P.M. and 12:00 midnight, the Sun will be found in the fourth house area.

The Sun in a P.M. birth should be located in the western half of the chart.

Time and Space of Astrology

The time and space of astrology is not to be confused with time and space on Earth. Minutes and seconds of arc are not to be confused with minutes and seconds of time. A degree is subdivided into minutes and seconds of arc.

In a form used in astrology we have the following table:

60″ (seconds) =	1′ (minute)
60′ (minutes) =	1° (degree)
30° (degrees) =	1 sign of the Zodiac
12 signs of the Zodiac =	1 circle of the Zodiac, or 360° (degrees)

Every sign of the Zodiac contains 30 degrees; this never changes, however the positions of the signs of the Zodiac with relation to the houses change with the diurnal rotation of the Earth. Therefore, as the Earth turns on its axis, making one complete turn in twenty-four hours, the entire twelve signs make a complete circle also. Putting it simply, in a twenty-four-hour period, every sign of the Zodiac will have been on the ascendant, each sign remaining there approximately two hours. Because of the revolution of the Earth upon its axis, a new degree of the Zodiac rises every four minutes. There are 30 degrees within each sign; 30 degrees × 4 minutes = 120 minutes, or 2 hours.

3

Triplicities and Quadruplicities and Their Use

The signs of the Zodiac are divided into several groupings, or patterns. These groupings are called triplicities, quadruplicities, and polarities. These groupings must be committed to memory or studied in such a manner that they can be recalled at will. The triplicities are also known as the elements, and they deal with the tendencies of the temperament. The quadruplicities deal with the basic modes of activity. The polarities deal with the basic nature of human behavior—that is, active-aggressive or passive-receptive—in handling different areas of experience. Each sign of the Zodiac is classified in all three ways; in other words, each sign is a part of all three groups.

When a preponderance of planets is found in a sign belonging to one of these groups, it becomes an outstanding factor in the quality of expression in some area of experience.

The Fire Triplicity is made up of the signs Aries, Leo, and Sagittarius. The individuals born under Fire signs seek to display leadership in some way. There is enthusiasm, creativity, and energy poured into this leadership potential.

In Aries this desire for leadership manifests itself as the ability to spearhead new efforts and endeavors in a decisive way. The house that carries Aries on its cusp is the area of experience where the individual will initiate new endeavors without waiting for an outside influence to motivate him or her into action.

In Leo this leadership ability is manifested in a managerial capacity for acting as a central dramatic figure around which an organization or a group of people gathers. The house with Leo on the cusp will be a place of power spotlighting the individual.

In Sagittarius this leadership is expressed as the ability to act as a spiritual, philosophic leader in the areas of philosophy, law, or higher education. The house with Sagittarius on its cusp will be colored by a concern with the ideas around which human society is built.

The Earth Triplicity is made up of the signs Taurus, Virgo, and Capricorn. Individuals born under these signs display skill in using and managing material and financial resources in a practical way in order to achieve practical and concrete results. They are usually occupied with financial, business, and professional matters.

In Taurus this practicality is demonstrated as an ability to accumulate and manage money and other material resources. The house with Taurus on its cusp is the area where the individual eventually will be able to accumulate money and resources that will bring financial and emotional security.

In Virgo this practicality is demonstrated as intelligence and skill in labor that somehow is instrumental in constructing the material objects that are essential to man. It is also demonstrated in maintaining the physical body. The house with Virgo on its cusp is the area where the individual will demonstrate skill and intelligence.

In Capricorn this practicality is demonstrated as the ability to structure and organize ordinary or big-business affairs. The house with Capricorn on its cusp is the area where the individual manifests ability in organization and takes on the responsibility and discipline that should lead to eventual fulfillment.

The Air Triplicity is made up of the signs Gemini, Libra, and Aquarius. Individuals born under these signs are concerned with the intellectual capacity of man and human relations. This includes the communication of ideas and social interrelations.

In Gemini this intellectualism is demonstrated as the ability to acquire, utilize, and communicate factual information. The house with Gemini on its cusp is the area where the individual will manifest mental abilities and intellectual attributes that give the ability to repattern ideas or communication.

In Libra this intellectualism manifests as a natural ability in psychology and related disciplines. It is also the ability to weigh, balance, and make just comparisons. The house with Libra on its cusp is the area where the individual has a marked social awareness.

In Aquarius this intellectualism is manifested as an impersonal concern for the well-being of humanity as well as an intuitive grasp of universal principles that underlie all manifestation. The house with Aquarius on its cusp is the area where the individual must be free to express an understanding of cosmic law.

The Water Triplicity is made up of the signs Cancer, Scorpio, and Pisces. Individuals born under these signs are concerned with sensitivity, intuition, and the deeper psychic aspects of life, and exhibit deep emotions.

In Cancer this quality of emotions manifests as strong feelings about home and family. The house with Cancer on its cusp will be the area where the individual will express these emotions and sensitivity.

In Scorpio this quality of emotions manifests as strong feelings concerning joint resources, death, and the deeper occult mysteries of life, which include regeneration of the self on all levels of being. The house with Scorpio on its cusp deals with these matters in a fundamental and pertinent way.

In Pisces this quality of emotions manifests itself as a sympathetic awareness of the environment. There is an extreme sensitivity and impressionability that is influenced by the unconscious. There is also an unconscious telepathic communication with others. There is a strong mystical feeling toward the infinite. The house with Pisces on its cusp will be influenced by the unconscious with an extreme sensitivity to the matters concerning that house.

When a horoscope does not contain planets in one of these elements, it is an important point in interpretation.

When there are no planets in Fire signs in a horoscope, the individual feels a need to build in self-assertion. He or she needs to expand self through unique forms of self-expression. Once this self-expression is found and some measure of success is achieved, the individual takes self-importance for granted.

When there are no planets in Earth signs in a horoscope, the individual needs to build in basic principles of lasting values that will build a foundation to bring reality, practicality, and stability into the life.

When there are no planets in Air signs in a horoscope, the individual must justify his or her existence by achieving or having some constructive outlet. This is generally done through a career. Until it is done, the individual is uncomfortable.

When there are no planets in Water signs in a horoscope, the individual's personal emotions can be unresponsive to the feelings and mood changes of those close to him or her. This individual accepts emotional subtleties but does not understand them; however, if confronted with personal issues and problems, he or she can offer good solutions.

If the missing element is found on the Ascendant, the individual is in touch with the lack, and because of this awareness is able to round out the life.

The Fire signs are always approximately 120 degrees apart, or five signs away from each other. In the Natural Zodiac the Fire signs are always trine to each other. From one sign to the next sign is 30 degrees.

Example: From Aries to Taurus is exactly 30 degrees; from Taurus to Gemini is 30 degrees; from Gemini to Cancer is 30 degrees; from Cancer to Leo is 30 degrees—making a total of 120 degrees, which is the span of a trine. There is also a span of 120 degrees between Leo and Sagittarius, and between Sagittarius and Aries, making a total of 360 degrees, which completes the zodiacal circle.

The Earth signs, Taurus, Virgo, and Capricorn, follow this same pattern; they are all trine to each other. The Air signs, Gemini, Libra, and Aquarius, also trine each other; and the Water signs, Cancer, Scorpio, and Pisces, follow the same pattern.

When the personal horoscope is calculated for an individual, the planets that are found in two or more Fire signs are always in trine position to each other; however, it does not mean that they make a trine aspect unless the planets are within 6 degrees of each other. If the Sun or the Moon is involved, an orb of 10 degrees is allowed.

Example: Mars in Leo 12 degrees and 24 minutes would make a trine to Jupiter 16 degrees and 4 minutes of Sagittarius. The orb is 3 degrees and 40 minutes from being an exact trine. In such a trine a 6-degree orb is allowed between planets, and a 10-degree orb if the Sun or Moon is involved. The same holds true for all the elements.

Exceptions are made when one or both planets making the trine aspect are found in the Angle Houses, first, tenth, seventh, or fourth. In this case an extra degree is allowed, making it 7 degrees for the planets and 11 degrees if the Sun or Moon is involved.

Example: If the Sun is trine to Mars, 10 degrees is allowed; however, when either one is found in an Angle House, then 11 degrees is the orb allowed.

There is an exception to this rule: There can be what is called a "hidden aspect" between two planets in two different elements. This happens only when two planets are in trine aspect to each other by degrees and

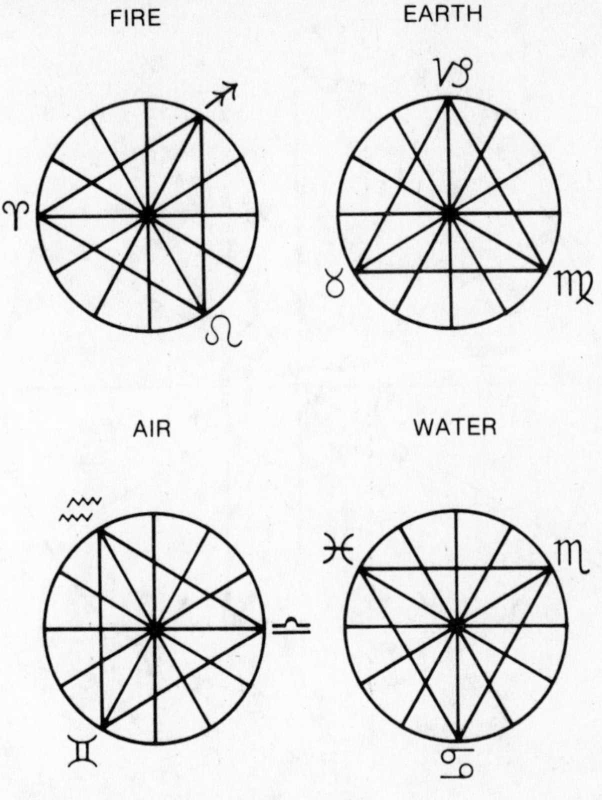

not by sign. When this happens, it is always because the planets in trine aspect to each other are located with one planet in the last degrees of one sign and the other planet in the first few degrees of another sign.

Example: Uranus 28 degrees of Capricorn is trine to Saturn 3 degrees of Gemini.

28 degrees of Capricorn to 28 degrees of Aquarius	=	30 degrees
28 degrees of Aquarius to 28 degrees of Pisces	=	30 degrees
28 degrees of Pisces to 28 degrees of Aries	=	30 degrees
28 degrees of Aries to 28 degrees of Taurus	=	30 degrees
28 degrees of Taurus to 3 degrees of Gemini	=	5 degrees
A trine consists of 120 degrees.	TOTAL	125 degrees

This is a difference of 5 degrees, and 6 degrees is allowed for the trine.

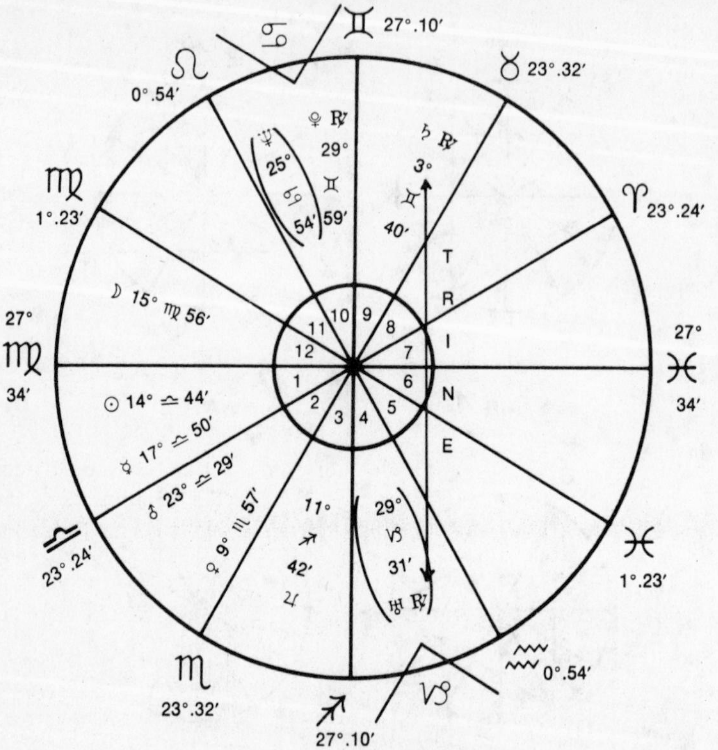

Example of "Hidden Trine"

Note that Uranus in Capricorn is in the Earth Triplicity, and Saturn is in the Air Triplicity; however, they are in trine aspect by degrees. This type of "hidden aspect" can be found between any of the elements, providing they follow the sequential order of the Zodiac.

Many astrologers use wider orbs; they allow up to 14 degrees for aspects involving the Sun or Moon, and 10 degrees for planets in aspect to each other. In the authors' combined experience of eighty-four years in counseling and teaching, they have observed subtle leanings with these wide orbs; however, they are not overtly active or expressed in the life. The more exact the aspect, the stronger will be the expression of that which is promised in the aspect.

Another pattern or grouping is called the quadruplicities. These consist of the Cardinal, Fixed, and Mutable signs, indicating modes of activity. Each quadruplicity consists of four signs of the Zodiac.

The Cardinal signs are Aries, Cancer, Libra, and Capricorn. The houses that have these signs on the cusp, or intercepted in the house, indicate the department of life where action takes place. In these departments the individual has a realistic grasp of the immediate situation and its potential for action. The departments of life that carry these signs are those in which the individual has the ability to act directly and decisively upon present circumstances. The houses carrying these signs are those in which the individual is concerned with the "here and now" of the situation. The past or future ramifications of the action or decision are not taken into consideration immediately. When positive, this can be expressed as constructive initiative. When negative, it can be expressed as thoughtless action.

The Fixed Quadruplicity consists of Taurus, Leo, Scorpio, and Aquarius. These are called the Fixed signs. The houses that have these signs on the cusp, or intercepted in the house, indicate the departments of the life where the individual is not easily swayed once he or she has made up his or her mind about something. In the houses or departments in which these signs are found, the individual will exert a sustained effort through unwavering perseverance over an extended period of time. In these departments the individual is concerned with future goals; thus, he or she can be said to be goal-oriented in these areas of life. When positive, Fixity can be expressed as constancy and reliability; expressed negatively, it can be manifested as stubbornness and rigidity.

The Mutable Quadruplicity consists of the signs Gemini, Virgo, Sagittarius, and Pisces. These are called the Mutable signs. The houses that have these signs on the cusp, or intercepted in the house, indicate the departments of the life where there is a richness of experience in dealing with a variety of circumstances. The Mutable signs deal with memory and the utilization of past experiences. The departments of life that have these signs on the house cusp are those in which the individual will have a mental, adaptable approach to life experiences, and thus will use past experience as a guide in handling the affairs of these houses. This comes from previous experience in similar circumstances. Positive past skills and events will allow the individual to meld into circumstances and to work around obstacles. When expressed negatively, there is always the danger of the memory of past unpleasant experiences interfering with the present.

When two different quadruplicities influence a house, one type of quadruplicity on the cusp and another intercepted in the same house, the indication would be alternating modes of action. This action would be stimulated by transiting planets; however, the sign on the cusp is the predominating influence even if it is in the last degrees of a sign.

The signs belonging to the Cardinal, Fixed, or Mutable quadruplicities are always 90 degrees apart or 180 degrees apart. These signs are always either in square position to each other or they fall opposite each other.

From one Cardinal sign to the next, following in sequential order for the Cardinal signs, there is a span of 90 degrees.

Example: From Aries, which is the first Cardinal sign of the Zodiac, to Taurus is exactly 30 degrees; from Taurus to Gemini is exactly 30 degrees; from Gemini to Cancer, which is the next Cardinal sign in the Zodiac, is exactly 30 degrees—making a total of 90 degrees, indicating that Aries is 90 degrees away from Cancer, and they are in square position to each other. A square consists of 90 degrees of the Zodiac.

Starting from the second Cardinal sign, Cancer, to the next sign, Leo, is exactly 30 degrees; from Leo to Virgo is exactly 30 degrees; from Virgo to Libra, which is the next Cardinal sign in the Zodiac, is exactly 30 degrees—making a total of 90 degrees, indicating that Cancer and Libra are in square position to each other. When counting from Aries, the first Cardinal sign, to Cancer, the second Cardinal sign, then to Libra, the third Cardinal sign, there is a span of six signs, or 180 degrees, indicating that the sign Aries is always opposite the sign Libra.

Starting with Libra, the third Cardinal sign in the Natural Zodiac, to the sign Scorpio is exactly 30 degrees; from Scorpio to Sagittarius is exactly 30 degrees; from Sagittarius to the sign Capricorn, which is the fourth Cardinal sign, is a span of four signs, or 90 degrees.

When counting from the sign Capricorn or the sign Cancer, the space between these two signs equals 180 degrees, or six signs. Therefore, Cancer and Capricorn are always in opposition to each other, the same as Aries and Libra are opposite to each other. These signs are always opposite to each other in the Natural Zodiac, as well as in an individual chart, regardless of the system used.

Proceeding with the same rule, from Capricorn to Aquarius there are 30 degrees; from Aquarius to Pisces there are 30 degrees; and from Pisces to Aries is exactly 30 degrees—spanning four signs.

Aries is always square to Cancer and Capricorn, and in opposition to the sign Libra. Cancer is always square to Aries and Libra, and in opposition to the sign Capricorn. Libra is always square to Cancer and Capricorn, and in opposition to Aries. Capricorn is always square to Libra and Aries, and in opposition to the sign Cancer. This holds true for any type of astrological system used.

There are four signs in the Cardinal Quadruplicity; from one Cardinal sign to the next is 90 degrees, and 90 degrees multiplied by four makes a total of 360 degrees, completing the zodiacal circle.

The Fixed signs, Taurus, Leo, Scorpio, and Aquarius, follow this same pattern; they are always square or in opposition to each other. Taurus is always square to Leo and Aquarius, and in opposition to Scorpio; Leo is always square to Taurus and Scorpio, and in opposition to Aquarius; Scorpio is always square to Leo and Aquarius, and in opposition to Taurus; Aquarius is always square to Scorpio and Taurus, and in opposition to Leo.

The Mutable signs also follow this same pattern; they are always square or in opposition to each other. Gemini is always square to Virgo and Pisces, and in opposition to Sagittarius; Virgo is always square to Gemini and Sagittarius, and in opposition to Pisces; Sagittarius is always square to Virgo and Pisces, and in opposition to Gemini; and Pisces is always square to Sagittarius and Gemini, and in opposition to Virgo.

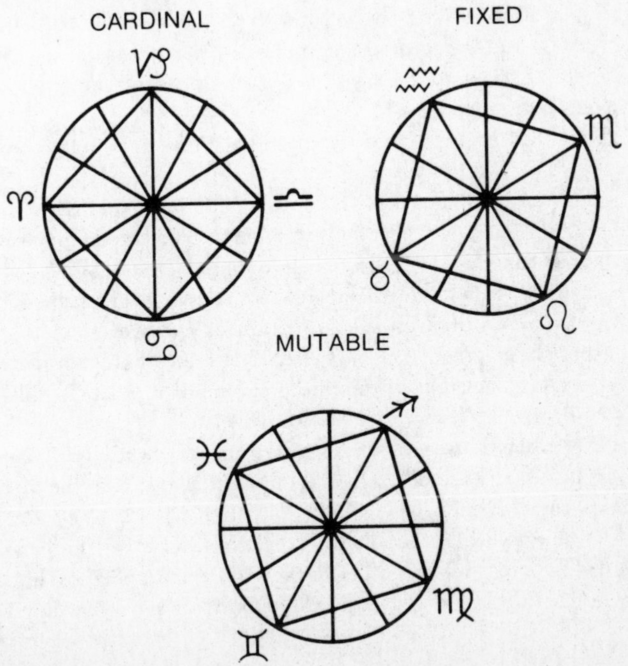

When the personal horoscope is calculated for an individual and there is a preponderance of planets in one of the quadruplicities, it is indicative of a strong characteristic trait.

Example: When four or more of the ten planetary bodies are found in Fixed signs, and the rest are divided between the other two quadruplicities, it would indicate that the individual would not be easily swayed once he or she has made a decision and that he or she is capable of exerting a sustained interest and effort over an extended period of time; thus, the individual is goal-oriented or concerned with the future.

When the personal horoscope is calculated for an individual, the planets found in the three quadruplicities, Cardinal, Fixed, and Mutable, are always in opposition or square position to each other; however, as in the triplicities, this does not mean that the planets found in the quadruplicity are in square or opposition aspect to each other unless the planets are within a 6-degree orb of each other. If the Sun or Moon is involved, an orb of 10 degrees between the planets is allowed.

Example: If the planet Mars is in the Cardinal sign of Libra 10 degrees and 8 minutes, and Uranus is in the Cardinal sign of Capricorn 15 degrees and 20 minutes, these planets will be in square aspect to each other. *Procedure:* From Libra to Scorpio is 30 degrees; from Scorpio to Sagittarius is 30 degrees; from Sagittarius to Capricorn is 30 degrees—making a total of 90 degrees. This indicates that these planets are in square position. They are also within square aspect to each other, as an orb of 6 degrees is allowed.

This same rule applies if planets are in the Fixed or Mutable quadruplicities.

Exceptions to this rule occur when planets are in square aspect but in different quadruplicities. This type of square is called a "hidden aspect."

Example: If the Moon is in the Mutable sign of Pisces 28 degrees, and the planet Jupiter is in the Cardinal sign of Cancer 2 degrees, the planets are not in square position by sign quadruplicity; however, they are in square aspect by degrees. It is important that these "hidden aspects" be searched out and included in the interpretation of a chart. In this case there is a 4-degree orb between these two planets.

As in the triplicity aspects, this can happen only when one planet is in the last few degrees of one sign and the other planet is in the first few degrees of another sign.

When dealing with the opposition aspect, a similar rule applies. The planets will be opposite each other in the same quadruplicity. This positioning automatically puts the planets in opposition; however, only when the planets are within a 6-degree orb of each other do they form an opposition aspect. The opposition aspect generally covers a span of six signs in sequential order, unless there is a "hidden aspect." In that case it would involve seven signs, and the planets in the opposition would be in two different quadruplicities.

Positive and Receptive Signs, or the Polarities

Another division or grouping of the signs is the positive, masculine signs and the receptive, feminine signs. Sometimes the grouping is labeled masculine and feminine signs or positive and negative signs. These two divisions concern themselves with active versus passive, the generative versus the receptive nature of human behavior.

The positive, masculine signs are the Fire and Air signs, Aries, Gemini, Leo, Libra, Sagittarius, and Aquarius.

The receptive, feminine signs are the Earth and Water signs, Taurus, Cancer, Virgo, Scorpio, Capricorn, and Pisces.

The positive, masculine signs are aggressive and self-initiating. Wherever these signs are found, the individual will take action to achieve a desired result, or will initiate action to change conditions he or she feels need to be changed. The house cusps that carry the positive, masculine signs indicate the area of the life where the individual initiates action and displays positive, aggressive tendencies. In these departments of the life the individual will manifest leadership abilities and tend to be a self-starter. If the majority of the planets are found in positive, masculine signs, the individual initiates action without waiting for any kind of outside stimulus.

The receptive, feminine signs, which are the Earth and Water signs, work with the principle of attraction. They attract the things they need rather than aggressively seeking them. These signs are responsive to outside stimuli, and they take action only when stimulated by some kind of outside influence. They are receptive and interact as a result of outside influence. This does not mean that they do not accomplish their desired ends. They can be strong and forceful when confronted with circumstances that require taking action. They do not set out actively to conquer. The house cusps that carry the receptive, feminine signs indicate the areas of the life where individuals make decisions in response to outside stimuli. They usually attract and interact with that with which they must deal; therefore, they are called receptive, feminine signs.

PART III

SIGN, HOUSE, AND PLANETARY PATTERNS

4

Sun Signs and Rising Signs

The sign that the Sun is in at the time an individual is born is labeled the Sun sign. For instance, if an individual is born on April 1, the Sun is in the sign Aries; therefore the Sun sign is Aries, and one would say that the individual is an Aries person.

The Sun sign indicates the way the individual expresses his or her basic energy potential, as well as the creative drive to develop and grow as an individual. The Sun sign represents the dynamic expression of the will in learning the lessons the individual must master.

Special forms of energy are associated with each zodiacal sign. These signs represent twelve different classifications of human activity. The signs of the Zodiac divide humanity into twelve major classes. However, the great work of character building and fulfillment in the life includes an understanding of all twelve signs because each individual has all twelve signs somewhere in his or her personal horoscope.

Each sign of the Zodiac is associated with one of the twelve divisions of the horoscope, called houses. Each house represents a particular field of activity in which experience may be gathered. The sign found on any of the twelve houses indicates a particular response to the activity of that house and colors that area of experience.

When the horoscope is cast for the exact time and place of birth, the sign that is rising on the Eastern horizon at the time and place of birth is placed on the cusp of the first house, and it is called the "rising sign," or the Ascendant.

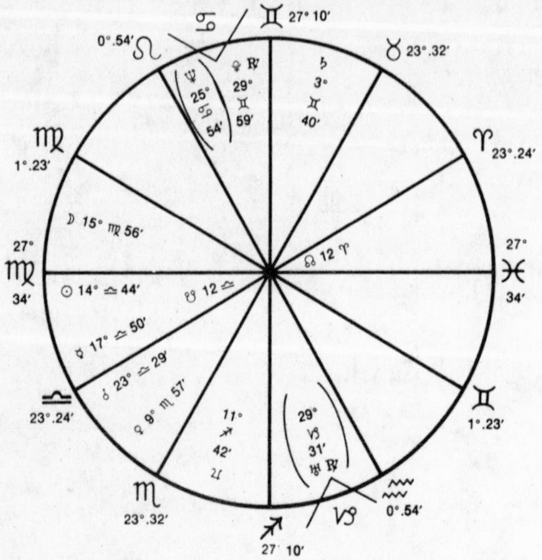

Note that Sagittarius is on the fourth-house cusp, and the sign Capricorn is intercepted in the fourth house.

The rising sign, or Ascendant, deals with the self-awareness and self-image of the individual. It indicates the way the individual views reality and deals with the nowness of each new moment and the decision-making that goes on in any life. The rising sign also deals with the appearance of the physical body and its mannerisms.

The Sun rules the dynamic energy in the process of creation, and the Sun sign determines the manner in which this energy is expressed.

Each zodiacal sign has two characteristics, one according to the triplicity to which it belongs and the other according to the quadruplicity to which it belongs.*

Although many astrologers use the Sun sign, the rising sign, and the first house interchangeably, they are three distinct things, as stated.

Once the rising sign has been ascertained by using the mathematical formula given in Chapter 13, the rising sign is placed on the first-house cusp and is followed by the next sign of the zodiac, which belongs on the second-house cusp. For example, if the sign Scorpio is rising, the sign Sagittarius will be on the second-house cusp; the sign Capricorn will be

* See the chapter on triplicities and quadruplicities in this text.

on the third-house cusp; Aquarius will be on the fourth-house cusp; Pisces will be on the fifth-house cusp; Aries will be on the sixth-house cusp; Taurus will be on the seventh-house cusp; Gemini will be on the eighth-house cusp; Cancer will be on the ninth-house cusp; Leo will be on the tenth-house cusp; Virgo will be on the eleventh-house cusp; and Libra will be on the twelfth-house cusp.

This sequential order of the signs never changes; however, the farther the birthplace is from the Equator, the more uneven the houses become. It is possible to have the same sign fall on two house cusps. If this situation takes place, then there will be what is called an "intercepted sign," indicating that there are two or more signs influencing that house. Thus there will be two expressions in the handling of the affairs of that house. The sign that takes precedence at any given time is determined by the transiting planets affecting the sign.

If there are intercepted signs in the horoscope, the opposite signs will also be intercepted in opposite houses.

The Ascendant and Midheaven Tables

These tables are a simple and accurate means for determining the Midheaven (10th House Cusp) and Ascendant (Rising Sign) of a horoscope for anyone born within the locales of the cities listed.

This is the first time, to our knowledge, that tables as comprehensive as these have been made available.

These tables make it possible for those who are not familiar with the mathematics of astrology to determine, without calculation, their approximate (and sometimes *exact*) Midheaven and Ascendant—which are the Angles of the horoscope.

The Ascendant and Midheaven Tables are mathematically designed to provide both an accurate Midheaven and Ascendant for birth horoscopes located on or near the 42nd Parallel of North Latitude. Individuals born in cities and towns near or on this degree of latitude* can, at a glance, determine the approximate degree of their rising sign, known as the Ascendant, and their Midheaven, the sign on the 10th House cusp. The 42nd Parallel of North Latitude crosses what is probably the most densely populated area in the United States.

* The larger cities and towns located within one degree of this 42nd Parallel of North Latitude are listed on separate pages (pages 40–43). Individuals born in surrounding towns of these cities can also use these tables.

How to Use the Ascendant and Midheaven Tables

First, search for the calendar month of birth—this is listed at the top of each page of the tables.

After locating the month of birth in the tables, search across the top of the pages for that particular month until you locate the page containing the "Calendar Date" of the individual's birth.

Next, search the extreme left column of that particular page carrying the individual's birth date for the "Hour of Birth" and select the double-row corresponding to the birth hour. Note: The top half of the page deals with A.M. births, and the lower half deals with P.M. births.

Follow the column listing under the "Calendar Date" to where it intersects the double-row of figures to the right of the "Hour of Birth." Where these two intersect, there are two positions listed. The top figure refers to the degree (and sign) of the Midheaven or 10th House cusp. The lower figure refers to the degree known as the Ascendant (the sign that was rising on the Eastern horizon at the time of the individual's birth).

The Midheaven and Ascendant signs are listed under the first "Calendar Dates" column on *each* page. Because there are 30° in each sign, there are occasions when the Midheaven or Ascendant will change signs in the tables. When this happens, the tables will list the change where it first occurs (in reading a row from left to right) and is recorded in the tables—at either 0° or 1° of a particular sign. Usually, the Midheaven and Ascendant *signs* will be found on the far-left "Calendar Date" column.

Accuracy of Tables for Births Worldwide

These Tables only provide an accurate Midheaven (10th House cusp) and Ascendant (Rising Sign) for those born on or near the 42nd Parallel of North Latitude.

Individuals born *anywhere* in the world can use the Midheaven portion of these tables simply by determining the Midheaven from these tables, then referring to a Table of Houses that contains the correct latitude of birth.

In this case, find the Midheaven degree listed in a Table of Houses (containing the correct birth latitude) that corresponds to the Midheaven as found in these tables. Put the Midheaven degree and sign on the 10th House cusp of a blank "wheel." Then, fill in the rest of the house cusps as listed in the Table of Houses. Note that only the 11th, 12th, 1st (Asc.), 2nd, and 3rd house cusps will be listed in this Table of Houses. Once these are filled in on the blank "wheel," then put the *same degree* of the *opposite sign* on each of the opposing house cusps—that is, the 4th (which opposes the 10th), the 5th (which opposes the 11th), the 6th (which opposes the 12th), and so fourth. This will complete the "wheel."

The Minor House Cusps—11th, 12th, 2nd, 3rd, etc.

For those born on or near the 42nd Parallel of North Latitude and wishing to determine the other house cusps, simply follow the procedure described under "Accuracy of Tables for Births Worldwide."*

SAMPLES: CALENDAR DATE JANUARY of any year CALENDAR DATE

	17	18	19	20	21	22	23	24	
8	28♏22	29 19	0♐16	1 13	2 09	3 06	4 02	4 58	MC
A.M.	5♒55	7 13	8 32	9 52	11 13	12 35	13 58	15 23	ASC
9	12♐38	13 33	14 28	15 23	16 17	17 12	18 07	19 02	MC
A.M.	27♒41	29 16	0♓51	2 27	4 05	5 43	7 22	9 02	ASC

To determine the Midheaven and Ascendant of a client born January 21 at 8 A.M. at 42° North Latitude, first search for the month January at the top of the page, then pinpoint the "Calendar Date" "21" and the column beneath it. Next, referring to the extreme left column under "Hour of Birth," find "8 A.M." and follow the double-row immediately to its right to the point where it intersects the column beneath the "Calendar Date" "21." This provides the values 2°09′ (the top figure) for the Midheaven and 11°13′ (the bottom figure) for the Ascendant. But what signs? Proceed to the far-left "Calendar Date" column, where Scorpio is listed for the Midheaven and Aquarius for the Ascendant. Proceeding to the right along *this* double-row, there is a noted sign change in the "19" column of the Midheaven row; therefore, the Midheaven is not Scorpio, but Sagittarius because the sign has changed. There is no such change in the Ascendant's sign. Hence, the Midheaven for this time and date is (approximately) 2°♐09′, and the Ascendant is (approximately) 11°♒13′.

To determine the Midheaven and Ascendant of a client born January 23 at 9 A.M. at 42° North Latitude, first search for the month January at the top of the page, then pinpoint the "Calendar Date" "23" and the column beneath it. Next, referring to the extreme left column under "Hour of Birth," find "9 A.M." and follow the double-row immediately to its right to the point where it intersects the column beneath the "Calendar Date" "23." This provides the values 18°07′ (the top figure) for the Midheaven and 7°22′ (the bottom figure) for the Ascendant. But what signs? Proceed to the far-left "Calendar Data" column, where Sagittarius

* Or, see our book *Your Instant Midheaven Ascendant and House Cusps.*

is listed for the Midheaven and Aquarius for the Ascendant. Proceeding to the right along *this* double-row toward the intersection point of the double-row and the column marked "23," there is a noted change in the "19" column of the Ascendant row; therefore, the Ascendant is not Aquarius, but Pisces because the sign has changed. There is no such change in the Midheaven's sign. Hence, the Midheaven for this time and date is (approximately) 18° ♐07′, and the Ascendant is (approximately) 7° ♓22′.

These Tables use the Base Year 1980—a leap year—and Greenwich Mean Time in their computation. The following are the cities and towns for which these tables would apply:

Massachusetts:

Boston	Holyoke
Quincy	Cambridge
New Bedford	Northampton
Worcester	Pittsfield
Framingham	Fall River
Plymouth	Brockton
Springfield	Taunton

Rhode Island:

Newport	Warwick
Providence	Pawtucket
Cranston	Coventry

Connecticut:

Norwich	Bristol
Willimantic	Meriden
Hartford	Middletown
New Britain	South Manchester
Torrington	Winsted
Waterbury	

New York:

Hudson	Watkins Glen
Albany	Corning
Kingston	Bath
Norwich	Belmont
Delhi	Jamestown
Cortland	Poughkeepsie
Binghamton	Monticello
Oswego	Newburgh
Elmira	Liberty
Ithaca	

Pennsylvania:

Scranton
Wilkes-Barre
Laporte
Williamsport
Wellsboro
Emporium
Bradford
Meadville
Erie
Oil City
Ridgway

Ohio:

Ashtabula
Cleveland
Lorain
Elyria
Sandusky
Fremont
Toledo
Portage
Defiance

Michigan:

Detroit
Mt. Clemens
Pontiac
Ann Arbor
Monroe
Adrian
Hillsdale
Jackson
Lansing
Charlotte
Albion
Battle Creek
Kalamazoo
Niles
Coldwater
Benton Harbor
St. Joseph
Wyandotte

Indiana:

Angola
Lagrange
Elkhart
Goshen
South Bend
La Porte
Valparaiso
Michigan City
Hammond

Illinois:

Chicago
Chicago Heights
Wheaton
Joliet
DeKalb
Elgin
Dixon
Sterling
Waukegan
Belvidere
Rockford
Freeport
Galena
Rock Island
Clinton
Aurora

Iowa:

Dubuque	Davenport
Independence	Clinton
Waterloo	Cedar Rapids
Cedar Falls	Iowa City
Webster City	Grinnell
Fort Dodge	Marshalltown
Sioux City	Des Moines
Boone	Oelwein
Muscatine	

South Dakota:

Elk Point	Vermillion

Nebraska:

Ponca	Harrisburg
Wayne	Taylor
Omaha	Burwell
Blair	Tryon
Fremont	Arthur
West Point	Fullerton
David City	Bartlett
Alliance	Broken Bow
Brewster	Gandy
Gering	Neligh

Wyoming:

Carbon	Kemmerer
Laramie	Rock Springs
Saratoga	Green River
Guernsey	Rawlins
Douglas	Splitrock
Diamondville	

Utah:

Logan	Hyrum
Smithfield	Ogden
Richmond	Brigham City

Idaho:

Preston	Fairview
Malad City	Oakley
Paris	Twin Falls
Montpelier	

Oregon:

Lakeview	Ashland
Andrews	Jacksonville
Klamath Falls	Grants Pass
Medford	Gold Beach

California:

Alturas	Crescent City
Mt. Shasta	Henley
Eureka	

All of these locations fall within approximately 30′ arc of the 42nd Parallel of Latitude. This may be extended, with varying loss of accuracy (up to about 20′ of arc on the Ascendant), to locations falling within 1° of the 42nd Parallel of Latitude, but the degrees noted will (at least) be reasonably accurate on the Ascendant.

For More Exact Calculation of the Midheaven and Ascendant Using These Tables

For those who know how to determine Local Mean Time, it is possible through the use of these tables to find the accurate Midheaven and Ascendant within two minutes of time (about 30′ of arc).

To do this, one must:

1. Find the Standard Time of birth (correct for Daylight Saving Time, War Time, "power shortage" time, or any other "advanced" time, where applicable);
2. Find the Local Mean Time by adding to or subtracting from the Standard Time of birth the Local Mean Time variation (as appropriate);
3. Locate in the Ascendant and Midheaven Tables the *date* and *nearest hour* to the Local Mean Time of birth;
4. Divide the number of minutes before or after the hour by four; and,
5. a. If the Local Mean Time of birth is *before* the hour, count from the Midheaven/Ascendant found in Step 3 to the *left* (in the *same row*) the number of "date-columns" equal to the result of Step 4. The Midheaven and Ascendant found there will be accurate figures for these two angles in the horoscope.
   b. If the Local Mean Time of birth is *after* the hour, count from the Midheaven/Ascendant found in Step 3 to the *right* (in the *same row*) the number of "date-columns" equal to the result of Step 4. The Midheaven and Ascendant found there will be accurate figures for these two angles in the horoscope.

NOTE: If necessary, flip forward or back a page to make this determination, but remember to *stay in the same "hour-row"* if you must do this.

CALENDAR DATE — JANUARY of any year — CALENDAR DATE

HOUR OF BIRTH	1	2	3	4	5	6	7	8	
12 MID	9♋13	10 07	11 02	11 57	12 51	13 46	14 41	15 36	MC
	7♎51	8 38	9 24	10 10	10 56	11 43	12 29	13 15	ASC
1 AM	23♋14	24 10	25 06	26 02	26 58	27 55	28 51	29 48	MC
	19♎36	20 22	21 08	21 54	22 40	23 26	24 12	24 58	ASC
2 AM	7♌42	8 40	9 38	10 37	11 36	12 34	13 33	14 33	MC
	1♏17	2 03	2 49	3 35	4 20	5 06	5 52	6 38	ASC
3 AM	22♌48	23 49	24 50	25 51	26 53	27 54	28 56	29 58	MC
	12♏55	13 41	14 27	15 12	15 58	16 44	17 30	18 15	ASC
4 AM	8♍34	9 37	10 40	11 44	12 47	13 51	14 55	15 59	MC
	24♏35	25 21	26 07	26 53	27 40	28 26	29 13	29 59	ASC
5 AM	24♍48	25 53	26 57	28 02	29 06	0♎11	1 15	2 19	MC
	6♐27	7 14	8 02	8 50	9 38	10 26	11 14	12 02	ASC
6 AM	11♎11	12 15	13 19	14 22	15 26	16 30	17 34	18 37	MC
	18♐49	19 39	20 30	21 21	22 12	23 03	23 55	24 47	ASC
7 AM	27♎16	28 19	29 21	0♏23	1 25	2 26	3 28	4 29	MC
	2♑10	3 05	4 01	4 58	5 54	6 52	7 50	8 48	ASC
8 AM	12♏48	13 48	14 48	15 47	16 46	17 45	18 44	19 42	MC
	17♑12	18 16	19 21	20 27	21 33	22 40	23 48	24 56	ASC
9 AM	27♏40	28 37	29 34	0♐31	1 28	2 24	3 20	4 17	MC
	4♒58	6 15	7 33	8 52	10 13	11 34	12 56	14 20	ASC
10 AM	11♐57	12 52	13 47	14 42	15 37	16 32	17 27	18 21	MC
	26♒32	28 06	29 40	1♓16	2 53	4 30	6 09	7 48	ASC
11 AM	25♐51	26 45	27 40	28 34	29 28	0♑22	1 17	2 11	MC
	21♓57	23 42	25 27	27 12	28 58	0♈44	2 29	4 15	ASC
12 NOON	9♑40	10 35	11 29	12 24	13 19	14 14	15 09	16 04	MC
	18♈33	20 14	21 55	23 34	25 13	26 51	28 28	0♉03	ASC
1 PM	23♑42	24 38	25 34	26 30	27 26	28 23	29 19	0♒16	MC
	12♉35	14 01	15 26	16 49	18 12	19 33	20 54	22 13	ASC
2 PM	8♒11	9 09	10 08	11 06	12 05	13 04	14 03	15 02	MC
	2♊32	3 42	4 52	6 01	7 09	8 16	9 22	10 28	ASC
3 PM	23♒19	24 20	25 21	26 22	27 23	28 25	29 27	0♓29	MC
	19♊04	20 03	21 02	22 01	22 58	23 56	24 53	25 49	ASC
4 PM	9♓06	10 09	11 12	12 16	13 19	14 23	15 27	16 30	MC
	3♋19	4 12	5 04	5 56	6 48	7 39	8 31	9 21	ASC
5 PM	25♓21	26 25	27 29	28 34	29 38	0♈43	1 47	2 52	MC
	16♋12	17 01	17 50	18 38	19 26	20 14	21 02	21 50	ASC
6 PM	11♈43	12 47	13 51	14 54	15 58	17 02	18 05	19 09	MC
	28♋20	29 06	29 53	0♌40	1 26	2 12	2 59	3 45	ASC
7 PM	27♈48	28 50	29 52	0♉54	1 55	2 57	3 58	4 59	MC
	10♌05	10 51	11 37	12 23	13 08	13 54	14 40	15 26	ASC
8 PM	13♉18	14 18	15 17	16 16	17 15	18 14	19 13	20 12	MC
	21♌43	22 29	23 15	24 00	24 46	25 32	26 18	27 03	ASC
9 PM	28♉09	29 06	0♊03	0 59	1 56	2 52	3 49	4 45	MC
	3♍22	4 08	4 54	5 40	6 26	7 12	7 58	8 44	ASC
10 PM	12♊24	13 19	14 14	15 09	16 04	16 59	17 54	18 49	MC
	15♍05	15 51	16 37	17 23	18 09	18 55	19 42	20 28	ASC
11 PM	26♊18	27 13	28 07	29 01	29 55	0♋50	1 44	2 38	MC
	26♍51	27 37	28 23	29 10	29 56	0♎42	1 29	2 15	ASC

CALENDAR DATE — JANUARY of any year — CALENDAR DATE

HOUR OF BIRTH	9	10	11	12	13	14	15	16	
12 MID	16♋31	17 26	18 21	19 17	20 12	21 08	22 03	22 59	MC
	14♎01	14 47	15 34	16 20	17 06	17 52	18 38	19 24	ASC
1 AM	0♌45	1 42	2 39	3 36	4 34	5 31	6 29	7 27	MC
	25♎44	26 30	27 16	28 02	28 48	29 34	0♏20	1 05	ASC
2 AM	15♌32	16 32	17 31	18 31	19 31	20 31	21 32	22 33	MC
	7♏23	8 09	8 55	9 40	10 26	11 12	11 58	12 43	ASC
3 AM	1♍00	2 02	3 04	4 06	5 09	6 12	7 15	8 18	MC
	19♏01	19 47	20 33	21 19	22 05	22 51	23 37	24 23	ASC
4 AM	17♍02	18 06	19 10	20 15	21 19	22 23	23 27	24 32	MC
	0♐46	1 32	2 19	3 06	3 53	4 40	5 27	6 14	ASC
5 AM	3♎24	4 28	5 33	6 37	7 41	8 46	9 50	10 54	MC
	12♐51	13 39	14 28	15 17	16 07	16 56	17 46	18 36	ASC
6 AM	19♎40	20 44	21 47	22 50	23 53	24 55	25 58	27 00	MC
	25♐39	26 32	27 25	28 18	29 12	0♑06	1 01	1 55	ASC
7 AM	5♏30	6 31	7 32	8 32	9 33	10 33	11 33	12 33	MC
	9♑47	10 46	11 46	12 47	13 48	14 50	15 52	16 56	ASC
8 AM	20♏41	21 39	22 37	23 35	24 33	25 30	26 28	27 25	MC
	26♑06	27 16	28 28	29 40	0♒53	2 07	3 22	4 38	ASC
9 AM	5♐13	6 09	7 05	8 00	8 56	9 52	10 47	11 42	MC
	15♒45	17 10	18 37	20 05	21 34	23 04	24 36	26 08	ASC
10 AM	19♐16	20 10	21 05	21 59	22 54	23 48	24 43	25 37	MC
	9♓28	11 10	12 51	14 34	16 17	18 01	19 45	21 29	ASC
11 AM	3♑05	4 00	4 54	5 48	6 43	7 37	8 31	9 26	MC
	6♈00	7 45	9 30	11 15	12 58	14 42	16 24	18 07	ASC
12 NOON	16♑59	17 54	18 49	19 45	20 40	21 36	22 31	23 27	MC
	1♉38	3 12	4 45	6 16	7 47	9 17	10 45	12 12	ASC
1 PM	1♒13	2 10	3 07	4 05	5 02	6 00	6 58	7 56	MC
	23♉32	24 49	26 06	27 21	28 35	29 49	1♊01	2 13	ASC
2 PM	16♒02	17 01	18 01	19 01	20 01	21 02	22 02	23 03	MC
	11♊33	12 37	13 40	14 43	15 45	16 47	17 48	18 48	ASC
3 PM	1♓31	2 33	3 35	4 38	5 40	6 43	7 46	8 49	MC
	26♊45	27 41	28 36	29 30	0♋25	1 19	2 12	3 05	ASC
4 PM	17♓34	18 38	19 43	20 47	21 51	22 55	23 59	25 04	MC
	10♋12	11 02	11 52	12 42	13 32	14 21	15 11	16 00	ASC
5 PM	3♈56	5 01	6 05	7 09	8 13	9 18	10 22	11 26	MC
	22♋38	23 25	24 12	25 00	25 47	26 34	27 21	28 08	ASC
6 PM	20♈12	21 15	22 18	23 21	24 24	25 27	26 29	27 31	MC
	4♌31	5 17	6 03	6 49	7 35	8 21	9 07	9 53	ASC
7 PM	6♉00	7 01	8 02	9 02	10 03	11 03	12 03	13 03	MC
	16♌11	16 57	17 43	18 28	19 14	20 00	20 45	21 31	ASC
8 PM	21♉10	22 08	23 06	24 04	25 02	25 59	26 57	27 54	MC
	27♌49	28 35	29 21	0♍07	0 52	1 38	2 24	3 10	ASC
9 PM	5♊41	6 37	7 33	8 28	9 24	10 19	11 15	12 10	MC
	9♍30	10 16	11 02	11 48	12 34	13 20	14 06	14 53	ASC
10 PM	19♊43	20 38	21 32	22 27	23 21	24 15	25 10	26 04	MC
	21♍15	22 01	22 47	23 33	24 20	25 06	25 52	26 39	ASC
11 PM	3♋32	4 27	5 21	6 15	7 10	8 04	8 59	9 53	MC
	3♎01	3 48	4 34	5 20	6 07	6 53	7 39	8 26	ASC

CALENDAR DATE — JANUARY of any year — CALENDAR DATE

HOUR OF BIRTH	17 ° '	18 ° '	19 ° '	20 ° '	21 ° '	22 ° '	23 ° '	24 ° '	
12	23♋55	24 51	25 47	26 43	27 40	28 36	29 33	0♌30	MC
MID	20♎10	20 56	21 42	22 28	23 14	24 00	24 46	25 32	ASC
1	8♌25	9 23	10 22	11 20	12 19	13 18	14 17	15 17	MC
AM	1♏51	2 37	3 23	4 09	4 54	5 40	6 26	7 11	ASC
2	23♌33	24 34	25 35	26 37	27 38	28 40	29 41	0♍43	MC
AM	13♏29	14 15	15 00	15 46	16 32	17 18	18 04	18 49	ASC
3	9♍21	10 24	11 27	12 31	13 34	14 38	15 42	16 46	MC
AM	25♏09	25 55	26 41	27 28	28 14	29 00	29 47	0♐34	ASC
4	25♍36	26 40	27 45	28 49	29 54	0♎58	2 03	3 07	MC
AM	7♐02	7 49	8 37	9 25	10 13	11 01	11 50	12 38	ASC
5	11♎58	13 02	14 06	15 10	16 13	17 17	18 20	19 24	MC
AM	19♐26	20 17	21 07	21 59	22 50	23 41	24 33	25 26	ASC
6	28♎03	29 05	0♏07	1 08	2 10	3 12	4 13	5 14	MC
AM	2♑51	3 47	4 43	5 39	6 37	7 34	8 33	9 31	ASC
7	13♏33	14 32	15 31	16 31	17 30	18 28	19 27	20 26	MC
AM	18♑00	19 04	20 09	21 16	22 22	23 30	24 38	25 48	ASC
8	28♏22	29 19	0♐16	1 13	2 09	3 06	4 02	4 58	MC
AM	5♒55	7 13	8 32	9 52	11 13	12 35	13 58	15 23	ASC
9	12♐38	13 33	14 28	15 23	16 17	17 12	18 07	19 02	MC
AM	27♒41	29 16	0♓51	2 27	4 05	5 43	7 22	9 02	ASC
10	26♐31	27 26	28 20	29 14	0♑08	1 03	1 57	2 51	MC
AM	23♓14	25 00	26 45	28 31	0♈16	2 02	3 48	5 33	ASC
11	10♑21	11 15	12 10	13 05	13 59	14 54	15 49	16 44	MC
AM	19♈48	21 29	23 08	24 47	26 25	28 02	29 39	1♉14	ASC
12	24♑23	25 19	26 15	27 11	28 08	29 05	0♒01	0 58	MC
NOON	13♉38	15 04	16 28	17 51	19 12	20 33	21 53	23 12	ASC
1	8♒54	9 52	10 51	11 50	12 49	13 48	14 47	15 46	MC
PM	3♊24	4 34	5 43	6 51	7 58	9 05	10 11	11 16	ASC
2	24♒04	25 05	26 06	27 07	28 09	29 11	0♓12	1 14	MC
PM	19♊48	20 47	21 45	22 43	23 41	24 38	25 35	26 31	ASC
3	9♓52	10 56	11 59	13 03	14 06	15 10	16 14	17 18	MC
PM	3♋58	4 51	5 43	6 35	7 26	8 17	9 08	9 59	ASC
4	26♓08	27 13	28 17	29 22	0♈26	1 31	2 35	3 39	MC
PM	16♋48	17 37	18 25	19 14	20 02	20 50	21 38	22 25	ASC
5	12♈30	13 34	14 38	15 42	16 45	17 49	18 52	19 56	MC
PM	28♋54	29 41	0♌27	1 14	2 00	2 47	3 33	4 19	ASC
6	28♈34	29 36	0♉38	1 39	2 41	3 42	4 44	5 45	MC
PM	10♌39	11 25	12 11	12 56	13 42	14 28	15 14	15 59	ASC
7	14♉02	15 02	16 01	17 00	17 59	18 58	19 56	20 55	MC
PM	22♌17	23 03	23 48	24 34	25 20	26 06	26 51	27 37	ASC
8	28♉51	29 48	0♊45	1 41	2 38	3 34	4 30	5 26	MC
PM	3♍56	4 42	5 28	6 14	7 00	7 46	8 32	9 18	ASC
9	13♊05	14 00	14 55	15 50	16 45	17 40	18 34	19 29	MC
PM	15♍39	16 25	17 11	17 57	18 44	19 30	20 16	21 02	ASC
10	26♊58	27 53	28 47	29 41	0♋36	1 30	2 24	3 18	MC
PM	27♍25	28 11	28 58	29 44	0♎30	1 17	2 03	2 49	ASC
11	10♋48	11 43	12 37	13 32	14 27	15 22	16 17	17 12	MC
PM	9♎12	9 58	10 44	11 31	12 17	13 03	13 49	14 35	ASC

CALENDAR DATE — JANUARY of any year — CALENDAR DATE

HOUR OF BIRTH	25 ° '	26 ° '	27 ° '	28 ° '	29 ° '	30 ° '	31 ° '	1 ° '	
12	1♌27	2 24	3 21	4 19	5 16	6 14	7 12	8 10	MC
MID	26♎18	27 04	27 50	28 36	29 22	0♏08	0 53	1 39	ASC
1	16♌16	17 16	18 16	19 16	20 16	21 16	22 17		MC
AM	7♏57	8 43	9 29	10 14	11 00	11 46	12 31		ASC
2	1♍46	2 48	3 50	4 53	5 55	6 58	8 01		MC
AM	19♏35	20 21	21 07	21 53	22 39	23 25	24 11		ASC
3	17♍50	18 54	19 58	21 02	22 06	23 11	24 15		MC
AM	1♐20	2 07	2 54	3 41	4 28	5 15	6 02		ASC
4	4♎12	5 16	6 20	7 25	8 29	9 33	10 37		MC
AM	13♐27	14 16	15 05	15 54	16 43	17 33	18 23		ASC
5	20♎27	21 30	22 33	23 36	24 39	25 42	26 44		MC
AM	26♐18	27 11	28 04	28 58	29 52	0♑46	1 41		ASC
6	6♏15	7 16	8 16	9 17	10 17	11 17	12 17		MC
AM	10♑31	11 31	12 31	13 32	14 34	15 36	16 39		ASC
7	21♏24	22 22	23 20	24 18	25 15	26 13	27 10		MC
AM	26♑58	28 09	29 21	0♒34	1 47	3 02	4 18		ASC
8	5♐54	6 50	7 46	8 42	9 37	10 33	11 28		MC
AM	16♒48	18 15	19 42	21 11	22 41	24 12	25 44		ASC
9	19♐56	20 51	21 45	22 40	23 34	24 29	25 23		MC
AM	10♓43	12 25	14 07	15 50	17 34	19 18	21 02		ASC
10	3♑45	4 40	5 34	6 28	7 23	8 17	9 12		MC
AM	7♈18	9 03	10 47	12 31	14 15	15 58	17 40		ASC
11	17♑40	18 35	19 30	20 26	21 21	22 17	23 13		MC
AM	2♉48	4 21	5 53	7 24	8 53	10 22	11 50		ASC
12	1♒55	2 52	3 50	4 47	5 45	6 43	7 41		MC
NOON	24♉29	25 46	27 01	28 16	29 30	0♊43	1 55		ASC
1	16♒46	17 46	18 46	19 46	20 46	21 46	22 47		MC
PM	12♊20	13 24	14 27	15 29	16 31	17 32	18 32		ASC
2	2♓17	3 19	4 21	5 24	6 27	7 30	8 33		MC
PM	27♊26	28 22	29 16	0 11	1 05	1 58	2 52		ASC
3	18♓22	19 26	20 30	21 34	22 38	23 43	24 47		MC
PM	10♋49	11 39	12 29	13 19	14 09	14 58	15 47		ASC
4	4♈44	5 48	6 52	7 57	9 01	10 05	11 09		MC
PM	23♋13	24 00	24 47	25 35	26 22	27 09	27 55		ASC
5	20♈59	22 02	23 05	24 08	25 10	26 13	27 15		MC
PM	5♌05	5 51	6 37	7 23	8 09	8 55	9 41		ASC
6	6♉45	7 46	8 47	9 47	10 47	11 47	12 47		MC
PM	16♌45	17 31	18 17	19 02	19 48	20 34	21 19		ASC
7	21♉53	22 51	23 49	24 47	25 44	26 42	27 39		MC
PM	28♌23	29 09	29 55	0♍40	1 26	2 12	2 58		ASC
8	6♊22	7 18	8 14	9 09	10 05	11 00	11 56		MC
PM	10♍04	10 50	11 36	12 22	13 08	13 54	14 41		ASC
9	20♊24	21 18	22 13	23 07	24 01	24 56	25 50		MC
PM	21♍49	22 35	23 21	24 08	24 54	25 40	26 27		ASC
10	4♋13	5 07	6 01	6 56	7 50	8 45	9 39		MC
PM	3♎36	4 22	5 08	5 55	6 41	7 27	8 13		ASC
11	18♋07	19 02	19 58	20 53	21 49	22 45	23 41		MC
PM	15♎22	16 08	16 54	17 40	18 26	19 12	19 58		ASC

CALENDAR DATE FEBRUARY of any year CALENDAR DATE

HOUR OF BIRTH	1	2	3	4	5	6	7	8	
12 MID	8♌10	9 08	10 06	11 05	12 04	13 03	14 02	15 01	MC
	1♏39	2 25	3 11	3 57	4 42	5 28	6 14	7 00	ASC
1 AM	23♌17	24 18	25 19	26 21	27 22	28 24	29 25	0♍27	MC
	13♏17	14 03	14 49	15 34	16 20	17 06	17 52	18 37	ASC
2 AM	9♍04	10 08	11 11	12 14	13 18	14 22	15 25	16 29	MC
	24♏57	25 43	26 29	27 16	28 02	28 48	29 35	0♐21	ASC
3 AM	25♍19	26 24	27 28	28 33	29 37	0♎42	1 46	2 50	MC
	6♐50	7 37	8 25	9 13	10 01	10 49	11 37	12 25	ASC
4 AM	11♎41	12 45	13 49	14 53	15 57	17 00	18 04	19 07	MC
	19♐13	20 04	20 54	21 45	22 37	23 28	24 20	25 12	ABC
5 AM	27♎46	28 49	29 51	0♏52	1 54	2 56	3 57	4 58	MC
	2♑36	3 32	4 28	5 25	6 22	7 19	8 17	9 16	ASC
6 AM	13♏17	14 17	15 16	16 15	17 14	18 13	19 12	20 10	MC
	17♑43	18 47	19 52	20 58	22 05	23 12	24 21	25 30	ASC
7 AM	28♏07	29 04	0♐01	0 58	1 55	2 51	3 47	4 44	MC
	5♒35	6 52	8 11	9 31	10 52	12 13	13 36	15 00	ASC
8 AM	12♐23	13 18	14 13	15 08	16 03	16 58	17 53	18 36	MC
	27♒17	28 51	0♓26	2 02	3 39	5 17	6 56	8 36	ASC
9 AM	26♐17	27 11	28 06	29 00	29 54	0♑49	1 43	2 37	MC
	22♓47	24 32	26 18	28 03	29 49	1♈34	3 20	5 06	ASC
10 AM	10♑06	11 01	11 56	12 50	13 45	14 40	15 35	16 30	MC
	19♈22	21 03	22 43	24 22	26 00	27 37	29 14	0♉49	ASC
11 AM	24♑08	25 04	26 01	26 57	27 53	28 50	29 47	0♒43	MC
	13♉16	14 42	16 06	17 29	18 51	20 12	21 32	22 51	ASC
12 NOON	8♒39	9 37	10 36	11 34	12 33	13 32	14 31	15 31	MC
	3♊06	4 16	5 25	6 33	7 41	8 48	9 54	10 59	ASC
1 PM	23♒48	24 49	25 50	26 51	27 53	28 55	29 56	0♓58	MC
	19♊32	20 31	21 30	22 28	23 26	24 23	25 20	26 16	ASC
2 PM	9♓36	10 39	11 43	12 46	13 50	14 53	15 57	17 01	MC
	3♋44	4 37	5 29	6 21	7 13	8 04	8 55	9 46	ASC
3 PM	25♓52	26 56	28 00	29 05	0♈09	1 14	2 18	3 23	MC
	16♋36	17 24	18 13	19 01	19 49	20 37	21 25	22 13	ASC
4 PM	12♈13	13 17	14 21	15 25	16 29	17 32	18 36	19 39	MC
	28♋42	29 29	0♌15	1 02	1 48	2 35	3 21	4 07	ASC
5 PM	28♈17	29 20	0♉21	1 23	2 25	3 26	4 28	5 29	MC
	10♌27	11 13	11 59	12 45	13 30	14 16	15 02	15 47	ASC
6 PM	13♉47	14 46	15 46	16 45	17 44	18 42	19 41	20 40	MC
	22♌05	22 51	23 36	24 22	25 08	25 54	26 39	27 25	ASC
7 PM	28♉36	29 33	0♊30	1 26	2 23	3 19	4 16	5 12	MC
	3♍44	4 30	5 16	6 02	6 48	7 34	8 20	9 06	ASC
8 PM	12♊51	13 46	14 41	15 36	16 31	17 25	18 20	19 15	MC
	15♍27	16 13	16 59	17 45	18 32	19 18	20 04	20 50	ASC
9 PM	26♊44	27 39	28 33	29 27	0♋21	1 16	2 10	3 04	MC
	27♍13	27 59	28 46	29 32	0♎18	1 05	1 51	2 37	ASC
10 PM	10♋34	11 28	12 23	13 18	14 13	15 07	16 02	16 58	MC
	9♎00	9 46	10 32	11 19	12 05	12 51	13 37	14 23	ASC
11 PM	24♋36	25 33	26 29	27 25	28 22	29 18	0♌15	1 12	MC
	20♎44	21 30	22 16	23 02	23 48	24 34	25 20	26 06	ASC

CALENDAR DATE FEBRUARY of any year CALENDAR DATE

HOUR OF BIRTH	9	10	11	12	13	14	15	16	
12 MID	16♌01	17 00	18 00	19 00	20 00	21 00	22 01	23 02	MC
	7♏45	8 31	9 17	10 02	10 48	11 34	12 20	13 05	ASC
1 AM	1♍29	2 32	3 34	4 36	5 39	6 42	7 45	8 48	MC
	19♏23	20 09	20 55	21 41	22 27	23 13	23 59	24 45	ASC
2 AM	17♍33	18 37	19 41	20 45	21 50	22 54	23 58	25 03	MC
	1♐08	1 55	2 42	3 28	4 15	5 03	5 50	6 37	ASC
3 AM	3♎55	4 59	6 04	7 08	8 12	9 16	10 21	11 25	MC
	13♐14	14 03	14 52	15 41	16 30	17 20	18 10	19 00	ASC
4 AM	20♎11	21 14	22 17	23 20	24 23	25 25	26 28	27 30	MC
	26♐04	26 57	27 50	28 44	29 38	0♑32	1 27	2 22	ASC
5 AM	5♏59	7 00	8 01	9 01	10 02	11 02	12 02	13 01	MC
	10♑15	11 15	12 15	13 16	14 18	15 20	16 23	17 26	ASC
6 AM	21♏09	22 07	23 05	24 03	25 00	25 58	26 55	27 53	MC
	26♑40	27 50	29 02	0♒15	1 28	2 43	3 58	5 14	ASC
7 AM	5♐40	6 36	7 31	8 27	9 23	10 18	11 14	12 09	MC
	16♒26	17 52	19 19	20 48	22 17	23 48	25 20	26 52	ASC
8 AM	19♐42	20 37	21 31	22 26	23 20	24 14	25 09	26 03	MC
	10♓17	11 58	13 40	15 23	17 07	18 50	20 35	22 20	ASC
9 AM	3♑31	4 26	5 20	6 14	7 09	8 03	8 58	9 52	MC
	6♈51	8 36	10 20	12 04	13 48	15 31	17 14	18 55	ASC
10 AM	17♑25	18 20	19 16	20 11	21 07	22 02	22 58	23 54	MC
	2♉23	3 57	5 29	7 00	8 30	9 59	11 27	12 54	ASC
11 AM	1♒40	2 38	3 35	4 32	5 30	6 28	7 26	8 24	MC
	24♉09	25 26	26 42	27 57	29 11	0♊24	1 36	2 47	ASC
12 NOON	16♒30	17 30	18 30	19 30	20 30	21 31	22 31	23 32	MC
	12♊04	13 07	14 11	15 13	16 15	17 16	18 17	19 17	ASC
1 PM	2♓00	3 03	4 05	5 08	6 10	7 13	8 16	9 19	MC
	27♊12	28 07	29 02	29 57	0♋51	1 44	2 38	3 31	ASC
2 PM	18♓05	19 09	20 13	21 17	22 22	23 26	24 30	25 35	MC
	10♋36	11 26	12 16	13 06	13 56	14 45	15 34	16 23	ASC
3 PM	4♈27	5 31	6 36	7 40	8 44	9 48	10 53	11 57	MC
	23♋00	23 48	24 35	25 22	26 09	26 56	27 43	28 30	ASC
4 PM	20♈42	21 45	22 48	23 51	24 54	25 56	26 59	28 01	MC
	4♌53	5 39	6 25	7 11	7 57	8 43	9 29	10 15	ASC
5 PM	6♉30	7 30	8 31	9 31	10 32	11 32	12 32	13 31	MC
	16♌33	17 19	18 05	18 50	19 36	20 22	21 07	21 53	ASC
6 PM	21♉38	22 36	23 34	24 32	25 29	26 27	27 24	28 21	MC
	28♌11	28 57	29 43	0♍29	1 14	2 00	2 46	3 32	ASC
7 PM	6♊08	7 04	7 59	8 55	9 50	10 46	11 41	12 36	MC
	9♍52	10 38	11 24	12 10	12 56	13 42	14 29	15 15	ASC
8 PM	20♊09	21 04	21 58	22 53	23 47	24 42	25 36	26 30	MC
	21♍37	22 23	23 09	23 56	24 42	25 28	26 15	27 01	ASC
9 PM	3♋58	4 53	5 47	6 42	7 36	8 30	9 25	10 19	MC
	3♎24	4 10	4 56	5 43	6 29	7 15	8 01	8 48	ASC
10 PM	17♋53	18 48	19 43	20 39	21 34	22 30	23 26	24 22	MC
	15♎10	15 56	16 42	17 28	18 14	19 00	19 46	20 32	ASC
11 PM	2♌09	3 06	4 04	5 01	5 59	6 57	7 55	8 53	MC
	26♎52	27 38	28 24	29 10	29 56	0♏42	1 27	2 13	ASC

CALENDAR DATE — FEBRUARY of any year — CALENDAR DATE

HOUR OF BIRTH	17	18	19	20	21	22	23	24	
12	24♌02	25 04	26 05	27 06	28 08	29 09	0♍11	1 13	MC
MID	13♏51	14 37	15 22	16 08	16 54	17 40	18 25	19 11	ASC
1	9♍51	10 54	11 58	13 01	14 05	15 09	16 13	17 16	MC
AM	25♏31	26 17	27 04	27 50	28 36	29 23	0♐09	0 56	ASC
2	26♍07	27 11	28 16	29 20	0♎25	1 29	2 34	3 38	MC
AM	7♐25	8 12	9 00	9 48	10 36	11 24	12 13	13 01	ASC
3	12♎29	13 33	14 37	15 40	16 44	17 47	18 51	19 54	MC
AM	19♐50	20 41	21 32	22 23	23 15	24 06	24 58	25 51	ASC
4	28♎32	29 34	0♏36	1 38	2 40	3 41	4 42	5 43	MC
AM	3♑17	4 13	5 10	6 07	7 04	8 02	9 01	10 00	ASC
5	14♏01	15 01	16 00	16 59	17 58	18 57	19 55	20 54	MC
AM	18♑30	19 35	20 41	21 47	22 55	24 03	25 12	26 21	ASC
6	28♏50	29 47	0♐43	1 40	2 36	3 33	4 29	5 25	MC
AM	6♒32	7 50	9 10	10 30	11 52	13 15	14 39	16 03	ASC
7	13♐04	13 59	14 54	15 49	16 44	17 39	18 33	19 28	MC
AM	28♒26	0♓01	1 37	3 14	4 52	6 31	8 10	9 51	ASC
8	26♐57	27 52	28 46	29 40	0♑34	1 29	2 23	3 17	MC
AM	24♓05	25 50	27 36	29 21	1♈07	2 53	4 38	6 23	ASC
9	10♑47	11 41	12 36	13 31	14 26	15 21	16 16	17 11	MC
AM	20♈36	22 17	23 56	25 34	27 12	28 49	0♉24	1 59	ASC
10	24♑50	25 46	26 42	27 39	28 35	29 32	0♒29	1 26	MC
AM	14♉19	15 44	17 07	18 30	19 51	21 11	22 31	23 49	ASC
11	9♒22	10 21	11 19	12 18	13 17	14 16	15 15	16 15	MC
AM	3♊57	5 07	6 16	7 23	8 30	9 37	10 42	11 47	ASC
12	24♒33	25 34	26 35	27 37	28 38	29 40	0♓42	1 44	MC
NOON	20♊16	21 15	22 13	23 11	24 08	25 05	26 02	26 57	ASC
1	10♓23	11 26	12 30	13 33	14 37	15 41	16 44	17 48	MC
PM	4♋23	5 16	6 08	6 59	7 51	8 42	9 33	10 23	ASC
2	26♓39	27 44	28 48	29 53	0♈57	2 01	3 06	4 10	MC
PM	17♋11	18 00	18 49	19 37	20 25	21 13	22 00	22 48	ASC
3	13♈01	14 05	15 08	16 12	17 16	18 19	19 23	20 26	MC
PM	29♋17	0♌03	0 50	1 36	2 23	3 09	3 55	4 41	ASC
4	29♈03	0♉05	1 07	2 09	3 10	4 12	5 13	6 14	MC
PM	11♌01	11 47	12 33	13 18	14 12	14 50	15 36	16 21	ASC
5	14♉31	15 30	16 29	17 28	18 27	19 26	20 24	21 23	MC
PM	22♌39	23 25	24 10	24 56	25 42	26 28	27 13	27 59	ASC
6	29♉18	0♊15	1 12	2 08	3 05	4 01	4 57	5 53	MC
PM	4♍18	5 04	5 50	6 36	7 22	8 08	8 54	9 40	ASC
7	13♊32	14 27	15 21	16 16	17 11	18 06	19 01	19 55	MC
PM	16♍01	16 47	17 33	18 20	19 06	19 52	20 38	21 25	ASC
8	27♊24	28 19	29 13	0♋07	1 02	1 56	2 50	3 44	MC
PM	27♍47	28 34	29 20	0♎06	0 53	1 39	2 25	3 12	ASC
9	11♋14	12 09	13 03	13 58	14 53	15 48	16 43	17 38	MC
PM	9♎34	10 20	11 06	11 53	12 39	13 25	14 11	14 58	ASC
10	25♋18	26 14	27 10	28 07	29 03	0♌00	0 57	1 54	MC
PM	21♎18	22 04	22 50	23 36	24 22	25 08	25 54	26 40	ASC
11	9♌51	10 50	11 49	12 47	13 46	14 46	15 45	16 45	MC
PM	2♏59	3 45	4 30	5 16	6 02	6 48	7 33	8 19	ASC

CALENDAR DATE — FEBRUARY of any year — CALENDAR DATE

HOUR OF BIRTH	25	26	27	28	29	1	
12	2♍15	3 18	4 20	5 23	6 26	7 28	MC
MID	19♏57	20 43	21 29	22 15	23 01	23 47	ASC
1	18♍20	19 25	20 29	21 33	22 37		MC
AM	1♐43	2 29	3 16	4 03	4 50		ASC
2	4♎42	5 47	6 51	7 55	9 00		MC
AM	13♐50	14 39	15 28	16 18	17 07		ASC
3	20♎57	22 01	23 03	24 06	25 09		MC
AM	26♐43	27 37	28 30	29 24	0♑18		ASC
4	6♏44	7 45	8 45	9 46	10 46		MC
AM	10♑59	11 59	13 00	14 02	15 04		ASC
5	21♏52	22 50	23 48	24 45	25 43		MC
AM	27♑32	28 43	29 56	1♒09	2 23		ASC
6	6♐21	7 17	8 13	9 08	10 04		MC
AM	17♒29	18 56	20 25	21 54	23 24		ASC
7	20♐22	21 17	22 11	23 06	24 00		MC
AM	11♓32	13 14	14 56	16 40	18 23		ASC
8	4♑11	5 06	6 00	6 55	7 49		MC
AM	8♈08	9 53	11 37	13 21	15 04		ASC
9	18♑06	19 01	19 57	20 52	21 48		MC
AM	3♉32	5 05	6 36	8 07	9 36		ASC
10	2♒23	3 20	4 17	5 15	6 13		MC
AM	25♉06	26 22	27 37	28 52	0♊05		ASC
11	17♒15	18 14	19 14	20 15	21 15		MC
AM	12♊51	13 54	14 57	15 59	17 00		ASC
12	2♓46	3 49	4 51	5 54	6 57		MC
NOON	27♊53	28 48	29 42	0♋37	1 30		ASC
1	18♓52	19 57	21 01	22 05	23 09		MC
PM	11♋13	12 03	12 53	13 43	14 32		ASC
2	5♈15	6 19	7 23	8 28	9 32		MC
PM	23♋35	24 23	25 10	25 57	26 44		ASC
3	21♈29	22 32	23 35	24 38	25 40		MC
PM	5♌27	6 13	6 59	7 45	8 31		ASC
4	7♉15	8 15	9 16	10 16	11 16		MC
PM	17♌07	17 53	18 38	19 24	20 10		ASC
5	22♉21	23 19	24 17	25 14	26 12		MC
PM	28♌45	29 31	0♍17	1 02	1 48		ASC
6	6♊49	7 45	8 40	9 36	10 31		MC
PM	10♍26	11 12	11 58	12 44	13 30		ASC
7	20♊50	21 44	22 39	23 33	24 27		MC
PM	22♍11	22 57	23 44	24 30	25 16		ASC
8	4♋39	5 33	6 27	7 22	8 16		MC
PM	3♎58	4 44	5 30	6 17	7 03		ASC
9	18♋34	19 29	20 24	21 20	22 16		MC
PM	15♎44	16 30	17 16	18 02	18 48		ASC
10	2♌51	3 49	4 46	5 44	6 42		MC
PM	27♎26	28 12	28 58	29 44	0♏30		ASC
11	17♌44	18 44	19 44	20 45	21 45		MC
PM	9♏05	9 50	10 36	11 22	12 08		ASC

CALENDAR DATE — MARCH of any year — CALENDAR DATE

HOUR OF BIRTH	1	2	3	4	5	6	7	8	
12	7♍28	8 31	9 35	10 38	11 41	12 45	13 48	14 52	MC
MID	23♏47	24 33	25 19	26 05	26 52	27 38	28 24	29 11	ASC
1	23♍41	24 46	25 50	26 55	27 59	29 03	0♎08	1 12	MC
AM	5♐38	6 25	7 12	8 00	8 48	9 36	10 24	11 12	ASC
2	10♎04	11 08	12 12	13 16	14 20	15 24	16 27	17 31	MC
AM	17♐57	18 47	19 37	20 28	21 19	22 10	23 01	23 53	ASC
3	26♎12	27 14	28 16	29 18	0♏20	1 22	2 24	3 25	MC
AM	1♑13	2 08	3 03	3 59	4 55	5 52	6 49	7 47	ASC
4	11♏46	12 46	13 46	14 45	15 44	16 44	17 42	18 41	MC
AM	16♑06	17 10	18 14	19 18	20 24	21 30	22 37	23 45	ASC
5	26♏40	27 38	28 35	29 32	0♐29	1 25	2 22	3 18	MC
AM	3♒38	4 54	6 12	7 30	8 49	10 09	11 31	12 53	ASC
6	10♐59	11 54	12 50	13 45	14 40	15 35	16 29	17 24	MC
AM	24♒56	26 28	28 02	29 36	1♓12	2 49	4 26	6 05	ASC
7	24♐55	25 49	26 43	27 37	28 32	29 26	0♑20	1 15	MC
AM	20♓08	21 52	23 37	25 23	27 08	28 54	0♈39	2 25	ASC
8	8♑43	9 38	10 33	11 27	12 22	13 17	14 11	15 06	MC
AM	16♈47	18 29	20 10	21 51	23 30	25 09	26 47	28 24	ASC
9	22♑43	23 39	24 35	25 31	26 28	27 24	28 20	29 17	MC
AM	11♉04	12 31	13 57	15 22	16 46	18 09	19 30	20 51	ASC
10	7♒11	8 09	9 07	10 05	11 04	12 03	13 02	14 01	MC
AM	1♊17	2 29	3 39	4 49	5 58	7 06	8 13	9 24	ASC
11	22♒15	23 16	24 17	25 18	26 19	27 21	28 22	29 24	MC
AM	18♊01	19 01	20 01	21 00	21 58	22 56	23 54	24 50	ASC
12	8♓00	9 03	10 06	11 10	12 13	13 17	14 20	15 24	MC
NOON	2♋24	3 17	4 10	5 02	5 54	6 46	7 37	8 28	ASC
1	24♓14	25 18	26 22	27 27	28 31	29 36	0♈40	1 45	MC
PM	15♋21	16 10	16 59	17 48	18 36	19 24	20 12	21 00	ASC
2	10♈36	11 40	12 44	13 48	14 52	15 55	16 59	18 03	MC
PM	27♋31	28 18	29 04	29 51	0♌38	1 24	2 10	2 57	ASC
3	26♈43	27 45	28 47	29 49	0♉51	1 53	2 54	3 56	MC
PM	9♌17	10 03	10 49	11 35	12 21	13 06	13 52	14 38	ASC
4	12♉16	13 16	14 15	15 15	16 14	17 13	18 12	19 11	MC
PM	20♌56	21 41	22 27	23 13	23 58	24 44	25 30	26 16	ASC
5	27♉09	28 06	29 03	0♊00	0 57	1 54	2 50	3 46	MC
PM	2♍34	3 20	4 06	4 52	5 38	6 24	7 10	7 56	ASC
6	11♊27	12 22	13 17	14 12	15 07	16 02	16 57	17 52	MC
PM	14♍17	15 03	15 49	16 35	17 21	18 08	18 54	19 40	ASC
7	25♊22	26 16	27 10	28 05	28 59	29 53	0♋47	1 42	MC
PM	26♍02	26 49	27 35	28 21	29 08	29 54	0♎40	1 27	ASC
8	9♋11	10 05	11 00	11 55	12 49	13 44	14 39	15 34	MC
PM	7♎49	8 36	9 22	10 08	10 54	11 41	12 27	13 13	ASC
9	23♋11	24 07	25 03	25 59	26 56	27 52	28 49	29 45	MC
PM	19♎34	20 20	21 06	21 52	22 38	23 24	24 10	24 56	ASC
10	7♌40	8 38	9 36	10 35	11 33	12 32	13 31	14 30	MC
PM	1♏15	2 01	2 47	3 33	4 19	5 04	5 50	6 36	ASC
11	22♌46	23 47	24 48	25 49	26 50	27 52	28 53	29 55	MC
PM	12♏53	13 39	14 25	15 10	15 56	16 42	17 28	18 14	ASC

CALENDAR DATE — MARCH of any year — CALENDAR DATE

HOUR OF BIRTH	9	10	11	12	13	14	15	16	
12	15♍56	17 00	18 04	19 08	20 12	21 16	22 20	23 25	MC
MID	29♏57	0♐44	1 30	2 17	3 04	3 51	4 38	5 25	ASC
1	2♎17	3 21	4 26	5 30	6 34	7 39	8 43	9 47	MC
AM	12♐00	12 49	13 37	14 26	15 15	16 05	16 54	17 44	ASC
2	18♎34	19 38	20 41	21 44	22 47	23 50	24 53	25 55	MC
AM	24♐45	25 37	26 30	27 23	28 16	29 10	0♑04	0 58	ASC
3	4♏26	5 27	6 28	7 29	8 30	9 30	10 30	11 30	MC
AM	8♑45	9 44	10 44	11 44	12 44	13 46	14 47	15 50	ASC
4	19♏40	20 38	21 37	22 35	23 33	24 30	25 28	26 26	MC
AM	24♑54	26 03	27 13	28 25	29 37	0♒50	2 04	3 19	ASC
5	4♐14	5 11	6 06	7 02	7 58	8 54	9 49	10 45	MC
AM	14♒17	15 41	17 07	18 34	20 02	21 31	23 01	24 32	ASC
6	18♐19	19 14	20 08	21 03	21 57	22 52	23 46	24 40	MC
AM	7♓44	9 24	11 05	12 47	14 30	16 13	17 56	19 40	ASC
7	2♑09	3 03	3 57	4 52	5 46	6 40	7 35	8 29	MC
AM	4♈11	5 56	7 41	9 26	11 10	12 54	14 38	16 20	ASC
8	16♑01	16 56	17 52	18 47	19 42	20 38	21 33	22 29	MC
AM	29♈59	1 34	3 08	4 41	6 13	7 43	9 13	10 41	ASC
9	0♒14	1 11	2 08	3 05	4 02	5 00	5 58	6 55	MC
AM	22♉10	23 29	24 46	26 02	27 18	28 32	29 46	0♊58	ASC
10	15♒00	15 59	16 59	17 59	18 59	19 59	20 59	22 00	MC
AM	10♊25	11 30	12 34	13 38	14 41	15 43	16 44	17 45	ASC
11	0♓26	1 28	2 30	3 33	4 35	5 38	6 41	7 43	MC
AM	25♊47	26 43	27 38	28 34	29 28	0♋23	1 16	2 10	ASC
12	16♓28	17 32	18 36	19 40	20 44	21 48	22 53	23 57	MC
NOON	9♋19	10 10	11 00	11 50	12 40	13 30	14 19	15 09	ASC
1	2♈49	3 53	4 58	6 02	7 07	8 11	9 15	10 19	MC
PM	21♋48	22 36	23 23	24 10	24 58	25 45	26 32	27 19	ASC
2	19♈06	20 09	21 13	22 16	23 19	24 21	25 24	26 27	MC
PM	3♌43	4 29	5 15	6 01	6 47	7 33	8 19	9 05	ASC
3	4♉57	5 58	6 59	7 59	9 00	10 00	11 00	12 00	MC
PM	15♌24	16 09	16 55	17 41	18 27	19 12	19 58	20 44	ASC
4	20♉09	21 07	22 06	23 04	24 02	24 59	25 57	26 54	MC
PM	27♌01	27 47	28 33	29 19	0♍05	0 50	1 36	2 22	ASC
5	4♊42	5 39	6 34	7 30	8 26	9 22	10 17	11 12	MC
PM	8♍42	9 28	10 14	11 00	11 46	12 32	13 18	14 05	ASC
6	18♊46	19 41	20 35	21 30	22 24	23 19	24 13	25 08	MC
PM	20♍26	21 13	21 59	22 45	23 31	24 18	25 04	25 50	ASC
7	2♋36	3 30	4 25	5 19	6 13	7 08	8 02	8 57	MC
PM	2♎13	2 59	3 46	4 32	5 18	6 05	6 51	7 37	ASC
8	16♋29	17 24	18 19	19 15	20 10	21 05	22 01	22 57	MC
PM	13♎59	14 46	15 32	16 18	17 04	17 50	18 36	19 22	ASC
9	0♌42	1 39	2 36	3 34	4 31	5 29	6 27	7 24	MC
PM	25♎42	26 28	27 14	28 00	28 46	29 32	0♏18	1 03	ASC
10	15♌30	16 29	17 29	18 29	19 29	20 29	21 29	22 30	MC
PM	7♏21	8 07	8 53	9 39	10 24	11 10	11 56	12 41	ASC
11	0♍57	1 59	3 01	4 04	5 06	6 09	7 12	8 15	MC
PM	18♏59	19 45	20 31	21 17	22 03	22 49	23 35	24 21	ASC

CALENDAR DATE MARCH of any year CALENDAR DATE

HOUR OF BIRTH	17	18	19	20	21	22	23	24	
12	24♍29	25 33	26 38	27 42	28 47	29 51	0♎56	2 00	MC
MID	6♐13	7 00	7 48	8 35	9 23	10 11	10 59	11 48	ASC
1	10♎51	11 55	12 59	14 03	15 07	16 11	17 14	18 18	MC
AM	18♐34	19 24	20 15	21 05	21 56	22 48	23 39	24 31	ASC
2	26♎58	28 00	29 02	0 04	1 06	2 08	3 09	4 10	MC
AM	1♑53	2 49	3 44	4 41	5 37	6 34	7 32	8 30	ASC
3	12♏30	13 30	14 30	15 29	16 28	17 27	18 26	19 25	MC
AM	16♑53	17 57	19 01	20 07	21 13	22 20	23 27	24 36	ASC
4	27♏23	28 20	29 17	0 14	1 11	2 07	3 03	4 00	MC
AM	4♒35	5 51	7 09	8 28	9 48	11 09	12 32	13 55	ASC
5	11♐40	12 35	13 30	14 25	15 20	16 15	17 10	18 05	MC
AM	26♒04	27 37	29 12	0♓47	2 23	4 01	5 39	7 18	ASC
6	25♐35	26 29	27 23	28 18	29 12	0♑06	1 00	1 55	MC
AM	21♓25	23 10	24 55	26 41	28 26	0♈12	1 58	3 43	ASC
7	9♑24	10 18	11 13	12 08	13 02	13 57	14 52	15 47	MC
AM	18♈02	19 44	21 24	23 04	24 43	26 21	27 58	29 35	ASC
8	23♑25	24 21	25 17	26 13	27 09	28 06	29 02	29 59	MC
AM	12♉09	13 35	15 00	16 24	17 47	19 09	20 30	21 50	ASC
9	7♒54	8 52	9 50	10 49	11 47	12 46	13 45	14 44	MC
AM	2♊10	3 21	4 31	5 40	6 48	7 56	9 02	10 08	ASC
10	23♒00	24 01	25 02	26 03	27 05	28 06	29 08	0♓10	MC
AM	18♊45	19 45	20 44	21 43	22 41	23 39	24 36	25 32	ASC
11	8♓47	9 50	10 53	11 56	13 00	14 04	15 07	16 11	MC
AM	3♋03	3 56	4 48	5 41	6 32	7 24	8 15	9 06	ASC
12	25♓01	26 06	27 10	28 15	29 19	0♈23	1 28	2 32	MC
NOON	15♋58	16 46	17 35	18 23	19 12	20 00	20 48	21 36	ASC
1	11♈23	12 27	13 31	14 35	15 39	16 43	17 46	18 50	MC
PM	28♋06	28 52	29 39	0♌26	1 12	1 58	2 45	3 31	ASC
2	27♈29	28 31	29 33	0♉35	1 37	2 38	3 40	4 41	MC
PM	9♌51	10 37	11 23	12 09	12 55	13 40	14 26	15 12	ASC
3	13♉00	14 00	14 59	15 59	16 58	17 57	18 55	19 54	MC
PM	21♌29	22 15	23 01	23 47	24 32	25 18	26 04	26 50	ASC
4	27♉51	28 48	29 45	0♊42	1 39	2 35	3 32	4 28	MC
PM	3♍08	3 54	4 40	5 26	6 12	6 58	7 44	8 30	ASC
5	12♊08	13 03	13 58	14 53	15 48	16 43	17 37	18 32	MC
PM	14♍51	15 37	16 23	17 09	17 56	18 42	19 28	20 14	ASC
6	26♊02	26 56	27 50	28 45	29 39	0♋33	1 28	2 22	MC
PM	26♍37	27 23	28 09	28 56	29 42	0♎28	1 15	2 01	ASC
7	9♋51	10 46	11 40	12 35	13 30	14 25	15 20	16 15	MC
PM	8♎24	9 10	9 56	10 42	11 29	12 15	13 01	13 47	ASC
8	23♋53	24 49	25 45	26 41	27 38	28 34	29 31	0♌27	MC
PM	20♎08	20 54	21 40	22 27	23 13	23 59	24 44	25 30	ASC
9	8♌23	9 21	10 19	11 18	12 17	13 16	14 15	15 14	MC
PM	1♏49	2 35	3 21	4 07	4 52	5 38	6 24	7 10	ASC
10	23♌31	24 32	25 33	26 34	27 36	28 37	29 39	0♍41	MC
PM	13♏27	14 13	14 59	15 44	16 30	17 16	18 02	18 47	ASC
11	9♍18	10 21	11 25	12 28	13 32	14 36	15 39	16 43	MC
PM	25♏07	25 53	26 39	27 26	28 12	28 59	29 45	0♐32	ASC

CALENDAR DATE MARCH of any year CALENDAR DATE

HOUR OF BIRTH	25	26	27	28	29	30	31	1 (April)	
12	3♎05	4 09	5 13	6 18	7 22	8 26	9 30	10 35	MC
MID	12♐36	13 25	14 14	15 03	15 52	16 41	17 31	18 21	ASC
1	19♎21	20 25	21 28	22 31	23 34	24 36	25 39		MC
AM	25♐23	26 16	27 09	28 02	28 56	29 50	0♑44		ASC
2	5♏12	6 13	7 13	8 14	9 14	10 15	11 15		MC
AM	9♑29	10 28	11 28	12 29	13 30	14 31	15 34		ASC
3	20♏23	21 21	22 20	23 18	24 15	25 13	26 11		MC
AM	25♑45	26 55	28 06	29 18	0♒31	1 44	2 59		ASC
4	4♐56	5 52	6 48	7 44	8 39	9 35	10 30		MC
AM	15♒19	16 44	18 11	19 39	21 07	22 37	24 08		ASC
5	18♐59	19 54	20 49	21 43	22 38	23 32	24 26		MC
AM	8♓58	10 39	12 21	14 03	15 46	17 29	19 13		ASC
6	2♑49	3 43	4 38	5 32	6 26	7 21	8 15		MC
AM	5♈29	7 14	8 59	10 43	12 27	14 11	15 54		ASC
7	16♑42	17 37	18 33	19 28	20 23	21 19	22 14		MC
AM	1♉10	2 44	4 17	5 49	7 20	8 50	10 18		ASC
8	0♒56	1 53	2 50	3 47	4 45	5 43	6 40		MC
AM	23♉08	24 26	25 43	26 58	28 13	29 27	0♊40		ASC
9	15♒44	16 43	17 43	18 43	19 43	20 44	21 44		MC
AM	11♊13	12 18	13 21	14 24	15 27	16 28	17 29		ASC
10	1♓12	2 14	3 16	4 19	5 21	6 24	7 27		MC
AM	26♊28	27 24	28 19	29 14	0♋08	1 02	1 56		ASC
11	17♓15	18 19	19 23	20 27	21 32	22 36	23 40		MC
AM	9♋57	10 47	11 37	12 27	13 17	14 07	14 56		ASC
12	3♈37	4 41	5 46	6 50	7 54	8 58	10 03		MC
NOON	22♋23	23 11	23 58	24 45	25 33	26 20	27 07		ASC
1	19♈53	20 56	21 59	23 02	24 05	25 08	26 10		MC
PM	4♌17	5 03	5 49	6 36	7 22	8 07	8 53		ASC
2	5♉42	6 43	7 44	8 44	9 45	10 45	11 45		MC
PM	15♌58	16 43	17 29	18 15	19 00	19 46	20 32		ASC
3	20♉52	21 51	22 49	23 47	24 44	25 42	26 39		MC
PM	27♌35	28 21	29 07	29 53	0♍39	1 24	2 10		ASC
4	5♊24	6 20	7 16	8 11	9 07	10 03	10 58		MC
PM	9♍16	10 02	10 48	11 34	12 20	13 06	13 53		ASC
5	19♊27	20 21	21 16	22 10	23 05	23 59	24 53		MC
PM	21♍01	21 47	22 33	23 19	24 06	24 52	25 38		ASC
6	3♋16	4 10	5 05	5 59	6 53	7 48	8 42		MC
PM	2♎47	3 34	4 20	5 06	5 53	6 39	7 25		ASC
7	17♋10	18 05	19 00	19 56	20 51	21 47	22 42		MC
PM	14♎34	15 20	16 06	16 52	17 38	18 24	19 10		ASC
8	1♌24	2 22	3 19	4 16	5 14	6 12	7 09		MC
PM	26♎16	27 02	27 48	28 34	29 20	0♏06	0 52		ASC
9	16♌14	17 13	18 13	19 13	20 13	21 14	22 14		MC
PM	7♏55	8 41	9 27	10 13	10 58	11 44	12 30		ASC
10	1♍43	2 45	3 48	4 50	5 53	6 56	7 59		MC
PM	19♏33	20 19	21 05	21 51	22 37	23 23	24 09		ASC
11	17♍47	18 51	19 55	20 59	22 04	23 08	24 12		MC
PM	1♐18	2 05	2 52	3 39	4 26	5 13	6 00		ASC

CALENDAR DATE — APRIL of any year — CALENDAR DATE

HOUR OF BIRTH	1	2	3	4	5	6	7	8	
12 MID	10♎35	11 39	12 43	13 47	14 50	15 54	16 58	18 01	MC
	18♐21	19 11	20 01	20 52	21 43	22 34	23 26	24 18	ASC
1 AM	26♎42	27 44	28 46	29 48	0♏50	1 52	2 53	3 54	MC
	1♑39	2 34	3 30	4 26	5 22	6 19	7 17	8 15	ASC
2 AM	12♏15	13 15	14 14	15 14	16 13	17 12	18 11	19 09	MC
	16♑37	17 40	18 45	19 50	20 56	22 02	23 10	24 18	ASC
3 AM	27♏08	28 05	29 02	29 59	0♐56	1 52	2 49	3 45	MC
	4♒15	5 31	6 49	8 08	9 27	10 48	12 10	13 33	ASC
4 AM	11♐26	12 21	13 16	14 11	15 06	16 01	16 56	17 51	MC
	25♒40	27 13	28 47	0♓22	1 58	3 35	5 13	6 52	ASC
5 AM	25♐21	26 15	27 09	28 04	28 58	29 52	0♑46	1 41	MC
	20♓58	22 43	24 28	26 13	27 59	29 44	1♈30	3 16	ASC
6 AM	9♑10	10 04	10 59	11 53	12 48	13 43	14 38	15 33	MC
	17♈36	19 18	20 58	22 38	24 18	25 56	27 33	29 10	ASC
7 AM	23♑10	24 06	25 02	25 58	26 55	27 51	28 48	29 44	MC
	11♉45	13 13	14 38	16 02	17 26	18 48	20 09	21 29	ASC
8 AM	7♒38	8 37	9 35	10 33	11 32	12 31	13 30	14 29	MC
	1♊52	3 03	4 13	5 22	6 31	7 38	8 45	9 51	ASC
9 AM	22♒45	23 45	24 46	25 48	26 49	27 50	28 52	29 54	MC
	18♊30	19 30	20 29	21 28	22 26	23 24	24 21	25 18	ASC
10 AM	8♓30	9 33	10 37	11 40	12 43	13 47	14 51	15 55	MC
	2♋49	3 42	4 35	5 27	6 19	7 11	8 02	8 53	ASC
11 AM	24♓44	25 49	26 53	27 58	29 02	0♈07	1 11	2 16	MC
	15♋45	16 34	17 22	18 11	18 59	19 47	20 35	21 23	ASC
12 NOON	11♈07	12 11	13 15	14 19	15 22	16 26	17 30	18 33	MC
	27♋53	28 40	29 27	0♌13	1 00	1 46	2 33	3 19	ASC
1 PM	27♈13	28 15	29 17	0♉19	1 21	2 22	3 24	4 25	MC
	9♌39	10 25	11 11	11 57	12 43	13 28	14 14	15 00	ASC
2 PM	12♉45	13 44	14 44	15 43	16 42	17 41	18 40	19 39	MC
	21♌17	22 03	22 49	23 35	24 20	25 06	25 52	26 38	ASC
3 PM	27♉37	28 34	29 31	0♊27	1 24	2 21	3 17	4 13	MC
	2♍56	3 42	4 28	5 14	6 00	6 46	7 32	8 18	ASC
4 PM	11♊53	12 48	13 44	14 39	15 34	16 28	17 23	18 18	MC
	14♍39	15 25	16 11	16 57	17 44	18 30	19 16	20 02	ASC
5 PM	25♊48	26 42	27 36	28 31	29 25	0♋19	1 13	2 08	MC
	26♍25	27 11	27 57	28 44	29 30	0♎16	1 03	1 49	ASC
6 PM	9♋37	10 31	11 26	12 21	13 16	14 10	15 05	16 00	MC
	8♎12	8 58	9 44	10 30	11 17	12 03	12 49	13 35	ASC
7 PM	23♋38	24 34	25 30	26 26	27 23	28 19	29 16	0♌13	MC
	19♎56	20 42	21 29	22 15	23 01	23 47	24 33	25 18	ASC
8 PM	8♌07	9 06	10 04	11 03	12 01	13 00	13 59	14 59	MC
	1♏37	2 23	3 09	3 55	4 40	5 26	6 12	6 58	ASC
9 PM	23♌15	24 16	25 17	26 18	27 20	28 21	29 23	0♍25	MC
	13♏15	14 01	14 47	15 32	16 18	17 04	17 50	18 36	ASC
10 PM	9♍02	10 05	11 08	12 12	13 15	14 19	15 23	16 27	MC
	24♏55	25 41	26 27	27 14	28 00	28 46	29 33	0♐19	ASC
11 PM	25♍17	26 21	27 26	28 30	29 34	0♎39	1 43	2 48	MC
	6♐48	7 35	8 23	9 11	9 59	10 47	11 35	12 23	ASC

CALENDAR DATE — APRIL of any year — CALENDAR DATE

HOUR OF BIRTH	9	10	11	12	13	14	15	16	
12 MID	19♎05	20 08	21 11	22 14	23 17	24 20	25 23	26 25	MC
	25♐10	26 02	26 55	27 48	28 42	29 36	0♑30	1 25	ASC
1 AM	4♏56	5 57	6 58	7 58	8 59	9 59	10 59	11 59	MC
	9♑14	10 13	11 12	12 13	13 14	14 15	15 17	16 20	ASC
2 AM	20♏08	21 06	22 05	23 03	24 00	24 58	25 56	26 53	MC
	25♑27	26 37	27 47	28 59	0♒12	1 25	2 40	3 55	ASC
3 AM	4♐41	5 37	6 33	7 29	8 25	9 20	10 16	11 11	MC
	14♒57	16 22	17 48	19 16	20 44	22 14	23 44	25 16	ASC
4 AM	18♐45	19 40	20 34	21 29	22 23	23 18	24 12	25 06	MC
	8♓32	10 13	11 54	13 36	15 19	17 02	18 46	20 31	ASC
5 AM	2♑35	3 29	4 23	5 18	6 12	7 06	8 01	8 55	MC
	5♈01	6 46	8 31	10 16	12 00	13 44	15 27	17 09	ASC
6 AM	16♑28	17 23	18 18	19 13	20 09	21 04	22 00	22 56	MC
	0♉45	2 19	3 53	5 25	6 56	8 26	9 55	11 23	ASC
7 AM	0♒41	1 38	2 35	3 33	4 30	5 28	6 25	7 23	MC
	22♉48	24 06	25 23	26 39	27 54	29 08	0♊21	1 33	ASC
8 AM	15♒28	16 28	17 28	18 27	19 28	20 28	21 28	22 29	MC
	10♊56	12 01	13 05	14 08	15 10	16 12	17 14	18 14	ASC
9 AM	0♓56	1 58	3 00	4 03	5 05	6 08	7 11	8 14	MC
	26♊14	27 10	28 05	29 00	29 54	0♋48	1 42	2 36	ASC
10 AM	16♓58	18 02	19 07	20 11	21 15	22 19	23 23	24 28	MC
	9♋44	10 34	11 24	12 14	13 04	13 54	14 43	15 32	ASC
11 AM	3♈20	4 24	5 29	6 33	7 37	8 42	9 46	10 50	MC
	22♋11	22 58	23 46	24 33	25 20	26 07	26 54	27 41	ASC
12 NOON	19♈36	20 40	21 43	22 46	23 49	24 51	25 54	26 56	MC
	4♌05	4 51	5 37	6 24	7 10	7 56	8 41	9 27	ASC
1 PM	5♉26	6 27	7 28	8 29	9 29	10 29	11 29	12 29	MC
	15♌46	16 31	17 17	18 03	18 48	19 34	20 20	21 06	ASC
2 PM	20♉37	21 35	22 34	23 31	24 29	25 27	26 24	27 22	MC
	27♌23	28 09	28 55	29 41	0♍27	1 12	1 58	2 44	ASC
3 PM	5♊09	6 05	7 01	7 57	8 53	9 48	10 44	11 39	MC
	9♍04	9 50	10 36	11 22	12 08	12 54	13 41	14 27	ASC
4 PM	19♊13	20 07	21 02	21 56	22 51	23 45	24 39	25 34	MC
	20♍49	21 35	22 21	23 07	23 54	24 40	25 26	26 13	ASC
5 PM	3♋02	3 56	4 51	5 45	6 39	7 34	8 28	9 23	MC
	2♎35	3 22	4 08	4 54	5 41	6 27	7 13	8 00	ASC
6 PM	16♋55	17 50	18 46	19 41	20 37	21 32	22 28	23 24	MC
	14♎22	15 08	15 54	16 40	17 26	18 12	18 58	19 44	ASC
7 PM	1♌10	2 07	3 04	4 01	4 59	5 56	6 54	7 52	MC
	26♎04	26 50	27 36	28 22	29 08	29 54	0♏40	1 25	ASC
8 PM	15♌58	16 58	17 58	18 58	19 58	20 58	21 58	22 59	MC
	7♏43	8 29	9 15	10 01	10 46	11 32	12 18	13 03	ASC
9 PM	1♍27	2 29	3 31	4 34	5 37	6 39	7 42	8 45	MC
	19♏21	20 07	20 53	21 39	22 25	23 11	23 57	24 43	ASC
10 PM	17♍30	18 34	19 39	20 43	21 47	22 51	23 56	25 00	MC
	1♐06	1 53	2 40	3 27	4 14	5 01	5 48	6 35	ASC
11 PM	3♎52	4 57	6 01	7 05	8 10	9 14	10 18	11 22	MC
	13♐12	14 01	14 50	15 39	16 28	17 18	18 08	18 58	ASC

CALENDAR DATE APRIL of any year CALENDAR DATE

HOUR OF BIRTH	17	18	19	20	21	22	23	24	
12	27♎28	28 30	29 32	0♏34	1 36	2 37	3 38	4 40	MC
MID	2♑20	3 15	4 11	5 08	6 05	7 02	8 00	8 58	ASC
1	12♏59	13 59	14 58	15 57	16 56	17 55	18 54	19 53	MC
AM	17♑24	18 28	19 33	20 38	21 45	22 52	24 00	25 09	ASC
2	27♏50	28 47	29 44	0♐41	1 38	2 34	3 30	4 27	MC
AM	5♒11	6 29	7 47	9 07	10 27	11 49	13 11	14 35	ASC
3	12♐07	13 02	13 57	14 52	15 47	16 42	17 36	18 31	MC
AM	26♒49	28 22	29 57	1♓33	3 10	4 48	6 26	8 06	ASC
4	26♐01	26 55	27 49	28 44	29 38	0♑32	1 26	2 21	MC
AM	22♓15	24 00	25 46	27 31	29 17	1♈03	2 48	4 34	ASC
5	9♑50	10 45	11 39	12 34	13 29	14 23	15 18	16 13	MC
AM	18♈51	20 32	22 12	23 52	25 30	27 08	28 45	0♉20	ASC
6	23♑52	24 48	25 44	26 40	27 36	28 33	29 29	0♒26	MC
AM	12♉50	14 16	15 41	17 04	18 27	19 48	21 08	22 27	ASC
7	8♒21	9 20	10 18	11 17	12 16	13 14	14 14	15 13	MC
AM	2♊44	3 55	5 04	6 13	7 21	8 28	9 34	10 39	ASC
8	23♒30	24 30	25 32	26 33	27 34	28 36	29 38	0♓40	MC
AM	19♊14	20 14	21 13	22 11	23 09	24 06	25 03	25 59	ASC
9	9♓17	10 20	11 23	12 27	13 31	14 34	15 38	16 42	MC
AM	3♋29	4 21	5 13	6 05	6 57	7 49	8 40	9 30	ASC
10	25♓32	26 37	27 41	28 45	29 50	0♈54	1 59	3 03	MC
AM	16♋21	17 10	17 58	18 47	19 35	20 23	21 11	21 58	ASC
11	11♈54	12 58	14 02	15 06	16 09	17 13	18 17	19 20	MC
AM	28♋28	29 15	0♌01	0 48	1 34	2 21	3 07	3 53	ASC
12	27♈59	29 01	0♉03	1 05	2 06	3 08	4 09	5 10	MC
NOON	10♌13	10 59	11 45	12 31	13 16	14 02	14 48	15 34	ASC
1	13♉29	14 28	15 28	16 27	17 26	18 25	19 23	20 22	MC
PM	21♌51	22 37	23 23	24 08	24 54	25 40	26 26	27 11	ASC
2	28♉19	29 16	0♊13	1 09	2 06	3 02	3 59	4 55	MC
PM	3♍30	4 16	5 02	5 48	6 34	7 20	8 06	8 52	ASC
3	12♊34	13 29	14 24	15 19	16 14	17 09	18 04	18 58	MC
PM	15♍13	15 59	16 45	17 31	18 18	19 04	19 50	20 36	ASC
4	26♊28	27 22	28 17	29 11	0♋05	0 59	1 54	2 48	MC
PM	26♍59	27 45	28 32	29 18	0♎04	0 51	1 37	2 23	ASC
5	10♋17	11 12	12 07	13 01	13 56	14 51	15 46	16 41	MC
PM	8♎46	9 32	10 18	11 05	11 51	12 37	13 23	14 09	ASC
6	24♋20	25 16	26 12	27 08	28 05	29 01	29 58	0♌55	MC
PM	20♎30	21 17	22 03	22 49	23 35	24 21	25 06	25 52	ASC
7	8♌51	9 49	10 47	11 46	12 45	13 44	14 43	15 43	MC
PM	2♏11	2 57	3 43	4 29	5 14	6 00	6 46	7 31	ASC
8	24♌00	25 01	26 02	27 04	28 05	29 07	0♍09	1 11	MC
PM	13♏49	14 35	15 21	16 06	16 52	17 38	18 24	19 09	ASC
9	9♍48	10 52	11 55	12 59	14 02	15 06	16 10	17 14	MC
PM	25♏29	26 15	27 02	27 48	28 34	29 21	0♐07	0 54	ASC
10	26♍04	27 09	28 13	29 18	0♎22	1 27	2 31	3 35	MC
PM	7♐23	8 10	8 58	9 46	10 34	11 22	12 11	12 59	ASC
11	12♎26	13 30	14 34	15 38	16 41	17 45	18 48	19 52	MC
PM	19♐48	20 39	21 30	22 21	23 12	24 04	24 56	25 49	ASC

CALENDAR DATE APRIL of any year CALENDAR DATE

HOUR OF BIRTH	25	26	27	28	29	30	1	
12	5♏41	6 42	7 42	8 43	9 43	10 44	11 44	MC
MID	9♑57	10 57	11 57	12 58	13 59	15 01	16 04	ASC
1	20♏51	21 49	22 47	23 45	24 43	25 41		MC
AM	26♑18	27 29	28 40	29 53	1♒06	2 20		ASC
2	5♐23	6 19	7 15	8 10	9 06	10 01		MC
AM	16♒00	17 26	18 53	20 21	21 50	23 21		ASC
3	19♐26	20 20	21 15	22 09	23 04	23 58		MC
AM	9♓46	11 28	13 10	14 52	16 35	18 19		ASC
4	3♑15	4 09	5 04	5 58	6 52	7 47		MC
AM	6♈19	8 04	9 49	11 33	13 17	15 00		ASC
5	17♑09	18 04	18 59	19 54	20 50	21 45		MC
AM	1♉55	3 29	5 01	6 33	8 03	9 32		ASC
6	1♒23	2 20	3 18	4 15	5 13	6 10		MC
AM	23♉46	25 03	26 19	27 34	28 49	0♊02		ASC
7	16♒12	17 12	18 12	19 12	20 12	21 12		MC
AM	11♊44	12 48	13 52	14 54	15 56	16 58		ASC
8	1♓42	2 44	3 46	4 49	5 52	6 54		MC
AM	26♊55	27 51	28 46	29 40	0♋34	1 28		ASC
9	17♓46	18 50	19 54	20 58	22 02	23 07		MC
AM	10♋21	11 11	12 01	12 51	13 41	14 30		ASC
10	4♈08	5 12	6 16	7 21	8 25	9 29		MC
AM	22♋46	23 34	24 21	25 08	25 55	26 42		ASC
11	20♈23	21 26	22 29	23 32	24 35	25 38		MC
AM	4♌39	5 25	6 12	6 58	7 44	8 29		ASC
12	6♉11	7 12	8 13	9 13	10 13	11 14		MC
NOON	16♌19	17 05	17 51	18 37	19 22	20 08		ASC
1	21♉20	22 18	23 16	24 14	25 12	26 09		MC
PM	27♌57	28 43	29 29	0♍15	1 01	1 46		ASC
2	5♊51	6 47	7 42	8 38	9 34	10 29		MC
PM	9♍38	10 24	11 10	11 56	12 42	13 29		ASC
3	19♊53	20 47	21 42	22 36	23 31	24 25		MC
PM	21♍23	22 09	22 55	23 42	24 28	25 14		ASC
4	3♋42	4 36	5 31	6 25	7 20	8 14		MC
PM	3♎10	3 56	4 42	5 29	6 15	7 01		ASC
5	17♋36	18 31	19 27	20 22	21 18	22 13		MC
PM	14♎56	15 42	16 28	17 14	18 00	18 46		ASC
6	1♌52	2 49	3 46	4 44	5 41	6 39		MC
PM	26♎38	27 24	28 10	28 56	29 42	0♏28		ASC
7	16♌42	17 42	18 42	19 42	20 42	21 43		MC
PM	8♏17	9 03	9 49	10 34	11 20	12 06		ASC
8	2♍13	3 15	4 18	5 20	6 23	7 26		MC
PM	19♏55	20 41	21 27	22 13	22 59	23 45		ASC
9	18♍18	19 22	20 26	21 30	22 35	23 39		MC
PM	1♐41	2 27	3 14	4 01	4 48	5 36		ASC
10	4♎40	5 44	6 49	7 53	8 57	10 01		MC
PM	13♐48	14 37	15 26	16 16	17 05	17 55		ASC
11	20♎55	21 58	23 01	24 04	25 06	26 09		MC
PM	26♐41	27 34	28 28	29 22	0♑16	1 10		ASC

HOUR OF BIRTH

CALENDAR DATE — MAY of any year — CALENDAR DATE

Hour	1	2	3	4	5	6	7	8	
12	11♏44	12 43	13 43	14 43	15 42	16 41	17 40	18 39	MC
MID	16♑04	17 07	18 11	19 16	20 21	21 27	22 34	23 42	ASC
1	26♏38	27 35	28 32	29 29	0♐26	1 23	2 19	3 16	MC
AM	3♒35	4 51	6 08	7 27	8 46	10 06	11 27	12 50	ASC
2	10♐57	11 52	12 47	13 42	14 37	15 32	16 27	17 22	MC
AM	24♒52	26 24	27 58	29 33	1♓08	2 45	4 22	6 01	ASC
3	24♐52	25 47	26 41	27 35	28 30	29 24	0♑18	1 12	MC
AM	20♓03	21 48	23 33	25 18	27 04	28 49	0♈35	2 21	ASC
4	8♑41	9 36	10 30	11 25	12 20	13 14	14 09	15 04	MC
AM	16♈43	18 24	20 06	21 46	23 26	25 05	26 43	28 20	ASC
5	22♑41	23 37	24 33	25 29	26 25	27 22	28 18	29 15	MC
AM	11♉01	12 28	13 54	15 19	16 42	18 05	19 27	20 47	ASC
6	7♒08	8 06	9 04	10 03	11 01	12 00	12 59	13 58	MC
AM	1♊14	2 26	3 36	4 46	5 55	7 03	8 10	9 17	ASC
7	22♒13	23 14	24 15	25 16	26 17	27 18	28 20	29 22	MC
AM	17♊58	18 59	19 58	20 57	21 56	22 54	23 51	24 48	ASC
8	7♓57	9 00	10 04	11 07	12 10	13 14	14 18	15 21	MC
AM	2♋22	3 15	4 07	5 00	5 52	6 44	7 35	8 26	ASC
9	24♓11	25 15	26 20	27 24	28 29	29 33	0♈38	1 42	MC
AM	15♋19	16 08	16 57	17 46	18 34	19 22	20 10	20 58	ASC
10	10♈33	11 37	12 41	13 45	14 49	15 53	16 57	18 00	MC
AM	27♋29	28 16	29 03	29 49	0♌36	1 22	2 09	2 55	ASC
11	26♈40	27 43	28 45	29 47	0♉49	1 50	2 52	3 53	MC
AM	9♌15	10 01	10 47	11 33	12 19	13 05	13 50	14 36	ASC
12	12♉14	13 13	14 13	15 12	16 12	17 11	18 09	19 08	MC
NOON	20♌54	21 39	22 25	23 11	23 57	24 42	25 28	26 14	ASC
1	27♉07	28 04	29 01	29 58	0♊55	1 51	2 48	3 44	MC
PM	2♍32	3 18	4 04	4 50	5 36	6 22	7 08	7 54	ASC
2	11♊24	12 20	13 15	14 10	15 05	16 00	16 55	17 49	MC
PM	14♍15	15 01	15 47	16 33	17 19	18 06	18 52	19 38	ASC
3	25♊19	26 14	27 08	28 02	28 57	29 51	0♋45	1 39	MC
PM	26♍01	26 47	27 33	28 20	29 06	29 52	0♎39	1 25	ASC
4	9♋08	10 03	10 58	11 52	12 47	13 42	14 37	15 32	MC
PM	7♎47	8 34	9 20	10 06	10 53	11 39	12 25	13 11	ASC
5	23♋09	24 05	25 01	25 57	26 53	27 50	28 46	29 43	MC
PM	19♎32	20 18	21 05	21 51	22 37	23 23	24 09	24 55	ASC
6	7♌37	8 35	9 34	10 32	11 31	12 30	13 29	14 28	MC
PM	1♏14	1 59	2 45	3 31	4 17	5 02	5 48	6 34	ASC
7	22♌43	23 44	24 45	25 46	26 48	27 49	28 51	29 53	MC
PM	12♏51	13 37	14 23	15 09	15 54	16 40	17 26	18 12	ASC
8	8♍29	9 32	10 35	11 39	12 42	13 46	14 49	15 53	MC
PM	24♏31	25 17	26 03	26 50	27 36	28 22	29 09	29 55	ASC
9	24♍43	25 48	26 52	27 56	29 01	0♎05	1 10	2 14	MC
PM	6♐23	7 10	7 58	8 46	9 34	10 22	11 10	11 58	ASC
10	11♎05	12 09	13 13	14 17	15 21	16 25	17 28	18 32	MC
PM	18♐45	19 35	20 26	21 17	22 08	22 59	23 51	24 43	ASC
11	27♎11	28 14	29 16	0♏18	1 19	2 21	3 23	4 24	MC
PM	2♑05	3 01	3 57	4 53	5 50	6 47	7 45	8 43	ASC

HOUR OF BIRTH

CALENDAR DATE — MAY of any year — CALENDAR DATE

Hour	9	10	11	12	13	14	15	16	
12	19♏37	20 36	21 34	22 32	23 30	24 28	25 26	26 23	MC
MID	24♑51	26 00	27 10	28 22	29 34	0♒47	2 01	3 16	ASC
1	4♐12	5 08	6 04	7 00	7 56	8 51	9 47	10 42	MC
AM	14♒13	15 38	17 03	18 30	19 58	21 27	22 57	24 28	ASC
2	18♐17	19 11	20 06	21 01	21 55	22 49	23 44	24 38	MC
AM	7♓40	9 20	11 01	12 43	14 25	16 08	17 52	19 36	ASC
3	2♑07	3 01	3 55	4 49	5 44	6 38	7 33	8 27	MC
AM	4♈06	5 52	7 37	9 22	11 06	12 50	14 33	16 16	ASC
4	15♑59	16 54	17 49	18 45	19 40	20 35	21 31	22 27	MC
AM	29♈56	1♉30	3 04	4 37	6 09	7 40	9 09	10 38	ASC
5	0♒12	1 08	2 05	3 03	4 00	4 58	5 55	6 53	MC
AM	22♉07	23 25	24 43	25 59	27 15	28 29	29 43	0♊56	ASC
6	14♒57	15 57	16 57	17 56	18 56	19 56	20 57	21 57	MC
AM	10♊22	11 27	12 32	13 35	14 38	15 40	16 42	17 43	ASC
7	0♓23	1 26	2 28	3 30	4 33	5 35	6 38	7 41	MC
AM	25♊45	26 41	27 36	28 31	29 26	0♋20	1 14	2 08	ASC
8	16♓25	17 29	18 33	19 37	20 41	21 46	22 50	23 54	MC
AM	9♋17	10 08	10 58	11 48	12 38	13 28	14 17	15 07	ASC
9	2♈46	3 51	4 55	6 00	7 04	8 08	9 12	10 17	MC
AM	21♋46	22 34	23 21	24 09	24 56	25 43	26 30	27 17	ASC
10	19♈03	20 07	21 10	22 13	23 16	24 19	25 21	26 24	MC
AM	3♌41	4 27	5 13	6 00	6 46	7 32	8 18	9 03	ASC
11	4♉54	5 55	6 56	7 57	8 58	9 58	10 58	11 58	MC
AM	15♌22	16 08	16 53	17 39	18 25	19 10	19 56	20 42	ASC
12	20♉07	21 05	22 03	23 01	23 59	24 57	25 54	26 52	MC
NOON	27♌00	27 45	28 31	29 17	0♍03	0 49	1 34	2 20	ASC
1	4♊40	5 36	6 32	7 28	8 24	9 19	10 15	11 10	MC
PM	8♍40	9 26	10 12	10 58	11 44	12 30	13 17	14 03	ASC
2	18♊44	19 39	20 33	21 28	22 22	23 17	24 11	25 05	MC
PM	20♍24	21 11	21 57	22 43	23 30	24 16	25 02	25 49	ASC
3	2♋34	3 28	4 22	5 17	6 11	7 05	8 00	8 54	MC
PM	2♎11	2 58	3 44	4 30	5 17	6 03	6 49	7 35	ASC
4	16♋27	17 22	18 17	19 12	20 08	21 03	21 59	22 55	MC
PM	13♎57	14 44	15 30	16 16	17 02	17 48	18 34	19 20	ASC
5	0♌40	1 37	2 34	3 31	4 29	5 26	6 24	7 22	MC
PM	25♎40	26 26	27 12	27 58	28 44	29 30	0♏16	1 02	ASC
6	15♌27	16 27	17 26	18 26	19 26	20 27	21 27	22 28	MC
PM	7♏20	8 05	8 51	9 37	10 22	11 08	11 54	12 40	ASC
7	0♍54	1 57	2 59	4 01	5 04	6 07	7 09	8 12	MC
PM	18♏57	19 43	20 29	21 15	22 01	22 47	23 33	24 19	ASC
8	16♍57	18 01	19 05	20 09	21 14	22 18	23 22	24 26	MC
PM	0♐42	1 28	2 15	3 02	3 49	4 36	5 23	6 11	ASC
9	3♎19	4 23	5 27	6 32	7 36	8 40	9 45	10 49	MC
PM	12♐47	13 35	14 24	15 13	16 03	16 52	17 42	18 32	ASC
10	19♎35	20 38	21 42	22 45	23 47	24 50	25 53	26 55	MC
PM	25♐35	26 28	27 20	28 14	29 08	0♑02	0 56	1 51	ASC
11	5♏25	6 26	7 27	8 27	9 28	10 28	11 28	12 28	MC
PM	9♑42	10 41	11 41	12 42	13 43	14 45	15 47	16 50	ASC

CALENDAR DATE — MAY of any year — CALENDAR DATE

HOUR OF BIRTH	17	18	19	20	21	22	23	24	
12 MID	27♏20	28 18	29 15	0♐11	1 08	2 05	3 01	3 57	MC
	4♒31	5 48	7 06	8 25	9 45	11 06	12 28	13 51	ASC
1 AM	11♐38	12 33	13 28	14 23	15 18	16 13	17 08	18 03	MC
	26♒00	27 34	29 08	0♓43	2 19	3 57	5 35	7 14	ASC
2 AM	25♐33	26 27	27 21	28 15	29 10	0♑04	0 58	1 52	MC
	21♓21	23 06	24 51	26 36	28 22	0♈08	1 53	3 39	ASC
3 AM	9♑22	10 16	11 11	12 05	13 00	13 55	14 50	15 45	MC
	17♈58	19 40	21 20	23 00	24 39	26 17	27 55	29 31	ASC
4 AM	23♑23	24 18	25 14	26 11	27 07	28 03	29 00	29 57	MC
	12♉05	13 31	14 57	16 21	17 44	19 06	20 27	21 46	ASC
5 AM	7♒51	8 49	9 48	10 46	11 45	12 44	13 43	14 42	MC
	2♊07	3 18	4 28	5 37	6 45	7 53	9 00	10 05	ASC
6 AM	22♒58	23 59	25 00	26 01	27 02	28 04	29 06	0♓07	MC
	18♊43	19 43	20 42	21 41	22 39	23 36	24 33	25 30	ASC
7 AM	8♓44	9 47	10 50	11 54	12 57	14 01	15 05	16 09	MC
	3♋01	3 54	4 46	5 38	6 30	7 22	8 13	9 04	ASC
8 AM	24♓59	26 03	27 07	28 12	29 16	0♈21	1 25	2 30	MC
	15♋56	16 44	17 33	18 21	19 10	19 58	20 46	21 34	ASC
9 AM	11♈21	12 25	13 29	14 33	15 36	16 40	17 44	18 47	MC
	28♋04	28 50	29 37	0♌24	1 10	1 56	2 43	3 29	ASC
10 AM	27♈26	28 29	29 31	0♉33	1 34	2 36	3 37	4 39	MC
	9♌49	10 35	11 21	12 07	12 53	13 38	14 24	15 10	ASC
11 AM	12♉58	13 57	14 57	15 56	16 55	17 54	18 53	19 52	MC
	21♌27	22 13	22 59	23 45	24 30	25 16	26 02	26 48	ASC
12 NOON	27♉49	28 46	29 43	0♊40	1 36	2 33	3 29	4 26	MC
	3♍06	3 52	4 38	5 24	6 10	6 56	7 42	8 28	ASC
1 PM	12♊05	13 01	13 56	14 51	15 46	16 40	17 35	18 30	MC
	14♍49	15 35	16 21	17 07	17 54	18 40	19 26	20 12	ASC
2 PM	26♊00	26 54	27 48	28 43	29 37	0♋31	1 25	2 20	MC
	26♍35	27 21	28 08	28 54	29 40	0≏27	1 13	1 59	ASC
3 PM	9♋49	10 43	11 38	12 33	13 28	14 22	15 17	16 12	MC
	8≏22	9 08	9 54	10 41	11 27	12 13	12 59	13 45	ASC
4 PM	23♋50	24 46	25 43	26 39	27 35	28 32	29 28	0♌25	MC
	20≏07	20 53	21 39	22 25	23 11	23 57	24 43	25 29	ASC
5 PM	8♌20	9 18	10 17	11 16	12 14	13 13	14 12	15 12	MC
	1♏47	2 33	3 19	4 05	4 51	5 36	6 22	7 08	ASC
6 PM	23♌28	24 29	25 30	26 32	27 33	28 35	29 36	0♍38	MC
	13♏25	14 11	14 57	15 42	16 28	17 14	18 00	18 46	ASC
7 PM	9♍16	10 19	11 22	12 26	13 29	14 33	15 37	16 41	MC
	25♏05	25 51	26 38	27 24	28 10	28 57	29 43	0♐30	ASC
8 PM	25♍31	26 35	27 40	28 44	29 49	0≏53	1 57	3 02	MC
	6♐58	7 46	8 33	9 21	10 09	10 57	11 46	12 34	ASC
9 PM	11≏53	12 57	14 01	15 04	16 08	17 12	18 15	19 19	MC
	19♐22	20 13	21 03	21 54	22 46	23 37	24 29	25 21	ASC
10 PM	27≏57	29 00	0♏02	1 03	2 05	3 07	4 08	5 09	MC
	2♑46	3 42	4 38	5 35	6 32	7 30	8 28	9 27	ASC
11 PM	13♏28	14 27	15 27	16 26	17 25	18 24	19 22	20 21	MC
	17♑54	18 59	20 04	21 10	22 17	23 24	24 33	25 42	ASC

CALENDAR DATE — MAY of any year — CALENDAR DATE

HOUR OF BIRTH	25	26	27	28	29	30	31	1	
12 MID	4♐54	5 50	6 46	7 41	8 37	9 33	10 28	11 23	MC
	15♒16	16 41	18 07	19 35	21 04	22 33	24 04	25 36	ASC
1 AM	18♐57	19 52	20 46	21 41	22 35	23 30	24 24		MC
	8♓54	10 35	12 16	13 59	15 42	17 25	19 09		ASC
2 AM	2♑47	3 41	4 35	5 30	6 24	7 18	8 13		MC
	5♈24	7 09	8 54	10 39	12 23	14 06	15 49		ASC
3 AM	16♑40	17 35	18 30	19 26	20 21	21 17	22 12		MC
	1♉06	2 40	4 13	5 45	7 16	8 46	10 15		ASC
4 AM	0♒54	1 51	2 48	3 45	4 43	5 40	6 38		MC
	23♉05	24 23	25 40	26 55	28 10	29 24	0♊37		ASC
5 AM	15♒41	16 41	17 41	18 41	19 41	20 41	21 41		MC
	11♊11	12 15	13 19	14 22	15 24	16 26	17 27		ASC
6 AM	1♓09	2 12	3 14	4 16	5 19	6 22	7 25		MC
	26♊26	27 22	28 17	29 12	0♋06	1 00	1 54		ASC
7 AM	17♓13	18 17	19 21	20 25	21 29	22 33	23 38		MC
	9♋55	10 45	11 35	12 25	13 15	14 04	14 54		ASC
8 AM	3♈34	4 39	5 43	6 47	7 52	8 56	10 00		MC
	22♋21	23 09	23 56	24 44	25 31	26 18	27 05		ASC
9 AM	19♈50	20 54	21 57	23 00	24 02	25 05	26 08		MC
	4♌15	5 01	5 48	6 34	7 20	8 06	8 52		ASC
10 AM	5♉40	6 40	7 41	8 42	9 42	10 42	11 42		MC
	15♌56	16 41	17 27	18 13	18 58	19 44	20 30		ASC
11 AM	20♉50	21 48	22 46	23 44	24 42	25 39	26 37		MC
	27♌33	28 19	29 05	29 51	0♍37	1 23	2 08		ASC
12 NOON	5♊22	6 18	7 13	8 09	9 05	10 00	10 56		MC
	9♍14	10 00	10 46	11 32	12 18	13 05	13 51		ASC
1 PM	19♊24	20 19	21 14	22 08	23 02	23 57	24 51		MC
	20♍59	21 45	22 31	23 18	24 04	24 50	25 36		ASC
2 PM	3♋14	4 08	5 02	5 57	6 51	7 46	8 40		MC
	2≏46	3 32	4 18	5 04	5 51	6 37	7 23		ASC
3 PM	17♋07	18 03	18 58	19 53	20 49	21 44	22 40		MC
	14≏32	15 18	16 04	16 50	17 36	18 22	19 08		ASC
4 PM	1♌22	2 19	3 16	4 14	5 11	6 09	7 07		MC
	26≏14	27 00	27 46	28 32	29 18	0♏04	0 50		ASC
5 PM	16♌11	17 11	18 11	19 11	20 11	21 11	22 12		MC
	7♏53	8 39	9 25	10 11	10 56	11 42	12 28		ASC
6 PM	1♍40	2 43	3 45	4 48	5 50	6 53	7 56		MC
	19♏31	20 17	21 03	21 49	22 35	23 21	24 07		ASC
7 PM	17♍45	18 49	19 53	20 57	22 01	23 05	24 10		MC
	1♐16	2 03	2 50	3 37	4 24	5 11	5 58		ASC
8 PM	4≏06	5 11	6 15	7 19	8 24	9 28	10 32		MC
	13♐23	14 12	15 01	15 50	16 39	17 29	18 19		ASC
9 PM	20≏22	21 25	22 28	23 31	24 34	25 36	26 39		MC
	26♐14	27 07	28 00	28 54	29 47	0♑42	1 37		ASC
10 PM	6♏10	7 11	8 12	9 12	10 12	11 12	12 12		MC
	10♑26	11 26	12 26	13 27	14 29	15 31	16 34		ASC
11 PM	21♏19	22 17	23 15	24 13	25 11	26 08	27 06		MC
	26♑52	28 03	29 15	0♒28	1 41	2 56	4 12		ASC

CALENDAR DATE — JUNE of any year — CALENDAR DATE

HOUR OF BIRTH	1	2	3	4	5	6	7	8	
12 MID	11♐23	12 19	13 14	14 09	15 04	15 59	16 54	17 48	MC
	25♒36	27 09	28 43	0♓18	1 54	3 31	5 09	6 48	ASC
1 AM	25♐18	26 13	27 07	28 01	28 56	29 50	0♑44	1 38	MC
	20♓54	22 38	24 24	26 09	27 54	29 40	1♈26	3 11	ASC
2 AM	9♑07	10 02	10 56	11 51	12 46	13 41	14 36	15 30	MC
	17♈32	19 13	20 54	22 34	24 14	25 52	27 29	29 06	ASC
3 AM	23♑08	24 04	25 00	25 56	26 52	27 49	28 45	29 06	MC
	11♉43	13 09	14 35	15 59	17 22	18 44	20 06	21 26	ASC
4 AM	7♒36	8 34	9 32	10 31	11 30	12 28	13 27	14 27	MC
	1♊49	3 00	4 10	5 19	6 28	7 35	8 42	9 48	ASC
5 AM	22♒42	23 43	24 44	25 45	26 46	27 48	28 49	29 51	MC
	18♊27	19 27	20 27	21 25	22 24	23 21	24 19	25 15	ASC
6 AM	8♓28	9 31	10 34	11 37	12 41	13 44	14 48	15 52	MC
	2♋47	3 40	4 33	5 25	6 17	7 08	8 00	8 51	ASC
7 AM	24♓42	25 46	26 51	27 55	29 00	0♈04	1 08	2 13	MC
	15♋43	16 32	17 20	18 09	18 57	19 45	20 33	21 21	ASC
8 AM	11♈04	12 08	13 12	14 16	15 20	16 23	17 27	18 30	MC
	27♋52	28 38	29 25	0♌12	0 58	1 44	2 31	3 17	ASC
9 AM	27♈10	28 12	29 14	0♉16	1 18	2 20	3 21	4 23	MC
	9♌37	10 23	11 09	11 55	12 41	13 26	14 12	14 58	ASC
10 AM	12♉42	13 42	14 41	15 41	16 40	17 39	18 38	19 36	MC
	21♌16	22 01	22 47	23 33	24 18	25 04	25 50	26 36	ASC
11 AM	27♉34	28 31	29 28	0♊25	1 22	2 18	3 15	4 11	MC
	2♍54	3 40	4 26	5 12	5 58	6 44	7 30	8 16	ASC
12 NOON	11♊51	12 46	13 41	14 36	15 31	16 26	17 21	18 16	MC
	14♍37	15 23	16 09	16 55	17 42	18 28	19 14	20 00	ASC
1 PM	25♊46	26 40	27 34	28 28	29 23	0♋17	1 11	2 05	MC
	26♍23	27 09	27 55	28 42	29 28	0♎14	1 01	1 47	ASC
2 PM	9♋35	10 29	11 24	12 19	13 13	14 08	15 03	15 58	MC
	8♎10	8 56	9 42	10 28	11 15	12 01	12 47	13 33	ASC
3 PM	23♋36	24 32	25 28	26 24	27 20	28 17	29 14	0♌10	MC
	19♎55	20 41	21 27	22 13	22 59	23 45	24 31	25 17	ASC
4 PM	8♌05	9 03	10 02	11 00	11 59	12 58	13 57	14 56	MC
	1♏35	2 21	3 07	3 53	4 39	5 24	6 10	6 56	ASC
5 PM	23♌12	24 13	25 14	26 16	27 17	28 19	29 20	0♍22	MC
	13♏13	13 59	14 45	15 31	16 16	17 02	17 48	18 34	ASC
6 PM	8♍59	10 02	11 06	12 09	13 13	14 16	15 20	16 24	MC
	24♏53	25 39	26 26	27 12	27 58	28 45	29 31	0♐18	ASC
7 PM	25♍14	26 18	27 23	28 27	29 32	0♎36	1 41	2 45	MC
	6♐46	7 33	8 21	9 09	9 57	10 45	11 33	12 21	ASC
8 PM	11♎36	12 40	13 44	14 48	15 52	16 55	17 59	19 02	MC
	19♐09	19 59	20 50	21 41	22 32	23 24	24 16	25 08	ASC
9 PM	27♎41	28 43	29 45	0♏47	1 49	2 51	3 52	4 53	MC
	2♑32	3 27	4 24	5 20	6 17	7 15	8 13	9 11	ASC
10 PM	13♏12	14 12	15 11	16 10	17 09	18 08	19 07	20 06	MC
	17♑38	18 42	19 47	20 53	21 59	23 07	24 15	25 24	ASC
11 PM	28♏03	29 00	29 57	0♐53	1 50	2 46	3 43	4 39	MC
	5♒28	6 46	8 04	9 24	10 45	12 07	13 30	14 54	ASC

CALENDAR DATE — JUNE of any year — CALENDAR DATE

HOUR OF BIRTH	9	10	11	12	13	14	15	16	
12 MID	18♐43	19 38	20 32	21 27	22 21	23 16	24 10	25 04	MC
	8♓28	10 09	11 50	13 32	15 15	16 58	18 42	20 26	ASC
1 AM	2♑33	3 27	4 21	5 16	6 10	7 04	7 59	8 53	MC
	4♈57	6 42	8 27	10 12	11 56	13 40	15 23	17 05	ASC
2 AM	16♑26	17 21	18 16	19 11	20 07	21 02	21 58	22 53	MC
	0♉41	2 16	3 49	5 21	6 53	8 23	9 52	11 20	ASC
3 AM	0♒39	1 36	2 33	3 30	4 28	5 25	6 23	7 21	MC
	22♉45	24 03	25 20	26 36	27 51	29 05	0♊18	1 30	ASC
4 AM	15♒26	16 25	17 25	18 25	19 25	20 25	21 26	22 26	MC
	10♊54	11 58	13 02	14 05	15 08	16 10	17 11	18 12	ASC
5 AM	0♓53	1 55	2 58	4 00	5 03	6 05	7 08	8 11	MC
	26♊12	27 07	28 03	28 58	29 52	0♋46	1 40	2 33	ASC
6 AM	16♓56	18 00	19 04	20 08	21 12	22 17	23 21	24 25	MC
	9♋42	10 32	11 22	12 12	13 02	13 52	14 41	15 30	ASC
7 AM	3♈17	4 22	5 26	6 30	7 35	8 39	9 43	10 47	MC
	22♋09	22 56	23 44	24 31	25 18	26 06	26 52	27 39	ASC
8 AM	19♈34	20 37	21 40	22 43	23 46	24 49	25 51	26 54	MC
	4♌03	4 49	5 36	6 22	7 08	7 54	8 40	9 26	ASC
9 AM	5♉24	6 25	7 25	8 26	9 26	10 27	11 27	12 27	MC
	15♌44	16 29	17 15	18 01	18 47	19 32	20 18	21 04	ASC
10 AM	20♉35	21 33	22 31	23 29	24 27	25 25	26 22	27 19	MC
	27♌21	28 07	28 53	29 39	0♍25	1 11	1 57	2 42	ASC
11 AM	5♊07	6 03	6 59	7 55	8 50	9 46	10 41	11 37	MC
	9♍02	9 48	10 34	11 20	12 06	12 53	13 39	14 25	ASC
12 NOON	19♊10	20 05	20 59	21 54	22 48	23 43	24 37	25 31	MC
	20♍47	21 33	22 19	23 05	23 52	24 38	25 24	26 11	ASC
1 PM	3♋00	3 54	4 48	5 43	6 37	7 32	8 26	9 20	MC
	2♎33	3 20	4 06	4 52	5 39	6 25	7 11	7 58	ASC
2 PM	16♋53	17 48	18 43	19 39	20 34	21 30	22 26	23 21	MC
	14♎20	15 06	15 52	16 38	17 24	18 10	18 56	19 43	ASC
3 PM	1♌07	2 04	3 02	3 59	4 56	5 54	6 52	7 50	MC
	26♎03	26 48	27 34	28 20	29 06	29 52	0♏38	1 24	ASC
4 PM	15♌56	16 55	17 55	18 55	19 55	20 56	21 56	22 57	MC
	7♏42	8 27	9 13	9 59	10 44	11 30	12 16	13 02	ASC
5 PM	1♍24	2 26	3 29	4 31	5 34	6 37	7 40	8 43	MC
	19♏19	20 05	20 51	21 37	22 23	23 09	23 55	24 41	ASC
6 PM	17♍28	18 32	19 36	20 40	21 44	22 49	23 53	24 57	MC
	1♐04	1 51	2 38	3 25	4 12	4 59	5 46	6 33	ASC
7 PM	3♎50	4 54	5 58	7 03	8 07	9 11	10 15	11 19	MC
	13♐10	13 59	14 48	15 37	16 26	17 16	18 06	18 56	ASC
8 PM	20♎06	21 09	22 12	23 15	24 18	25 20	26 23	27 25	MC
	26♐00	26 53	27 46	28 40	29 33	0♑28	1 22	2 17	ASC
9 PM	5♏54	6 55	7 56	8 56	9 57	10 57	11 57	12 57	MC
	10♑10	11 10	12 10	13 11	14 13	15 15	16 18	17 21	ASC
10 PM	21♏04	22 02	23 00	23 58	24 56	25 53	26 51	27 48	MC
	26♑34	27 44	28 56	0♒09	1 22	2 36	3 52	5 08	ASC
11 PM	5♐35	6 31	7 27	8 23	9 18	10 14	11 09	12 04	MC
	16♒19	17 45	19 12	20 40	22 10	23 41	25 12	26 45	ASC

CALENDAR DATE JUNE of any year CALENDAR DATE

HOUR OF BIRTH	17	18	19	20	21	22	23	24	
12	25♐59	26 53	27 47	28 41	29 36	0♑30	1 24	2 19	MC
MID	22♓11	23 56	25 42	27 27	29 13	0♈59	2 44	4 30	ASC
1	9♑48	10 42	11 37	12 32	13 26	14 21	15 16	16 11	MC
AM	18♈47	20 28	22 08	23 48	25 26	27 04	28 41	0♉17	ASC
2	23♑49	24 45	25 41	26 38	27 34	28 31	29 27	0♒24	MC
AM	12♉47	14 12	15 37	17 01	18 23	19 45	21 05	22 24	ASC
3	8♒19	9 17	10 16	11 14	12 13	13 12	14 11	15 11	MC
AM	2♊41	3 52	5 01	6 10	7 18	8 25	9 31	10 37	ASC
4	23♒27	24 28	25 29	26 30	27 32	28 33	29 35	0♓37	MC
AM	19♊12	20 11	21 10	22 09	23 06	24 04	25 01	25 57	ASC
5	9♓14	10 18	11 21	12 24	13 28	14 32	15 35	16 39	MC
AM	3♋26	4 19	5 11	6 03	6 55	7 46	8 38	9 28	ASC
6	25♓30	26 34	27 38	28 43	29 47	0♈52	1 56	3 01	MC
AM	16♋19	17 08	17 56	18 45	19 33	20 21	21 09	21 57	ASC
7	11♈51	12 55	13 59	15 03	16 07	17 11	18 14	19 17	MC
AM	28♋26	29 13	29 59	0♌46	1 32	2 19	3 05	3 51	ASC
8	27♈56	28 58	0♉00	1 02	2 04	3 05	4 07	5 08	MC
AM	10♌11	10 57	11 43	12 29	13 15	14 00	14 46	15 32	ASC
9	13♉26	14 26	15 25	16 25	17 24	18 22	19 21	20 20	MC
AM	21♌49	22 35	23 21	24 07	24 52	25 38	26 24	27 10	ASC
10	28♉16	29 13	0♊10	1 07	2 04	3 00	3 56	4 53	MC
AM	3♍28	4 14	5 00	5 46	6 32	7 18	8 04	8 50	ASC
11	12♊32	13 27	14 22	15 17	16 12	17 07	18 01	18 56	MC
AM	15♍11	15 57	16 43	17 30	18 16	19 02	19 48	20 35	ASC
12	26♊26	27 20	28 14	29 09	0♋03	0 57	1 51	2 46	MC
NOON	26♍57	27 43	28 30	29 16	0♎02	0 49	1 35	2 21	ASC
1	10♋15	11 10	12 04	12 59	13 54	14 49	15 44	16 39	MC
PM	8♎44	9 30	10 16	11 03	11 49	12 35	13 21	14 08	ASC
2	24♋17	25 13	26 10	27 06	28 02	28 59	29 56	0♌52	MC
PM	20♎29	21 15	22 01	22 47	23 33	24 19	25 05	25 51	ASC
3	8♌48	9 47	10 45	11 44	12 43	13 42	14 41	15 40	MC
PM	2♏09	2 55	3 41	4 27	5 12	5 58	6 44	7 30	ASC
4	23♌58	24 59	26 00	27 01	28 03	29 04	0♍06	1 08	MC
PM	13♏58	14 33	15 19	16 04	16 50	17 36	18 22	19 08	ASC
5	9♍46	10 49	11 53	12 56	14 00	15 04	16 07	17 11	MC
PM	25♏27	26 14	27 00	27 46	28 32	29 19	0♐05	0 52	ASC
6	26♍02	27 06	28 11	29 15	0♎19	1 24	2 28	3 33	MC
PM	7♐21	8 08	8 56	9 44	10 32	11 20	12 09	12 57	ASC
7	12♎23	13 27	14 31	15 35	16 39	17 42	18 46	19 49	MC
PM	19♐46	20 37	21 28	22 19	23 10	24 02	24 54	25 46	ASC
8	28♎27	29 29	0♏31	1 33	2 35	3 36	4 37	5 38	MC
PM	3♑13	4 09	5 05	6 02	7 00	7 58	8 56	9 55	ASC
9	13♏56	14 56	15 55	16 54	17 53	18 52	19 50	20 49	MC
PM	18♑25	19 30	20 36	21 42	22 49	23 57	25 06	26 16	ASC
10	28♏45	29 42	0♐39	1 42	2 32	3 28	4 24	5 21	MC
PM	6♒26	7 44	9 03	10 24	11 45	13 08	14 32	15 56	ASC
11	12♐59	13 55	14 50	15 44	16 39	17 34	18 29	19 23	MC
PM	28♒19	29 53	1♓29	3 06	4 44	6 23	8 02	9 42	ASC

CALENDAR DATE JUNE of any year CALENDAR DATE

HOUR OF BIRTH	25	26	27	28	29	30	1	
12	3♑13	4 07	5 01	5 56	6 50	7 45	8 39	MC
MID	6♈15	8 00	9 45	11 29	13 13	14 56	16 39	ASC
1	17♑06	18 02	18 57	19 52	20 48	21 43		MC
AM	1♉51	3 25	4 57	6 29	7 59	9 29		ASC
2	1♒21	2 18	3 15	4 13	5 10	6 08		MC
AM	23♉43	25 00	26 16	27 31	28 46	29 59		ASC
3	16♒10	17 10	18 09	19 09	20 10	21 10		MC
AM	11♊42	12 46	13 49	14 52	15 54	16 55		ASC
4	1♓39	2 41	3 44	4 46	5 49	6 52		MC
AM	26♊53	27 48	28 43	29 38	0♋32	1 26		ASC
5	17♓43	18 47	19 51	20 56	22 00	23 04		MC
AM	10♋19	11 09	11 59	12 49	13 39	14 28		ASC
6	4♈05	5 09	6 14	7 18	8 22	9 27		MC
AM	22♋44	23 32	24 19	25 06	25 53	26 40		ASC
7	20♈21	21 24	22 27	23 30	24 33	25 35		MC
AM	4♌37	5 24	6 10	6 56	7 42	8 28		ASC
8	6♉09	7 10	8 10	9 11	10 11	11 11		MC
AM	16♌18	17 03	17 49	18 35	19 20	20 06		ASC
9	21♉18	22 16	23 14	24 12	25 10	26 07		MC
AM	27♌55	28 41	29 27	0♍13	0 59	1 45		ASC
10	5♊49	6 44	7 40	8 36	9 31	10 27		MC
AM	9♍36	10 22	11 08	11 54	12 41	13 27		ASC
11	19♊51	20 45	21 40	22 34	23 29	24 23		MC
AM	21♍21	22 07	22 54	23 40	24 26	25 12		ASC
12	3♋40	4 34	5 29	6 23	7 17	8 12		MC
NOON	3♎08	3 54	4 40	5 27	6 13	6 59		ASC
1	17♋34	18 29	19 24	20 20	21 15	22 11		MC
PM	14♎54	15 40	16 26	17 12	17 58	18 45		ASC
2	1♌49	2 47	3 44	4 41	5 39	6 37		MC
PM	26♎37	27 22	28 08	28 54	29 40	0♏26		ASC
3	16♌40	17 40	18 39	19 40	20 40	21 40		MC
PM	8♏15	9 01	9 47	10 32	11 18	12 04		ASC
4	2♍10	3 13	4 15	5 18	6 20	7 23		MC
PM	19♏53	20 39	21 25	22 11	22 57	23 43		ASC
5	18♍15	19 19	20 23	21 28	22 32	23 36		MC
PM	1♐39	2 26	3 12	3 59	4 47	5 34		ASC
6	4♎37	5 42	6 46	7 50	8 54	9 59		MC
PM	13♐46	14 35	15 24	16 14	17 03	17 53		ASC
7	20♎52	21 55	22 58	24 01	25 04	26 06		MC
PM	26♐39	27 32	28 26	29 19	0♑14	1 08		ASC
8	6♏39	7 40	8 41	9 41	10 41	11 41		MC
PM	10♑54	11 55	12 55	13 57	14 59	16 01		ASC
9	21♏47	22 45	23 43	24 41	25 38	26 36		MC
PM	27♑26	28 37	29 50	1♒03	2 17	3 32		ASC
10	6♐17	7 12	8 08	9 04	9 59	10 55		MC
PM	17♒22	18 49	20 17	21 47	23 17	24 48		ASC
11	20♐18	21 13	22 07	23 01	23 56	24 50		MC
PM	11♓24	13 05	14 48	16 31	18 15	19 59		ASC

HOUR OF BIRTH	CALENDAR DATE 1	2	3	JULY of any year 4	5	6	CALENDAR DATE 7	8	
12	8♑39	9 34	10 28	11 23	12 17	13 12	14 07	15 02	MC
MID	16♈39	18 21	20 02	21 42	23 22	25 01	26 39	28 16	ASC
1	22♑39	23 35	24 31	25 27	26 23	27 19	28 16	29 12	MC
AM	10♉57	12 24	13 50	15 15	16 39	18 02	19 24	20 44	ASC
2	7♒06	8 04	9 02	10 01	10 59	11 58	12 57	13 56	MC
AM	1♊11	2 23	3 34	4 43	5 52	7 00	8 08	9 14	ASC
3	22♒11	23 11	24 12	25 13	26 14	27 16	28 17	29 19	MC
AM	17♊56	18 56	19 56	20 55	21 53	22 51	23 49	24 46	ASC
4	7♓55	8 58	10 01	11 04	12 08	13 11	14 15	15 19	MC
AM	2♋20	3 13	4 05	4 58	5 50	6 42	7 33	8 24	ASC
5	24♓08	25 13	26 17	27 22	28 26	29 30	0♈35	1 39	MC
AM	15♋17	16 06	16 55	17 44	18 32	19 20	20 08	20 56	ASC
6	10♈31	11 35	12 39	13 43	14 47	15 50	16 54	17 58	MC
AM	27♋27	28 14	29 01	29 47	0♌34	1 20	2 07	2 53	ASC
7	26♈38	27 40	28 42	29 44	0♉46	1 48	2 49	3 51	MC
AM	9♌14	9 59	10 45	11 31	12 17	13 03	13 48	14 34	ASC
8	12♉11	13 11	14 11	15 10	16 09	17 08	18 07	19 06	MC
AM	20♌52	21 38	22 23	23 09	23 55	24 40	25 26	26 12	ASC
9	27♉04	28 02	28 59	29 56	0♊52	1 49	2 45	3 42	MC
AM	2♍30	3 16	4 02	4 48	5 34	6 20	7 06	7 52	ASC
10	11♊22	12 18	13 13	14 08	15 03	15 58	16 52	17 47	MC
AM	14♍13	14 59	15 45	16 31	17 18	18 04	18 50	19 36	ASC
11	25♊17	26 12	27 06	28 00	28 54	29 49	0♋43	1 37	MC
AM	25♍59	26 45	27 31	28 18	29 04	29 50	0♎37	1 23	ASC
12	9♋06	10 01	10 55	11 50	12 45	13 40	14 34	15 29	MC
NOON	7♎46	8 32	9 18	10 04	10 51	11 37	12 23	13 09	ASC
1	23♋07	24 03	24 59	25 55	26 51	27 48	28 44	29 41	MC
PM	19♎31	20 17	21 03	21 49	22 35	23 21	24 07	24 53	ASC
2	7♌35	8 33	9 31	10 30	11 28	12 27	13 26	14 25	MC
PM	1♏12	1 57	2 43	3 29	4 15	5 01	5 46	6 32	ASC
3	22♌41	23 42	24 43	25 44	26 45	27 47	28 48	29 50	MC
PM	12♏50	13 35	14 21	15 07	15 53	16 38	17 24	18 10	ASC
4	8♍26	9 29	10 33	11 36	12 40	13 43	14 47	15 51	MC
PM	24♏29	25 15	26 02	26 48	27 34	28 20	29 07	29 53	ASC
5	24♍41	25 45	26 49	27 54	28 58	0♎03	1 07	2 12	MC
PM	6♐21	7 08	7 56	8 44	9 32	10 20	11 08	11 56	ASC
6	11♎03	12 07	13 11	14 15	15 18	16 22	17 26	18 29	MC
PM	18♐43	19 33	20 24	21 15	22 06	22 57	23 49	24 41	ASC
7	27♎09	28 11	29 13	0♏15	1 17	2 19	3 20	4 21	MC
PM	2♑03	2 58	3 54	4 51	5 47	6 45	7 42	8 41	ASC
8	12♏41	13 41	14 40	15 40	16 39	17 38	18 37	19 35	MC
PM	17♑04	18 08	19 13	20 19	21 25	22 32	23 39	24 48	ASC
9	27♏33	28 30	29 27	0♐24	1 21	2 17	3 14	4 10	MC
PM	4♒48	6 05	7 23	8 43	10 03	11 24	12 46	14 10	ASC
10	11♐50	12 45	13 40	14 35	15 30	16 25	17 20	18 15	MC
PM	26♒21	27 54	29 29	1♓04	2 41	4 18	5 57	7 36	ASC
11	25♐44	26 39	27 33	28 27	29 22	0♑16	1 10	2 04	MC
PM	21♓44	23 29	25 14	27 00	28 45	0♈31	2 17	4 02	ASC

HOUR OF BIRTH	CALENDAR DATE 9	10	11	JULY of any year 12	13	14	CALENDAR DATE 15	16	
12	15♑57	16 52	17 47	18 42	19 38	20 33	21 29	22 24	MC
MID	29♈52	1♉27	3 01	4 34	6 05	7 36	9 06	10 34	ASC
1	0♒09	1 06	2 03	3 00	3 58	4 55	5 53	6 51	MC
AM	22♉04	23 22	24 40	25 56	27 12	28 26	29 40	0♊53	ASC
2	14♒55	15 55	16 54	17 54	18 54	19 54	20 54	21 55	MC
AM	10♊20	11 25	12 29	13 33	14 36	15 38	16 39	17 40	ASC
3	0♓21	1 23	2 25	3 28	4 30	5 33	6 35	7 38	MC
AM	25♊42	26 38	27 34	28 29	29 24	0♋18	1 12	2 06	ASC
4	16♓23	17 27	18 31	19 35	20 39	21 43	22 47	23 52	MC
AM	9♋15	10 06	10 56	11 46	12 36	13 26	14 15	15 05	ASC
5	2♈44	3 48	4 53	5 57	7 01	8 06	9 10	10 14	MC
AM	21♋44	22 32	23 19	24 07	24 54	25 41	26 28	27 15	ASC
6	19♈01	20 04	21 07	22 11	23 13	24 16	25 19	26 21	MC
AM	3♌39	4 25	5 12	5 58	6 44	7 30	8 16	9 02	ASC
7	4♉52	5 53	6 54	7 55	8 55	9 55	10 56	11 56	MC
AM	15♌20	16 06	16 51	17 37	18 23	19 09	19 54	20 40	ASC
8	20♉04	21 03	22 01	22 59	23 57	24 55	25 52	26 50	MC
AM	26♌58	27 44	28 29	29 15	0♍01	0 47	1 33	2 19	ASC
9	4♊38	5 34	6 30	7 26	8 21	9 17	10 13	11 08	MC
AM	8♍38	9 24	10 10	10 56	11 42	12 29	13 15	14 01	ASC
10	18♊42	19 37	20 31	21 26	22 20	23 14	24 09	25 03	MC
AM	20♍23	21 09	21 55	22 41	23 28	24 14	25 00	25 47	ASC
11	2♋32	3 26	4 20	5 14	6 09	7 03	7 58	8 52	MC
AM	2♎09	2 56	3 42	4 28	5 15	6 01	6 47	7 34	ASC
12	16♋24	17 20	18 15	19 10	20 05	21 01	21 57	22 52	MC
NOON	13♎56	14 42	15 28	16 14	17 00	17 46	18 33	19 19	ASC
1	0♌38	1 35	2 32	3 29	4 27	5 24	6 22	7 20	MC
PM	25♎39	26 25	27 10	27 56	28 42	29 28	0♏14	1 00	ASC
2	15♌25	16 24	17 24	18 24	19 24	20 24	21 25	22 25	MC
PM	7♏18	8 03	8 49	9 35	10 21	11 06	11 52	12 38	ASC
3	0♍52	1 54	2 56	3 59	5 01	6 04	7 07	8 10	MC
PM	18♏56	19 42	20 27	21 13	21 59	22 45	23 31	24 17	ASC
4	16♍55	17 59	19 03	20 07	21 11	22 15	23 20	24 24	MC
PM	0♐40	1 27	2 13	3 00	3 47	4 34	5 21	6 09	ASC
5	3♎16	4 20	5 25	6 29	7 34	8 38	9 42	10 46	MC
PM	12♐45	13 33	14 22	15 11	16 01	16 50	17 40	18 30	ASC
6	19♎33	20 36	21 39	22 42	23 45	24 48	25 50	26 53	MC
PM	25♐33	26 25	27 18	28 12	29 05	29 59	0♑54	1 49	ASC
7	5♏22	6 23	7 24	8 25	9 25	10 26	11 26	12 26	MC
PM	9♑40	10 39	11 39	12 39	3 41	14 42	15 45	16 48	ASC
8	20♏34	21 32	22 30	23 28	24 26	25 23	26 21	27 18	MC
PM	25♑57	27 08	28 19	29 31	0♒44	1 58	3 13	4 28	ASC
9	5♐06	6 02	6 58	7 54	8 49	9 45	10 40	11 36	MC
PM	15♒34	17 00	18 27	19 54	21 23	22 53	24 24	25 57	ASC
10	19♐09	20 04	20 58	21 53	22 47	23 42	24 36	25 30	MC
PM	9♓16	10 57	12 39	14 21	16 04	17 48	19 32	21 17	ASC
11	2♑59	3 53	4 47	5 42	6 36	7 30	8 25	9 19	MC
PM	5♈47	7 33	9 17	11 02	12 46	14 29	16 12	17 54	ASC

CALENDAR DATE — JULY of any year — CALENDAR DATE

HOUR OF BIRTH	17	18	19	20	21	22	23	24	
12	23♑20	24 16	25 12	26 08	27 05	28 01	28 58	29 54	MC
MID	12♉02	13 28	14 53	16 17	17 40	19 02	20 23	21 43	ASC
1	7♒49	8 47	9 45	10 44	11 43	12 41	13 40	14 40	MC
AM	2♊04	3 15	4 25	5 34	6 43	7 50	8 57	10 03	ASC
2	22♒55	23 56	24 57	25 58	27 00	28 01	29 03	0♓05	MC
AM	18♊41	19 40	20 40	21 38	22 36	23 34	24 31	25 28	ASC
3	8♓41	9 45	10 48	11 51	12 55	13 58	15 02	16 06	MC
AM	2♋59	3 52	4 44	5 36	6 28	7 20	8 11	9 02	ASC
4	24♓56	26 00	27 05	28 09	29 14	0♈18	1 23	2 27	MC
AM	15♋54	16 42	17 31	18 20	19 08	19 56	20 44	21 32	ASC
5	11♈18	12 22	13 26	14 30	15 34	16 37	17 41	18 44	MC
AM	28♋02	28 49	29 35	0♌22	1 08	1 55	2 41	3 27	ASC
6	27♈24	28 26	29 28	0♉30	1 32	2 33	3 35	4 36	MC
AM	9♌48	10 33	11 19	12 05	12 51	13 37	14 22	15 08	ASC
7	12♉55	13 55	14 55	15 54	16 53	17 52	18 51	19 49	MC
AM	21♌26	22 11	22 57	23 43	24 29	25 14	26 00	26 46	ASC
8	27♉47	28 44	29 41	0♊38	1 34	2 31	3 27	4 23	MC
AM	3♍04	3 50	4 36	5 22	6 08	6 54	7 40	8 26	ASC
9	12♊03	12 58	13 53	14 48	15 43	16 38	17 33	18 28	MC
AM	14♍47	15 33	16 19	17 06	17 52	18 38	19 24	20 11	ASC
10	25♊58	26 52	27 46	28 40	29 35	0♋29	1 23	2 17	MC
AM	26♍33	27 19	28 06	28 52	29 38	0♎25	1 11	1 57	ASC
11	9♋47	10 41	11 36	12 31	13 25	14 20	15 15	16 10	MC
AM	8♎20	9 06	9 52	10 39	11 25	12 11	12 57	13 44	ASC
12	23♋48	24 44	25 40	26 37	27 33	28 29	29 26	0♌23	MC
NOON	20♎04	20 51	21 37	22 23	23 09	23 55	24 41	25 27	ASC
1	8♌18	9 16	10 15	11 13	12 12	13 11	14 10	15 09	MC
PM	1♏46	2 31	3 17	4 03	4 49	5 34	6 20	7 06	ASC
2	23♌26	24 27	25 28	26 29	27 31	28 32	29 34	0♍36	MC
PM	13♏23	14 09	14 55	15 41	16 26	17 12	17 58	18 44	ASC
3	9♍13	10 16	11 20	12 23	13 27	14 30	15 34	16 38	MC
PM	25♏03	25 50	26 36	27 22	28 08	28 55	29 41	0♐28	ASC
4	25♍28	26 33	27 37	28 41	29 46	0♎50	1 55	2 59	MC
PM	6♐56	7 44	8 31	9 19	10 07	10 55	11 44	12 32	ASC
5	11♎50	12 54	13 58	15 02	16 06	17 09	18 13	19 16	MC
PM	19♐20	20 11	21 01	21 52	22 44	23 35	24 27	25 19	ASC
6	27♎55	28 57	29 59	1♏01	2 03	3 04	4 05	5 07	MC
PM	2♑44	3 40	4 36	5 33	6 30	7 27	8 25	9 24	ASC
7	13♏25	14 25	15 24	16 23	17 22	18 21	19 20	20 18	MC
PM	17♑52	18 56	20 01	21 07	22 14	23 22	24 30	25 39	ASC
8	28♏15	29 12	0♐09	1 06	2 02	2 59	3 55	4 51	MC
PM	5♒45	7 03	8 22	9 42	11 03	12 25	13 48	15 12	ASC
9	12♐31	13 26	14 21	15 16	16 11	17 06	18 00	18 55	MC
PM	27♒30	29 04	0♓39	2 16	3 53	5 31	7 10	8 50	ASC
10	26♐25	27 19	28 13	29 07	0♑02	0 56	1 50	2 45	MC
PM	23♓01	24 47	26 32	28 18	0♈03	1 49	3 35	5 20	ASC
11	10♑14	11 09	12 03	12 58	13 53	14 48	15 43	16 38	MC
PM	19♈36	21 16	22 56	24 35	26 13	27 51	29 27	1♉02	ASC

CALENDAR DATE — JULY of any year — CALENDAR DATE

HOUR OF BIRTH	25	26	27	28	29	30	31	1	
12	0♒51	1 48	2 45	3 43	4 40	5 38	6 36	7 34	MC
MID	23♉02	24 20	25 37	26 52	28 07	29 21	0♊34	1 43	ASC
1	15♒39	16 39	17 38	18 38	19 38	20 39	21 39		MC
AM	11♊08	12 12	13 16	14 19	15 22	16 23	17 24		ASC
2	1♓07	2 09	3 11	4 14	5 16	6 19	7 22		MC
AM	26♊24	27 20	28 15	29 10	0♋04	0 58	1 52		ASC
3	17♓10	18 14	19 18	20 22	21 26	22 31	23 35		MC
AM	9♋53	10 43	11 33	12 23	13 13	14 02	14 52		ASC
4	3♈32	4 35	5 40	6 45	7 49	8 53	9 57		MC
AM	22♋19	23 07	23 54	24 42	25 29	26 16	27 03		ASC
5	19♈48	20 51	21 54	22 57	24 00	25 03	26 05		MC
AM	4♌13	5 00	5 46	6 32	7 18	8 04	8 50		ASC
6	5♉37	6 38	7 39	8 39	9 40	10 40	11 40		MC
AM	15♌54	16 39	17 25	18 11	18 57	19 42	20 28		ASC
7	20♉48	21 46	22 44	23 42	24 40	25 37	26 35		MC
AM	27♌32	28 17	29 03	29 49	0♍35	1 21	2 07		ASC
8	5♊19	6 15	7 11	8 07	9 03	9 58	10 53		MC
AM	9♍12	9 58	10 44	11 30	12 17	13 03	13 49		ASC
9	19♊22	20 17	21 11	22 06	23 00	23 55	24 49		MC
AM	20♍57	21 43	22 29	23 16	24 02	24 48	25 35		ASC
10	3♋12	4 06	5 00	5 55	6 49	7 43	8 38		MC
AM	2♎44	3 30	4 16	5 03	5 49	6 35	7 21		ASC
11	17♋05	18 00	18 56	19 51	20 47	21 42	22 38		MC
AM	14♎30	15 16	16 02	16 48	17 34	18 21	19 07		ASC
12	1♌20	2 17	3 14	4 12	5 09	6 07	7 05		MC
NOON	26♎13	26 59	27 44	28 30	29 16	0♏02	0 48		ASC
1	16♌09	17 08	18 08	19 08	20 08	21 09	22 09		MC
PM	7♏52	8 37	9 23	10 09	10 54	11 40	12 26		ASC
2	1♍38	2 40	3 43	4 45	5 48	6 51	7 53		MC
PM	19♏30	20 15	21 01	21 47	22 33	23 19	24 05		ASC
3	17♍42	18 46	19 50	20 54	21 58	23 03	24 07		MC
PM	1♐14	2 01	2 48	3 35	4 22	5 09	5 56		ASC
4	4♎04	5 08	6 12	7 17	8 21	9 25	10 29		MC
PM	13♐21	14 10	14 59	15 48	16 37	17 27	18 17		ASC
5	20♎19	21 23	22 26	23 29	24 31	25 34	26 36		MC
PM	26♐12	27 05	27 58	28 51	29 45	0♑40	1 34		ASC
6	6♏08	7 08	8 09	9 10	10 10	11 10	12 10		MC
PM	10♑23	11 23	12 24	13 25	14 26	15 28	16 31		ASC
7	21♏17	22 15	23 13	24 11	25 08	26 06	27 03		MC
PM	26♑49	28 00	29 12	0♒25	1 38	2 53	4 09		ASC
8	5♐47	6 43	7 39	8 35	9 30	10 26	11 21		MC
PM	16♒37	18 04	19 31	21 00	22 30	24 01	25 32		ASC
9	19♐50	20 44	21 39	22 33	23 27	24 22	25 16		MC
PM	10♓31	12 12	13 55	15 37	17 21	19 05	20 49		ASC
10	3♑39	4 33	5 27	6 22	7 16	8 11	9 05		MC
PM	7♈05	8 50	10 35	12 19	14 02	15 45	17 28		ASC
11	17♑33	18 28	19 23	20 19	21 14	22 10	23 06		MC
PM	2♉36	4 09	5 42	7 13	8 42	10 11	11 39		ASC

CALENDAR DATE AUGUST of any year CALENDAR DATE

HOUR OF BIRTH	1	2	3	4	5	6	7	8	
12 MID	7♒34	8 32	9 30	10 29	11 27	12 26	13 25	14 24	MC
	1♊43	2 57	4 07	5 16	6 25	7 33	8 40	9 46	ASC
1 AM	22♒40	23 40	24 41	25 43	26 44	27 45	28 47	29 49	MC
	18♊25	19 25	20 24	21 23	22 21	23 19	24 16	25 13	ASC
2 AM	8♓25	9 28	10 31	11 35	12 38	13 42	14 46	15 49	MC
	2♋45	3 38	4 31	5 23	6 15	7 06	7 58	8 49	ASC
3 AM	24♓39	25 44	26 48	27 53	28 57	0♈01	1 06	2 10	MC
	15♋41	16 30	17 18	18 07	18 55	19 43	20 31	21 19	ASC
4 AM	11♈02	12 06	13 10	14 13	15 17	16 21	17 25	18 28	MC
	27♋50	28 36	29 23	0♌10	0 56	1 43	2 29	3 15	ASC
5 AM	27♈08	28 10	29 12	0♉14	1 16	2 17	3 19	4 20	MC
	9♌36	10 21	11 07	11 53	12 39	13 25	14 10	14 56	ASC
6 AM	12♉40	13 40	14 39	15 38	16 38	17 37	18 35	19 34	MC
	21♌14	21 59	22 45	23 31	24 17	25 02	25 48	26 34	ASC
7 AM	27♉32	28 29	29 26	0♊23	1 20	2 16	3 12	4 09	MC
	2♍53	3 38	4 24	5 10	5 56	6 42	7 28	8 14	ASC
8 AM	11♊49	12 44	13 39	14 34	15 29	16 24	17 19	18 13	MC
	14♍35	15 21	16 07	16 54	17 40	18 26	19 12	19 59	ASC
9 AM	25♊43	26 38	27 32	28 26	29 21	0♋15	1 09	2 03	MC
	26♍21	27 07	27 54	28 40	29 26	0♎13	0 59	1 45	ASC
10 AM	9♋32	10 27	11 22	12 16	13 11	14 06	15 01	15 56	MC
	8♎08	8 54	9 40	10 27	11 13	11 59	12 45	13 32	ASC
11 AM	23♋34	24 30	25 26	26 22	27 18	28 15	29 11	0♌08	MC
	19♎53	20 39	21 25	22 11	22 57	23 43	24 29	25 15	ASC
12 NOON	8♌03	9 01	9 59	10 58	11 57	12 56	13 55	14 54	MC
	1♏34	2 19	3 05	3 51	4 37	5 23	6 08	6 54	ASC
1 PM	23♌10	24 11	25 12	26 13	27 15	28 16	29 18	0♍20	MC
	13♏12	13 57	14 43	15 29	16 14	17 00	17 46	18 32	ASC
2 PM	8♍57	10 00	11 03	12 07	13 10	14 14	15 18	16 21	MC
	24♏51	25 38	26 24	27 10	27 56	28 43	29 29	0♐16	ASC
3 PM	25♍12	26 16	27 20	28 25	29 29	0♎34	1 38	2 43	MC
	6♐44	7 31	8 19	9 07	9 55	10 43	11 31	12 19	ASC
4 PM	11♎34	12 38	13 41	14 45	15 49	16 53	17 56	19 00	MC
	19♐07	19 57	20 48	21 39	22 30	23 22	24 13	25 06	ASC
5 PM	27♎39	28 41	29 43	0♏45	1 47	2 48	3 50	4 51	MC
	2♑30	3 25	4 21	5 18	6 15	7 12	8 10	9 09	ASC
6 PM	13♏10	14 09	15 09	16 08	17 07	18 06	19 05	20 03	MC
	17♑35	18 39	19 44	20 50	21 57	23 04	24 12	25 21	ASC
7 PM	28♏01	28 58	29 54	0♐51	1 48	2 44	3 41	4 37	MC
	5♒25	6 43	8 01	9 21	10 42	12 03	13 26	14 50	ASC
8 PM	12♐16	13 12	14 07	15 02	15 57	16 51	17 46	18 41	MC
	27♒05	28 39	0♓14	1 51	3 28	5 05	6 44	8 24	ASC
9 PM	26♐11	27 05	27 59	28 53	29 48	0♑42	1 36	2 30	MC
	22♓34	24 19	26 05	27 50	29 36	1♈22	3 07	4 53	ASC
10 PM	10♑00	10 54	11 49	12 44	13 39	14 33	15 28	16 23	MC
	19♈09	20 50	22 30	24 10	25 48	27 25	29 02	0♉37	ASC
11 PM	24♑02	24 58	25 54	26 50	27 46	28 43	29 40	0♒37	MC
	13♉06	14 31	15 56	17 19	18 41	20 02	21 23	22 42	ASC

CALENDAR DATE AUGUST of any year CALENDAR DATE

HOUR OF BIRTH	9	10	11	12	13	14	15	16	
12 MID	15♒24	16 23	17 23	18 23	19 23	20 23	21 23	22 24	MC
	10♊51	11 56	13 00	14 03	15 05	16 07	17 09	18 09	ASC
1 AM	0♓51	1 53	2 55	3 58	5 00	6 03	7 06	8 09	MC
	26♊09	27 05	28 00	28 55	29 50	0♋44	1 38	2 31	ASC
2 AM	16♓53	17 57	19 01	20 05	21 10	22 14	23 18	24 23	MC
	9♋40	10 30	11 20	12 10	13 00	13 50	14 39	15 28	ASC
3 AM	3♈15	4 19	5 24	6 28	7 32	8 36	9 41	10 45	MC
	22♋07	22 55	23 42	24 29	25 17	26 04	26 51	27 37	ASC
4 AM	19♈31	20 35	21 38	22 41	23 44	24 46	25 49	26 51	MC
	4♌01	4 48	5 34	6 20	7 06	7 52	8 38	9 24	ASC
5 AM	5♉21	6 22	7 23	8 24	9 24	10 24	11 24	12 24	MC
	15♌42	16 28	17 13	17 59	18 45	19 30	20 16	21 02	ASC
6 AM	20♉32	21 31	22 29	23 27	24 25	25 22	26 20	27 17	MC
	27♌20	28 05	28 51	29 37	0♍23	1 09	1 55	2 41	ASC
7 AM	5♊05	6 01	6 57	7 53	8 48	9 44	10 39	11 34	MC
	9♍00	9 46	10 32	11 18	12 05	12 51	13 37	14 23	ASC
8 AM	19♊08	20 03	20 57	21 52	22 46	23 41	24 35	25 29	MC
	20♍45	21 31	22 17	23 04	23 50	24 36	25 23	26 09	ASC
9 AM	2♋58	3 52	4 46	5 41	6 35	7 29	8 24	9 18	MC
	2♎32	3 18	4 04	4 51	5 37	6 23	7 10	7 56	ASC
10 AM	16♋51	17 46	18 41	19 37	20 32	21 28	22 23	23 19	MC
	14♎18	15 04	15 50	16 36	17 22	18 09	18 55	19 41	ASC
11 AM	1♌05	2 02	2 59	3 57	4 54	5 52	6 50	7 48	MC
	26♎01	26 47	27 33	28 18	29 04	29 50	0♏36	1 22	ASC
12 NOON	15♌53	16 53	17 53	18 53	19 53	20 53	21 54	22 54	MC
	7♏40	8 25	9 11	9 57	10 43	11 28	12 14	13 00	ASC
1 PM	1♍22	2 24	3 26	4 29	5 31	6 34	7 37	8 40	MC
	19♏18	20 04	20 49	21 35	22 21	23 07	23 53	24 39	ASC
2 PM	17♍25	18 29	19 33	20 38	21 42	22 46	23 50	24 55	MC
	1♐02	1 49	2 36	3 23	4 10	4 57	5 44	6 31	ASC
3 PM	3♎47	4 51	5 56	7 00	8 04	9 09	10 13	11 17	MC
	13♐08	13 57	14 46	15 35	16 24	17 14	18 04	18 54	ASC
4 PM	20♎03	21 06	22 09	23 12	24 15	25 18	26 20	27 23	MC
	25♐58	26 51	27 44	28 37	29 31	0♑26	1 20	2 15	ASC
5 PM	5♏52	6 53	7 53	8 54	9 54	10 54	11 54	12 54	MC
	10♑08	11 08	12 08	13 09	14 10	15 12	16 15	17 18	ASC
6 PM	21♏02	22 00	22 58	23 56	24 53	25 51	26 48	27 46	MC
	26♑31	27 42	28 53	0♒06	1 19	2 33	3 49	5 05	ASC
7 PM	5♐33	6 29	7 25	8 20	9 16	10 11	11 07	12 02	MC
	16♒15	17 41	19 09	20 37	22 06	23 37	25 08	26 41	ASC
8 PM	19♐35	20 30	21 24	22 19	23 13	24 08	25 02	25 56	MC
	10♓05	11 46	13 28	15 11	16 54	18 38	20 22	22 07	ASC
9 PM	3♑25	4 19	5 13	6 08	7 02	7 57	8 51	9 46	MC
	6♈38	8 23	10 08	11 52	13 35	15 19	17 01	18 43	ASC
10 PM	17♑18	18 14	19 09	20 04	21 00	21 56	22 51	23 47	MC
	2♉12	3 45	5 18	6 49	8 19	9 48	11 16	12 43	ASC
11 PM	1♒34	2 31	3 28	4 25	5 23	6 21	7 19	8 17	MC
	24♉00	25 17	26 33	27 48	29 02	0♊15	1 27	2 39	ASC

CALENDAR DATE — AUGUST of any year — CALENDAR DATE

HOUR OF BIRTH

	17	18	19	20	21	22	23	24	
12	23♒25	24 26	25 27	26 28	27 29	28 31	29 33	0♓35	MC
MID	19♊09	20 09	21 08	22 06	23 04	24 01	24 58	25 55	ASC
1	9♓12	10 15	11 18	12 22	13 25	14 29	15 33	16 37	MC
AM	3♋24	4 17	5 09	6 01	6 53	7 44	8 36	9 26	ASC
2	25♓27	26 31	27 36	28 40	29 45	0♈49	1 54	2 58	MC
AM	16♋17	17 06	17 54	18 40	19 31	20 19	21 07	21 55	ASC
3	11♈49	12 53	13 57	15 01	16 04	17 08	18 11	19 15	MC
AM	28♋24	29 11	29 58	0♌44	1 31	2 17	3 03	3 49	ASC
4	27♈54	28 56	29 58	1♉00	2 01	3 03	4 04	5 05	MC
AM	10♌10	10 55	11 41	12 27	13 13	13 59	14 44	15 30	ASC
5	13♉24	14 24	15 23	16 22	17 21	18 20	19 19	20 17	MC
AM	21♌48	22 33	23 19	24 05	24 50	25 36	26 22	27 08	ASC
6	28♉14	29 11	0♊08	1 05	2 01	2 58	3 54	4 50	MC
AM	3♍26	4 12	4 58	5 44	6 30	7 16	8 02	8 48	ASC
7	12♊30	13 25	14 20	15 15	16 10	17 04	17 59	18 54	MC
AM	15♍09	15 55	16 42	17 28	18 14	19 00	19 46	20 33	ASC
8	26♊24	27 18	28 12	29 06	0♋01	0 55	1 49	2 43	MC
AM	26♍55	27 42	28 28	29 14	0♎01	0 47	1 33	2 20	ASC
9	10♋13	11 07	12 02	12 57	13 52	14 47	15 41	16 37	MC
AM	8♎42	9 28	10 15	11 01	11 47	12 33	13 20	14 06	ASC
10	24♋15	25 11	26 07	27 04	28 00	28 57	29 53	0♌50	MC
AM	20♎27	21 13	21 59	22 45	23 31	24 17	25 03	25 49	ASC
11	8♌46	9 44	10 43	11 41	12 40	13 39	14 38	15 38	MC
AM	2♏08	2 53	3 39	4 25	5 11	5 56	6 42	7 28	ASC
12	23♌55	24 56	25 57	26 59	28 00	29 02	0♍04	1 06	MC
NOON	13♏45	14 31	15 17	16 03	16 48	17 34	18 20	19 06	ASC
1	9♍43	10 47	11 50	12 54	13 57	15 01	16 05	17 09	MC
PM	25♏26	26 12	26 58	27 44	28 31	29 17	0♐04	0 50	ASC
2	25♍59	27 04	28 08	29 12	0♎17	1 21	2 26	3 30	MC
PM	7♐19	8 07	8 54	9 42	10 30	11 18	12 07	12 55	ASC
3	12♎21	13 25	14 29	15 32	16 36	17 40	18 43	19 47	MC
PM	19♐44	20 35	21 26	22 17	23 08	24 00	24 52	25 44	ASC
4	28♎25	29 27	0♏29	1 31	2 32	3 34	4 35	5 36	MC
PM	3♑11	4 07	5 03	6 00	6 57	7 55	8 54	9 53	ASC
5	13♏54	14 53	15 53	16 52	17 51	18 49	19 48	20 46	MC
PM	18♑23	19 27	20 33	21 39	22 46	23 54	25 03	26 13	ASC
6	28♏43	29 40	0 36	1♐33	2 30	3 26	4 22	5 18	MC
PM	6♒22	7 41	9 00	10 21	11 42	13 05	14 28	15 53	ASC
7	12♐57	13 52	14 47	15 42	16 37	17 32	18 27	19 21	MC
PM	28♒15	29 50	1♓25	3 02	4 40	6 18	7 58	9 38	ASC
8	26♐51	27 45	28 39	29 34	0♑28	1 22	2 16	3 11	MC
PM	23♓52	25 37	27 23	29 08	0♈54	2 40	4 25	6 11	ASC
9	10♑40	11 35	12 29	13 24	14 19	15 14	16 09	17 04	MC
PM	20♈24	22 04	23 44	25 23	27 00	28 37	0♉13	1 47	ASC
10	24♑43	25 39	26 35	27 32	28 28	29 25	0♒22	1 19	MC
PM	14♉09	15 34	16 57	18 20	19 41	21 02	22 21	23 39	ASC
11	9♒15	10 13	11 12	12 11	13 10	14 09	15 08	16 08	MC
PM	3♊49	4 59	6 07	7 15	8 22	9 29	10 34	11 39	ASC

CALENDAR DATE — AUGUST of any year — CALENDAR DATE

HOUR OF BIRTH

	25	26	27	28	29	30	31	1	
12	1♓37	2 39	3 41	4 44	5 46	6 49	7 52	8 55	MC
MID	26♊51	27 46	28 41	29 36	0♋30	1 24	2 17	3 10	ASC
1	17♓41	18 45	19 49	20 53	21 57	23 01	24 06		MC
AM	10♋17	11 07	11 57	12 47	13 37	14 26	15 15		ASC
2	4♈02	5 07	6 11	7 15	8 20	9 24	10 28		MC
AM	22♋42	23 30	24 17	25 04	25 51	26 38	27 25		ASC
3	20♈18	21 21	22 24	23 27	24 30	25 33	26 35		MC
AM	4♌36	5 22	6 08	6 54	7 40	8 26	9 12		ASC
4	6♉06	7 07	8 08	9 08	10 09	11 09	12 09		MC
AM	16♌16	17 01	17 47	18 33	19 19	20 04	20 50		ASC
5	21♉16	22 14	23 12	24 10	25 07	26 05	27 02		MC
AM	27♌54	28 39	29 25	0♍11	0 57	1 43	2 29		ASC
6	5♊46	6 42	7 38	8 34	9 29	10 25	11 20		MC
AM	9♍34	10 20	11 06	11 53	12 39	13 25	14 11		ASC
7	19♊48	20 43	21 38	22 32	23 26	24 21	25 15		MC
AM	21♍19	22 05	22 52	23 38	24 24	25 11	25 57		ASC
8	3♋38	4 32	5 26	6 21	7 15	8 10	9 04		MC
AM	3♎06	3 52	4 39	5 25	6 11	6 57	7 44		ASC
9	17♋32	18 27	19 22	20 18	21 13	22 09	23 05		MC
AM	14♎52	15 38	16 24	17 10	17 57	18 43	19 29		ASC
10	1♌47	2 44	3 42	4 39	5 37	6 35	7 33		MC
AM	26♎35	27 21	28 06	28 52	29 38	0♏24	1 10		ASC
11	16♌37	17 37	18 37	19 37	20 37	21 38	22 38		MC
AM	8♏14	8 59	9 45	10 31	11 16	12 02	12 48		ASC
12	2♍08	3 10	4 13	5 15	6 18	7 21	8 24		MC
NOON	19♏52	20 37	21 23	22 09	22 55	23 41	24 27		ASC
1	18♍13	19 17	20 21	21 25	22 29	23 34	24 38		MC
PM	1♐37	2 24	3 11	3 58	4 45	5 32	6 19		ASC
2	4♎35	5 39	6 43	7 48	8 52	9 56	11 00		MC
PM	13♐44	14 33	15 22	16 12	17 01	17 51	18 41		ASC
3	20♎50	21 53	22 56	23 59	25 01	26 04	27 06		MC
PM	26♐37	27 30	28 23	29 17	0♑11	1 06	2 01		ASC
4	6♏37	7 38	8 38	9 39	10 39	11 39	12 39		MC
PM	10♑52	11 52	12 53	13 54	14 56	15 59	17 02		ASC
5	21♏45	22 43	23 41	24 38	25 36	26 33	27 31		MC
PM	27♑23	28 35	29 47	1♒00	2 14	3 29	4 45		ASC
6	6♐14	7 10	8 06	9 01	9 57	10 52	11 48		MC
PM	17♒19	18 46	20 14	21 43	23 13	24 45	26 17		ASC
7	20♐16	21 10	22 05	22 59	23 54	24 48	25 42		MC
PM	11♓19	13 01	14 44	16 27	18 11	19 55	21 40		ASC
8	4♑05	4 59	5 54	6 48	7 42	8 37	9 31		MC
PM	7♈56	9 40	11 25	13 09	14 52	16 35	18 17		ASC
9	17♑59	18 55	19 50	20 45	21 41	22 37	23 33		MC
PM	3♉21	4 54	6 25	7 56	9 25	10 54	12 21		ASC
10	2♒16	3 13	4 10	5 08	6 06	7 04	8 02		MC
PM	24♉57	26 13	27 28	28 43	29 56	1♊08	2 20		ASC
11	17♒07	18 07	19 07	20 07	21 08	22 08	23 09		MC
PM	12♊43	13 46	14 49	15 51	16 53	17 54	18 54		ASC

CALENDAR DATE — SEPTEMBER of any year — CALENDAR DATE

HOUR OF BIRTH	1	2	3	4	5	6	7	8	
12 MID	8♓55	9 59	11 02	12 05	13 09	14 12	15 16	16 20	MC
	3♋10	4 03	4 56	5 48	6 40	7 31	8 22	9 13	ASC
1 AM	25♓10	26 15	27 19	28 23	29 28	0♈32	1 37	2 41	MC
	16♋04	16 53	17 42	18 30	19 18	20 06	20 54	21 42	ASC
2 AM	11♈32	12 36	13 40	14 44	15 48	16 51	17 55	18 58	MC
	28♋12	28 59	29 45	0♌32	1 18	2 05	2 51	3 37	ASC
3 AM	27♈38	28 40	29 42	0♉44	1 45	2 47	3 48	4 49	MC
	9♌58	10 43	11 29	12 15	13 01	13 47	14 32	15 18	ASC
4 AM	13♉09	14 08	15 08	16 07	17 06	18 05	19 03	20 02	MC
	21♌36	22 21	23 07	23 53	24 39	25 24	26 10	26 56	ASC
5 AM	27♉59	28 56	29 53	0♊50	1 47	2 43	3 39	4 36	MC
	3♍14	4 00	4 46	5 32	6 18	7 04	7 50	8 36	ASC
6 AM	12♊15	13 10	14 06	15 00	15 55	16 50	17 45	18 40	MC
	14♍57	15 43	16 30	17 16	18 02	18 48	19 34	20 21	ASC
7 AM	26♊09	27 04	27 58	28 52	29 47	0♋41	1 35	2 29	MC
	26♍43	27 29	28 16	29 02	29 48	0♎35	1 21	2 08	ASC
8 AM	9♋59	10 53	11 48	12 43	13 37	14 32	15 27	16 22	MC
	8♎30	9 16	10 03	10 49	11 35	12 21	13 08	13 54	ASC
9 AM	24♋00	24 57	25 53	26 49	27 45	28 42	29 39	0♌35	MC
	20♎15	21 01	21 47	22 33	23 19	24 05	24 51	25 37	ASC
10 AM	8♌31	9 29	10 27	11 26	12 25	13 24	14 23	15 22	MC
	1♏56	2 41	3 27	4 13	4 59	5 44	6 30	7 16	ASC
11 AM	23♌39	24 40	25 41	26 43	27 44	28 46	29 48	0♍49	MC
	13♏33	14 19	15 05	15 51	16 36	17 22	18 08	18 54	ASC
12 NOON	9♍27	10 30	11 34	12 37	13 41	14 44	15 48	16 52	MC
	25♏13	26 00	26 46	27 32	28 19	29 05	29 51	0♐38	ASC
1 PM	25♍42	26 47	27 51	28 56	0♎00	1 05	2 09	3 13	MC
	7♐07	7 54	8 42	9 30	10 18	11 06	11 54	12 43	ASC
2 PM	12♎04	13 08	14 12	15 16	16 20	17 23	18 27	19 30	MC
	19♐31	20 22	21 12	22 03	22 55	23 46	24 38	25 31	ASC
3 PM	28♎09	29 11	0♏13	1 14	2 16	3 18	4 19	5 20	MC
	2♑56	3 52	4 48	5 45	6 42	7 40	8 38	9 37	ASC
4 PM	13♏38	14 38	15 37	16 36	17 35	18 34	19 33	20 31	MC
	18♑06	19 10	20 16	21 22	22 29	23 37	24 45	25 55	ASC
5 PM	28♏28	29 25	0♐22	1 18	2 15	3 11	4 08	5 04	MC
	6♒02	7 20	8 39	10 00	11 21	12 43	14 06	15 31	ASC
6 PM	12♐43	13 38	14 33	15 28	16 23	17 18	18 12	19 07	MC
	27♒50	29 25	1♓00	2 37	4 14	5 53	7 32	9 12	ASC
7 PM	26♐37	27 31	28 25	29 19	0♑14	1 08	2 02	2 56	MC
	23♓25	25 10	26 55	28 41	0♈27	2 12	3 58	5 43	ASC
8 PM	10♑26	11 21	12 15	13 10	14 05	15 00	15 55	16 50	MC
	19♈58	21 38	23 18	24 57	26 35	28 12	29 48	1♉23	ASC
9 PM	24♑28	25 25	26 21	27 17	28 14	29 10	0♒07	1 04	MC
	13♉47	15 12	16 36	17 59	19 20	20 41	22 01	23 19	ASC
10 PM	9♒00	9 58	10 57	11 55	12 54	13 53	14 53	15 52	MC
	3♊31	4 40	5 49	6 58	8 05	9 11	10 17	11 22	ASC
11 PM	24♒10	25 11	26 12	27 13	28 15	29 17	0♓18	1 21	MC
	19♊53	20 53	21 51	22 49	23 47	24 44	25 40	26 36	ASC

CALENDAR DATE — SEPTEMBER of any year — CALENDAR DATE

HOUR OF BIRTH	9	10	11	12	13	14	15	16	
12 MID	17♓24	18 28	19 32	20 36	21 40	22 45	23 49	24 53	MC
	10♋04	10 54	11 44	12 34	13 24	14 13	15 03	15 52	ASC
1 AM	3♈46	4 50	5 54	6 59	8 03	9 07	10 11	11 16	MC
	22♋30	23 17	24 05	24 52	25 39	26 26	27 13	28 00	ASC
2 AM	20♈02	21 05	22 08	23 11	24 14	25 16	26 19	27 21	MC
	4♌24	5 10	5 56	6 42	7 28	8 14	9 00	9 46	ASC
3 AM	5♉51	6 51	7 52	8 53	9 53	10 53	11 53	12 53	MC
	16♌04	16 50	17 35	18 21	19 07	19 52	20 38	21 24	ASC
4 AM	21♉00	21 59	22 57	23 55	24 52	25 50	26 47	27 44	MC
	27♌42	28 27	29 13	29 59	0 45	1 31	2 17	3 03	ASC
5 AM	5♊32	6 28	7 23	8 19	9 15	10 10	11 06	12 01	MC
	9♍22	10 08	10 54	11 41	12 27	13 13	13 59	14 45	ASC
6 AM	19♊34	20 29	21 23	22 18	23 12	24 07	25 01	25 55	MC
	21♍07	21 53	22 40	23 26	24 12	24 58	25 45	26 31	ASC
7 AM	3♋24	4 18	5 12	6 07	7 01	7 55	8 50	9 44	MC
	2♎54	3 40	4 26	5 13	5 59	6 45	7 32	8 18	ASC
8 AM	17♋17	18 13	19 08	20 03	20 59	21 54	22 50	23 46	MC
	14♎40	15 26	16 12	16 58	17 45	18 31	19 17	20 03	ASC
9 AM	1♌32	2 29	3 27	4 24	5 22	6 20	7 17	8 16	MC
	26♎23	27 09	27 55	28 40	29 26	0♏12	0 58	1 44	ASC
10 AM	16♌22	17 22	18 21	19 21	20 22	21 22	22 23	23 23	MC
	8♏02	8 47	9 33	10 19	11 04	11 50	12 36	13 22	ASC
11 AM	1♍52	2 54	3 56	4 59	6 02	7 04	8 07	9 10	MC
	19♏40	20 26	21 11	21 57	22 43	23 29	24 15	25 01	ASC
12 NOON	17♍56	19 00	20 04	21 08	22 13	23 17	24 21	25 26	MC
	1♐25	2 11	2 58	3 45	4 32	5 20	6 07	6 54	ASC
1 PM	4♎18	5 22	6 27	7 31	8 35	9 39	10 44	11 48	MC
	13♐31	14 20	15 09	15 59	16 48	17 38	18 28	19 18	ASC
2 PM	20♎33	21 36	22 39	23 42	24 45	25 48	26 50	27 52	MC
	26♐23	27 16	28 10	29 03	29 57	0♑52	1 47	2 42	ASC
3 PM	6♏21	7 22	8 22	9 23	10 23	11 23	12 23	13 23	MC
	10♑37	11 36	12 37	13 38	14 40	15 42	16 45	17 49	ASC
4 PM	21♏30	22 28	23 26	24 23	25 21	26 19	27 16	28 13	MC
	27♑05	28 16	29 28	0♒41	1 55	3 09	4 25	5 42	ASC
5 PM	6♐00	6 56	7 51	8 47	9 43	10 38	11 33	12 29	MC
	16♒56	18 23	19 51	21 20	22 50	24 21	25 53	27 26	ASC
6 PM	20♐02	20 56	21 51	22 45	23 39	24 34	25 28	26 22	MC
	10♓53	12 35	14 17	16 00	17 44	19 28	21 12	22 57	ASC
7 PM	3♑51	4 45	5 39	6 34	7 28	8 23	9 17	10 12	MC
	7♈28	9 13	10 58	12 42	14 25	16 08	17 50	19 32	ASC
8 PM	17♑45	18 40	19 36	20 31	21 27	22 22	23 18	24 14	MC
	2♉57	4 30	6 02	7 32	9 02	10 31	11 58	13 25	ASC
9 PM	2♒01	2 58	3 55	4 53	5 51	6 48	7 46	8 45	MC
	24♉37	25 53	27 09	28 23	29 37	0♊50	2 02	3 12	ASC
10 PM	16♒52	17 51	18 51	19 52	20 52	21 52	22 53	23 54	MC
	12♊26	13 30	14 33	15 35	16 37	17 38	18 38	19 38	ASC
11 PM	2♓23	3 25	4 28	5 30	6 33	7 36	8 39	9 42	MC
	27♊32	28 27	29 22	0♋16	1 10	2 03	2 57	3 50	ASC

CALENDAR DATE — SEPTEMBER of any year — CALENDAR DATE

HOUR OF BIRTH	17	18	19	20	21	22	23	24	
12 MID	25♓58	27 02	28 07	29 11	0♈16	1 20	2 24	3 29	MC
	16♋40	17 29	18 18	19 06	19 54	20 42	21 30	22 17	ASC
1 AM	12♈20	13 23	14 27	15 31	16 35	17 38	18 42	19 45	MC
	28♋47	29 33	0♌20	1 06	1 53	2 39	3 25	4 12	ASC
2 AM	28♈23	29 26	0♉28	1 29	2 31	3 32	4 34	5 35	MC
	10♌32	11 17	12 03	12 49	13 35	14 20	15 06	15 52	ASC
3 AM	13♉53	14 52	15 51	16 51	17 49	18 48	19 47	20 45	MC
	22♌10	22 55	23 41	24 27	25 12	25 58	26 44	27 30	ASC
4 AM	28♉42	29 38	0♊35	1 32	2 28	3 25	4 21	5 17	MC
	3♍48	4 34	5 20	6 06	6 52	7 38	8 24	9 10	ASC
5 AM	12♊56	13 51	14 46	15 41	16 36	17 31	18 25	19 20	MC
	15♍31	16 18	17 04	17 50	18 36	19 22	20 09	20 55	ASC
6 AM	26♊50	27 44	28 38	29 32	0♋27	1 21	2 15	3 09	MC
	27♍17	28 04	28 50	29 36	0♎23	1 09	1 55	2 42	ASC
7 AM	10♋39	11 34	12 28	13 23	14 18	15 13	16 08	17 03	MC
	9♎04	9 51	10 37	11 23	12 09	12 56	13 42	14 28	ASC
8 AM	24♋42	25 38	26 34	27 31	28 27	29 24	0♌21	1 17	MC
	20♎49	21 35	22 21	23 07	23 53	24 39	25 25	26 11	ASC
9 AM	9♌14	10 12	11 11	12 10	13 09	14 08	15 07	16 06	MC
	2♏30	3 15	4 01	4 47	5 33	6 18	7 04	7 50	ASC
10 AM	24♌24	25 25	26 27	27 28	28 30	29 31	0♍33	1 35	MC
	14♏07	14 53	15 39	16 25	17 10	17 56	18 42	19 28	ASC
11 AM	10♍14	11 17	12 21	13 24	14 28	15 32	16 35	17 39	MC
	25♏48	26 34	27 20	28 06	28 53	29 39	0♐26	1 13	ASC
12 NOON	26♍30	27 34	28 39	29 43	0♎48	1 52	2 57	4 01	MC
	7♐42	8 29	9 17	10 05	10 53	11 42	12 30	13 19	ASC
1 PM	12♎52	13 55	14 59	16 03	17 07	18 10	19 14	20 17	MC
	20♐09	20 59	21 50	22 41	23 33	24 25	25 17	26 10	ASC
2 PM	28♎55	29 57	0 58	2 00	3 02	4 03	5 04	6 05	MC
	3♑37	4 34	5 30	6 27	7 25	8 23	9 22	10 21	ASC
3 PM	14♏22	15 22	16 21	17 20	18 19	19 18	20 16	21 14	MC
	18♑54	19 59	21 05	22 11	23 19	24 27	25 36	26 46	ASC
4 PM	29♏10	0♐07	1 04	2 00	2 57	3 53	4 49	5 45	MC
	7♒00	8 19	9 39	11 00	12 22	13 45	15 09	16 34	ASC
5 PM	13♐24	14 19	15 14	16 09	17 03	17 58	18 53	19 47	MC
	29♒00	0♓35	2 12	3 49	5 27	7 06	8 46	10 27	ASC
6 PM	27♐17	28 11	29 05	0♑00	0 54	1 48	2 42	3 37	MC
	24♓42	26 28	28 13	29 59	1♈45	3 30	5 16	7 01	ASC
7 PM	11♑06	12 01	12 56	13 51	14 45	15 40	16 35	17 31	MC
	21♈12	22 52	24 31	26 09	27 47	29 23	0♉58	2 32	ASC
8 PM	25♑10	26 06	27 02	27 59	28 55	29 52	0♒49	1 46	MC
	14♉50	16 14	17 37	18 59	20 20	21 40	22 59	24 17	ASC
9 PM	9♒43	10 41	11 40	12 39	13 38	14 37	15 37	16 36	MC
	4♊22	5 32	6 40	7 47	8 54	10 00	11 05	12 10	ASC
10 PM	24♒55	25 56	26 57	27 59	29 01	0♓02	1 04	2 07	MC
	20♊37	21 36	22 34	23 32	24 29	25 25	26 22	27 17	ASC
11 PM	10♓45	11 49	12 52	13 56	15 00	16 03	17 07	18 11	MC
	4♋42	5 34	6 26	7 18	8 09	9 00	9 51	10 41	ASC

CALENDAR DATE — SEPTEMBER of any year — CALENDAR DATE

HOUR OF BIRTH	25	26	27	28	29	30	1	
12 MID	4♈33	5 38	6 42	7 46	8 51	9 55	10 59	MC
	23♋05	23 52	24 40	25 27	26 14	27 01	27 48	ASC
1 AM	20♈48	21 52	22 55	23 57	25 00	26 03		MC
	4♌58	5 44	6 30	7 16	8 02	8 48		ASC
2 AM	6♉36	7 36	8 37	9 37	10 38	11 38		MC
	16♌36	17 23	18 09	18 55	19 40	20 26		ASC
3 AM	21♉43	22 42	23 40	24 37	25 35	26 32		MC
	28♌16	29 01	29 47	0♍33	1 19	2 05		ASC
4 AM	6♊13	7 09	8 04	9 00	9 56	10 51		MC
	9♍56	10 42	11 29	12 15	13 01	13 47		ASC
5 AM	20♊15	21 09	22 04	22 58	23 52	24 47		MC
	21♍41	22 28	23 14	24 00	24 46	25 33		ASC
6 AM	4♋04	4 58	5 52	6 47	7 41	8 36		MC
	3♎28	4 14	5 01	5 47	6 33	7 20		ASC
7 AM	17♋58	18 53	19 49	20 44	21 40	22 36		MC
	15♎14	16 00	16 46	17 33	18 19	19 05		ASC
8 AM	2♌15	3 12	4 09	5 07	6 04	7 02		MC
	26♎57	27 43	28 28	29 14	0♏00	0 46		ASC
9 AM	17♌06	18 06	19 06	20 06	21 06	22 07		MC
	8♏35	9 21	10 07	10 53	11 38	12 24		ASC
10 AM	2♍38	3 40	4 43	5 45	6 48	7 51		MC
	20♏14	20 59	21 45	22 31	23 17	24 03		ASC
11 AM	18♍43	19 47	20 52	21 56	23 00	24 04		MC
	1♐59	2 46	3 33	4 20	5 07	5 54		ASC
12 NOON	5♎06	6 10	7 14	8 18	9 23	10 27		MC
	14♐08	14 57	15 46	16 35	17 25	18 15		ASC
1 PM	21♎20	22 23	23 26	24 29	25 31	26 34		MC
	27♐02	27 56	28 49	29 43	0♑37	1 32		ASC
2 PM	7♏06	8 07	9 07	10 07	11 08	12 08		MC
	11♑21	12 21	13 22	14 24	15 26	16 29		ASC
3 PM	22♏13	23 11	24 08	25 06	26 04	27 01		MC
	27♑57	29 09	0♒22	1 35	2 50	4 05		ASC
4 PM	6♐41	7 37	8 33	9 28	10 24	11 19		MC
	18♒00	19 28	20 56	22 26	23 57	25 29		ASC
5 PM	20♐42	21 36	22 31	23 25	24 20	25 14		MC
	12♓08	13 50	15 33	17 17	19 01	20 45		ASC
6 PM	4♑31	5 25	6 20	7 14	8 08	9 03		MC
	8♈46	10 30	12 15	13 58	15 41	17 24		ASC
7 PM	18♑26	19 21	20 17	21 12	22 08	23 03		MC
	4♉06	5 38	7 09	8 39	10 08	11 35		ASC
8 PM	2♒43	3 40	4 38	5 36	6 33	7 31		MC
	25♉33	26 49	28 04	29 18	0♊31	1 43		ASC
9 PM	17♒36	18 36	19 36	20 36	21 37	22 37		MC
	13♊14	14 17	15 19	16 21	17 22	18 23		ASC
10 PM	3♓09	4 11	5 14	6 17	7 19	8 22		MC
	28♊13	29 07	0♋02	0 56	1 50	2 43		ASC
11 PM	19♓15	20 20	21 24	22 28	23 32	24 37		MC
	11♋31	12 21	13 11	14 00	14 50	15 39		ASC

CALENDAR DATE OCTOBER of any year CALENDAR DATE

HOUR OF BIRTH	1	2	3	4	5	6	7	8	
12	10♈59	12 03	13 07	14 11	15 15	16 18	17 22	18 25	MC
MID	27♋48	28 35	29 21	0♌08	0 54	1 41	2 27	3 13	ASC
1	27♈05	28 07	29 09	0♉11	1 13	2 15	3 16	4 18	MC
AM	9♌34	10 20	11 05	11 51	12 37	13 23	14 09	14 54	ASC
2	12♉37	13 37	14 37	15 36	16 35	17 34	18 33	19 32	MC
AM	21♌12	21 58	22 43	23 29	24 15	25 01	25 46	26 32	ASC
3	27♉30	28 27	29 24	0♊21	1 17	2 14	3 10	4 06	MC
AM	2♍51	3 37	4 22	5 08	5 54	6 40	7 26	8 12	ASC
4	11♊47	12 42	13 37	14 32	15 27	16 22	17 16	18 11	MC
AM	14♍33	15 19	16 05	16 52	17 38	18 24	19 10	19 57	ASC
5	25♊41	26 35	27 30	28 24	29 18	0♋13	1 07	2 01	MC
AM	26♍19	27 05	27 52	28 38	29 24	0♎11	0 57	1 43	ASC
6	9♋30	10 25	11 19	12 14	13 09	14 04	14 59	15 54	MC
AM	8♎06	8 52	9 39	10 25	11 11	11 57	12 43	13 30	ASC
7	23♋31	24 27	25 23	26 20	27 16	28 12	29 09	0♌06	MC
AM	19♎51	20 37	21 23	22 09	22 55	23 41	24 27	25 13	ASC
8	8♌00	8 59	9 57	10 56	11 54	12 53	13 52	14 51	MC
AM	1♏32	2 18	3 03	3 49	4 35	5 21	6 06	6 52	ASC
9	23♌08	24 08	25 09	26 11	27 12	28 14	29 15	0♍17	MC
AM	13♏10	13 55	14 41	15 27	16 13	16 58	17 44	18 30	ASC
10	8♍54	9 57	11 01	12 04	13 08	14 11	15 15	16 19	MC
AM	24♏49	25 36	26 22	27 08	27 54	28 41	29 27	0♐14	ASC
11	25♍09	26 13	27 18	28 22	29 27	0♎31	1 35	2 40	MC
AM	6♐42	7 29	8 17	9 05	9 53	10 41	11 29	12 17	ASC
12	11♎31	12 35	13 39	14 43	15 46	16 50	17 54	18 57	MC
NOON	19♐05	19 55	20 46	21 37	22 28	23 20	24 11	25 03	ASC
1	27♎36	28 38	29 40	0♏42	1 44	2 46	3 47	4 48	MC
PM	2♑27	3 23	4 19	5 15	6 12	7 10	8 08	9 06	ASC
2	13♏07	14 07	15 06	16 06	17 04	18 04	19 02	20 01	MC
PM	17♑32	18 37	19 42	20 48	21 54	23 01	24 09	25 18	ASC
3	27♏58	28 55	29 52	0♐49	1 45	2 42	3 38	4 34	MC
PM	5♒22	6 40	7 58	9 18	10 38	12 00	13 23	14 47	ASC
4	12♐14	13 09	14 04	14 59	15 54	16 49	17 44	18 39	MC
PM	27♒02	28 36	0♓11	1 47	3 24	5 01	6 40	8 20	ASC
5	26♐08	27 03	27 57	28 51	29 45	0♑40	1 34	2 28	MC
PM	22♓30	24 15	26 00	27 46	29 32	1♈17	3 03	4 48	ASC
6	9♑58	10 52	11 47	12 41	13 36	14 31	15 26	16 21	MC
PM	19♈05	20 46	22 26	24 06	25 44	27 21	28 58	0♉34	ASC
7	23♑59	24 55	25 51	26 48	27 44	28 41	29 37	0♒34	MC
PM	13♉02	14 28	15 52	17 16	18 38	19 59	21 19	22 38	ASC
8	8♒29	9 28	10 26	11 25	12 24	13 23	14 22	15 21	MC
PM	2♊54	4 04	5 14	6 22	7 30	8 37	9 43	10 48	ASC
9	23♒38	24 39	25 40	26 41	27 43	28 44	29 46	0♓48	MC
PM	19♊22	20 22	21 21	22 19	23 17	24 14	25 11	26 07	ASC
10	9♓26	10 29	11 32	12 36	13 39	14 43	15 47	16 51	MC
PM	3♋36	4 28	5 21	6 13	7 04	7 56	8 47	9 37	ASC
11	25♓41	26 45	27 50	28 54	29 59	1♈03	2 08	3 12	MC
PM	16♋28	17 16	18 05	18 53	19 41	20 29	21 17	22 05	ASC

CALENDAR DATE OCTOBER of any year CALENDAR DATE

HOUR OF BIRTH	9	10	11	12	13	14	15	16	
12	19♈29	20 32	21 35	22 38	23 41	24 44	25 46	26 49	MC
MID	4♌00	4 46	5 32	6 18	7 04	7 50	8 36	9 22	ASC
1	5♉19	6 20	7 21	8 21	9 22	10 22	11 22	12 22	MC
AM	15♌40	16 26	17 11	17 57	18 43	19 29	20 14	21 00	ASC
2	20♉30	21 28	22 26	23 24	24 22	25 20	26 17	27 15	MC
AM	27♌18	28 04	28 49	29 35	0♍21	1 07	1 53	2 39	ASC
3	5♊03	5 59	6 54	7 50	8 46	9 41	10 37	11 32	MC
AM	8♍58	9 44	10 31	11 17	12 03	12 49	13 35	14 21	ASC
4	19♊06	20 00	20 55	21 49	22 44	23 38	24 33	25 27	MC
AM	20♍43	21 29	22 15	23 02	23 48	24 34	25 21	26 07	ASC
5	2♋55	3 50	4 44	5 38	6 33	7 27	8 22	9 16	MC
AM	2♎30	3 16	4 02	4 49	5 35	6 21	7 08	7 54	ASC
6	16♋49	17 44	18 39	19 34	20 30	21 25	22 21	23 17	MC
AM	14♎16	15 02	15 48	16 34	17 21	18 07	18 53	19 39	ASC
7	1♌03	2 00	2 57	3 54	4 52	5 49	6 47	7 45	MC
AM	25♎59	26 45	27 31	28 17	29 02	29 48	0♏34	1 20	ASC
8	15♌51	16 50	17 50	18 50	19 50	20 51	21 51	22 52	MC
AM	7♏38	8 24	9 09	9 55	10 41	11 26	12 12	12 58	ASC
9	1♍19	2 21	3 24	4 26	5 29	6 32	7 35	8 38	MC
AM	19♏16	20 02	20 48	21 33	22 19	23 05	23 51	24 37	ASC
10	17♍23	18 27	19 31	20 35	21 39	22 43	23 48	24 52	MC
AM	1♐00	1 47	2 34	3 21	4 08	4 55	5 42	6 30	ASC
11	3♎44	4 49	5 53	6 57	8 02	9 06	10 10	11 14	MC
AM	13♐06	13 55	14 44	15 33	16 22	17 12	18 02	18 52	ASC
12	20♎00	21 04	22 07	23 10	24 12	25 15	26 18	27 20	MC
NOON	25♐56	26 49	27 42	28 35	29 29	0♑23	1 18	2 13	ASC
1	5♏49	6 50	7 51	8 51	9 52	10 52	11 52	12 52	MC
PM	10♑06	11 05	12 05	13 06	14 08	15 10	16 12	17 16	ASC
2	20♏59	21 57	22 55	23 53	24 51	25 49	26 46	27 43	MC
PM	26♑28	27 39	28 50	0♒03	1 16	2 30	3 46	5 02	ASC
3	5♐31	6 27	7 22	8 18	9 14	10 09	11 05	12 00	MC
PM	16♒12	17 38	19 05	20 33	22 03	23 33	25 05	26 37	ASC
4	19♐33	20 28	21 22	22 17	23 11	24 06	25 00	25 54	MC
PM	10♓00	11 42	13 24	15 06	16 50	18 34	20 18	22 03	ASC
5	3♑22	4 17	5 11	6 05	7 00	7 54	8 49	9 43	MC
PM	6♈34	8 19	10 03	11 48	13 31	15 14	16 57	18 39	ASC
6	17♑16	18 11	19 07	20 02	20 58	21 53	22 49	23 45	MC
PM	2♉08	3 42	5 14	6 45	8 16	9 45	11 13	12 40	ASC
7	1♒31	2 28	3 26	4 23	5 21	6 18	7 16	8 14	MC
PM	23♉56	25 14	26 30	27 45	28 59	0♊12	1 24	2 36	ASC
8	16♒21	17 20	18 20	19 20	20 20	21 21	22 21	23 22	MC
PM	11♊53	12 57	14 00	15 03	16 05	17 06	18 07	19 07	ASC
9	1♓50	2 53	3 55	4 58	6 00	7 03	8 06	9 09	MC
PM	27♊03	27 58	28 53	29 48	0♋42	1 36	2 29	3 22	ASC
10	17♓55	18 59	20 03	21 07	22 11	23 16	24 20	25 24	MC
PM	10♋28	11 18	12 08	12 58	13 48	14 37	15 26	16 15	ASC
11	4♈17	5 21	6 25	7 30	8 34	9 38	10 42	11 46	MC
PM	22♋53	23 40	24 27	25 15	26 02	26 49	27 36	28 22	ASC

CALENDAR DATE — OCTOBER of any year — CALENDAR DATE

HOUR OF BIRTH	17	18	19	20	21	22	23	24	
12 MID	27♈51	28 53	29 55	0♉57	1 59	3 00	4 02	5 03	MC
	10♌08	10 53	11 39	12 25	13 11	13 57	14 42	15 28	ASC
1 AM	13♉22	14 21	15 21	16 29	17 19	18 18	19 16	20 15	MC
	21♌46	22 31	23 17	24 03	24 49	25 34	26 20	27 06	ASC
2 AM	28♉12	29 09	0♊06	1 02	1 59	2 55	3 52	4 48	MC
	3♍25	4 10	4 56	5 42	6 28	7 14	8 00	8 46	ASC
3 AM	12♊27	13 23	14 18	15 13	16 07	17 02	17 57	18 52	MC
	15♍07	15 53	16 40	17 26	18 12	18 58	19 45	20 31	ASC
4 AM	26♊21	27 16	28 10	29 04	29 58	0♋53	1 47	2 41	MC
	26♍53	27 40	28 26	29 12	29 59	0♎45	1 31	2 18	ASC
5 AM	10♋11	11 05	12 00	12 55	13 49	14 44	15 39	16 34	MC
	8♎40	9 26	10 13	10 59	11 45	12 31	13 18	14 04	ASC
6 AM	24♋13	25 09	26 05	27 01	27 58	28 54	29 51	0♌48	MC
	20♎25	21 11	21 57	22 43	23 29	24 15	25 01	25 47	ASC
7 AM	8♌43	9 42	10 40	11 39	12 38	13 37	14 36	15 35	MC
	2♏06	2 51	3 37	4 23	5 09	5 54	6 40	7 26	ASC
8 AM	23♌53	24 54	25 55	26 56	27 58	28 59	0♍01	1 03	MC
	13♏43	14 29	15 15	16 01	16 46	17 32	18 18	19 04	ASC
9 AM	9♍41	10 44	11 47	12 51	13 55	14 58	16 02	17 06	MC
	25♏24	26 10	26 56	27 42	28 29	29 15	0♐02	0 48	ASC
10 AM	25♍56	27 01	28 05	29 10	0♎14	1 19	2 23	3 28	MC
	7♐17	8 05	8 52	9 40	10 28	11 16	12 05	12 53	ASC
11 AM	12♎18	13 22	14 26	15 30	16 34	17 37	18 41	19 44	MC
	19♐42	20 33	21 24	22 15	23 06	23 58	24 50	25 42	ASC
12 NOON	28♎22	29 24	0♏26	1 28	2 30	3 31	4 32	5 33	MC
	3♑08	4 04	5 01	5 58	6 55	7 53	8 51	9 50	ASC
1 PM	13♏51	14 51	15 50	16 49	17 48	18 47	19 46	20 44	MC
	18♑20	19 25	20 30	21 37	22 44	23 52	25 00	26 10	ASC
2 PM	28♏40	29 37	0♐34	1 31	2 27	3 24	4 20	5 16	MC
	6♒19	7 38	8 57	10 17	11 39	13 01	14 25	15 49	ASC
3 PM	12♐55	13 50	14 45	15 40	16 35	17 30	18 24	19 19	MC
	28♒11	29 46	1♓21	2 58	4 36	6 14	7 54	9 34	ASC
4 PM	26♐48	27 43	28 37	29 31	0♑26	1 20	2 14	3 08	MC
	23♓48	25 33	27 18	29 04	0♈50	2 35	4 21	6 06	ASC
5 PM	10♑38	11 33	12 27	13 22	14 17	15 12	16 07	17 02	MC
	20♈20	22 00	23 40	25 18	26 56	28 33	0♉09	1 44	ASC
6 PM	24♑41	25 37	26 33	27 29	28 26	29 23	0♒19	1 16	MC
	14♉06	15 30	16 54	18 17	19 38	20 59	22 18	23 36	ASC
7 PM	9♒13	10 11	11 10	12 08	13 07	14 06	15 06	16 05	MC
	3♊46	4 56	6 04	7 12	8 20	9 26	10 31	11 36	ASC
8 PM	24♒23	25 24	26 25	27 27	28 28	29 30	0♓32	1 34	MC
	20♊06	21 05	22 04	23 02	23 59	24 56	25 52	26 48	ASC
9 PM	10♓12	11 16	12 19	13 23	14 26	15 30	16 34	17 38	MC
	4♋15	5 07	5 59	6 51	7 42	8 33	9 24	10 15	ASC
10 PM	26♓29	27 33	28 38	29 42	0♈46	1 51	2 55	4 00	MC
	17♋04	17 52	18 41	19 29	20 17	21 05	21 53	22 40	ASC
11 PM	12♈50	13 54	14 58	16 02	17 05	18 09	19 12	20 16	MC
	29♋09	29 56	0 42	1 29	2 15	3 01	3 48	4 34	ASC

CALENDAR DATE — OCTOBER of any year — CALENDAR DATE

HOUR OF BIRTH	25	26	27	28	29	30	31	1	
12 MID	6♉04	7 05	8 05	9 06	10 06	11 06	12 06	13 06	MC
	16♌14	17 00	17 45	18 31	19 17	20 02	20 48	21 34	ASC
1 AM	21♉13	22 11	23 09	24 07	25 05	26 02	27 00		MC
	27♌52	28 37	29 23	0♍09	0 55	1 41	2 27		ASC
2 AM	5♊44	6 40	7 36	8 31	9 27	10 22	11 18		MC
	9♍32	10 19	11 05	11 51	12 37	13 23	14 09		ASC
3 AM	19♊46	20 41	21 35	22 30	23 24	24 19	25 13		MC
	21♍17	22 03	22 50	23 36	24 22	25 09	25 55		ASC
4 AM	3♋36	4 30	5 24	6 19	7 13	8 07	9 02		MC
	3♎04	3 50	4 37	5 23	6 09	6 56	7 42		ASC
5 AM	17♋29	18 25	19 20	20 15	21 11	22 07	23 02		MC
	14♎50	15 36	16 22	17 09	17 55	18 41	19 27		ASC
6 AM	1♌45	2 42	3 39	4 37	5 34	6 32	7 30		MC
	26♎33	27 19	28 05	28 50	29 36	0♏22	1 08		ASC
7 AM	16♌35	17 35	18 35	19 35	20 35	21 35	22 36		MC
	8♏12	8 57	9 43	10 29	11 14	12 00	12 46		ASC
8 AM	2♍05	3 08	4 10	5 13	6 15	7 18	8 21		MC
	19♏50	20 36	21 21	22 07	22 53	23 39	24 25		ASC
9 AM	18♍10	19 14	20 18	21 22	22 27	23 31	24 35		MC
	1♐35	2 22	3 09	3 56	4 43	5 30	6 17		ASC
10 AM	4♎32	5 36	6 41	7 45	8 49	9 53	10 58		MC
	13♐42	14 31	15 20	16 10	16 59	17 49	18 39		ASC
11 AM	20♎47	21 50	22 53	23 56	24 59	26 01	27 04		MC
	26♐35	27 28	28 21	29 15	0♑09	1 04	1 59		ASC
12 NOON	6♏34	7 35	8 36	9 36	10 36	11 36	12 36		MC
	10♑50	11 50	12 50	13 52	14 53	15 56	16 59		ASC
1 PM	21♏42	22 40	23 38	24 36	25 34	26 31	27 28		MC
	27♑20	28 32	29 44	0♒57	2 11	3 26	4 42		ASC
2 PM	6♐12	7 08	8 04	8 59	9 55	10 50	11 45		MC
	17♒15	18 42	20 10	21 39	23 09	24 41	26 13		ASC
3 PM	20♐14	21 08	22 03	22 57	23 51	24 46	25 40		MC
	11♓15	12 57	14 40	16 23	18 06	19 51	21 35		ASC
4 PM	4♑03	4 57	5 51	6 46	7 40	8 35	9 29		MC
	7♈51	9 36	11 20	13 04	14 48	16 30	18 12		ASC
5 PM	17♑57	18 52	19 48	20 43	21 39	22 34	23 30		MC
	3♉17	4 50	6 22	7 52	9 22	10 50	12 17		ASC
6 PM	2♒13	3 11	4 08	5 06	6 03	7 01	7 59		MC
	24♉54	26 10	27 25	28 40	29 53	1♊06	2 17		ASC
7 PM	17♒05	18 05	19 05	20 05	21 05	22 06	23 06		MC
	12♊40	13 44	14 47	15 49	16 50	17 51	18 51		ASC
8 PM	2♓36	3 39	4 41	5 44	6 47	7 50	8 53		MC
	27♊44	28 39	29 34	0♋28	1 22	2 15	3 08		ASC
9 PM	18♓42	19 46	20 50	21 55	22 59	24 03	25 08		MC
	11♋05	11 55	12 45	13 35	14 24	15 13	16 02		ASC
10 PM	5♈04	6 09	7 13	8 17	9 21	10 25	11 30		MC
	23♋28	24 15	25 02	25 49	26 36	27 23	28 10		ASC
11 PM	21♈19	22 22	23 25	24 27	25 30	26 33	27 35		MC
	5♌20	6 06	6 52	7 38	8 24	9 10	9 56		ASC

CALENDAR DATE NOVEMBER of any year CALENDAR DATE

HOUR OF BIRTH	1	2	3	4	5	6	7	8	
12	13♉06	14 06	15 05	16 04	17 03	18 02	19 01	20 00	MC
MID	21♌34	22 20	23 05	23 51	24 37	25 22	26 08	26 54	ASC
1	27♉57	28 54	29 51	0♊48	1 44	2 41	3 37	4 33	MC
AM	3♍13	3 59	4 44	5 30	6 16	7 02	7 48	8 34	ASC
2	12♊13	13 08	14 03	14 58	15 53	16 48	17 43	18 37	MC
AM	14♍55	15 41	16 28	17 14	18 00	18 46	19 33	20 19	ASC
3	26♊07	27 02	27 56	28 50	29 44	0♋39	1 33	2 27	MC
AM	26♍41	27 28	28 14	29 00	29 47	0♎33	1 19	2 06	ASC
4	9♋56	10 51	11 46	12 40	13 35	14 30	15 25	16 20	MC
AM	8♎28	9 14	10 01	10 47	11 33	12 19	13 06	13 52	ASC
5	23♋58	24 54	25 50	26 47	27 43	28 40	29 36	0♌33	MC
AM	20♎13	20 59	21 45	22 31	23 17	24 03	24 49	25 35	ASC
6	8♌28	9 27	10 25	11 24	12 22	13 21	14 21	15 20	MC
AM	1♏54	2 40	3 25	4 11	4 57	5 43	6 28	7 14	ASC
7	23♌37	24 38	25 39	26 40	27 42	28 43	29 45	0♍47	MC
AM	13♏32	14 17	15 03	15 49	16 35	17 20	18 06	18 52	ASC
8	9♍24	10 28	11 31	12 34	13 38	14 42	15 46	16 49	MC
AM	25♏12	25 58	26 44	27 30	28 17	29 03	29 50	0♐36	ASC
9	25♍40	26 44	27 49	28 53	29 57	1♎02	2 06	3 11	MC
AM	7♐05	7 52	8 40	9 28	10 16	11 04	11 52	12 41	ASC
10	12♎02	13 06	14 09	15 13	16 17	17 21	18 24	19 27	MC
AM	19♐29	20 20	21 10	22 01	22 53	23 44	24 36	25 29	ASC
11	28♎06	29 08	0 10	1 12	2 14	3 15	4 16	5 18	MC
AM	2♑54	3 50	4 46	5 43	6 40	7 38	8 36	9 35	ASC
12	13♏36	14 35	15 35	16 34	17 33	18 32	19 30	20 29	MC
NOON	18♑03	19 08	20 13	21 19	22 26	23 34	24 42	25 52	ASC
1	28♏26	29 23	0♐19	1 16	2 13	3 09	4 05	5 01	MC
PM	5♒59	7 17	8 36	9 56	11 17	12 40	14 03	15 27	ASC
2	12♐41	13 36	14 31	15 26	16 21	17 15	18 10	19 05	MC
PM	27♒47	29 21	0♓56	2 33	4 10	5 49	7 28	9 08	ASC
3	26♐34	27 29	28 23	29 17	0♑11	1 06	2 00	2 54	MC
PM	23♓20	25 06	26 51	28 37	0♈22	2 08	3 53	5 39	ASC
4	10♑24	11 18	12 13	13 08	14 03	14 57	15 52	16 47	MC
PM	19♈54	21 34	23 14	24 53	26 31	28 08	29 44	1♉19	ASC
5	24♑26	25 22	26 18	27 15	28 11	29 08	0♒05	1 01	MC
PM	13♉43	15 08	16 32	17 55	19 17	20 38	21 57	23 16	ASC
6	8♒57	9 56	10 54	11 53	12 52	13 51	14 50	15 50	MC
PM	3♊28	4 38	5 47	6 55	8 02	9 09	10 14	11 20	ASC
7	24♒07	25 08	26 09	27 11	28 12	29 14	0♓16	1 18	MC
PM	19♊51	20 50	21 49	22 47	23 44	24 41	25 38	26 34	ASC
8	9♓56	10 59	12 03	13 06	14 10	15 14	16 17	17 21	MC
PM	4♋01	4 54	5 46	6 37	7 29	8 20	9 11	10 02	ASC
9	26♓12	27 16	28 21	29 25	0♈30	1 34	2 39	3 43	MC
PM	16♋51	17 40	18 28	19 16	20 05	20 52	21 40	22 28	ASC
10	12♈34	13 38	14 41	15 45	16 49	17 52	18 56	19 59	MC
PM	28♋57	29 44	0♌30	1 17	2 03	2 49	3 35	4 22	ASC
11	28♈37	29 39	0 41	1 43	2 44	3 46	4 47	5 48	MC
PM	10♌42	11 27	12 13	12 59	13 45	14 30	15 16	16 02	ASC

CALENDAR DATE NOVEMBER of any year CALENDAR DATE

HOUR OF BIRTH	9	10	11	12	13	14	15	16	
12	20♉58	21 56	22 54	23 52	24 50	25 47	26 45	27 42	MC
MID	27♌40	28 26	29 11	29 57	0♍43	1 29	2 15	3 01	ASC
1	5♊29	6 25	7 21	8 17	9 12	10 08	11 03	11 59	MC
AM	9♍20	10 07	10 53	11 39	12 25	13 11	13 57	14 43	ASC
2	19♊32	20 27	21 21	22 16	23 10	24 04	24 59	25 53	MC
AM	21♍05	21 51	22 38	23 24	24 10	24 57	25 43	26 29	ASC
3	3♋21	4 16	5 10	6 04	6 59	7 53	8 48	9 42	MC
AM	2♎52	3 38	4 25	5 11	5 57	6 44	7 30	8 16	ASC
4	17♋15	18 10	19 06	20 01	20 56	21 52	22 48	23 44	MC
AM	14♎38	15 24	16 10	16 56	17 43	18 29	19 15	20 01	ASC
5	1♌30	2 27	3 24	4 22	5 19	6 17	7 15	8 13	MC
AM	26♎21	27 07	27 53	28 38	29 24	0♏10	0 56	1 42	ASC
6	16♌19	17 19	18 19	19 19	20 19	21 20	22 20	23 21	MC
AM	8♏00	8 45	9 31	10 17	11 03	11 48	12 34	13 20	ASC
7	1♍49	2 51	3 54	4 56	5 59	7 02	8 05	9 08	MC
AM	19♏38	20 24	21 10	21 55	22 41	23 27	24 13	25 00	ASC
8	17♍53	18 57	20 02	21 06	22 10	23 14	24 19	25 23	MC
AM	1♐23	2 10	2 56	3 43	4 30	5 18	6 05	6 52	ASC
9	4♎15	5 20	6 24	7 28	8 33	9 37	10 41	11 45	MC
AM	13♐29	14 18	15 07	15 57	16 46	17 36	18 26	19 16	ASC
10	20♎31	21 34	22 37	23 40	24 43	25 45	26 48	27 50	MC
AM	26♐21	27 14	28 07	29 01	29 55	0♑49	1 44	2 39	ASC
11	6♏18	7 19	8 20	9 20	10 21	11 21	12 21	13 20	MC
AM	10♑34	11 34	12 34	13 36	14 37	15 40	16 43	17 46	ASC
12	21♏27	22 25	23 23	24 21	25 19	26 16	27 13	28 11	MC
NOON	27♑02	28 13	29 25	0♒38	1 52	3 06	4 22	5 39	ASC
1	5♐57	6 53	7 49	8 45	9 40	10 36	11 31	12 26	MC
PM	16♒53	18 19	19 47	21 16	22 46	24 17	25 49	27 22	ASC
2	19♐59	20 54	21 48	22 43	23 37	24 32	25 26	26 20	MC
PM	10♓49	12 31	14 13	15 56	17 39	19 23	21 08	22 53	ASC
3	3♑49	4 43	5 37	6 32	7 26	8 20	9 15	10 09	MC
PM	7♈24	9 09	10 53	12 37	14 21	16 04	17 46	19 27	ASC
4	17♑43	18 38	19 33	20 29	21 24	22 20	23 16	24 12	MC
PM	2♉53	4 26	5 58	7 29	8 58	10 27	11 55	13 21	ASC
5	1♒59	2 56	3 53	4 51	5 48	6 46	7 44	8 42	MC
PM	24♉34	25 50	27 06	28 20	29 34	0♊47	1 59	3 09	ASC
6	16♒49	17 49	18 49	19 49	20 49	21 50	22 51	23 51	MC
PM	12♊24	13 27	14 30	15 33	16 34	17 35	18 36	19 36	ASC
7	2♓20	3 22	4 25	5 28	6 30	7 33	8 36	9 39	MC
PM	27♊29	28 25	29 19	0♋14	1 08	2 01	2 55	3 47	ASC
8	18♓25	19 29	20 34	21 38	22 42	23 46	24 51	25 55	MC
PM	10♋52	11 42	12 32	13 22	14 11	15 01	15 50	16 38	ASC
9	4♈47	5 52	6 56	8 00	9 05	10 09	11 13	12 17	MC
PM	23♋15	24 03	24 50	25 37	26 24	27 11	27 58	28 45	ASC
10	21♈02	22 05	23 08	24 11	25 14	26 16	27 19	28 21	MC
PM	5♌08	5 54	6 40	7 26	8 12	8 58	9 44	10 30	ASC
11	6♉49	7 50	8 50	9 50	10 51	11 51	12 51	13 50	MC
PM	16♌48	17 33	18 19	19 05	19 50	20 36	21 22	22 08	ASC

CALENDAR DATE — NOVEMBER of any year — CALENDAR DATE

HOUR OF BIRTH	17	18	19	20	21	22	23	24	
12 MID	28♉39	29 36	0♊33	1 30	2 26	3 22	4 19	5 15	MC
	3♍47	4 33	5 18	6 04	6 50	7 36	8 22	9 08	ASC
1 AM	12♊54	13 49	14 44	15 39	16 34	17 28	18 23	19 18	MC
	15♍29	16 16	17 02	17 48	18 34	19 21	20 07	20 53	ASC
2 AM	26♊47	27 42	28 36	29 30	0♋24	1 19	2 13	3 07	MC
	27♍16	28 02	28 48	29 35	0♎21	1 07	1 54	2 40	ASC
3 AM	10♋37	11 31	12 26	13 21	14 16	15 11	16 06	17 01	MC
	9♎02	9 49	10 35	11 21	12 07	12 54	13 40	14 26	ASC
4 AM	24♋40	25 36	26 32	27 28	28 25	29 21	0♌18	1 15	MC
	20♎47	21 33	22 19	23 05	23 51	24 37	25 23	26 09	ASC
5 AM	9♌11	10 10	11 08	12 07	13 06	14 05	15 04	16 04	MC
	2♏28	3 13	3 59	4 45	5 31	6 16	7 02	7 48	ASC
6 AM	24♌22	25 23	26 24	27 26	28 27	29 29	0♍31	1 33	MC
	14♏05	14 51	15 37	16 23	17 08	17 54	18 40	19 26	ASC
7 AM	10♍11	11 14	12 18	13 21	14 25	15 29	16 33	17 37	MC
	25♏46	26 32	27 18	28 05	28 51	29 37	0♐24	1 11	ASC
8 AM	26♍27	27 32	28 36	29 41	0♎45	1 50	2 54	3 58	MC
	7♐40	8 27	9 15	10 03	10 51	11 40	12 28	13 17	ASC
9 AM	12♎49	13 53	14 57	16 00	17 04	18 08	19 11	20 14	MC
	20♐06	20 57	21 48	22 39	23 31	24 23	25 15	26 07	ASC
10 AM	28♎52	29 54	0♏56	1 58	2 59	4 00	5 01	6 03	MC
	3♑35	4 31	5 28	6 25	7 23	8 21	9 19	10 19	ASC
11 AM	14♏20	15 19	16 19	17 18	18 16	19 15	20 14	21 12	MC
	18♑51	19 56	21 02	22 09	23 16	24 24	25 34	26 44	ASC
12 NOON	29♏07	0♐05	1 01	1 58	2 54	3 51	4 47	5 43	MC
	6♒57	8 15	9 35	10 56	12 18	13 41	15 05	16 30	ASC
1 PM	13♐21	14 16	15 11	16 06	17 01	17 56	18 51	19 45	MC
	28♒56	0♓31	2 08	3 45	5 23	7 02	8 42	10 23	ASC
2 PM	27♐15	28 09	29 03	29 57	0♑52	1 46	2 40	3 34	MC
	24♓38	26 24	28 09	29 55	1♈40	3 26	5 11	6 57	ASC
3 PM	11♑04	11 59	12 53	13 48	14 43	15 38	16 33	17 28	MC
	21♈08	22 48	24 27	26 05	27 43	29 19	0♉54	2 29	ASC
4 PM	25♑08	26 04	27 00	27 57	28 53	29 50	0♒47	1 44	MC
	14♉46	16 11	17 34	18 56	20 17	21 37	22 56	24 13	ASC
5 PM	9♒41	10 39	11 38	12 37	13 36	14 35	15 34	16 34	MC
	4♊20	5 29	6 37	7 45	8 51	9 57	11 03	12 07	ASC
6 PM	24♒52	25 53	26 55	27 56	28 58	0♓00	1 02	2 04	MC
	20♊35	21 33	22 32	23 29	24 26	25 23	26 19	27 15	ASC
7 PM	10♓43	11 46	12 50	13 53	14 57	16 01	17 05	18 09	MC
	4♋40	5 32	6 24	7 16	8 07	8 58	9 49	10 39	ASC
8 PM	27♓00	28 04	29 08	0♈13	1 17	2 22	3 26	4 31	MC
	17♋27	18 16	19 04	19 52	20 40	21 28	22 15	23 03	ASC
9 PM	13♈21	14 25	15 29	16 32	17 36	18 39	19 43	20 46	MC
	29♋31	0♌18	1 04	1 51	2 37	3 23	4 10	4 56	ASC
10 PM	29♈23	0♉25	1 27	2 28	3 30	4 31	5 32	6 33	MC
	11♌15	12 01	12 47	13 33	14 19	15 04	15 50	16 36	ASC
11 PM	14♉50	15 49	16 48	17 47	18 46	19 44	20 43	21 41	MC
	22♌53	23 39	24 25	25 11	25 56	26 42	27 28	28 14	ASC

CALENDAR DATE — NOVEMBER of any year — CALENDAR DATE

HOUR OF BIRTH	25	26	27	28	29	30	1	
12 MID	6♊11	7 07	8 02	8 58	9 54	10 49	11 44	MC
	9♍55	10 41	11 27	12 13	12 59	13 45	14 31	ASC
1 AM	20♊12	21 07	22 01	22 56	23 50	24 45		MC
	21♍39	22 26	23 12	23 58	24 45	25 31		ASC
2 AM	4♋02	4 56	5 50	6 45	7 39	8 33		MC
	3♎26	4 13	4 59	5 45	6 31	7 18		ASC
3 AM	17♋56	18 51	19 47	20 42	21 38	22 33		MC
	15♎12	15 58	16 44	17 31	18 17	19 03		ASC
4 AM	2♌12	3 09	4 07	5 04	6 02	7 00		MC
	26♎55	27 41	28 27	29 12	29 58	0♏44		ASC
5 AM	17♌04	18 03	19 03	20 04	21 04	22 04		MC
	8♏34	9 19	10 05	10 51	11 36	12 22		ASC
6 AM	2♍35	3 37	4 40	5 43	6 45	7 48		MC
	20♏12	20 58	21 43	22 29	23 15	24 01		ASC
7 AM	18♍41	19 45	20 49	21 53	22 57	24 02		MC
	1♐57	2 44	3 31	4 18	5 05	5 53		ASC
8 AM	5♎03	6 07	7 12	8 16	9 20	10 24		MC
	14♐06	14 55	15 44	16 33	17 23	18 13		ASC
9 AM	21♎17	22 20	23 23	24 26	25 29	26 31		MC
	27♐00	27 53	28 47	29 41	0♑35	1 30		ASC
10 AM	7♏03	8 04	9 05	10 05	11 05	12 05		MC
	11♑18	12 19	13 20	14 21	15 23	16 26		ASC
11 AM	22♏10	23 08	24 06	25 04	26 01	26 59		MC
	27♑54	29 06	0♒19	1 32	2 47	4 02		ASC
12 NOON	6♐39	7 35	8 30	9 26	10 21	11 17		MC
	17♒57	19 24	20 53	22 22	23 53	25 25		ASC
1 PM	20♐40	21 34	22 29	23 23	24 17	25 12		MC
	12♓04	13 46	15 29	17 12	18 56	20 41		ASC
2 PM	4♑29	5 23	6 17	7 12	8 06	9 01		MC
	8♈42	10 26	12 10	13 54	15 37	17 19		ASC
3 PM	18♑23	19 19	20 14	21 10	22 05	23 01		MC
	4♉02	5 34	7 05	8 35	10 04	11 32		ASC
4 PM	2♒41	3 38	4 36	5 33	6 31	7 29		MC
	25♉30	26 46	28 01	29 15	0♊28	1 40		ASC
5 PM	17♒33	18 33	19 33	20 34	21 34	22 35		MC
	13♊11	14 14	15 17	16 18	17 19	18 20		ASC
6 PM	3♓06	4 09	5 11	6 14	7 17	8 20		MC
	28♊10	29 05	0♋00	0 54	1 47	2 41		ASC
7 PM	19♓13	20 17	21 21	22 25	23 30	24 34		MC
	11♋29	12 19	13 09	13 58	14 48	15 37		ASC
8 PM	5♈35	6 39	7 44	8 48	9 52	10 56		MC
	23♋50	24 38	25 25	26 12	26 59	27 46		ASC
9 PM	21♈49	22 52	23 55	24 58	26 00	27 03		MC
	5♌42	6 28	7 14	8 00	8 46	9 32		ASC
10 PM	7♉34	8 34	9 35	10 35	11 35	12 35		MC
	17♌21	18 07	18 53	19 39	20 24	21 10		ASC
11 PM	22♉39	23 37	24 35	25 32	26 30	27 27		MC
	28♌59	29 45	0♍31	1 17	2 03	2 49		ASC

CALENDAR DATE DECEMBER of any year CALENDAR DATE

HOUR OF BIRTH	1	2	3	4	5	6	7	8	
12 MID	11♊44	12 40	13 35	14 30	15 25	16 19	17 14	18 09	MC
	14♍31	15 17	16 04	16 50	17 36	18 22	19 08	19 55	ASC
1 AM	25♊39	26 33	27 28	28 22	29 16	0♋10	1 05	1 59	MC
	26♍17	27 03	27 50	28 36	29 22	0♎09	0 55	1 41	ASC
2 AM	9♋28	10 23	11 17	12 12	13 07	14 01	14 56	15 51	MC
	8♎04	8 50	9 37	10 23	11 09	11 55	12 42	13 28	ASC
3 AM	23♋29	24 25	25 21	26 17	27 14	28 10	29 07	0♌03	MC
	19♎49	20 35	21 21	22 07	22 53	23 39	24 25	25 11	ASC
4 AM	7♌58	8 56	9 55	10 53	11 52	12 51	13 50	14 49	MC
	1♏30	2 16	3 02	3 47	4 33	5 19	6 05	6 50	ASC
5 AM	23♌05	24 06	25 07	26 08	27 10	28 11	29 13	0♍15	MC
	13♏08	13 54	14 39	15 25	16 11	16 57	17 42	18 28	ASC
6 AM	8♍51	9 55	10 58	12 01	13 05	14 09	15 12	16 16	MC
	24♏48	25 34	26 20	27 06	27 53	28 39	29 25	0♐12	ASC
7 AM	25♍06	26 11	27 15	28 19	29 24	0♎28	1 33	2 37	MC
	6♐40	7 27	8 15	9 03	9 51	10 39	11 27	12 15	ASC
8 AM	11♎28	12 32	13 36	14 40	15 44	16 48	17 51	18 55	MC
	19♐03	19 53	20 44	21 35	22 26	23 17	24 09	25 01	ASC
9 AM	27♎34	28 36	29 38	0♏40	1 42	2 43	3 45	4 46	MC
	2♑25	3 21	4 17	5 13	6 10	7 08	8 06	9 04	ASC
10 AM	13♏05	14 04	15 04	16 03	17 02	18 01	19 00	19 58	MC
	17♑30	18 34	19 39	20 45	21 51	22 59	24 07	25 16	ASC
11 AM	27♏56	28 53	29 50	0♐47	1 43	2 40	3 36	4 32	MC
	5♒19	6 36	7 55	9 14	10 35	11 57	13 19	14 43	ASC
12 NOON	12♐12	13 07	14 02	14 57	15 52	16 47	17 42	18 36	MC
	26♒58	28 32	0♓07	1 43	3 20	4 57	6 36	8 16	ASC
1 PM	26♐06	27 00	27 55	28 49	29 43	0♑37	1 32	2 26	MC
	22♓26	24 11	25 56	27 42	29 27	1♈13	2 59	4 44	ASC
2 PM	9♑55	10 50	11 45	12 39	13 34	14 29	15 24	16 19	MC
	19♈01	20 42	22 22	24 02	25 40	27 18	28 54	0♉30	ASC
3 PM	23♑57	24 53	25 49	26 45	27 42	28 38	29 35	0♒32	MC
	12♉59	14 24	15 49	17 12	18 35	19 56	21 16	22 35	ASC
4 PM	8♒27	9 25	10 24	11 22	12 21	13 20	14 19	15 19	MC
	2♊51	4 01	5 11	6 19	7 27	8 34	9 40	10 46	ASC
5 PM	23♒35	24 36	25 38	26 39	27 40	28 42	29 44	0♓46	MC
	19♊20	20 19	21 18	22 17	23 14	24 12	25 08	26 05	ASC
6 PM	9♓23	10 26	11 30	12 33	13 37	14 40	15 44	16 48	MC
	3♋34	4 26	5 19	6 11	7 02	7 54	8 45	9 35	ASC
7 PM	25♓38	26 43	27 47	28 52	29 56	1♈01	2 05	3 10	MC
	16♋26	17 14	18 03	18 51	19 39	20 28	21 15	22 03	ASC
8 PM	12♈00	13 04	14 08	15 12	16 16	17 19	18 23	19 26	MC
	28♋33	29 19	0♌06	0 52	1 39	2 25	3 11	3 58	ASC
9 PM	28♈05	29 07	0♉09	1 11	2 12	3 14	4 15	5 16	MC
	10♌18	11 04	11 49	12 35	13 21	14 07	14 52	15 38	ASC
10 PM	13♉35	14 34	15 34	16 33	17 32	18 31	19 29	20 28	MC
	21♌56	22 41	23 27	24 13	24 59	25 44	26 30	27 16	ASC
11 PM	28♉24	29 21	0♊18	1 15	2 11	3 08	4 04	5 00	MC
	3♍35	4 21	5 07	5 52	6 38	7 24	8 10	8 56	ASC

CALENDAR DATE DECEMBER of any year CALENDAR DATE

HOUR OF BIRTH	9	10	11	12	13	14	15	16	
12 MID	19♊04	19 58	20 53	21 47	22 42	23 36	24 30	25 25	MC
	20♍41	21 27	22 14	23 00	23 46	24 32	25 19	26 05	ASC
1 AM	2♋53	3 47	4 42	5 36	6 30	7 25	8 19	9 14	MC
	2♎28	3 14	4 00	4 47	5 33	6 19	7 06	7 52	ASC
2 AM	16♋46	17 42	18 37	19 32	20 28	21 23	22 19	23 15	MC
	14♎14	15 00	15 46	16 32	17 19	18 05	18 51	19 37	ASC
3 AM	1♌00	1 57	2 55	3 52	4 49	5 47	6 45	7 43	MC
	25♎57	26 43	27 29	28 15	29 00	29 46	0♏32	1 18	ASC
4 AM	15♌48	16 48	17 48	18 48	19 48	20 48	21 49	22 49	MC
	7♏36	8 22	9 07	9 53	10 39	11 25	12 10	12 56	ASC
5 AM	1♍17	2 19	3 21	4 24	5 26	6 29	7 32	8 35	MC
	19♏14	20 00	20 46	21 32	22 17	23 03	23 50	24 36	ASC
6 AM	17♍20	18 24	19 28	20 32	21 37	22 41	23 45	24 49	MC
	0♐59	1 45	2 32	3 19	4 06	4 53	5 40	6 28	ASC
7 AM	3♎42	4 46	5 50	6 55	7 59	9 03	10 08	11 12	MC
	13♐04	13 53	14 42	15 31	16 20	17 10	18 00	18 50	ASC
8 AM	19♎58	21 01	22 04	23 07	24 10	25 13	26 15	27 17	MC
	25♐54	26 46	27 40	28 33	29 27	0♑21	1 16	2 11	ASC
9 AM	5♏47	6 48	7 48	8 49	9 49	10 49	11 49	12 49	MC
	10♑03	11 03	12 03	13 04	14 05	15 07	16 10	17 13	ASC
10 AM	20♏57	21 55	22 53	23 51	24 49	25 46	26 44	27 41	MC
	26♑25	27 36	28 47	0♒00	1 13	2 27	3 43	4 59	ASC
11 AM	5♐28	6 24	7 20	8 16	9 11	10 07	11 02	11 58	MC
	16♒08	17 34	19 01	20 30	21 59	23 29	25 01	26 34	ASC
12 NOON	19♐31	20 26	21 20	22 14	23 09	24 03	24 58	25 52	MC
	9♓56	11 38	13 20	15 02	16 45	18 29	20 14	21 58	ASC
1 PM	3♑20	4 15	5 09	6 03	6 58	7 52	8 47	9 41	MC
	6♈29	8 14	9 59	11 43	13 27	15 10	16 53	18 35	ASC
2 PM	17♑14	18 09	19 04	20 00	20 55	21 51	22 47	23 43	MC
	2♉04	3 38	5 10	6 42	8 12	9 41	11 09	12 36	ASC
3 PM	1♒29	2 26	3 23	4 21	5 18	6 16	7 14	8 12	MC
	23♉53	25 10	26 27	27 42	28 56	0♊09	1 21	2 33	ASC
4 PM	16♒18	17 18	18 18	19 18	20 18	21 18	22 19	23 20	MC
	11♊50	12 54	13 58	15 00	16 02	17 04	18 04	19 04	ASC
5 PM	1♓48	2 50	3 52	4 55	5 58	7 01	8 03	9 07	MC
	27♊01	27 56	28 51	29 46	0♋40	1 33	2 27	3 20	ASC
6 PM	17♓52	18 56	20 00	21 04	22 09	23 13	24 17	25 22	MC
	10♋26	11 16	12 06	12 56	13 46	14 35	15 24	16 13	ASC
7 PM	4♈14	5 18	6 23	7 27	8 31	9 35	10 40	11 44	MC
	22♋51	23 38	24 25	25 13	26 00	26 47	27 34	28 20	ASC
8 PM	20♈29	21 33	22 36	23 38	24 41	25 44	26 46	27 49	MC
	4♌44	5 30	6 16	7 02	7 48	8 34	9 20	10 06	ASC
9 PM	6♉17	7 18	8 19	9 19	10 19	11 19	12 19	13 19	MC
	16♌24	17 10	17 55	18 41	19 27	20 12	20 58	21 44	ASC
10 PM	21♉26	22 24	23 22	24 20	25 18	26 15	27 12	28 10	MC
	28♌02	28 48	29 33	0♍19	1 05	1 51	2 37	3 23	ASC
11 PM	5♊56	6 52	7 48	8 44	9 39	10 35	11 30	12 25	MC
	9♍43	10 29	11 15	12 01	12 47	13 33	14 19	15 05	ASC

CALENDAR DATE DECEMBER of any year CALENDAR DATE

HOUR OF BIRTH	17	18	19	20	21	22	23	24	
12 MID	26♊19	27 13	28 08	29 02	29 56	0♋51	1 45	2 39	MC
	26♍51	27 38	28 24	29 10	29 57	0♎43	1 29	2 16	ASC
1 AM	10♋08	11 03	11 58	12 52	13 47	14 42	15 37	16 32	MC
	8♎38	9 25	10 11	10 57	11 43	12 30	13 16	14 02	ASC
2 AM	24♋10	25 07	26 03	26 59	27 55	28 52	29 49	0♌46	MC
	20♎23	21 09	21 55	22 41	23 27	24 13	24 59	25 45	ASC
3 AM	8♌41	9 39	10 38	11 37	12 35	13 34	14 34	15 33	MC
	2♏04	2 50	3 35	4 21	5 07	5 53	6 38	7 24	ASC
4 AM	23♌50	24 51	25 52	26 54	27 55	28 57	29 59	1♍01	MC
	13♏42	14 27	15 13	15 59	16 45	17 30	18 16	19 02	ASC
5 AM	9♍38	10 42	11 45	12 48	13 52	14 56	16 00	17 03	MC
	25♏22	26 08	26 54	27 40	28 27	29 13	0♐00	0 46	ASC
6 AM	25♍54	26 58	28 03	29 07	0♎12	1 16	2 21	3 25	MC
	7♐15	8 03	8 50	9 38	10 26	11 15	12 03	12 51	ASC
7 AM	12♎16	13 20	14 24	15 27	16 31	17 35	18 38	19 41	MC
	19♐40	20 31	21 22	22 13	23 04	23 56	24 48	25 40	ASC
8 AM	28♎20	29 22	0♏24	1 26	2 27	3 29	4 30	5 31	MC
	3♑06	4 02	4 58	5 55	6 53	7 50	8 49	9 48	ASC
9 AM	13♏49	14 48	15 48	16 47	17 46	18 45	19 43	20 42	MC
	18♑17	19 22	20 28	21 34	22 41	23 49	24 58	26 07	ASC
10 AM	28♏38	29 35	0♐32	1 28	2 25	3 21	4 18	5 14	MC
	6♒16	7 34	8 54	10 14	11 35	12 58	14 21	15 46	ASC
11 AM	12♐53	13 48	14 43	15 38	16 33	17 27	18 22	19 17	MC
	28♒07	29 42	1♓18	2 54	4 32	6 10	7 50	9 30	ASC
12 NOON	26♐46	27 41	28 35	29 29	0♑23	1 18	2 12	3 06	MC
	23♓43	25 29	27 14	29 00	0♈46	2 31	4 17	6 02	ASC
1 PM	10♑36	11 30	12 25	13 20	14 15	15 10	16 05	17 00	MC
	20♈16	21 56	23 36	25 15	26 52	28 29	0♉05	1 40	ASC
2 PM	24♑38	25 35	26 31	27 27	28 24	29 20	0♒17	1 14	MC
	14♉02	15 27	16 51	18 13	19 35	20 55	22 15	23 33	ASC
3 PM	9♒10	10 09	11 07	12 06	13 05	14 04	15 03	16 03	MC
	3♊43	4 53	6 02	7 10	8 17	9 23	10 29	11 34	ASC
4 PM	24♒21	25 22	26 23	27 24	28 26	29 28	0♓30	1 32	MC
	20♊04	21 03	22 01	22 59	23 57	24 54	25 50	26 46	ASC
5 PM	10♓10	11 13	12 17	13 20	14 24	15 28	16 32	17 35	MC
	4♋13	5 05	5 57	6 49	7 40	8 31	9 22	10 13	ASC
6 PM	26♓26	27 31	28 35	29 39	0♈44	1 48	2 53	3 57	MC
	17♋02	17 50	18 39	19 27	20 15	21 03	21 51	22 38	ASC
7 PM	12♈48	13 52	14 55	15 59	17 03	18 06	19 10	20 13	MC
	29♋07	29 54	0♌40	1 27	2 13	2 59	3 46	4 32	ASC
8 PM	28♈51	29 53	0♉55	1 56	2 58	3 59	5 00	6 01	MC
	10♌52	11 37	12 23	13 09	13 55	14 41	15 26	16 12	ASC
9 PM	14♉19	15 18	16 17	17 16	18 15	19 14	20 12	21 11	MC
	22♌30	23 15	24 01	24 47	25 33	26 18	27 04	27 50	ASC
10 PM	29♉07	0♊03	1 00	1 57	2 53	3 50	4 46	5 42	MC
	4♍09	4 55	5 41	6 27	7 13	7 59	8 45	9 31	ASC
11 PM	13♊20	14 15	15 10	16 05	17 00	17 55	18 49	19 44	MC
	15♍52	16 38	17 24	18 10	18 56	19 43	20 29	21 15	ASC

CALENDAR DATE DECEMBER of any year CALENDAR DATE

HOUR OF BIRTH	25	26	27	28	29	30	31	
12 MID	3♋33	4 28	5 22	6 16	7 11	8 05	9 00	MC
	3♎02	3 48	4 35	5 21	6 07	6 54	7 40	ASC
1 AM	17♋27	18 22	19 18	20 13	21 09	22 04	23 00	MC
	14♎48	15 34	16 21	17 07	17 53	18 39	19 25	ASC
2 AM	1♌43	2 40	3 37	4 34	5 32	6 30	7 28	MC
	26♎31	27 17	28 03	28 49	29 34	0♏20	1 06	ASC
3 AM	16♌33	17 32	18 32	19 32	20 32	21 33	22 34	MC
	8♏10	8 56	9 41	10 27	11 13	11 58	12 44	ASC
4 AM	2♍03	3 05	4 07	5 10	6 13	7 16	8 19	MC
	19♏48	20 34	21 20	22 06	22 52	23 38	24 24	ASC
5 AM	18♍07	19 12	20 16	21 20	22 24	23 28	24 33	MC
	1♐33	2 20	3 07	3 54	4 41	5 28	6 15	ASC
6 AM	4♎29	5 34	6 38	7 42	8 47	9 51	10 55	MC
	13♐40	14 29	15 18	16 08	16 57	17 47	18 37	ASC
7 AM	20♎45	21 48	22 51	23 54	24 56	25 59	27 01	MC
	26♐33	27 26	28 19	29 13	0♑07	1 01	1 56	ASC
8 AM	6♏32	7 33	8 33	9 34	10 34	11 34	12 34	MC
	10♑47	11 47	12 48	13 49	14 51	15 54	16 57	ASC
9 AM	21♏40	22 38	23 36	24 34	25 31	26 29	27 26	MC
	27♑17	28 29	29 41	0♒54	2 08	3 23	4 39	ASC
10 AM	6♐10	7 06	8 01	8 57	9 52	10 48	11 43	MC
	17♒12	18 39	20 07	21 36	23 06	24 37	26 09	ASC
11 AM	20♐11	21 06	22 00	22 55	23 49	24 44	25 38	MC
	11♓11	12 53	14 36	16 19	18 02	19 46	21 31	ASC
12 NOON	4♑00	4 55	5 49	6 44	7 38	8 32	9 27	MC
	7♈47	9 32	11 16	13 00	14 43	16 26	18 08	ASC
1 PM	17♑55	18 50	19 45	20 41	21 36	22 32	23 28	MC
	3♉14	4 46	6 18	7 49	9 18	10 46	12 14	ASC
2 PM	2♒11	3 08	4 06	5 03	6 01	6 59	7 57	MC
	24♉50	26 07	27 22	28 37	29 50	1♊03	2 14	ASC
3 PM	17♒02	18 02	19 02	20 02	21 03	22 03	23 04	MC
	12♊38	13 41	14 44	15 46	16 48	17 49	18 49	ASC
4 PM	2♓34	3 36	4 39	5 41	6 44	7 47	8 50	MC
	27♊42	28 37	29 31	0♋26	1 20	2 13	3 06	ASC
5 PM	18♓39	19 44	20 48	21 52	22 56	24 01	25 05	MC
	11♋03	11 53	12 43	13 33	14 22	15 11	16 00	ASC
6 PM	5♈02	6 06	7 10	8 15	9 19	10 23	11 27	MC
	23♋26	24 13	25 00	25 48	26 35	27 21	28 08	ASC
7 PM	21♈16	22 19	23 22	24 25	25 28	26 30	27 32	MC
	5♌18	6 04	6 50	7 36	8 22	9 08	9 54	ASC
8 PM	7♉02	8 03	9 03	10 04	11 04	12 04	13 04	MC
	16♌58	17 43	18 29	19 15	20 01	20 46	21 32	ASC
9 PM	22♉09	23 07	24 05	25 03	26 00	26 57	27 55	MC
	28♌36	29 21	0♍07	0 53	1 39	2 25	3 11	ASC
10 PM	6♊38	7 33	8 29	9 25	10 20	11 16	12 11	MC
	10♍17	11 03	11 49	12 35	13 21	14 07	14 53	ASC
11 PM	20♊39	21 33	22 28	23 22	24 16	25 11	26 05	MC
	22♍02	22 48	23 34	24 20	25 07	25 53	26 39	ASC

5

Introduction to the Signs of the Zodiac

The sign that the Sun is *in* on the date of birth is called the Sun sign. The Sun determines the expression of the will and indicates the way an individual expresses basic energy potential and creative drive to grow and develop as an individual.

The will represented by the Sun is modified by the sign that the Sun is in, and represents the fundamental component of consciousness that colors all other activity.

The Sun has its own dynamic expression which is unfolded in the process of living, regardless of any kind of conditioning. In general, the Sun sign represents the individual's identity in the astrological classification of the twelve types of humanity. Every sign of the Zodiac is included in every individual's horoscope and will be located in some department of the life. The sign found in any house colors the activities of that house. For example, if Aries is found on the sixth house, the affairs of that house will be conducted with Aries energy.

This same principle applies to all twelve signs in the horoscope. Each sign of the Zodiac represents a life lesson that must be mastered and an energy that must be utilized in a harmonious manner. Each sign also has its pitfalls which the individual must learn to deal with if expression of that sign is to be used in a constructive way in the process of unfolding.

Aries: March 21 to April 19

Wherever Aries is found in a person's horoscope—whether it is the Sun sign, the Ascendant, on a house cusp, or intercepted in a house—the characteristics of the sign Aries will be manifested. Every sign of the Zodiac represents an output of power. Aries is the sign in which the Sun is exalted. This indicates that the Sun gets its power from the principle represented by Aries, which is new beginnings. The Sun, the giver of life, is exalted in this spring sign. This indicates that wherever Aries is found there will be a new cycle of evolutionary unfoldment.

The Sun is in the sign of Aries between March 21 and April 19. These are approximate dates. Aries is a Fire, Cardinal, and masculine sign. Its ruler is Mars and its co-ruler is Pluto. Aries is full of creative energy and enthusiasm. Within this sign there is a tremendous psychological drive to prove oneself through action. Because Aries is a Fire sign, the enthusiasm of this sign manifests itself by a desire to rush headlong into physical, mental, and emotional expression. Aries as the first of the Fire signs is enthusiastic, energetic, impulsive, militant, and either rash or courageous. Thus it is evident that this fiery force must be harnessed. There is a desire for authority and superiority, and because of this characteristic Aries individuals may try to use force rather than reason and diplomacy in dealing with others. If they do not possess the necessary wisdom to balance this craving for leadership, they can appear foolish to others.

Much of the Aries strength arises out of the refusal to admit defeat. Aries individuals are never daunted by failure; if they fail, they put that adventure behind them and immediately seek new avenues of expression. Because they are competitive, they must be first and best in everything they choose to do.

The Cardinal quality of Aries is demonstrated by the need for changing action. This can be either a handicap or an asset, depending on how this energy is used. When thought and action are ordered, there can be new use and direction of this fiery element. If this force is uncontrolled, the ideals represented by the Fire signs remain only ideals, and they are not brought into a living reality which is creative and operative with true power. When this exuberant force is managed and directed, it becomes a valuable asset in any pioneering adventure.

Impulsiveness is the worst enemy of Aries; only by reflection on the overall consequences of the actions taken can the lesson of love be learned. There is an impulsiveness and an inability to listen to and consider the advice of others. This headstrong attitude tends to involve Aries individuals in difficulties, as they grow restless under restraint.

Because the Aries nature is to lead and not to follow, Arians must not put an overemphasis on the idea that might makes right. When this happens, the result is chaos and disorder. They must learn to marshal their ideas and find their balance through second thoughts that are applied wisely. Thought and action wisely directed, true knowledge, and right attitude are requisites if the fiery element of this sign is to be understood and used properly.

Because the Sun is exalted in Aries the day will come when people will cease to be motivated by emotional desires. In that day we will not be compelled through aggressive Mars action; instead, spiritual inspiration will motivate us toward our goals.

Many hard lessons come to Arians through relationships, especially the marriage relationship, because the polar opposite sign is Libra, the sign of partnerships. There is a need to learn this lesson of love so that they can reach out to others with consideration. Aries, the warrior, especially needs to do battle with the enemy of selfish desire and thoughtlessness. There are few who understand the magic power of love, which can vanquish the most formidable enemy.

Aries, as a Cardinal sign, gives the ability to act directly and decisively upon present circumstances. Here one feels the need for action; here is where the individual will be opportunistic; here is where one initiates and organizes new projects. The department of life that carries Aries demands initiative without waiting for outside stimuli to motivate them to action. In this department there is the ability to be a self-starter and to have a realistic grasp of the immediate situation and its potential for action.

Because Aries is a positive masculine sign, the department that carries Aries is one in which the individual will be aggressive in action, initiating change; but care should be taken that all the activity and change bring progress and that old projects have been completed before embarking upon new enterprises.

The active, fiery, creative force that is inherent in the Aries nature gives Aries individuals the courage and enthusiasm to put the ideas and schemes that flood through their brains into action. Aries is the sign of the new cycle and of the pioneer who is resourceful in taking a failing enterprise, giving it a new twist, making it successful, and giving it a new beginning. This is partially due to Pluto being the co-ruler of Aries.

Refinements are necessary in all fields of science. The broad characteristics that are given to each sign do not apply entirely to all individuals. There is a pattern called *Decanates* in which each sign of thirty degrees is subdivided into three segments of ten degrees each. Each decanate has its sub-ruler influence that is determined by the triplicity or element to which the sign belongs.

The first decanate of Aries consists of 0 degrees of Aries to 10 degrees of Aries. This decanate applies to those born between March 21 and March 30. These are approximate dates. This decanate is known as the Aries-Aries or Mars-Mars-Pluto decanate. The drive of this decanate of Aries is based on a need to build up self-esteem by receiving recognition and admiration from others. If these individuals are praised, they will try to justify this praise by some commendable action. Self-respect and self-reliance are essential to the psychological well-being of the individuals born in this decanate of Aries. There is a need for social approval, and efforts are directed toward winning the acceptance of others, since that will justify self-esteem. This can be a strength or weakness, as the need for recognition can inspire them to worthwhile deeds or can goad them into reckless or foolish action. These individuals need to remember that discretion is the better part of valor. The flexing of their physical, mental, and emotional muscles can result in undesired ends. Their impulsiveness, impatience, and quick temper can be a detriment; however, this same energy gives them the ability to make new starts whenever necessary and the ability to initiate projects that others only dream about. Pluto, one of the rulers of this decanate, provides the resourcefulness, the desire, and the ability to upgrade their lives of action.

The second decanate of Aries consists of 10 degrees of Aries to 20 degrees of Aries. This decanate applies to those born approximately between March 31 and April 9. This decanate is known as the Aries-Leo or Mars-Pluto-Sun decanate. This decanate gives abundant energy, courage, and self-confidence, often with a self-centered, authoritative attitude. The individuals born under this decanate have more staying power than other Aries people because of the subinfluence of the Sun and Leo, which is a Fixed sign. Because of this Fixed-sign influence, they are more likely than the Aries type normally is to complete that which they start. They have a special type of leadership which enables them to hold the center of attention. They seek excitement and adventure through competitive sports, the performing arts, and romantic episodes. They are magnanimous and do things in a big way. Their motives are often colored with egotism and desire for greater personal prestige.

The third decanate of Aries consists of 20 degrees of Aries to 30 degrees of Aries. This decanate applies to those born between April 10 and

April 19. This decanate is known as the Aries-Sagittarius or Mars-Pluto-Jupiter-Neptune decanate.

In this decanate the Aries nature is tempered with cultural, educational, philosophical, and religious insight. These individuals are less self-centered than those in the other decanates. This is because they are genuinely concerned about the social order in their personal sphere of activity. They like to feel that they are authorities in some educational, religious, or social field of activity, and that they are originators of new concepts in these fields. Because of the Mutable quality of Sagittarius and the Cardinality of Aries, they can take effective action in a variety of circumstances. They have a great deal of enthusiasm for the beliefs and causes they espouse and an ability to initiate new educational, religious, and cultural projects. Their expansive activities are often motivated by a desire for greater personal prestige. They must guard against the possibility of narrow-minded, self-righteous, fanatical zeal on behalf of their cultural and educational values and religious beliefs.

Taurus: April 20 to May 20

Wherever Taurus is found in a person's horoscope—whether it is the Sun sign, the Ascendant, on a house cusp, or intercepted in a house—the characteristics of the sign Taurus will be manifested. Taurus is the sign in which the Moon is exalted, and this confers the ability to steady the feelings and to generate the vital energy needed to give ideas physical manifestation. The Moon is responsible for conveying form and physical manifestation to all living organisms on Earth, and it must have physical substance to work with to fulfill its function. Taurus, as the first of the Earth signs, provides the substance for lunar forces to work in.* Wherever Taurus is found in the horoscope is where the individual can obtain practical results in the projects undertaken; therefore, the Moon gains its power from and is exalted in the sign of Taurus.

The Sun is in the sign Taurus between April 20 and May 20. These are approximate dates. Taurus is an Earth, Fixed, and receptive, feminine sign. Its ruler is Venus. All Earth signs are concerned with matter through which the spirit must learn to function. Taurus is the most stable and practical sign in the Zodiac. Therefore Taurus is concerned with money and possessions, two factors that hold the individual firmly down to Earth. Because of physical necessities—the so-called practical aspects

* See the chapter on the exaltations of the planets in *The Astrologer's Handbook*, Francis Sakoian and L. Acker, New York: Harper & Row, 1973.

of life—Taurus individuals are forced to remember that they are of the Earth and that they need and must have material sustenance. Thus the individual's strong need for food, home, clothing, and possessions indicates that the individual must earn them through effort in some form or another, either through Mother Earth or service to other people. This is because Venus rules not only Taurus but also Libra, which rules others.

Unless the Taurus individuals have had spiritual discipline or been taught sound values during childhood conditioning, they will not aspire to spiritual heights but are concerned only with increasing and holding onto their money and possessions. They are not selfish in the ordinary material sense, yet they see to it that nothing interferes with their self-preservation. The instinct of Taureans is to hold themselves to what they feel they need and want, and no force in the world can budge them in any other direction.

Taurus is of the Earth element; therefore, Taureans are fond of the good things in life, and pleasure, satisfaction, and comfort are important to them. They are thrifty, mainly because of their love of possessions. They are fond of quality clothing and can be deeply impressed by the appearance of others. Being of the Earth element and ruled by Venus, they also admire the material progress of others.

Each sign has a different life lesson. The sign Taurus shows what material the individual is to control and dominate. In Taurus the individual plays the role of the builder, the administrator and preserver of the Earth's resources, and Taurus especially deals with the managing of material and financial resources that are necessary to make other functions of life possible. Because it is a receptive, feminine sign, talents connected with this expression are to be built in by working with things as they are and by working with the principle of attraction.

Taurus is not given to self-analysis, and Taureans seem to be unaware of their own inner motives. They feel that what they do is natural to them. Once something satisfies their deepest needs they hold onto it forever. Perhaps the most outstanding characteristic of Taureans is their singleness of purpose, their ability to persevere, and their loyalty which springs from one source, their need for security.

Taureans are very strong-willed; they can be persuaded but not driven. They do not interfere with others and are easy to live with providing one does not try to change them or make them over. Status, titles, and social standing are important to Taurean individuals. They are guided by outward show, tend to be a little pompous, and respond to flattery concerning their appearance. Taureans can be miserable if they marry someone beneath their station in life. Although Taurus is a feminine, receptive sign and inclined to be timid, Taureans are ruled by Venus and therefore do not hesitate to get involved in romantic situations. Once involved they can be very possessive and extremely jealous.

Because Venus rules Taurus, which rules all the beautiful and good things of life, there can be overindulgence. If this happens, the life lesson of Taurus is liable to be thwarted because the Earth signs must learn to serve, and if the body is clogged and diseased through luxury and overabundance, the lessons can not be accomplished. Every individual must work to gain control over the physical and lower self. The body is the most valuable possession, and Taurus as the builder must learn to build and perfect the temple of his or her own being, so that the physical body can serve and glorify the spirit that it houses.

The element of Earth teaches us to have mastery over physical matter. The house cusp that carries Taurus indicates the area in which this building must take place. This is the house that has untapped resources where one can build and accumulate and where one is permitted to become absorbed in the material life. However, the individual is not allowed to become possessed by these things. Success comes in this area of life through tapping the resources of the house carrying the sign of Taurus.

Because Taurus is a Fixed, goal-oriented sign, this success will come through unwavering perseverance over a long period of time. In this department of life the individual will be scientifically and commercially inclined and take a very solid, concrete view of life.

If the individuals' horoscopes do not show any modifying flexibility, they can be dogmatic, rigid, and unyielding. If they are not appreciated they can use passive resistance as a weapon and retreat into silence. The Fixed temperament of Taurus has a love of power that is apart from ambition. Taureans are slow to move, but under sufficient stimuli they may act with suddenness and rush into action in order to obtain some desired object.

The tendency of Taurus is to accumulate, make steady, and persevere rather than scatter and disrupt.

As in all the signs there is a pattern that divides the signs into three main groups called decanates.

The first decanate of Taurus consists of 0 degrees of Taurus to 10 degrees of Taurus. This decanate applies to those Taureans born between April 20 and April 30. These are approximate dates because of the uneven calendar. This decanate is known as the Taurus-Taurus or Venus-Venus decanate. There is a relentless determination to satisfy the desire for security, wealth, and status, which is the result of the double Fixed-Earth influence. Individuals born within this decanate are oriented toward achieving lasting results. There is a fondness for luxury and all material comforts. Artistic and musical talents are accentuated because of the strong Venus nature. There can also be problems in romantic and marriage relationships because of possessiveness and jealousy. In general the individuals born in this decanate are practical, down to earth, and adverse to wasted efforts or nonproductive enterprises. They are skillful in money management and make excellent bankers and financiers. They do not gamble or take foolish risks and are willing to work slowly and steadily to accomplish their goals.

The second decanate of Taurus is 10 degrees of Taurus to 20 degrees of Taurus. This decanate applies to those born from May 1 to May 10. This is the Taurus-Virgo or Venus-Mercury decanate. These individuals are also concerned with money and values as all Taureans are; however, they have a detailed analytical approach toward the realization of their goals of financial and emotional security.

The third decanate of Taurus is 20 degrees of Taurus to 30 degrees of Taurus. This decanate applies to those born between May 11 and May 20. This is the Taurus-Capricorn or Venus-Saturn-Uranus decanate. Because Mars is exalted in Capricorn, these individuals are ambitious, organized, and cautiously aggressive in their efforts to achieve financial and emotional security. They are good executives and business managers. They seek material security through dynamic action because of the Cardinality of Capricorn and the energy of Mars.

Gemini: May 21 to June 21

Wherever Gemini is found in a person's horoscope—whether it is the Sun sign, the Ascendant, on a house cusp, or intercepted in a house—the characteristics of the sign Gemini will be manifested. Gemini is the first of the intellectual Air signs; it is the sign of the conscious reasoning mind. The Sun is in the sign of Gemini between May 21 and June 21. These are approximate dates.

The house that carries Gemini is the department of life in which individuals become aware of their environment and where they reason and communicate about their interaction with others and the situations within their environments. Gemini as an Air sign is the first sign of relationships where one interacts with brothers, sisters, blood relatives, neighbors, and those in the immediate environment. The life lessons learned, or not learned, under Gemini affect the next intellectual Air sign Libra, the sign of partnerships, close personal relationships, and others in general. It can even extend to the next intellectual Air sign Aquarius, which deals with friends and group associates and affects the goals and objectives of the individual. Often problems arise with partners, friends, and close relationships because the early lessons of Gemini have not been learned.

The department of life that carries Gemini is very responsive to mental impressions. Gemini, being a Mutable sign, stores up experience that colors the response and course of action.

Gemini is ruled by the planet Mercury. It is a Mutable, intellectual Air, and positive, masculine sign. This sign of the mind gives individuals the power to reason and experiment so they can discover the most harmonious way of life. This is done through the development of the mind and a conscious cooperation with others.

The universal law that governs the sign Gemini teaches us that all knowledge is already in the universe. We are not the creators of ideas or thoughts; all ideas exist in the universal mind. We are producers; we cannot create even one blade of grass; however, we can produce a blade of grass as we tune in with the use of our minds to this particular type of creation. Everything originates in thought. One cannot even lift a finger without first the thought.

Because Gemini is a Mutable sign and deals with the past and the utilization of past experience, if the memories of the past have been unpleasant, it is difficult to choose the kind of thoughts that we allow to pass through the discriminating bar of the mind. Astrology teaches that what we have been in the past is what we will be in the future, until we direct our conscious thinking. Under the sign Gemini the admonition "watch and pray unceasingly" applies because the kind of thoughts we entertain affect our health, work, and relationships. This is because Mercury also rules the sign Virgo, which rules the house of health and work.

Wherever Gemini is found is where we must make a willing conscious effort toward thoughts and actions which are harmonious, kind, and loving when dealing with our reactions to others. In the realm of the mind the individual is called upon to destroy the mental bookkeeper of past evil and wipe out the robbers that steal the peace and joy that rightfully belongs to all. When thoughts are controlled, we will become masters of our destiny and rulers of our stellar forces. Until the mind is cleansed of all thieves and money changers, the consciousness that we call our own will receive all its ideas, thoughts, and impressions wholly independent of the individual's will and desire; it will influence the feeling and action, and we will have little or no power to prevent it.

Gemini, being a Mutable sign, is adaptable and can work around obstacles rather than confronting them directly. When Gemini expresses itself negatively, it expresses itself as worry, nervousness, and an inability to live in the present. Gemini individuals will communicate about their actions, thoughts, and relationships in an intellectual way, and there is an attitude of impersonal detachment and dispassion about these communications. When Gemini individuals master negative tendencies, they have the potential of reaching high social standing, especially if they acquire good training.

Because Mercury, the ruler of Gemini, is exalted in Aquarius and gets its power from Aquarius, the sign Gemini can indicate the nonconformist of the Zodiac. Whatever the Gemini is or is not, he or she will be different from anyone else around, because of the influence of Uranus ruled by Aquarius, the sign of Mercury's exaltation.

Air is the most subtle of all the elements, and individuals who have it prominent in their charts live in the world of mind, are governed by reason, and are seldom moved by ill-considered action; however, they must cultivate brotherhood, recognize weaknesses and strengths, and remain unmoved by petty slights, hurts, and jealousies if they are to learn the lesson of dispassion.

The desire for new experiences is grist for Geminis' mill. They want to make many connections, expand their circle, and be abreast of everything. They have a passion for locomotion and would like to be in two places at one time. They are always seeking knowledge and information with curiosity and a good memory.

The vice of Geminis is diffusion; they want to study, they want to play, they want to be in love, and yet want to be indifferent to it. At one moment they are charming and childlike and the next moment they are cynical and pessimistic. Because of their love of knowledge and their curiosity, self-education continues throughout life. The positive, masculine character of Gemini gives the ability to initiate intellectual activity. They will take the initiative in communications and in literary and scientific work. They do this in an intelligent and articulate manner. Without mental stimulation and change, they tend to be restless and nonconforming.

The first decanate of Gemini consists of 0 degrees of Gemini to 10 degrees of Gemini. This decanate applies to those born between May 21 and May 31. This decanate is known as the Gemini-Gemini or Mercury-Mercury decanate. This decanate gives unusual intellectual ability. These individuals have a nature which is adaptable, impressionable, intelligent, comprehensive, and comprehending. They possess a quick perception and a curious inquiring intellect that tends to be influenced by whatever impinges on their consciousness. Thus they can vacillate and be indecisive and scattered, with a nervousness of mind and body. These individuals tend to talk a lot and come and go a great deal. They have a talent for writing, secretarial work, reporting, advertising, and manual work that requires dexterity and skill, especially in the use of the hands.

The second decanate, consisting of 10 degrees of Gemini to 20 degrees of Gemini, is the Gemini-Libra or Mercury-Venus decanate. This decanate applies to those born between June 1 and June 10. In this decanate of Gemini, there is the grace of Venus combined with the intelligence of Mercury, giving these Geminis much charm and the ability to win others over to their point of view. They have a strong need for intellectual companionship and are curious about the thoughts and ideas of others. Their weakness lies in their tendency to be swayed or influenced by whomever they are with at the moment; thus they can acquire a reputation for being inconsistent. There is curiosity about romantic relationships and what they can offer, which adds to this kind of reputation. These Geminis have unusual talents in public relations, diplomacy, psychology, art, and literature.

The third decanate of Gemini consists of 20 degrees of Gemini to 30 degrees of Gemini. This decanate applies to those born between June 11 and June 21, and is the Gemini-Aquarius or Mercury-Uranus-Saturn decanate. These Geminis are open and impartial in the examination of ideas. Their mental outlook is universal and humanitarian. They have an organized intelligence with startling original, intuitive insights. This can manifest as a scientific ability, or an understanding of scientific and metaphysical laws. This gives them intuitive and surprising solutions to problems.

These Geminis can be eccentric and unpredictable at times, with little tolerance for those who interfere with their intellectual freedom. They demand for themselves the same freedom of inquiry and self-expression that they allow others. Because of Saturn's co-rulership of Aquarius, these individuals can be reserved and serious. They are less likely to engage in verbal frivolities than other Geminis because they reserve their speech until they have something important to say, and they do not like to engage in small talk.

Because of the Uranus influence, friends and group associates are important, and these Geminis often take an important part in organizational affairs. They tend to set intellectual goals for themselves that will achieve some worthwhile scientific, literary, or humanitarian objective.

Cancer: June 22 to July 22

Wherever Cancer is found in a person's horoscope—whether it is the Sun sign, the Ascendant, on a house cusp, or intercepted in a house—the characteristics of the sign Cancer will be manifested.

The Sun is in the sign of Cancer between June 22 and July 22. These are approximate dates. Cancer is a Water, Cardinal, and feminine, receptive sign. Its ruler is the Moon.

Cancer is the first of the Water signs and deals with feeling and intuitive awareness. The department of the life that carries Cancer is where the individual will have strong feelings about home and family. Cancer is a Cardinal, receptive, feminine sign, and although the Cardinal signs are signs of action and decision, Cancer takes action when motivated to do so by outside stimuli. Cancers attract the things they need rather than actively seeking them. They wait until they are confronted with circumstances before they act, or until they have an opportunity to change conditions. In other words, wherever the sign Cancer is found in the horoscope, the individuals will attract the people and circumstances necessary to further their desired ends. After they attract these people and circumstances, action takes place.

Cancer is sensitive and emotional; just like a crab which is all soft meat inside but surrounded by a protective hard shell. Cancers also present a hard exterior to the world, which hides the fact that they are tenderhearted and that the world might take advantage of them.

The absorbent quality of this Water sign reveals itself as an inherent collector storing up against future needs. In the average Cancer individual this manifests as caution, prudence, and careful husbanding of resources, and he or she can be quite active in this phase of life. Cancer can be as active as the squirrel preparing for the winter.

At times Cancer can be shrewd and grasping; however, if Cancer individuals are touched emotionally by friends or associates in need, there is nothing they won't do for them. They will shelter, house, and give of their possessions.

The consciousness of Cancer is fed by feelings and emotions, and there is a quality of attachment that retains and holds things long after others would release and let go, much like the crab who holds onto an object even though it loses a claw in the process.

The life lesson of Cancer and Water signs is the lesson of peace. Because Water absorbs every color and movement in the world around it, the harshness of the world is felt, and Cancers adopt some method of protection. In Cancer there is a special need for security, protection and a harmonious environment. Learning this lesson of peace does not mean a static or sluggish condition; it means the development of an inward relaxation and recuperative and energizing dynamic power. This can only be learned after the individual has touched the heights and depths of emotional experience. Until the secret to this inner security and peace is discovered, various methods of self-protection are employed. When the secret is finally discovered, no darkness or disturbing influence is allowed to enter the sanctuary that the Cancer has built. Once this sanctuary has been erected, there arises a strong maternal instinct which protects, shields, and nurtures anything or anyone that is loved and in need. All born under this sign have a need for a sanctuary. On the outer plane the home supplies this need, and this is why the home should be sacred and beautiful and a place of power which will re-create and nourish all who live in it.

Many born under the sign Cancer are denied a home that provides this kind of protection, sustenance, and refuge. These individuals have yet to learn to control their thoughts and emotions. When this is done, it will enable them to build secure, psychological walls in their life or home. This can only be done by obeying the spiritual laws that govern the home that we carry within us and that emanates from us no matter where the individual may be at any time.

Neptune and Jupiter are exalted in the sign Cancer. Neptune deals with the imagination, the picture-making apparatus of the mind. If the peace that is promised by the sign Cancer is to be attained and the expansion of Jupiter is to be realized, the negative conditioning from the home and past must be released and the contents of the unconscious mind, represented by Neptune and the Moon, must be cleansed and purified. This is the function of Water; when this is done, the imagination must be employed to visualize the new home in which the consciousness will dwell. Since all attainment must be won by the individual, meditation is a positive form of action that will help build this home of inner peace.

Cancer marks the Summer Solstice, the day when the Sun reaches the most northerly point of its journey and crosses over to a new direction. Therefore, Cancer individuals have the task of changing their old life for a new rhythm of expression. This takes place through the steady control of thoughts and emotions that protects the individual from all disharmony and preserves the sanctity of the soul.

Most Cancer people have a life lesson connecting them with property, home, mother, children, and family affairs. Cancers need a home and should be married because Cancer is the top homemaking sign of the Zodiac. It is in the home that the defensive instincts have an outlet. Here is where the nurturing and mothering instincts can be employed. When this expression is denied, this instinct can turn into fear or selfishness, and Cancers feel that their security is best served alone. They protect themselves from emotional hurt by withdrawing into themselves and pouring this nurturing energy in some other direction.

This is a sign that can be as strong as a giant or as weak as a child, and this can be on a physical or psychological level.

Wherever Cancer is found in the horoscope is where individuals must have the freedom to do things in their own way, as the ideas of others can confuse them. In this department of life the individual is averse to directional responsibilities. This is the "Please, Mother, I'd rather do it myself" sign.

The house that carries Cancer is one in which the individual can be emotional and possessive about the affairs of that house.

Because Cancers live in the world of emotions and feelings, they forget about the source from which all things come and tend to hoard for a rainy day. In this department of the life there is a desire to be in the swim of things, and there is a secret desire for fame. This is coupled with a subtle need to wield power and yet to be powerless. This is where one can be selfish or sympathetic, reserved yet rash, apathetic yet active.

One of the faults of Cancer individuals is that they lack the courage to say yes or no at critical moments. Because they are ruled by the inconstant Moon, their changing moods can be disarming. They also have the difficulty of catching the forces of the future represented by Jupiter, not knowing the importance of the present moment which is the eternal now.

The first decanate of Cancer consists of 0 degrees of Cancer to 10 degrees of Cancer. This decanate applies to those born between June 22 and July 1. This decanate is known as the Cancer-Cancer or Moon-Moon decanate.

This decanate has a double-Moon emphasis, indicating that these individuals are more emotional and sensitive than other Cancer individuals. They also have a greater concern with family and domestic affairs. Their moods undergo many changes and fluctuations. These individuals tend to take on the coloring and the moods of those in their immediate surroundings, making their environment a deciding factor in the state of their well-being. They have a tendency to be sentimentally attached to their possessions. There is a strong interest in cooking and food, and a tendency to overreact to a minor slight even when none is intended.

The second decanate of Cancer consists of 10 degrees to 20 degrees of Cancer. This decanate applies to those born between July 2 and July 12. This decanate is known as the Cancer-Scorpio or Moon-Mars-Pluto decanate.

Scorpio, which is part of this decanate, is a Fixed sign. These individuals have more willpower and determination than the average Cancer. Although Cancer and Scorpio are receptive signs and wait for things to come to them, the Mars-Pluto co-rulership of this decanate confers the ability to fight a relentless battle that is unyielding. Once these individuals set out to accomplish a task, they do so with power and thoroughness (if Mars or Pluto is found in this decanate, it is not as weak and debilitated as it would be in another decanate of Cancer). These individuals can be intensely emotional about sexual and romantic relationships. Jealousy and possessiveness could become a problem. They have considerable ability in do-it-yourself projects, and there is action in the home and resourcefulness in solving domestic problems. There can also be conflicts with parental figures. This decanate indicates an interest in mystical and occult pursuits, because Uranus is exalted in Scorpio and Pluto rules Scorpio, giving these individuals unusual psychic ability.

The third decanate of Cancer consists of 20 degrees of Cancer to 30 degrees of Cancer. This includes those born between July 13 and July 22. This decanate is known as the Cancer-Pisces or Moon-Neptune-Jupiter decanate.

These individuals are inclined to incorporate educational, religious, and spiritual values in their home and family life. The home is used as a place of spiritual healing and refuge; therefore they work to cultivate a peaceful and spiritual atmosphere in their domestic environment. They are kind and sympathetic with a great understanding for the emotional, physical, and spiritual needs of others. Some ignore the need for cleanliness and order in their environment. They also have active imaginations and artistic talents because Neptune and Jupiter are exalted in Cancer and these planets co-rule Pisces.

Leo: July 23 to August 22

Wherever Leo is found in a person's horoscope—whether it is the Sun sign, the Ascendant, on a house cusp, or intercepted in a house—the characteristics of the sign Leo will be manifested.

The Sun is in the sign of Leo between July 23 and August 22. These are approximate dates. Leo is the second of the Fire signs in their Fixed phase. It is a positive, masculine sign that is ruled by the Sun, the giver of life. The planet Pluto is exalted in Leo and derives its power from this Sun-ruled sign. Strength, power, and will are the attributes of the kingly sign of Leo. There is a warmth, a radiance, and willpower that make Leos natural leaders. Leo belongs to the Fire Triplicity and possesses the managerial capacity to act as a central dramatic figure around which an organization or group of people gathers.

Wherever Leo is found in the horoscope is where the creative ideas of an individual are dramatized and where the children of body and mind are manifested. Although in essence the fifth house deals with children of of the body, this concept deals with a wider application. An extension of this creativity is inherent in the sign Leo, and where it is found in the horoscope, and also the fifth house and the house that carries the Sun, these power points are true for all horoscopes. These are all the points of power and serve as a focus for individual creative expression. In these areas of the life the individual will have the strength, will, and optimism to meet all life's challenges. These are the power stations of the Zodiac and should be utilized as such by the individual.

Leo, being a positive, masculine sign, indicates that wherever it is found in the horoscope is where the individual is self-propelling and aggressive in expansive efforts. Leo is fond of pleasure, sports, exercise, entertaining, and adventure. As a Fixed sign, the Leo is very strong in likes and dislikes.

Leo rules the heart, and the whole being of Leo is set to obey the dictates of the heart. If the lesson of love is to be learned under the sign Leo, Leos must renounce vanity and pride and learn the right use of power, which is one of the hardest lessons for Leos. Lust for power, authority, and control destroys everything which is human and spiritual. Leos need to draw in the humanitarian qualities of their opposite sign Aquarius. If this is done, they will include those who feel a need to bask in their light. Leos can be cruel, and their cruelty is never subtle, but always open and hard like the Sun that can burn the unprotected and naked.

When the power of Pluto, which is exalted in Leo, is utilized in the proper way, then Leo becomes the true king who helps, raises, and refines his or her fellow man, giving love just as the Sun gives its warmth to all.

Because of the power inherent in the Leo, these individuals have a great deal of faith in themselves. When things go wrong and there does not seem to be any visible solution to their problems, Providence opens up a new field of action for them. Just as the Sun infiltrates the darkest shadow, the Leos find their way.

All Leos get a chance at creative expression at some time in their life. This expression will come through the Leo power points in the chart. Through this opportunity individuals have a chance to "do their own thing." At such a time Leos will feel that they are the theater, the play, and the main characters around which everything revolves. During such a time Leos will draw to themselves those who are fired and inspired by their enthusiasm. Because Leos are natural leaders, they attract those to whom they will give strength, support, and warm encouragement that is often mixed with a little patronage. As long as Leos are in a position of authority, nothing is beyond them; they will leave no stone unturned to justify the confidence that has been placed in them.

Leos demand attention; they must have the spotlight, and the department of life the Sun is found in pinpoints the area where they should shine with no need to hide their Sun light under a bushel.

The faculty to do good is very strong because of Pluto's exaltation in Leo, which makes them want to improve the world around them. Their enthusiasm and inspiration help to mold public opinion. Leos are very aware of themselves; they are sensitive to the effect they make on others and study how to improve the effect. This is not done through self-analysis, it is done through role-playing and by this method they regenerate their character.

Leos who are not operating with true power can be bombastic; they have the ability to discard their errors and change their reasoning in a clever and subtle manner.

In the weak type of Leo there is the kind of individual who tries to win praise from what has been done by someone else. Sometimes Leo's powers of leadership are used in the pursuit of pleasure instead of service to humanity.

Leos can hurt others because of their strong prejudices. They can badger others to the point of exasperation in order to get their own way; this is because Leo is a Fixed sign.

Leos are fascinated with subtle people; they dislike repetition and one does not have to be obvious around them, they get the point.

Under the influence of Leo the whole being is set to obey the dictates of the heart. This is where the individual actor and performer makes a grand play on the stage of life.

One thing to be remembered about the sign Leo is that you may step on Leos' toes but never on the toes of the children of their mind or body. If you do this you will have a lion at bay.

The first decanate of Leo consists of 0 degrees of Leo to 10 degrees of Leo. This decanate applies to those born between July 23 and August 1. This decanate is known as the Leo-Leo or Sun-Sun decanate. The double-Fixed emphasis of this decanate indicates that those born under it or those who have planets in this decanate have a great deal of self-confidence, personal authority, determination, and staying power. They possess the power for creation, and thus they are able to give form and life to their ideas. Many of them become fine artists, actors, sculptors, inventors, and craftsmen. Those born in this decanate have unusual strength and willpower, and should they become ill they have tremendous recuperative powers. The negative expression of this decanate is stubbornness, ego-centeredness, pride, and the need to be the center of attention.

The second decanate of Leo consists of 10 degrees to 20 degrees of Leo. This decanate applies to those born between August 2 and August 12. This decanate is known as the Leo-Sagittarius or Sun-Jupiter-Neptune decanate. These Leos are concerned with cultural, educational, and religious leadership. The Jupiter and Neptune emphasis gives these individuals an innate understanding of the prevailing social and cultural trends in politics, religion, philosophy, and law. There is a subtle desire with these individuals to make an important contribution that will leave a personal mark in history even if in a small way. They have the ability to mold public opinion, and because of this others recognize their power and leadership ability. They have a strong sense of their own direction even against the tide of popular opinion. Their understanding of mass psychology gives them a sense of aloofness, and they often feel they are alone in a crowd. Because of the expansive nature of Jupiter these individuals often attempt large and impressive enterprises and endeavors. They can seek to impress others by entertaining in an opulent way. These tendencies, if carried too far, can cause the individual to overreach, incurring debts and obligations. The Jupiter emphasis can also give a love of travel and a desire for superiority in sports, education, religious, and cultural activities, or in the performing arts.

The third decanate of Leo consists of 20 degrees to 30 degrees of Leo. This decanate applies to those born between August 13 and August 22. This decanate is known as the Leo-Aries or Sun-Mars-Pluto decanate.

These individuals are endowed with personal magnetism and vitality.

They often have a strong muscular build with physical prowess. Because of the inherent masculinity of this decanate, the men born under it have a great appeal to women. The women born under this decanate can be authoritative, self-assertive, and often competitive with men in some manner. The fixity of Leo gives these individuals staying power to see a project to the end. They are self-sufficient and able to provide for their own needs. They are competitive and want to be first in whatever is important to them. They must learn to guard against the desire or egotistical need to be the central authority figure of their involvements. This decanate of Leo needs plenty of liquids because the planet Mars heats up the system and the body needs cooling down; however, excessive drinking of alcohol can cause their undoing.

Virgo: August 23 to September 22

Wherever Virgo is found in a person's horoscope—whether it is the Sun sign, the Ascendant, on a house cusp, or intercepted in a house—the characteristics of the sign Virgo will be manifested. The Sun is in the sign of Virgo between August 23 and September 22. These are approximate dates.

Virgo is a Mutable sign dealing with memory, the past, and the utilization of past experience. Mercury as the ruler of Virgo indicates the mental nature of this sign. Virgo deals with ideas by analyzing them and categorizing them. It is different from the sign Gemini, which is also ruled by Mercury; Gemini takes in and accepts all ideas and communicates about them.

The life lesson of Virgo is to build in the ability to discriminate and to perfect service to the world. Serving with love is not enough in this sign of perfection; what is required along with the perfection is efficiency in performance. Otherwise the Virgo is liable to be acclaimed for the gift of love but cursed for inefficiency.

Virgo as an Earth sign indicates practicality and concern with concrete results. Virgos are occupied with financial, business, and professional affairs. In Virgo this practicality is manifested in intelligence and skill in labor and also in matters of properly maintaining the physical body.

Buddha's noble injunction that the individual must have right views, followed by right thought, right speech, and right action especially applies to this Mutable-Earth sign. These are very important to the Virgo individual.

Because the Mutable signs deal with the past, the Virgo individual must forget and release that part of the past that obstructs the present. The keyword is elimination, and Virgos must eliminate all thoughts that interfere with health and work performance or their life lesson of service. This cannot be done by burying resentment in the thought chamber of the unconscious. This is because in Virgo, the Earth sign, we sow the seeds of our conscious thoughts and reap them in the unconscious represented by Pisces and Neptune, its polar opposite sign and ruler. The thoughts as seeds planted in the womb of the mind will give the individual a start in reading the unwritten book of life. Once the individual starts reading this book, he or she will know the experience of the ages lives in every atom of his or her being, influencing thoughts and reactions. The Virgo will also know that each instant of the present time is there to shape at will.

Virgo, an Earth sign and ruled by Mercury, needs to use the mind in manipulating the Earth, the physical life, and its problems. Wherever Virgo is found in the horoscope is where the mental concept is brought into physical manifestation. This area is where the individual must reject what is faulty and imperfect, and where the individual must use a mathematical accuracy in work and service if everything is to go smoothly. In this area the individual constantly seeks knowledge which is to bring physical matter under control of the mind. This interest in detail and perfection makes Virgos good at comparison and discrimination and gives them the ability to reject that which they consider faulty and imperfect.

Virgo, a Mutable-Earth sign, deals with memory and the past. The polar opposite sign is Pisces and its ruler Neptune, which deal with the imagination and also the past, and this is why Virgo is required to work on all phases of its body and soul.

The department of life or house that carries Virgo is an area that requires the individual to understand the process of the conscious mind, ruled by Mercury, and the subconscious mind, ruled by Neptune and also the Moon, because it rules our automatic subconscious reaction to outside stimuli. A lack of understanding of the workings of these two minds brings most of the chaos and misery in the world.

When the individual eats a meal the subconscious mind controls all the vital processes that convert the meal into tissue, bone, and blood. The subconscious mind knows how to perform, the process is automatic, it never sleeps, it is always on the job.

If individuals are to fully understand the workings of the conscious and unconscious mind, they must take the one immutable law into consideration: A seed brings forth fruit after its own kind. In the receptive, feminine sign of Virgo is where we bring forth the fruit of our thoughts and labor. Thought, like a seed, lies in the unconscious soil of our mind and reproduces after its own kind. Virgo, being a Mutable sign dealing with memory, warns us that memory can be dangerous if the thoughts are not sorted out and put into proper perspective. Again in Virgo the individual is admonished to watch what is allowed to pass through the conscious bar of the mind.

Medical science tells us that pain is Nature's alarm clock warning the individual that something is wrong. However, medical science does not inform the individual that the pain had its origin in wrong thinking and wrong performance. With this in mind, under Virgo the individual learns not to sow seeds that destroy the planter.

Under Virgo the individual learns discrimination and develops the ability to know the false from the true, and the essential from the nonessential. In using the mind to mold matter, the individual must employ absolute accuracy and care over detail, otherwise it will be impossible to achieve the perfection which is the lesson of Virgo. At the same time individuals should not get so absorbed in details that they blind themselves to the main issues of life. The secret of all health is contained in the Mutable signs. If individuals are wise, they will not wear out their bodies' energies with worry, fear, resentment, or overwork.

In the sign Virgo the individual must learn that personal cleanliness of health and body must be extended to the hygiene of the soul, and that the subconscious produces only that which is fed to it by the conscious mind. In this sign one learns that the conscious mind feeds the unconscious mind and that the conscious mind is the builder of the body even though the individual cannot consciously perceive the silent inner process that eventually affects the health and work performance. Virgo individuals identify themselves with their work. Virgo, a feminine, receptive, Earth sign, is acquisitive, attracting to individuals activities that will benefit them financially, socially, and economically. It is difficult for Virgo individuals to accumulate large sums of money because of their excessive spending, which alternates with saving sprees. Being an Earth sign, they love the good things of the Earth, and they are fond of good food and clothing. However, food is harmful to them when they are under extreme anguish or anger. Virgo deals with diet and hygiene, and because of this Virgo individuals are apt to become food faddists.

In the sign Virgo the opposite extreme can be found, for some Virgo individuals are so disorderly and sometimes lacking in proper hygiene that the true life lesson is yet to be learned, and they turn a deaf ear to the admonition that "cleanliness is next to godliness."

The first decanate of Virgo consists of 0 degrees of Virgo to 10 degrees of Virgo. This decanate applies to those born between August 23 and September 2 (these are approximate dates). This decanate is known as the Virgo-Virgo or Mercury-Mercury decanate. The individuals who have the Sun or planets in this decanate of Virgo are concerned with health, hygiene, proper diet, and work. These individuals handle their practical responsibilities in an efficient manner. They have a good memory for detail and are good at working with figures or work that requires precision or manual dexterity. These individuals enjoy intellectual conversations with friends, relatives, and co-workers; however, when dealing with strangers or emotional issues they are liable to be shy and retiring. They are particular about dress and have a sense of style. They have keen powers of observation and notice details that others miss. Dress design and the clothing industry attract those with this decanate prominent. This decanate also attracts careers related to medicine, health, hygiene, and the preparation and distribution of food. If Mercury is found in this decanate, the individual's skills will be of superior quality.

The second decanate of Virgo consists of 10 degrees of Virgo to 20 degrees of Virgo. This decanate applies to those born between September 3 and September 12. This decanate is known as the Virgo-Capricorn or Saturn-Uranus decanate. These Virgos make skillful administrators with good organizing ability. They have endless patience in handling details and performing precise tasks. They strive for success in their chosen field. The individuals with this decanate prominent in their horoscope are hard-working with a capacity for mental organization and concentration. This enables them to work as draftsmen, engineers, scientists, skilled craftsmen, and researchers. In personal mannerisms they are reserved, dignified, and lean toward traditional social and moral ethical values.

The third decanate of Virgo consists of 20 degrees of Virgo to 30 degrees of Virgo. This decanate applies to those born between September 13 and September 22. This decanate is known as the Virgo-Taurus or Mercury-Venus decanate. Individuals with the Sun or planets prominent in this decanate have a good business sense that enables them to know what products will appeal to the public. These individuals are more outgoing and concerned with creature comforts than the average Virgo. They also make good clothing designers because of the Taurus and Venus influence which enables them to lay out and cut cloth in a precise way. They are fond of personal possessions that are durable and have an aesthetic appeal with a lasting value.

Libra: September 23 to October 22

Wherever Libra is found in a person's horoscope—whether it is the Sun sign, the Ascendant, on a house cusp, or intercepted in a house—the characteristics of Libra will be manifested. The Sun is in the sign of Libra between September 23 and October 22. These are approximate dates.

Libra is the second of the Air signs, dealing with the element of Air in its Cardinal or active phase. It is a positive, masculine sign that takes action to achieve results. Venus is the ruler of Libra and represents the principle of attraction, and thus introduces another factor into the Libra experience. In this sign new energies are aroused, which demand that Libra interact in a disciplined and harmonious manner. These energies are aroused in the Libra individual, producing social interchange and group cooperation. In this sign the individual begins to operate within the greater whole and must learn the laws of cooperation in terms of relationships.

The intellectual Air signs deal with communication and ideas. Gemini as an Air sign deals with one idea in preference to another. Librans want both; they try to unite the two into one. This is why they are called the diplomats or public relations people of the Zodiac. All Air signs have the ability to circulate and move freely in and around people and things. Libra as a Cardinal sign indicates an individual of action with a purpose. Libra's activity is to cooperate; it is less separative than the sign Aries, which is its polar opposite Cardinal sign. The activity is intellectual, imaginative, and artistic. There is a devotion to an ideal, and so wherever Libra is found in the horoscope, the affairs of that house will be handled in an intellectual manner. The department or house that carries Libra is where individuals will be sociable and companionable and do their best work when associated with others in some type of partnership or close friendship.

All Air signs are learning the lesson of dispassion and peace. Wherever Libra is found in the horoscope is where the individual must learn balance. Here is where individuals must weigh themselves to see what is lacking in order to maintain harmony and poise.

Libra is the guidepost in the journey of life that marks the seeking of absolute justice and dispassion. In the sign Libra balance and justice in one's dealings with all people at all times require selflessness and courage. When this power is not used properly, the desire to please others in a personal sense degenerates to making self amenable to others in order to receive their approval.

Signs of the Zodiac should not be interpreted just on the basis of the ruling planet alone; the exalted ruler must also be taken into consideration. Saturn exalted in Libra deals with the law of cause and effect. Saturn in its relationship with Libra deals with the reaction of the self to others and that which is not self. Here the individual learns the laws that are governed by time and space. As the Libra individuals move in time and space, there is a need to identify with others, yet their need for their own space is essential if they are to retain their own identity, which must not be endangered in any way if they are to be peaceful and dispassionate. Libra has many facets that must be dealt with at one time. In itself it is an intellectual, positive Air sign; its ruler is Venus which deals with the principle of attraction. Therefore, Libra individuals' reactions to what they attract call for poise and balanced emotional perceptivity. Sex as a basic human contact also plays an important role for Libra individuals. The scales of Libra demand justice, responsibility, and organization. Libra, a Cardinal sign dealing with action and decision-making, cannot allow the slightest obligation to go by or be left undone, because things left undone will become the obstacle that affects their peace and balance.

In their interaction with others, Librans walk a tightrope, trying to walk a delicate balance while interacting with others and yet allowing others to solve their own problems of living. Because they often make good counselors and help others with their personal problems, to walk this tightrope is difficult.

Libra individuals are especially adept at analyzing what is happening in the society around them and are interested in all matters pertaining to psychological and human relationships.

The department of the horoscope that carries Libra is the area where the individual will find it difficult to support a disturbed or quarrelsome atmosphere for an extended period of time, as it will eventually affect his or her health. Often Librans give in rather than face prolonged discord. Because of this they often appear insincere.

Librans are always courteous, and rarely are they guilty of a desire to injure others. As a rule their temper is unruffled; however, once aroused it is like a tornado in its fury, leaving nothing unsaid; the memory goes back in time, recounting all the injustices suffered and under what circumstances they took place. Like the tornado, everything usually subsides. Libra becomes ill and indisposed for a few days, forgives and forgets until the tornado season arrives again. Because of this, there is a great deal of secret unhappiness in Libra. Libra Sun individuals differ from Libra Ascendant individuals in that they do not give in as the Libra rising individual is apt to. If one is to get along with Librans, one does not order Librans to do anything; one asks if they would be kind enough to cooperate in any endeavor. They will work with you until they die, but never for you.

Libra individuals who are consciously working with their potential are influenced by Saturn as much as they are by Venus. They will have a strong sense of justice and love of balance and proportion. Under Saturn they learn discipline and develop organizational powers. Unlike Taurus, who is also ruled by Venus, Libra individuals exercise the intellect in pursuit of beauty, giving them an intellectual appreciation and perception of beauty.

In the sign Libra illumination comes through intuition; this is because in Esoteric Astrology* Uranus is the ruler of Libra. In Libra the emotional desires are refined and the individual works at a balance between higher and lower responses. Thinking, feeling, and willing must be equalized in this sign.

Libra in seeking a mate or partner faces another lesson in human relationships, which is linked with this seventh house sign of rivalry or enmity, labeled the house of open enemies. Lessons of give-and-take in human relations come through this seventh-house, intellectual Air sign where the intellect must govern the emotions.

Every Libra at some time in his or her life goes through the crucifixion experience or betrayal by a partner or friend. Here Libra suffers through love and through this experience refines his or her field of relationships. Libra calls out for companionship on levels of equality among peers. For Libra, balancing is a continuing process. There must be a balance between work, rest, and recuperation, using the talents wisely.

Libra rules love and marriage, "and what crucifixions are in love," says Herrick. Love is literally the life of Libra, and those born under this Venus sign are crucified in the flesh through desires and emotional feelings. This is a daily crucifixion until purification refines the life of the individual to a place of peace and poise. There is no school on Earth that offers the lessons that can be learned in the marriage relationship. Libra individuals must not only become aware of the law of love, they must

* *Esoteric Astrology*, Alice A. Bailey, New York: Lucis Publishing Co., 1951.

realize themselves as this love. In the marriage relationship love reaches its highest perfection when the two partners are equal though different in expression of power, supporting each other.

In Proverbs: 2–23, it states that a false balance is an abomination unto the Lord, but just weight is his delight, and this applies to all dealings in business, interpersonal relationships, and man's consciousness.

The first decanate of Libra consists of 0 degrees of Libra to 10 degrees of Libra. This decanate applies to those born between September 23 and October 3. These are approximate dates. This decanate is known as the Libra-Libra or Venus-Venus decanate. These individuals are attracted to the study of psychology and social sciences, and they have a need to receive and express love. Marriage, partnerships, and close relationships are important throughout the whole life. Because the first 10 degrees of this sign represent a new cycle of expression dealing with the second half of the Zodiac, with all its ramifications of human relationships, balance is the keyword throughout the life. The individuals born under this decanate must be careful about acquiescing to the actions of others merely for the sake of popularity and acceptance. Those born under this decanate attract a beautiful and comfortable environment to themselves. They have refined tastes and need harmonious surroundings in which to carry out their functions. They are also socially and artistically inclined.

The second decanate of Libra consists of 10 degrees of Libra to 20 degrees of Libra. This decanate applies to those born between October 4 and October 13. These are approximate dates. This decanate is known as the Libra-Aquarius or Venus-Uranus-Saturn decanate. Because Aquarius is a Fixed sign these individuals have more perseverance than those of the other decanates. These individuals have a scientific turn of mind which often unfolds through an interest in electronics or in occult studies such as astrology. They possess unusual intuitive occult faculties as well as good organizational skills and a capacity for self-discipline. Because of Libra's concern with relationships, Librans have an excellent understanding of karmic law and principles of justice. For these reasons these individuals make excellent lawyers, judges, arbitrators, and negotiators. Because Uranus is involved in this decanate, they often meet close friends and partners in unusual and unexpected ways. They will have unusual friendships with people of all ages and from all walks of life. Those born under this decanate or having planets in this decanate are often associated with groups or organizations of some type.

The third decanate of Libra consists of 20 degrees of Libra to 30 degrees of Libra. This decanate applies to those born between October

14 and October 22. These are approximate dates. This is known as the Libra-Gemini or Venus-Mercury decanate. Because of the Mutable, Cardinal combination inherent in this decanate, monotonous routine or humdrum existence will bore these individuals. Because of this they need to discipline themselves in order to follow through on the projects they initiate. These individuals often have literary ability in the fields of advertising, publicity, poetry, art, music, criticism, or in other pursuits related to the arts. This decanate prominent indicates much short-distance traveling connected with social activities, business, and possibly lecturing. These individuals are able to adapt to many different social situations and to many types of people. They like variety and do not want to be tied down exclusively to one relationship. Because of this, many think of them as inconsistent and fickle in their romantic relationships and friendships.

Scorpio: October 23 to November 21

Wherever Scorpio is found in a person's horoscope—whether it is the Sun sign, the Ascendant, on a house cusp, or intercepted in a house—the characteristics of the sign Scorpio will be manifested. Every sign of the Zodiac represents an output of some kind of power. Scorpio is the second of the Water signs. It rules the emotional and psychic aspects of the individual. Uranus gets its power from Scorpio because it is exalted in this sign, giving Scorpio an unusual and sudden release of energy and power. The Sun is in the sign of Scorpio between October 23 and November 21. These are approximate dates. Scorpio is a Water, Fixed, and a feminine, receptive sign. Its ruler is the planet Pluto and its co-ruler is Mars. Scorpio is the natural eighth-house sign; however, in a natal horoscope it can be found on any house cusp. Scorpio is a Water sign; therefore, whatever department of the life that carries Scorpio, affairs and activities of that house will be handled in an emotional way. The individuals will be intuitive regarding matters of that house, and their decisions will be based on feelings and their emotional considerations. The department of life that carries Scorpio is where individuals will distill the essence of their experiences and eventually raise these experiences to a higher level of expression. Because Scorpio is a Fixed sign, the individual will be determined and goal-oriented. Here is where the individual will be concerned with future goals and will persist in unwavering efforts to achieve them.

Scorpio is a feminine, receptive sign; therefore, Scorpios are likely to accept the status quo in matters regarding the house that Scorpio occupies. However, Scorpios can become very forceful in dealing with the circumstances of that house when they become dissatisified enough with the conditions under which they must exist. These changes must be accomplished within the existing circumstances because Scorpio is a feminine, receptive sign, and because of this Scorpios have the ability to attract people and circumstances needed to bring about their desired ends.

Scorpio is a Fixed sign ruled by the dynamic planets Pluto and Mars, giving those of this sign great energy, and the fixity of Scorpio, giving them the tenacity to succeed even against great obstacles. Wherever Scorpio is found in the horoscope, the individual will not be deterred by threats or attempts to instill thoughts of fear or failure. Because of the Pluto rulership, Scorpio has the power to transform circumstances affecting his or her life for better or for worse and thus make a new start, indicated by Pluto, co-ruling Aries, the sign of new beginnings. Often there is a do-or-die attitude that can be very uncompromising.

Scorpio represents the Fixed phase of the Water signs, silent water that mirrors the activity of the world around it and remains unruffled and undisturbed by this reflection. Those born under its influence tend to hide their feelings under a calm unruffled exterior. It is very difficult to fathom what is going on behind this barrier of calm reserve. This silence and calm are what give Scorpio its outward power, driving force, and determination in any project undertaken. Inherent in Scorpio is the knowledge that silence preserves and concentrates power. Those who are just beginning to learn the life lesson of Scorpio can be secretive, cunning, and scheming and work in subtle ways, thus using this power for selfish ends.

In this sign of secrets, desire motivates the life of the individual. It gives strength and energy to perform its tasks. Uranus as the exalted ruler gives the power and insights to attain the goals and objectives of this Fixed sign. Mars as the Esoteric ruler of Scorpio is involved in the lesson of Scorpio as action in the regeneration of the whole being. Taurus, the Fixed, Earth sign and the polar opposite of Scorpio, represents the energy that is brought into concrete manifestation; therefore, Scorpio has the first test in regeneration of appetite, both sexual and food intake, also physical comfort and money. The individual tends to identify with form, and under Scorpio, where Uranus is exalted, one experiences loss and destruction of form in order to teach the individual not to identify with form which is constantly changing. Thus where Scorpio is found in the horoscope, one is dealing with regeneration and new beginnings.

The scorpion is one of the symbols of the sign Scorpio, representing one of the lower phases of the journey through life. This is where individuals are at the mercy of their desires and have no vision beyond the material plane. In this phase Scorpio uses its emotional power, strength, and determination to get what it wants. These characteristics are accompanied by secrecy in order to thwart any one or any thing interfering with its desires. There is in the individual not only secrecy but also an urge for privacy in affairs, and if interfered with in any way Scorpio can sting and manifest jealousy, spite, and hatred. These kinds of responses can only lead to suffering, loss, or destruction of material possessions and pleasure. This is when the serpent symbol or aspect of Scorpio manifests itself. Finally the love of secret things that are focused on the material is turned inward to discover the mystery of life and death and the purpose of existence. Thus the individual enters the path of regeneration and the battlefield where the lower desires dealing with the sense-life are challenged. When this encounter takes place all feelings and sensations are intensified and the individual works at making a heaven or hell out of existence. With increased knowledge and wisdom the warrior attempts to overcome the turbulent desires of the lower self.

When Scorpio individuals become aware of the hidden powers of regeneration within them and the inner life that permeates and enriches all forms, they will begin to feel the suffering of others and will want to attain the wisdom which will help heal other people, represented by the humanitarian qualities of Aquarius and Uranus, which is exalted in Scorpio. This is why there are so many healers, doctors, and surgeons in this sign.

Where one has Scorpio in the horoscope is where the individual takes work, loves, and ideals seriously and insists that others do the same. Scorpio's house represents the Achilles' heel of the Zodiac, where individuals are unable to take a joke about themselves. This department of life is serious business and shows where Scorpio can become an uncompromising adversary.

Scorpio is one of the most misunderstood signs of the Zodiac. The characteristics of this sign baffle even the individuals born under it if they do not understand or know how to use its tremendous power. Scorpio deals with the fundamental processes of transformation on all levels.

Scorpio individuals can be difficult to live with as they are never satisfied with themselves. They are constantly renewing, regenerating, and working to improve the status quo. They do not like to admit weakness, and the struggle is always going on to improve themselves and everyone around them. Although they despise weakness in themselves and others, they are generally compassionate and will extend themselves to help others. They will use their time, money, and all other resources to help, but once helped it is expected that others will help themselves. If others do not help themselves, they may be met with indifference the second time around.

Hidden within the Scorpio process is the new form of life yet to come. Science suggests that the first forms of life appeared in still water. Man as the most evolved of life forms comes under this Water sign labeled the sex sign. Scorpio rules the organs of creation and the sex drive, and because of this there is tremendous emotional force behind the romantic and sexual involvements of Scorpio. If this energy is not controlled, it can lead to possessiveness, jealousy, and even violence. Pluto as the ruler of Scorpio demands not only the refinement of these sexual desires but also the action that is to be taken to obtain these refinements. Once this action is taken the next symbol of Scorpio comes into play, and that is the eagle that flies high in the mountain tops. In this sign the individual eventually learns that the sex energy is a creative energy and not to be used as a plaything or for simple pleasure. The individual will learn that sex is a healing force, and the exchange of this energy between two people should be used as a sacred gift for healing.

All the Water signs deal with endings. Cancer is associated with the fourth house and the later part of life; Scorpio is associated with the eighth house and death, whether it be the death of an old condition or death of the physical body; Pisces is associated with the twelfth house and deals with the end of a cycle of expression.

Reserve and outer control are only the beginning of the transmutation process of Scorpio. In the sign Scorpio lays the promise of control over the whole being, where the last symbol of Scorpio manifests itself as the dove of peace.

The first decanate of Scorpio consists of 0 degrees of Scorpio to 10 degrees of Scorpio. This decanate applies to those born between October 23 and November 2. These are approximate dates. This decanate is known as the Scorpio-Scorpio or Pluto-Mars decanate. Those born under this decanate are resourceful and enterprising in business, also in matters connected with manufacturing, engineering, and scientific investigation. They possess much energy and direct that energy toward success. They have great staying power and the ability to work in spite of obstacles.

Those with planets in this decanate or born in this decanate have little tolerance for weakness or laziness in others and will not permit it in themselves. There can be a do-or-die attitude that can be very uncompromising. These individuals are determined and can be competitive, and they can be vindictive enemies if aroused. They can make it very uncomfortable for those who incur their displeasure; however, they should know that this attitude is equally destructive to themselves.

Individuals under this decanate have a special ability in finding resourceful ways of utilizing old or discarded items. Scorpio being a psychic sign indicates that those born under this sign consciously or unconsciously understand that all manifested things are an expression of energy, and energy is not lost, it just takes on another form. These individuals know that everything has its right use or it would not be in existence. Because of this they have little fear of change or death; they recognize this force as part of the ongoing evolutionary process leading to greater expansion of consciousness and the creation of perfection. Individuals under this decanate have a strong sex drive and can be jealous and possessive sex partners. They can be cold and indifferent to those they consider beneath their dignity. They can be secretive, especially with information that has strategic importance. Joint finances and corporate dealings are important to those born under this decanate or those with planets in this decanate.

The second decanate consists of 10 degrees of Scorpio to 20 degrees of Scorpio. This decanate applies to those born between November 3 and November 12. These are approximate dates. This decanate is known as the Scorpio-Pisces or Pluto-Mars-Neptune-Jupiter decanate. The individuals born under this decanate or with planets in this decanate are more kind and sympathetic than the usual Scorpio because of the Pisces influence. They will help those in need; however, they are sufficiently Scorpio to expect others to help themselves after initial help has been given them to start them on their way. If others do not help themselves, those with this decanate can become indifferent and unmoved the next time around. These individuals have strong intuitive abilities and are therefore often drawn to mysticism, occultism, or magic. They are especially interested in reincarnation, life after death, and communication with the dead. If Neptune, Uranus, Pluto, Jupiter, or Venus is located in this decanate there are special psychic abilities.

The third decanate of Scorpio consists of 20 degrees of Scorpio to 30 degrees of Scorpio. This decanate applies to those born between November 13 and November 21. These are approximate dates. This decanate is known as the Scorpio-Cancer or Pluto-Mars-Moon decanate. Because Neptune and Jupiter are exalted in Cancer, there are many similarities with the second Pisces decanate of Scorpio, where Neptune and Jupiter also rule. These individuals have strong intuitive tendencies because of the combination of the Neptune-Pluto-Uranus influences; however, they are more decisive than the second decanate of Scorpio because Cancer is a decision-making Cardinal sign. Individuals with this decanate prominent are concerned with home improvement and family affairs. They are emotionally sensitive and easily hurt, especially in regard to family relationships, although it is not apparent. These individuals can be moody and subject to rapid emotional changes. They are also likely to act on impulse because of the Mars rulership of Scorpio and the combined influence of the Moon. If the planets located in this decanate receive stress aspects from other planets, there can be conflicts in the family over inheritance, alimony, or goods belonging to the dead. There could even be disputes over the jurisdiction of children in cases of divorce.

Sagittarius: November 22 to December 21

Wherever Sagittarius is found in a person's horoscope—whether it is the Sun sign, the Ascendant, on a house cusp, or intercepted in a house —the characteristics of this sign will be manifested. Every sign of the Zodiac represents an output of power. Sagittarius is a Fire sign, indicating leadership potential, enthusiasm, creativity, and energy. Where Sagittarius is found in the horoscope is where the individual has the ability to act as a spiritual, philosophic leader in the area of religion, law, and higher education. Here is where the individual is concerned with the ideas around which human society is built. Sagittarius is a masculine, positive sign; therefore, wherever Sagittarius is found the individual will take the initiative without waiting for outside stimuli to motivate him or her into action. Jupiter is the ruling planet of Sagittarius and deals with the principle of expansion and preservation. Jupiter as ruler of Sagittarius and exalted in the sign of Cancer preserves all the seed potential of the individual until the time comes for the individual to express the life inherent in this seed potential. Saturn, which is closely related to the Jupiter process, rules time and has a great deal to do with this potential ruling the time of blossoming. The house with Sagittarius on its cusp contains the seed of growth and expansion and the promise of that which will make one whole.

Sagittarius is co-ruled by the planet Neptune, calling the imagination into play, and it is well to remember that what individuals cannot perceive they cannot become. Therefore it is important that where the sign of the Archer is found in the horoscope is where right attunement and proper selection of the target bring results. The expansiveness of Jupiter demands that Sagittarius expand into new worlds and new areas of thought and experience. Where Sagittarius is found is where the individual can demonstrate a greater degree of superior powers in efforts at expansion. It is well for the Sagittarian to remember that neglected gifts atrophy through disuse. Sagittarius, which deals with the higher inspirational mind, must correct this kind of neglect or irresponsibility; if this is not done, the Sagittarian will cease to function in a productive way and will lose intuitive insights. It is difficult to distinguish between true intuition and an overactive imagination which could cause the individual to arrive at faulty conclusions. Thus it is necessary for Sagittarians to still the mind and body and reach beyond the senses where they can pierce the illusionary appearance of their material existence.

The area of experience that carries the sign Sagittarius is where one can be forceful and self-confident, and where one is enthusiastic and vital. Here is where one can exercise true judgment and understanding which is distilled from experience; this is because Sagittarius is a Mutable sign and deals with skills and the utilization of past experience. However, because Sagittarius is a Mutable sign that deals with the past, Sagittarians must let go of all their destructive unconscious habits of the past. They must know that the moment that has just passed will never come again; therefore, faith and optimism are demanded if they are to fulfill and enjoy life. Because Neptune co-rules Sagittarius, dealing with hidden support or self-undoing, Sagittarius is the area of experience where individuals can grow and expand or can have the capacity to act as their own destroyer, through overoptimism, overamplification of facts, misjudgment, hypocrisy, and unfortunate speculations.

Wherever Sagittarius is found in the horoscope is where the individual must have freedom and independence. For many this freedom is expressed in sports or the desire to roam the world and explore the cultures of other countries and people. However, the time comes when individuals will tire of their physical freedom and will realize that they can travel the world over but can never escape from limitation, loneliness, and frustration. When this happens the energy is then redirected to exploring the richness of the kingdom within the self. At such a time, individuals will harmonize their own life and by example will infect the lives of others. Others will turn to them for guidance, philosophy, wisdom, and inspiration.

The Fire signs need to learn the lesson of love, and Sagittarius needs to speak words of consolation, and be a friend and law-giver to friends and companions. Sagittarius must learn that regardless of material assets or education, he or she must give of this abundance to improve something outside of self. One of the spiritual laws is centered around the Jupiter-Saturn process and that is that individuals cannot fulfill their deepest needs until they are willing to put into action a deed that will make something possible for another as an expression of gratitude for the abundance they receive.

The Sagittarians' approach to life is straightforward; it is never subtle. Idealism is powerfully marked, as are their religious and philosophic tendencies. They can resort to righteous anger if their ideals have been degraded. They will let their arrows go, and truth will be spoken as the polar opposite sign of Gemini comes into play. As the noncomformist, the Sagittarian shoots forth ideas, ideals, and principles from the bow. The verbiage represents the rebellion against the secretiveness of the previous sign Scorpio.

Sagittarians' natural good spirits generally allow them to live an abundant life. They have the ability to see the future through their understanding of current trends of thought. Their insights border on prophecy.

Sagittarians should keep busy and active, otherwise depression and dormant anxiety will emerge under adversities. Although they are invincible optimists, their innate restlessness makes them desire constant change, and they go through the experience of extremes of exaltation and despondency. Their motives originate in thought rather than feeling, which is why many educators and writers have Sagittarius prominent in their horoscopes.

Wherever Sagittarius is found in the horoscope is where the individual will be sustained by optimism, creativity, expansiveness, and foresight long after others have fallen by the wayside.

Because the Fire signs are under the dominant influence of the Sun and Mars, new avenues of creative expression and expansiveness are always opening up for them, and Jupiter is always there to help even though the help comes at the eleventh hour.

Many Sagittarians pull themselves up by their own bootstraps, but often this does not happen until after the fortieth year, until the last half of life, for which the first was made. This is because Jupiter is exalted in the sign Cancer, the sign ruling the natural fourth house which deals with the conditions prevailing in the last half of the life.

The first decanate of Sagittarius consists of 0 degrees of Sagittarius to

10 degrees of Sagittarius. This decanate applies to those born between November 22 and December 2. These are approximate dates. This decanate is known as the Sagittarius-Sagittarius or Jupiter-Jupiter-Neptune decanate. These individuals are continually setting new goals for themselves and aspiring to a more abundant future. Their optimism will not permit them to admit failure or to become disheartened by difficulties. Because of this optimism they can run the risk of overreaching and neglecting details, or they can make commitments that are impossible to fulfill. Those having planets in this decanate have an expansive philosophical outlook with an interest in religion, philosophy, higher education, and the prevailing social order. These individuals are fond of travel and have a strong interest in foreign countries, their cultures, history, and religion. They often further their own ambitions by becoming involved with religious, cultural, or educational institutions, or by helping to promote large-scale projects in such areas.

The second decanate of Sagittarius consists of 10 degrees of Sagittarius to 20 degrees of Sagittarius. This decanate applies to those born between December 3 and December 11. These are approximate dates. This is known as the Sagittarius-Aries or Jupiter-Neptune-Mars-Pluto decanate. This is a powerful decanate providing these individuals with optimism, drive, initiative, and self-confidence, with the ability to put their ideals into practical action. These individuals are fond of adventure and excitement and are likely to travel as a means of experiencing new and thrilling adventures. Because of Jupiter's exaltation in the sign of the home and homeland, there can be the danger of narrow-minded, patriotic views based on the individual's family background and cultural conditioning. These individuals are often militant crusaders for their particular religious, cultural, political, or educational beliefs, which can run the entire gamut of the religious and philosophic spectrum. Regardless of their beliefs they promote and proselytize them with a militant fanatic zeal, often annoying or alienating others. On the other hand, they are able to initiate and spearhead religious, cultural, or educational projects.

The third decanate of Sagittarius consists of 20 degrees of Sagittarius to 30 degrees of Sagittarius. This decanate applies to those born between December 12 and December 21. These are approximate dates. This decanate is known as the Sagittarius-Leo or Jupiter-Neptune-Sun decanate. Individuals with this decanate prominent have a great deal of determination and optimism. The Sun's influence often indicates that they achieve positions of power and influence in religious, educational, and cultural institutions. Often these individuals become prominent lawyers or judges expressing the authority of Leo through the law which is ruled by Jupiter. The Fixed nature of Leo gives these individuals greater determination and staying power than other Sagittarians, and if they combine good judgment with their optimism they can go a long way down the road to success. In this decanate there is always the danger of using religious and philosophic beliefs and institutional positions in a self-serving way. These individuals must be careful to avoid prejudice and biased viewpoints. There is also a tendency to become ego-identified with familiar and comfortable attitudes even in the face of evidence to the contrary. However, these individuals express their philosophic beliefs with power and authority and are often able to inspire confidence and renewed faith in others.

Capricorn: December 22 to January 19

Wherever Capricorn is found in a person's horoscope—whether it is the Sun sign, the Ascendant, on a house cusp, or intercepted in a house—the characteristics of the sign Capricorn will be manifested. Every sign of the Zodiac represents an output of power. The Sun is in the sign of Capricorn between December 22 and January 19. These are approximate dates.

Capricorn is the last of the Earth Triplicities. In this sign individuals reach their zenith in this cycle of dealing with their material resources and physical matter. Much like the Earth signs Taurus and Virgo, Capricorn is motivated by practical considerations, and the Cardinal quality of Capricorn indicates that these individuals achieve their objectives through constant activity, decision-making, and dealing with the here and now. However, the activity of Capricorn is different from that of the other Cardinal signs because of its ruler Saturn, which deals with time. Capricorn is less inclined to initiate activity because it is a feminine, receptive sign. Capricorn individuals will either attract or patiently wait for a situation to develop that they can turn to their own advantage by timely intervention. The department of life carrying the sign Capricorn is where the individual has the capacity for patient discipline that is motivated by a desire for material status. In this area individuals desire and need respect in the eyes of the world in which they move. In this department individuals take on practical managerial responsibilities in order to fulfill themselves. There is little of practical consequence that escapes their notice, and this is where they take advantage of every opportunity for practical advancement.

Saturn, the ruler of Capricorn, is the planet of just compensation. Much like Jupiter and Neptune, it deals with the law of cause and effect. Mars is exalted in the sign Capricorn, which gives the Capricorn the zest and resourcefulness for encounters in business activities and the manipulation of material resources. These encounters give Capricorn individuals the ability to cope with any situation as it arises, giving them solutions to problems that may seem insurmountable to others. This ability is due to Mars co-ruling the resourceful sign Scorpio and ruling the innovative sign Aries. Mars exalted in Capricorn gives them the ability to coordinate their energies with organized strategy, making them very effective.

The Sun in Capricorn gives individuals a longer than average life span, because Saturn which rules time is the ruler of Capricorn. Subconsciously Capricorns know this because Sagittarius is the preceding sign and is ruled by Jupiter and Neptune which are exalted in Cancer and deal with the last half of life. Thus they seek security and independence for their old age. Wherever Capricorn is found in the horoscope, individuals will work, plan, organize, sacrifice, and seek material security. This is where individuals will display economical and prudent habits, where they will have a sense of responsibility, where they will be painstaking and careful, precise and methodical in the execution of their work. Capricorn is the tenth-house sign of the Zodiac, dealing with honor, prestige, and status in the world in which these individuals move; thus their concentration, perseverance, and hard work must give them recognition in time. Although Capricorn is a Cardinal sign and though the impulsive Mars is exalted in this sign, because of Saturn's rulership Capricorns are deliberate and seldom act impulsively; they usually act with premeditated care and strictly in accordance with existing rules and regulations, with activity directed toward attainment.

All Earth signs must learn the lesson of service; therefore self-training, discipline, and organization are requirements in the sign Capricorn if these individuals are to build structure into their lives.

The symbol of Capricorn is the Mountain Goat, and like the mountain goat that moves cautiously from crag to crag, Capricorn has the innate urge to struggle and climb to the top, as consciously or unconsciously the inner motive is ambition that is directed to attain security, prestige, and power. Once they set an aim, whether it is social, business, political, or intellectual, they will work hard and not be deterred. Their faith in their own power and ability makes it difficult for them to accept failure of any kind, for they feel that in some way they did not utilize all the resources that were at their command, and this can be a very embarrassing situation for any Capricorn.

In the sign Capricorn there is the persistent feeling that one must develop and build a position in the world. In this development Capricorn becomes a creature of habit, and Saturn, the ruler of Capricorn, often crystallizes the habits developed by the Capricorn individual. Saturn deals with contraction and narrows Capricorn's activities and directs them toward the attainment of worldly power. Uranus, co-ruler of Capricorn, is the habit breaker, and when love of experience and attainment takes over the Capricorn brain, then the heart can become cold and unresponsive to the needs of others. When this phase is reached, the Capricorn individual is confronted with the subtle powers of the material world; the business aspect of these Capricorns so absorbs their consciousness that they forget their divine source of supply. When this happens there can be a sudden downfall which brings about the destruction of their pride, and at that time everything that seems stable and permanent crumbles under them. Their world of ambition may lie in ruin. Capricorn rules the knees, and when Capricorns fail to bend the knees of humility to the divine supply that made possible all their attainments, their world of power and ambition will fall.

Capricorn is the most spiritual sign in the Zodiac, for under it the individual learns that great wealth and fame are easier to attain than the spiritual life, and that dealing with physical matter without spiritual input can leave the individual with a sense of isolation and want. Under the sign Capricorn the individual gets an understanding of the spiritual laws that govern all matter and our dependence on our divine source.

Capricorn children often have a struggle in the early years of their lives maintaining good health; however, once they have passed the early critical stages they have a lot of physical endurance.

Because Capricorn is a negative, feminine sign Capricorns can be uncertain and distrustful of their future, and therefore they have a tendency to be frugal. However, they are generally financially sustained in their old age. They are worldly and cynical with a tendency to be selfish but are also capable of great devotion and generosity if they think it is merited. They have a respect for law, order, and convention, and a reverence for the past, as they feel there is much in the past that can be useful in the present. Underlying all the virtues and faults of Capricorns is the primary instinct to vindicate themselves with power.

The first decanate of Capricorn consists of 0 degrees of Capricorn to 10 degrees of Capricorn. This decanate applies to those born between December 22 and December 31. These are approximate dates. This decanate is known as the Capricorn-Capricorn or Saturn-Saturn-Uranus decanate. The individuals born under this decanate or with planets prominent in this decanate work long and hard to achieve their ends, and they are not afraid of the discipline and perseverance that are required to achieve their goals. They are ambitious with good organizational ability, coupled with political astuteness and ability to make the most advantageous use of opportunities around them. They are attracted to professions that will confer status, prestige, and security, and also the respect and admiration of the community they live in. Because Mars is exalted in Capricorn they have the ability to act swiftly, forcefully, and decisively once they have determined that the strategic time is at hand.

The second decanate of Capricorn consists of 10 degrees of Capricorn to 20 degrees of Capricorn. This decanate applies to those born between January 1 and January 10. These are approximate dates. This is known as the Capricorn-Taurus or Saturn-Uranus-Venus decanate. Those born in this decanate or who have planets prominent in this decanate seek status and security through wealth. Some attain this wealth through holding a high professional position or through a partnership or marriage. Many of those born under this decanate often become executors and administrators in large-scale enterprises or they manage their own business affairs. They make excellent accountants, financial analysts, and efficiency experts. Because of the Fixed sign Taurus they have tremendous staying power and perseverance that enable them to follow their endeavors through to a successful conclusion. They have a good sense of values and a strong desire to own property of quality that has enduring worth. This decanate should avoid the pitfalls of worshiping money and material status as an end in itself. If they become too materialistic, their emotional and spiritual values are liable to get lost and they become enslaved by their possessions.

The third decanate of Capricorn consists of 20 degrees of Capricorn to 30 degrees of Capricorn. This decanate applies to those born between January 11 and January 19. These are approximate dates. This decanate is known as the Capricorn-Virgo or Saturn-Uranus-Mercury decanate. These individuals are particularly concerned with establishing good procedures and efficiency in their areas of work. They are attracted to the medical profession and other fields where specialized skills and education confer status, financial advantage, and prestige. They also have a talent for organizing industrial production, and because of the Saturn-Mercury combination they may be skilled in mathematics and are attracted to engineering. Often they are absorbed into government clerical work as a part of the machinery of a bureaucratic organization. This decanate of Capricorn makes them clothes-conscious, and they like simplicity and elegance as a means of creating a good impression to further their business and career interests. They are inclined toward strict health and dietary regimes to improve their vitality, fitness, and appearance.

Aquarius: January 20 to February 18

Wherever Aquarius is found in a person's horoscope—whether it is the Sun sign, the Ascendant, on a house cusp, or intercepted in a house—the characteristics of the sign Aquarius will be manifested.

The Sun is in the sign of Aquarius between January 20 and February 18. These are approximate dates. Aquarius is an intellectual Air sign belonging to the Fixed Quadruplicity. It is an aggressive, masculine sign with Uranus as its ruler and Saturn as its co-ruler. Uranus is exalted in the sign Scorpio, Saturn is exalted in the sign Libra, and Mercury is exalted in the sign Aquarius. In this sign all the elements are brought into play. Fire is also brought into play by its polar opposite sign Leo. If the individuals born under this sign are not understood, they will be viewed as eccentric and unpredictable by others.

Aquarius rules the ankles of the body by which we move forward, which signifies the special responsibilities of Aquarius to move forward toward the advancement of the new age, when the brotherhood of man will be a reality. Under the sign Aquarius the individual should work with societies, groups, or others for some common ideal. This kind of aspiration will fill the need for companionship and friendship which is inherent in this sign.

Whatever department of the life carries the sign Aquarius is where the individual has a happy knack of fraternizing easily with others. In this department of life the individual is obliging, with consideration for others. This amiability makes Aquarians popular and well-liked. Affectation or snobbery is rare in Aquarians, for truth makes them dislike sham or hypocrisy of any form.

Every sign of the Zodiac represents an output of power. The intellectual Air signs represent the quality of thinking and communicating ideas, and Aquarians are very aware of this gift which raises us above the animal. They are aware of the power of thought and speech, and thus these individuals need periods of silence to be alone without interfering annoyance from others. Uranus rules this sign and brings a new kind of orientation to the individual. Under this sign the motivation must be pure; altruism must be present if the goals, objectives, hopes, and wishes which Aquarius rules are to be realized. In this sign the individual strives for the genuine dignity of humans. Aquarius, as an intellectual Air sign, does not deal with blood ties as does the intellectual Air sign of Gemini, or as the Libra with partnerships and marriage; it deals with the companionship and alliance of people. This sign strives to make friendships operative by recognizing the hidden divinity or the spiritual equality of every person.

Average Aquarians respond equally to the rulership of Saturn, which deals with material manifestation. Saturn limits them to what can be perceived by the five senses. Mercury's exaltation in Aquarius and rulership of Virgo causes them to dissect and analyze by cold reason; nevertheless there is a desire to discover truth, and many Aquarians are drawn to scientific investigation. In this Fixed, intellectual Air sign thought power is fixed and concentrated until the thinking becomes alive and the thoughts are manifested in the material world.

The Fixed signs in the horoscope are goal oriented and represent reservoirs of energy, and here individuals make their way in spite of overwhelming obstacles. Aquarius in its association with ideas deals with human endeavors that are mental and material in their expression, and Aquarians are alive with invention and innovation, the new and unusual. Saturn as co-ruler of Aquarius is a unique partner to the lightning-like, unannounced effects of its ruler Uranus. Saturn represents time but Uranus rules the power that is beyond time. Aquarius favors those advanced individuals who bring invention and reform, those who strive to express life through religion, art, and science. As intellectual Air signs they are the spokespeople for humanity. Leos, the polar opposite sign, give to those they love, but Aquarians give to all humanity. It is less personal, therefore less understood.

Aquarians are never greedy; they understand that true community can only be established through kindness, friendliness, and compassion instead of the jealous, competitive atmosphere that prevails today. All the prophets who taught humanity had the constructive qualities of Aquarius in their makeup. It gave them the power to light the way for humanity in a cosmic sense, and they responded to the biblical saying, "Lo, I make all things new."

The need for the Aquarius expression is great as the heart of humanity calls out from its materialism to the children of Aquarius who can develop the gifts that will heal, comfort, and sustain humanity.

Those born under Aquarius who have not learned the lesson of Saturn and have not yet earned the freedom that Uranus bestows still seek their own interests or advocate impractical utopian ideas. They are still spiritually asleep.

Aquarius as a Fixed, intellectual Air sign can be cool and dispassionate; this dispassion can bring about an intellectual deadlock, and when Aquarians have been convinced of the infallibility of their opinion, this dispassion can mean the loss of all they hold dear—personal honor, possessions, and friends. Although dispassion is a lesson that needs to be learned by Air signs, it needs to be coupled with intuition which will protect the individual from intellectual arrogance. If an intellectual deadlock comes about, Uranus with its catastrophic, lightning-like flash will in time break this deadlock. Uranus the habit breaker will inflict temporary chaos so that there can be a complete change in motivation and in the mental, emotional, and physical attitudes of the individual. The individual who can not respond to Uranus in a positive manner often reacts in an undisciplined, unpredictable, and irrational manner to this influence.

The symbol of Aquarius is the Water Bearer, signified by a man on whose shoulder is a water pitcher. In astrology water represents emotion and Aquarius represents the intellectual thinker in this symbol. The Water Bearer controls the water as it pours out of the pitcher, indicating that in the new age we will use our intellect to reason things out, control the emotion that backs up our reasoning, and allow emotion its proper expression in life. The reverse is true today. People get themselves into all kinds of untenable situations because of misdirected emotions, and then they evoke the intellect to bring back the peace and poise that was lost. When the intellect and emotions become the proper servant of the spirit, we will become the thinkers and knowers of truth.

Aquarians, coming under a Fixed sign, will pursue their mental goals with a steady purpose, unlike the vacillation of Gemini and the scale-tipping Libra. These individuals will not accept any idea or standard of conduct on faith alone. They respect only those ideas and principles that can be proven scientifically or through direct experience. They will not adhere to any authority they cannot respect, and for this reason this sign is associated with reformers and revolutionaries. They seldom change their minds but when they do, they do so abruptly and unexpectedly, so that it confuses and shocks others. Aquarius as a positive, masculine sign moves the individual to take the initiative in formulating new ideas and practices.

Mercury exalted in Aquarius confers intellectual abilities that are combined with intuitive inspiration and original ideas, giving Aquarians the ability to research important scientific discoveries and innovate new techniques, theories, and technologies.

The first decanate of Aquarius consists of 0 degrees of Aquarius to 10 degrees of Aquarius. This decanate applies to those born between January 20 and January 29. These are approximate dates. This decanate is known as the Aquarius-Aquarius or Uranus-Saturn-Uranus-Saturn decanate. Those born under this decanate or having planets prominent in this decanate seek new experiences as a means of expanding their knowledge and intellectual outlook. Because of the double Fixed-sign influence of this decanate, these individuals will adhere to what they consider right and will not permit their minds to be changed against their will. These individuals can break away from tradition and try new ways of doing things which often take the form of rebellion against materialistic values that use people as a means of gaining possessions and status. They are friendly and cooperative on a voluntary basis, but they will not submit to regimentation or blind authority in any way. They have a broad impartial outlook that gives no special advantages or disadvantages to anyone unless they have been earned. This is because of Saturn's exaltation in Libra, the sign of justice and the co-ruler of Aquarius. These individuals are capable of mental concentration which in turn brings them mental guidance. They have a strong interest in scientifically understanding the basic laws of nature as well as the scientific and spiritual laws that govern human destiny.

The second decanate of Aquarius consists of 10 degrees of Aquarius to 20 degrees of Aquarius. This decanate applies to those born between January 30 and February 8. These are approximate dates. This is known as the Aquarius-Gemini or Uranus-Saturn-Mercury decanate. The individuals born under this decanate or with planets prominent in this decanate are more adaptable than other Aquarians because Gemini is a Mutable sign. These individuals have an intense curiosity and have a desire to know the underlying causes of things of interest to them. This curiosity often leads to surprising and original solutions to problems. Mercury is exalted in Aquarius and rules Gemini, and this double Mercury influence makes these individuals intellectual and fond of discussion and communication with their friends and associates. This Mercury-Uranus combination indicates a quick, intuitive, original mind, often bestowing an unusual ability in scientific and occult studies. Many inventors have this decanate prominent in their horoscope. They acquire much knowledge through friendships and group associations, often involving travel or short trips because of the Mercury influence.

The third decanate of Aquarius consists of 20 degrees of Aquarius to 30 degrees of Aquarius. This decanate applies to those born between February 9 and February 18. This decanate is known as the Aquarius-Libra or Uranus-Saturn-Venus decanate. These individuals are interested in the fields of psychology, sociology, and human relations. They often become leaders and organizers of group endeavors. The double influence of Saturn's co-rulership of Aquarius and Saturn's exaltation in Libra and the goal orientation of Aquarius gives these individuals a strong sense of purpose and responsibility in achieving worthwhile scientific, social, humanitarian, or organizational goals. It also gives them strong ambition to achieve intellectual and social distinction in some way. These individuals are loyal in friendships and expect loyalty and responsibility in turn. They are friendly and sociable but appear formal and austere in their social behavior.

Pisces: February 19 to March 20

Wherever Pisces is found in a person's horoscope—whether it is the Sun sign, the Ascendant, on a house cusp, or intercepted in a house—the characteristics of the sign Pisces will be manifested. Every sign of the Zodiac represents an output of power. The Sun is in the sign of Pisces between February 19 and March 20. These are approximate dates.

Pisces is a Mutable, Water, feminine, receptive sign; it is ruled by Neptune and is co-ruled by Jupiter, and the planet Venus is exalted in this sign. It is the third of the Water signs manifested in their Mutable or changeable phase. The Water signs are learning the lesson of peace, that unchanging dynamic stillness behind all form and motion. They are motivated by their feelings, emotions, and intuitions. Pisces being Mutable draws upon past experience that is retained in the subconscious to make decisions and formulate a way of life. This may not be done on a conscious level; however, subtle forces are at work.

Wherever Pisces is found in the horoscope, the individual is susceptible to subliminal influences and emotional nuances from the environment. Water is related to the emotions and psychic energies; therefore wherever Pisces is found, individuals will be especially sensitive and responsive to the thoughts, feelings, and surroundings of their environment. These individuals unconsciously absorb the ideas and mental outlook of those with whom they come in contact. Often they will imitate their gestures and actions. Thus children born under this sign should be in an environment that is helpful and worthy of imitation and absorption.

Pisces individuals are engaged in an internal process of assimilation and understanding of a whole cycle of past experience in preparing for a new beginning. Neptune, which has to do with the past, and Jupiter, as co-ruler of Pisces, give strong religious feelings that are usually based on internal intuitive perception of spiritual reality, rather than external education or cultural conditioning. Many astrologers use the phrase "I believe" when speaking of Pisces. Jupiter is the planet of benevolence and compassion and has much to do with the development of the higher inspirational mind and unfoldment of the spiritual consciousness of the Pisces individual.

Venus is exalted in the sign Pisces and endows these individuals with an extreme sensitivity to beauty. Neptune, which rules Pisces and the imagination, is combined with this Venus influence, which gives the Piscean artistic or musical ability. Neptune can also bring wonderful spiritual vision to those who are ready to respond to its positive influence, giving them unconquerable faith, or they can get into a dreamy state neglecting the practical aspects of life. These individuals have a kind, easygoing nature with a tendency to let things drift. This tendency can be trying to those associates who are more practical. Pisces is a very psychic sign, and often Pisceans have visions of the future, telepathic ability, and an acute awareness of the past.

In the Water sign Pisces there are two great extremes of emotion. Sympathies can be played upon, or individuals put themselves in the place of another who suffers. This supersensitivity and emotionalism are the forces which Pisceans need to control and direct. The emotion of Pisces is never obvious like that of Cancer and never repressed like that of Scorpio; in Pisces it is often hidden like an underground river. Pisces eventually learns that every human being creates his or her own destiny, and every thought, feeling, and action will create its own pattern, and calls forth the needed compensating destiny which is ruled by Neptune and Jupiter.

Pisces rules our feet, the part of the body that sustains the whole. If the feet are not strong the rest of the body is thrown out of alignment; therefore it is very important for the individual to train the mind in concentration and train the body in quick obedience to the will. This Water sign calls for willed activity in a physical body in this physical world so that the inner resources can be developed to serve humanity in a quiet, unostentatious way. Cancer as a Water sign deals with old age, Scorpio as a Water sign deals with death and regeneration, and Pisces as the last of the Water signs deals with the rewards that are the result of past experiences. It is the natural ruler of the twelfth-house sign that indicates our hidden support or our self-undoing.

Wherever Pisces is found in the horoscope is where individuals have the desire to become absorbed into something bigger than themselves. In this department individuals have the opportunity to give and understand sympathy and to share the joys, suffering, and degradation of others. Some Pisceans want to lose themselves in sensation, drink, or drugs, allowing the negative phase of Neptune to operate in their life.

Virgo, the polar opposite sign of Pisces with its symbol of the maiden with the sheaves of wheat, represents the unending nourishment that has its source in the spiritual realms. When Pisces enters into this world of human suffering and labors to bring healing and relief, and brings the factor of faith into play, the purity, sustainment, and service represented by the sign Virgo lead the Pisces individual to the proper path of the spirit. These individuals are reminded of their mission to heal and to give moral help and direction to others. When this happens the conscious and subconscious mind will be in tune with the superconscious mind, maladjustment and unhappiness will be no more, and they will attain the peace which is the lesson of the Water signs through self-renunciation and service. Then Pisces becomes the symbol of hidden support.

Neptune, the planet of illusion, as ruler of Pisces, rules the imagination, and because of the tendency to become absorbed in something bigger than self many Pisceans become great actors, fulfilling their need to be absorbed into another reality.

Music, poetry, and art are other outlets for the Venus-Neptune-Jupiter influence, and most Pisceans are strongly attracted to these fields of activity.

Pisceans are easily influenced by external factors, and because they belong to a passive, feminine sign, they often suffer injuries rather than fight for their rights. However, when the supply of patience is exhausted they can become so provoked that it is impossible to calm them down, and they become very stubborn and will not allow anyone to reason with them.

The Mutable signs deal with the breath, and the blood needs oxygen. Thus when Piscean individuals learn to breathe deeply, they will find that they will become more positive and healthy. Conscious deep breathing is a necessity for the Pisces individual. Pisceans need the cooperation of the polar opposite sign Virgo in this conscious deep breathing if Pisceans are to overcome all the psychic influences that deter them from their mission in life and sap their vitality.

The first decanate of Pisces consists of 0 degrees of Pisces to 10 degrees of Pisces. This decanate applies to those born between February 19 and February 29. These are approximate dates. This decanate is known as the Pisces-Pisces or Neptune-Jupiter decanate. These individuals have a strong link with their subconscious mind and the subliminal impressions that flow from it. They are easily influenced by their environment which often subconsciously reminds them of past experience. This openness to impressions can make them feel ill at ease without consciously knowing why. Those born under this decanate are compassionate and sympathetic toward those less fortunate than themselves because of a subconscious remembrance of similar circumstances in their own past.

These individuals tend to be introspective and meditative. They have an intuitive ability coupled with a telepathic link that enables them to understand and enter into the feelings of others.

Venus is exalted in Pisces and Neptune the ruler enhances the visualization and clairvoyant faculties of these individuals, enabling them to create moods and illusions. Thus they make fine actors or can express themselves through art and music. Those with the Sun or planets prominent in this decanate can tap the accumulated wisdom of their subconscious. This ability needs to be understood and handled properly or it can become a two-edged sword, especially if the subconscious memories are associated with pain and unpleasantness If this is the case, the painful memories should be brought from the subconscious mind to the conscious mind, their origin determined and dealt with. Otherwise, there is the danger of neurotic or psychotic behavior. Those born under this decanate are often associated with hospitals, institutions, or work behind the scenes.

The second decanate of Pisces consists of 10 degrees of Pisces to 20 degrees of Pisces. This decanate applies to those born between March 1 and March 10. These are approximate dates. This decanate is known as the Pisces-Cancer or Neptune-Jupiter-Moon decanate. Jupiter and Neptune are exalted in Cancer, thus making this decanate similar to the first decanate. Cancer is a Cardinal sign, and because of this these individuals can act decisively when they feel a pressing, emotional need to do so. They often have close psychic, karmic, and emotional links with other members of their families. These individuals use their home as a place of spiritual retreat, contemplation, or some kind of imaginative or artistic expression. They lavish much time and energy on the home, making it artistic and pleasing. Many born under this decanate have a talent for gourmet cooking because of the Moon and Cancer influence which have a great deal to do with food and the preparation of it.

The third decanate of Pisces consists of 20 degrees of Pisces to 30 degrees of Pisces. This decanate applies to those born between March 11 and March 20. These are approximate dates. This decanate is known as the Pisces-Scorpio or Neptune-Jupiter-Pluto-Mars decanate. The planets in this decanate are all involved with the evolution of our higher intuitive and spiritual faculties. Those with this decanate prominent in the horoscope have great willpower, strength, and determination because of the Fixed Mars-Pluto-Uranus influence of Scorpio. These individuals will follow through with the projects they start, using the resourcefulness inherent in Scorpio. They will also utilize their skills and memory of past experiences, indicated by the Mutable sign Pisces. This planetary combination enables them to use past experiences to improve existing circumstances and also enables them to initiate new enterprises.

This decanate is the last decanate of the entire Zodiac, and it is intimately associated with the spiritual process of death and rebirth. Those born in this decanate are engaged in the process of regenerating and making the contents of the subconscious mind conscious in preparation for the new cycle of evolutionary experience that begins with Aries. The Mars, Pluto, and Scorpio influence inherent in this Piscean decanate indicates the complete Pluto process of death, regeneration, and renewal. All the accumulated debris of the subconscious mind that no longer serves a useful purpose must be consumed by the transmuting fire of Pluto. This is one of the most interesting, most powerful, and intense phases of the zodiacal cycle or spiral of evolutionary growth.

These individuals have a great emotional intensity that they must learn to direct in a calm and focused way. Just as there is great calm and peace at the center of the hurricane, these individuals must find the center or "I" of their own emotional storms. These storms can be brought into harmony by meditation and spiritual unfoldment. Many inspired geniuses have their Sun in this decanate, as this decanate confers profound insights into the fundamental laws of the universe.

6

The Twelve House Patterns

The most commonly used system in Western astrology is the Tropical Placidean system of house cusps, on which this work is based. Each house represents a department of life and indicates a certain type of activity and the circumstances around that activity. It is important to know what each house represents, what affairs of life are included in each house, and what sphere of activity is represented by each house.

Unlike the signs of the Zodiac, which consist of 30 degrees each, the houses in the personal horoscope are not always of equal arc when the horoscope is cast for the time, date, and place of birth. This is seen by the uneven degrees and minutes on the house cusps after the horoscope is cast. The mathematical formula determines the signs, degrees, and minutes found on each house cusp. However, for purposes of study the houses are treated as twelve divisions of the horoscope. Each of the twelve houses has its own meaning, and the *position and meaning* of a house *never change*.

The houses are numbered in a counterclockwise manner, beginning with the first house and starting at the easternmost point of the wheel and proceeding in sequential order down in a counterclockwise direction.*

* See the chart on "Division of the Natural Horoscope Wheel" on page 117.

The Division of the Horoscope Wheel into Houses

The horoscopic wheel is divided into twelve parts called houses. The houses represent the different areas of experience in an individual's life. The lines that separate one house from the other are called cusps, or simply cusp. The term commonly used is "cusp of the first house" or cusp of any of the other houses.

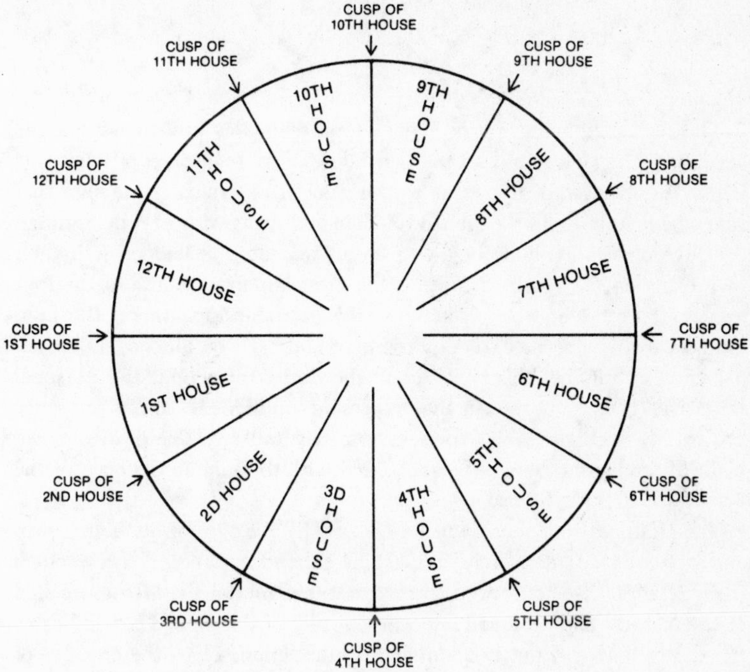

The First-House Pattern

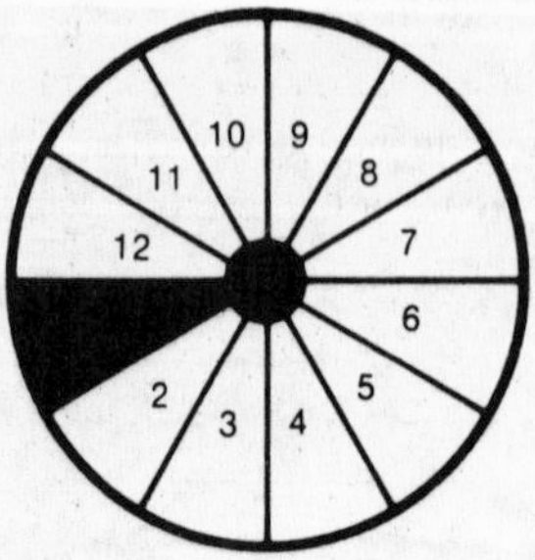

The darkened part of this wheel represents the first house and its activities. The sign found on the first house cusp, regardless of what sign it may be, is related in a sense to the sign Aries, which is the sign that rules the first house in the Natural Zodiac and deals with new beginnings. At this point individuals begin to operate as unique beings with their own experiences. The first house is the most important house of the four angles. It represents the personality, the personal appearance, the individual's awareness, the early environment and early childhood, the physical body and its health or lack of it, the desire for action, and personal initiative. This is the house that represents individuals' basic reference toward life and how their experiences are assimilated. The psychological traits of the first house will be associated with the sign on the cusp of the first house after the horoscope is cast.

The affairs of this house will be colored by the sign on its house cusp and its planetary ruler. They will also be colored by the sign Aries, which is the Natural first-house sign, also Mars the planet of the first-house sign of the Natural Zodiac, and Pluto, the co-ruler of this sign. Mars indicates the desire that will put the individual into action, Pluto the co-ruler of Aries indicates how the will is used to elevate the desires and actions to a higher level of expression. Next to be taken into consideration in the interpretation of this house and its activities is whether the sign on the cusp is a Cardinal, Fixed, or Mutable sign, indicating the modes of action.

If a Cardinal sign is rising, the individual will want and need activity and will be action-oriented and concerned with immediate circumstances.

If a Fixed sign is rising, individuals will be goal-oriented and determined with fixed aims in their life.

If a Mutable sign is rising, individuals will be aware of and utilize their skills in their projection into life. They will be versatile and adaptable.

Next, note whether the sign belongs to the Fire, Earth, Air, or Water element and whether the individual projects in an optimistic, creative, and inspirational manner, which would be Fire; or in a practical, down-to-earth manner, which would be Earth; or in an intellectual way with an interest in others and what they are experiencing, which would indicate an Air sign rising; or whether the projection is based on emotional response, which would indicate a Water sign rising.

The next step in understanding this house and its activities is to determine whether the rising sign is a positive, masculine sign, which would indicate that the individual would initiate activity without waiting for someone or something to prod him or her into action, or is the rising sign or ascendant a receptive, feminine sign, indicating that the individual will be stimulated into action by others, be confronted by circumstances that force him or her into action, or at times wait for the opportune time to go into action.

If the sign on the cusp of the first house is a positive, masculine sign and its planetary ruler is also placed in a positive, masculine sign, individuals will express themselves aggressively, initiate actions on their own, and carry through with some measure of leadership. They will be self-propelling individuals with a positive outlook.

If the sign on the Ascendant is a positive, masculine sign and the planetary ruler is placed in a receptive, feminine sign, individuals will take the initiative in affairs. However, after getting things started or verbalizing ideas for action, they will wait for circumstances or others to motivate them to further action. Or they will wait for the proper time to carry on with the activities they initiated. In other words, these individuals initiate action and then wait for development.

If the sign on the Ascendant is a receptive, feminine sign and the planetary ruler is in a positive, masculine sign, individuals are stimulated into action by others or are confronted by circumstances that force action or they go into action when they feel it is an opportune time to do so. Once the individual has been introduced to the possibilities of action, the ruler being in a positive, masculine sign indicates that the individual will then take the initiative and display leadership abilities in a positive, aggressive manner.

If the sign on the Ascendant is a receptive, feminine sign and its planetary ruler is placed in a receptive, feminine sign, individuals will rarely initiate action on their own. These individuals will be passive and interact with what comes their way. This does not mean that these individuals are not capable of acting forcibly; however, they usually wait for things to come to them or to be confronted with circumstances before going into action. These individuals can display great strength in passive perseverance.

These patterns are not to be judged as favorable or unfavorable. They merely represent the modus operandi of individuals and the way they reach out into life.

The next consideration in judging the first house is the aspects that are made to the Ascendant by planets. For this information see "Part II: Interpreting Aspects" of *The Astrologer's Handbook* that deals with planets in aspect to the Ascendant. Also see the chapter in this text, "Planet Patterns," that describes the ruler of the first house, whatever the planet may be.

The next consideration in dealing with the first house is to verify whether there are any planets in the first house. If there are planets in the first house, the pattern of this planet or planets must be studied as given in this text, and also the planet in the sign and house as given in *The Astrologer's Handbook*.

The next step is to determine what aspects if any the planets in the first house make to other planets in the horoscope. After the aspects have been determined, look up their meaning in "Part II: Interpreting Aspects" of *The Astrologer's Handbook*.

The planets found in the first house and the planets making aspects to them, the signs and houses in which these planets are found, the signs and houses these planets rule, and the signs and houses that contain their exalted rulers will all be part of the first-house expression of the individual. Combining all these factors is the art of astrological interpretation and should be at the command of every practicing astrologer.

The Second-House Pattern

The second house represents the material resources individuals require to sustain themselves. It indicates the ability to earn money and to acquire the material possessions the individual needs. The second house, regardless of the sign found on the cusp, corresponds to Taurus, which is the sign that belongs on the second house of the Natural Zodiac; therefore it is colored by the sign Taurus and the ruling planet, which is Venus. The second house deals with the earning and spending capacity

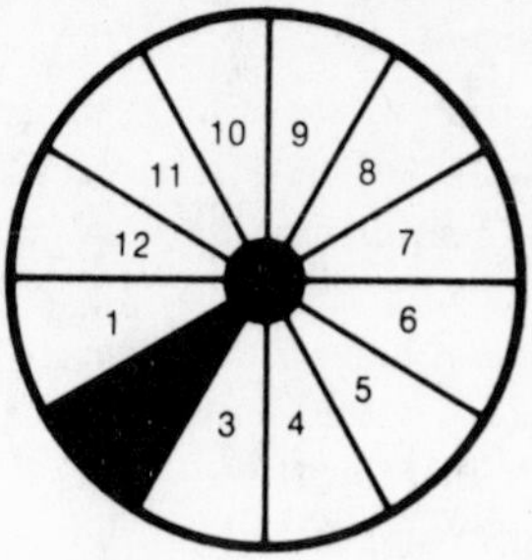

of individuals. It indicates the manner in which they meet their obligations and how they acquire and utilize material resources. The second house deals with values and especially what is of value to individuals. It represents their contact with their means of emotional and material security which they feel will bring them peace. This house deals with what individuals own, possess, or acquire. It has a lot to do with business activities and dealing with banks or other financial institutions. It has also to do with the pursuit of destiny, because Venus, which rules the Natural second house, is exalted in Pisces, and this colors the sign on the second house which indicates how the individual goes about pursuing destiny. When the planets in the heavens travel through this area of the horoscope or when they make aspects to this house, the activities of the house are intensified. This is true when planets contact any house.

If the sign on the second-house cusp is a Cardinal sign, individuals will be decisive, active, and sometimes impulsive in handling the affairs of the house. Individuals feel a need for action, and the present circumstances of these affairs are of primary concern to them. Individuals are likely to be opportunistic regarding these affairs.

If the sign on the second-house cusp is a Fixed sign, individuals will be determined and goal-oriented and the future development of these second-house affairs will be of primary concern to them.

If the sign on the second-house cusp is a Mutable sign, individuals' approach to their second-house affairs will be mental and adaptable. They will use past skills and experience in handling these affairs and will not be overly concerned with their present or future ramifications. However, past misfortunes could interfere with present or future success if they allow themselves to become trapped in their memories.

If the sign on the second-house cusp is a Fire sign, individuals will go about their second-house affairs in an energetic and enthusiastic manner, and they will display creativity, initiative, and leadership ability in the affairs of this house.

If the sign on the second-house cusp is an Earth sign, the affairs of the house will be handled in a practical way. Individuals' money-making activities are geared to comfort and security, and material possessions will be of consequence.

If the sign on the second house is an Air sign, individuals will handle the affairs of this house in an intellectual manner. The ideas and mental deliberations concerning these matters will be of primary concern. Individuals will study and communicate about them in an intellectual framework with a detached and dispassionate attitude.

If the sign on the second house is a Water sign, individuals will handle the affairs of the house in an emotional way. Decisions on matters involved in that house will be based on feelings, emotional considerations, and intuitive perceptions.

If the sign on the second house cusp is a positive, masculine sign, individuals will initiate activities in these second-house matters, and if they are unhappy with the circumstances of the second house, they will initiate action to improve the conditions of the affairs of the second house.

If the planetary ruler of the positive second-house sign is found in a positive, masculine sign, individuals will display leadership and aggressive tendencies in the acquisition of their material and emotional needs.

If the planetary ruler of the positive second-house sign is found in a receptive, feminine sign, individuals will initiate activities in regard to second-house matters; however, once they have initiated these activities, they will wait to attract the people and circumstances that will further their desired ends in pursuit of their emotional and material security.

If the sign on the second-house cusp is a receptive, feminine sign, individuals will accept the status quo of the affairs of this house; however, they will wait until the opportune time to change these circumstances that will improve these conditions or will attract someone who will prod them or help them to change the conditions.

If the planetary ruler of the receptive sign is in a positive, masculine sign, individuals will take the stimuli provided by others or the circumstances involving these affairs and initiate action in an aggressive way that will supply them with the emotional and material security that they feel they need. Any aspects to the planetary ruler or rulers of the house must be taken into consideration also.

If the planetary ruler of the receptive second-house sign is found in a receptive, feminine sign, individuals will accept the status quo, wait for opportunities to present themselves, and interact with what comes their way. In this manner they attract to themselves the emotional and material security they feel they need. Any aspects to the planetary ruler or rulers of the house must be taken into consideration also.

These patterns are not to be judged as favorable or unfavorable. They merely represent the modus operandi of individuals and the way individuals deal with the affairs of the second house.

In dealing with the second house, the next step to be considered is to ascertain whether there are any planets in the second house. The principles of these planets must be studied. (See the chapter on planets in their patterns in this text and planets in their signs and houses in *The Astrologer's Handbook.*)

The next step is to determine whether the planets are making any aspects to other planets. (These aspects are to be studied under the planets in their patterns in this text and planets in aspect to other planets in *The Astrologer's Handbook.*) The aspects must be interpreted, the houses that are interrelated by the planets forming the aspects; the houses that carry the signs that these planets rule and the houses where the exalted rulers of the planets involved in the aspect are found; and whether the planets involved in the aspect are Cardinal, Fixed, or Mutable signs; whether they are in Fire, Earth, Air, or Water signs; and finally whether they are in positive or receptive signs. All these factors must be integrated, indicating how the action of one department affects other departments of the life.

The Third-House Pattern

The third house deals with the conscious mind. It is in this house that individuals receive lessons in accurate perception. This type of perception implies that the conscious mind must exercise judgment and discrimination in choosing what the attention is allowed to dwell upon.

Metaphysics teaches that individuals are constantly creating themselves in the image of their focus of thoughts. The emotional responses and actions energize the thought patterns and bring them into material expression. Mercury, the ruler of the Natural third house, will indicate whether this expression will produce positive growth or confusion and negativity. Therefore the sign that is found on the third-house cusp and the ruler of that sign will color the thought processes of the individual. For this reason it is essential that the individual develop accurate, logical, and practical reasoning powers. Mercury is exalted in the sign Aquarius and signifies the intuitive flashes of sudden insights that can come only through a mind that is constructive in its thinking and is not glutted with erroneous concepts. These intuitive flashes are linked to Jupiter, the ruler of the opposite house and sign of Sagittarius which deals with growth and expansion. Thus the right choice of mental focus is a requisite if individuals are to mold their destiny in a constructive manner within their social environment.

The third house is concerned with the assimilation, processing, and circulation of information. It deals with the daily mental exchange that individuals have with others. Thus it rules brothers, sisters, all blood relatives (except mother and father), neighbors, neighborhood, short-distance traveling, general comings and goings, communication of all kinds, personal ideas, ideas for handling personal resources, study, practical decision-making, mental alertness or lack of it, rumors, news, changes of environment, arms, wrists, hands and fingers, speech and hearing, contracts and agreements, lungs and shoulders, and the nervous system.

Procedure for Delineating the Third House

Classify the sign pattern of the fourth house by:

1. The triplicity to which it belongs: Fire, Earth, Air, or Water pattern.
2. The quadruplicity to which it belongs: Cardinal, Fixed, or Mutable pattern.
3. Does the sign on the third house belong to the positive, masculine or receptive, feminine pattern?
4. Is the planetary ruler of the third-house sign in a positive, masculine or receptive, feminine sign?
5. Planets found in the third house and their aspects to other planets, if there are any.
6. The signs and houses in which the planets forming the aspects are found.

7. The signs and houses that the planets forming the aspects rule.
8. The signs and houses in which the exalted rulers of the planets involved in the aspects to the third-house planets are placed.
9. The aspects made to the planetary ruler or rulers of the third house.

For further assistance in delineating the factors involved in this house, refer to the procedure outlined in detail in the second-house pattern.

The Fourth-House Pattern

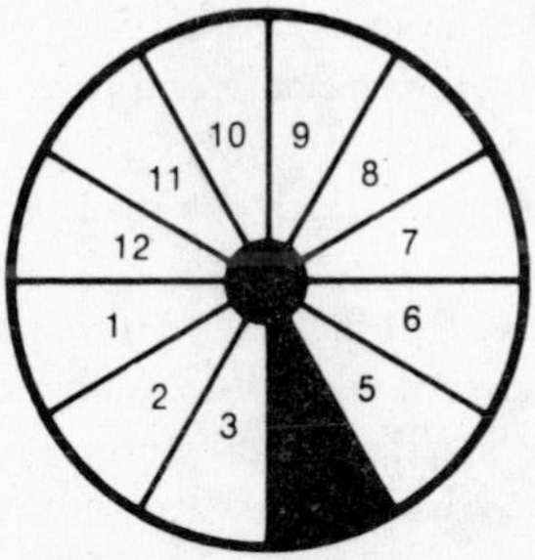

The fourth house is the house of the home. It indicates the conditions that exist in the domestic scene; however, the fourth house represents the home that individuals make for themselves, whether it is a room, an apartment, or a house. The fourth house represents the platform individuals use for collecting, organizing, and utilizing the things which individuals need to maintain and express themselves. The fourth house also represents the psychological home environment that individuals carry within themselves regardless of where they may live on the Earth's surface. In a broad sense it represents the mental and emotional conditioning with which individuals have become comfortable. A lot can be discerned about the mental and emotional characteristics of individuals from the environment that they create.

The fourth house represents the land itself and the stage upon which the drama of life is acted out. The fourth house rules the conditions that will prevail in the last half of life for which the first was made. The fourth house deals with the home, food, laundry, household items, the home environment, conditioned emotional habit patterns, ingrained emotional attitudes which determine individual responses, family affairs, relationships with parents, activity in the home, concerns related to the land and the Earth itself, and family tradition. The sign on the house cusp has a lot to do with the way the digestive organs function and is related to the stomach and breast.

Procedure for Delineating the Fourth House

Classify the sign pattern of the fourth house by:

1. The triplicity to which it belongs: Fire, Earth, Air, or Water pattern.
2. The quadruplicity to which it belongs: Cardinal, Fixed, or Mutable pattern.
3. Does the sign on the fourth house belong to the positive, masculine or receptive, feminine pattern?
4. Is the planetary ruler of the fourth-house sign in a positive, masculine or receptive, feminine sign?
5. Planets found in the fourth house and their aspects to other planets, if there are any.
6. The signs and houses in which the planets forming the aspects are found.
7. The signs and houses that the planets forming the aspects rule.
8. The signs and houses in which the exalted rulers of the planets involved in the aspects to the fourth-house planets are placed.
9. The aspects made to the planetary ruler or rulers of the fourth house.

For further assistance in delineating the factors involved in this house, refer to the procedure outlined in detail in the second-house pattern.

The Fifth-House Pattern

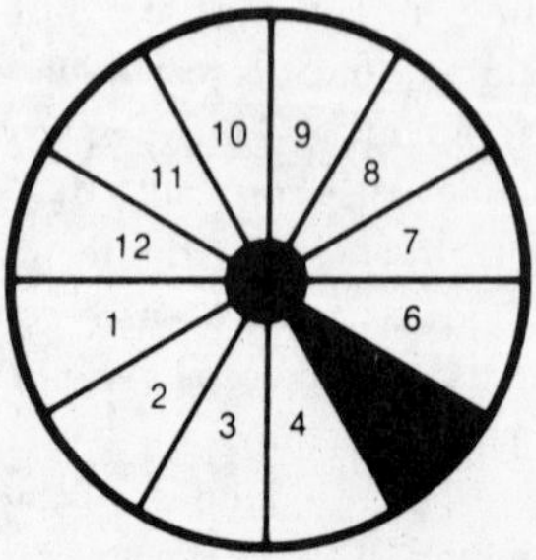

The fifth house is the house of creative expression, the house of mental and physical procreation which represents the children of the mind and body. This is the house of the creative arts, especially the performing arts. It is the house of love affairs and romantic attachments that can lead to marriage, but it does not deal with marriage per se. Marriage is a legal matter involving responsibility, as exemplified in the text on the Saturn pattern. The fifth house deals with pleasures, sex for pleasure, places of amusement, and social entertainment. The fifth house deals with children, their upbringing, and their early education. Both the third and the fifth deal with the primary education of the individual. The fifth house deals with education in a general sense. It has to do with teaching and sports. It deals with all functions, whether social or otherwise, in which the individual seeks a creative self-expression and social popularity. Above all the fifth house represents the areas of life where the dynamic powers of the individual can be expressed and dramatized in a creative expression of love. The fifth house also deals with financial speculation, stock-market activity, pregnancy and childbirth, pleasures, vacations, entertainment, and relaxation.

Procedure for Delineating the Fifth House

Classify the sign pattern of the fifth house by:

1. The triplicity to which it belongs: Fire, Earth, Air, or Water pattern.
2. The quadruplicity to which it belongs: Cardinal, Fixed, or Mutable pattern.
3. Does the sign on the fifth house belong to the positive, masculine or receptive, feminine pattern?
4. Is the planetary ruler of the fifth-house sign in a positive, masculine or receptive, feminine sign?
5. Planets found in the fifth house and their aspects to other planets, if there are any.
6. The signs and houses in which the planets forming the aspects are found.
7. The signs and houses that the planets forming the aspects rule.
8. The signs and houses in which the exalted rulers of the planets involved in the aspects to the fifth-house planets are found.
9. The aspects to the planetary ruler or rulers of the fifth house.

For further assistance in delineating the factors involved in this house, refer to the procedure outlined in the second-house pattern.

The Sixth-House Pattern

The sixth house is concerned with work and service and the ability to use the mind in a practical way in performing useful tasks. It deals with the individual's attitude toward work and service. It is concerned with the work and detail methodology that is necessary to bring into fruition that which was creatively envisioned in the fifth house. In the sixth house individuals learn to work with the intricate details of service to the

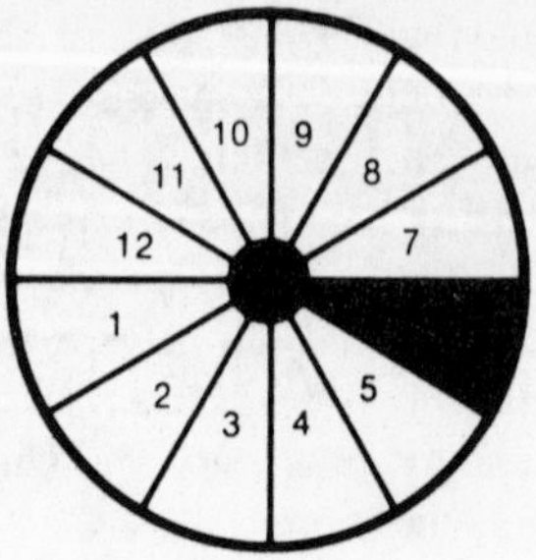

world. The sixth house is essential to the individuals' learning processes. It is through work, concentration, efficiency, and devotion in handling practical tasks and responsibility that the polar opposite sign Pisces and its rulers Neptune and Jupiter will be brought into play, which will stimulate the imagination to further creativity and expand the skills of individuals. Mercury is the primary planetary ruler of this sixth house, dealing with ideas and the communication of ideas that help to enlarge individuals' capacity and ability for service. Mercury as the ruler of the Natural sixth house deals with the proper care and maintenance of the physical body. The sixth house has to do with the health of the physical body or the lack of it, and in this sense is connected with the first house which rules the physical body. Mercury as the ruler of the Natural sixth house shows that individuals' ways of thinking have to do with their work attitudes and health.

The sixth house deals with work or services rendered, involuntary service, dietary habits, and personal hygiene, dealings with doctors or medical personnel, conditions in the work environment, occupational hazards, and clothing. It is related to the intestines, employees, subordinates, domestic animals, and co-workers.

Procedure for Delineating the Sixth House

Classify the sign pattern of the sixth house by:

1. The triplicity to which it belongs: Fire, Earth, Air, or Water pattern.
2. The quadruplicity to which it belongs: Cardinal, Fixed, or Mutable pattern.
3. Does the sign on the sixth house belong to the positive, masculine or receptive, feminine pattern?

4. Is the planetary ruler of the sixth-house sign in a positive, masculine or receptive, feminine sign?
5. Planets found in the sixth house and their aspects to other planets, if there are any.
6. The signs and houses in which the planets forming the aspects are found.
7. The signs and houses that the planets forming the aspects rule.
8. The signs and houses in which the exalted rulers of the planets involved in the aspects to the sixth-house planets are placed.
9. The aspects to the planetary ruler or rulers of the sixth house.

For further assistance in delineating the factors involved in this house, refer to the procedure outlined in detail in the second-house pattern.

The Seventh-House Pattern

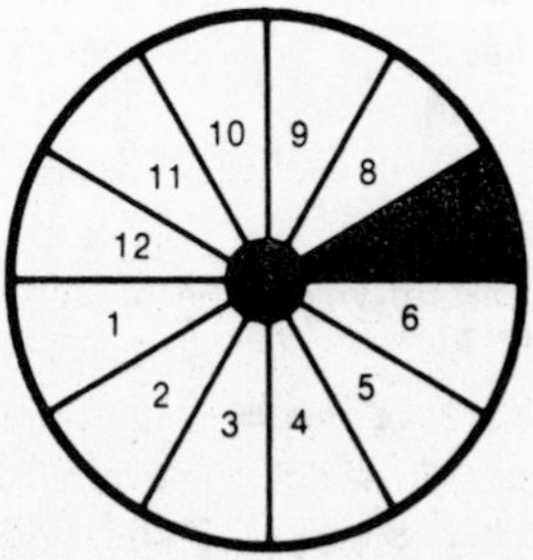

The seventh house deals with all relationships such as marriage, business partnerships, and close personal relationships, and it has to do with the public. The type of sign on the seventh-house cusp and the sign in which the planetary ruler is found describe the kind of business partner or marriage partner the individual is likely to attract. The seventh house deals with the individual's contact with the public; it has to do with legal affairs and the forming of contracts and agreements. (However, the third house deals with the contract itself.) It deals with business representatives and public relations people. The seventh house is the house of open adversaries, open enemies, and law suits. It has a great deal to do with the law of karma or compensation. This is because Saturn is exalted in Libra, which is the ruler of the Natural seventh house, and because the polar-opposite first house deals with the individuals themselves and what they do in the world, while the seventh house deals with what the world does to them.

The seventh house deals with responsibility to others, the need to cooperate with others, the reaction to others' personal action, social awareness, personal sense of justice and fair play, social activity connected with business or public relations, and conditions of the marriage relationship. It relates to the kidneys, a general description of the wife or husband, opponents and lower courts.

Procedure for Delineating the Seventh House

Classify the sign pattern of the seventh house by:

1. The triplicity to which it belongs: Fire, Earth, Air, or Water pattern.
2. The quadruplicity to which it belongs: Cardinal, Fixed, or Mutable pattern.
3. Does the sign on the seventh house belong to the positive, masculine or receptive, feminine pattern?
4. Is the planetary ruler of the seventh-house sign in a positive, masculine or receptive, feminine sign?
5. Planets found in the seventh house and their aspects to other planets, if there are any.
6. The signs and houses in which the planets forming the aspects are found.
7. The signs and houses that the planets forming the aspects rule.
8. The signs and houses in which the exalted rulers of the planets involved in the aspects to the seventh-house planets are placed.
9. The aspects to the planetary ruler or rulers of the seventh house.

For further assistance in delineating the factors involved in this house, refer to the procedure outlined in detail in the second-house pattern.

The Eighth-House Pattern

The eighth house deals with joint resources as opposed to personal property as indicated by the polar-opposite second house. Therefore the eighth house deals with money as a result of combined effort. It deals with inherited money or money belonging to business or marriage partners. It deals with insurances, taxes, and goods of the dead. It can indicate conflict over jointly held wealth if the eighth house receives stress aspects from other planets. It deals with death and matters connected with death, such as funerals, wills, and legacies. The sign on the eighth-house cusp indicates the way in which individuals terminate cycles of

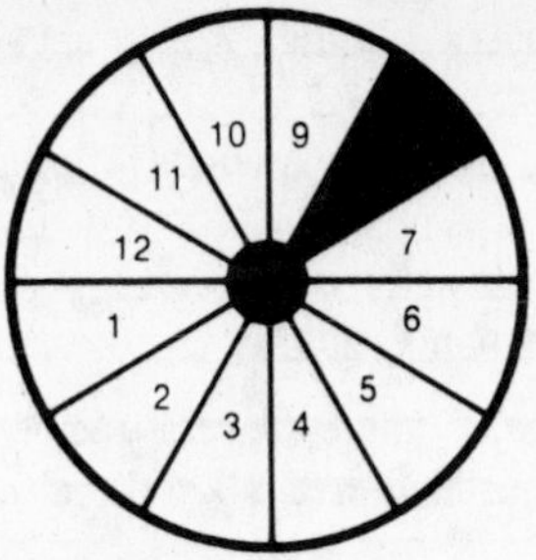

their lives and make new starts that add to the quality of their lives. The eighth house deals with subtle occult energy forces that are the internal causes of physical manifestation. It deals with higher mathematics, atomic physics, and internal mystical experiences. It deals with sex as used in procreation. This house also deals with communication with discarnate spirits.

The eighth house deals with transformation of personal motivation for better or worse; this is because Uranus is exalted in the sign Scorpio, which is the ruler of the Natural eighth house. It deals with recycling of old discarded or outworn items and resources, the handling of waste products, sexual energy, need for spiritual regeneration, interest in reincarnation and life after death, parapsychology and occult subjects, clairvoyance, and other paranormal abilities. It rules the external sex organs and rectum. It deals with creative energy and the sex force, the nature and manner of the individual's death, occupations connected with death, autopsies, and postmortems. The eighth house also deals with corporate money and funding.

Procedure for Delineating the Eighth House

Classify the sign pattern of the twelfth house by:

1. The triplicity to which it belongs: Fire, Earth, Air, or Water pattern.
2. The quadruplicity to which it belongs: Cardinal, Fixed, or Mutable pattern.
3. Does the sign on the eighth house belong to the positive, masculine or receptive, feminine pattern?
4. Is the planetary ruler of the eighth-house sign in a positive, masculine or receptive, feminine sign?
5. Planets found in the eighth house and their aspects to other planets, if there are any.

6. The signs and houses in which the planets forming the aspects are found.
7. The signs and houses that the planets forming the aspects rule.
8. The signs and houses in which the exalted rulers of the planets involved in the aspects to the eighth-house planets are placed.
9. The aspects to the planetary ruler or rulers of the eighth house.

For further assistance in delineating the factors involved in this house, refer to the procedure outlined in detail in the second-house pattern.

The Ninth-House Pattern

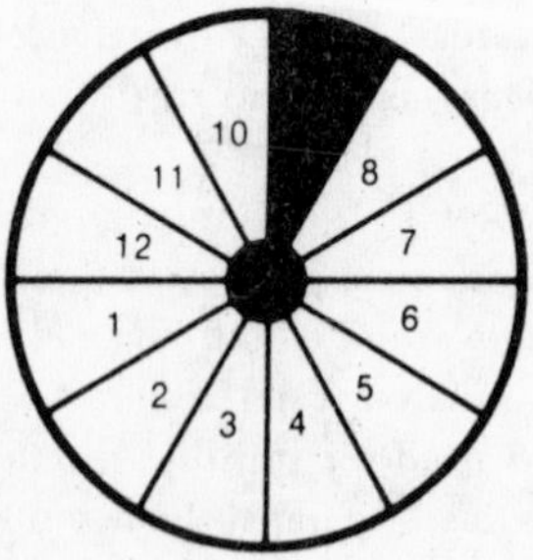

The ninth house deals with religion, philosophy, law, and self-motivated education. It deals with all institutions in which the social concepts developed in the course of civilization are embodied and taught. It deals with the abstract mind of intuition and inspiration because Jupiter and Neptune are ruler and co-ruler of the Natural ninth house. It deals with the individual's religious and philosophic beliefs. It deals with worldwide contacts, foreign countries, foreigners, and long-distance travel. It deals with publishing and publishers as they pertain to an individual. It deals with in-laws unless the in-laws live in close proximity, such as neighbors; then the in-laws can come under the third house. The ninth house deals with higher education; personal, cultural, religious, philosophic ideals and principles; moral codes; all codification of cultural thought and tradition; and personal conscience based on philosophic and religious values and cultural conditioning. The ninth house is related to the hips, thighs, buttocks, and the sciatic nerve. It rules clergymen, the church, and places far removed from the place of birth.

Procedure for Delineating the Ninth House

Classify the sign pattern of the ninth house by:

1. The triplicity to which it belongs: Fire, Earth, Air, or Water pattern.
2. The quadruplicity to which it belongs: Cardinal, Fixed, or Mutable pattern.
3. Does the sign on the ninth house belong to the positive, masculine or receptive, feminine pattern?
4. Is the planetary ruler of the ninth-house sign in a positive, masculine or receptive, feminine sign?
5. Planets found in the ninth house and their aspects to other planets, if there are any.
6. The signs and houses in which the planets forming the aspects are found.
7. The signs and houses that the planets forming the aspects rule.
8. The signs and houses in which the exalted rulers of the planets involved in the aspects to the ninth-house planets are placed.
9. The aspects to the planetary ruler or rulers of the ninth house.

For further assistance in delineating the factors involved in this house, refer to the procedure outlined in detail in the second-house pattern.

The Tenth-House Pattern

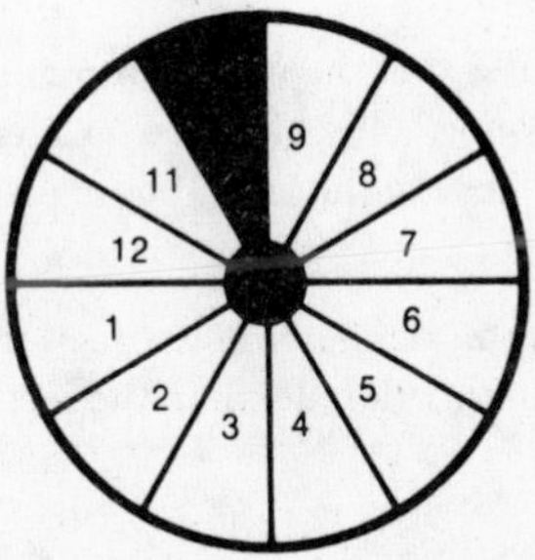

The tenth house deals with individuals' professional and public reputations and their careers. It deals with individuals' relationships to the business and political power structures that affect their world. The sign on the tenth house cusp and its planetary ruler indicate how the individual's ambition will be manifested. It indicates favor or disfavor from those in authority, employers, and people in high positions of power. It deals with those in the executive branch of the government, also with official governmental power structures. The tenth house represents individuals' status and standing in the world in which they move and how they carry out their responsibilities. The tenth house also deals with the parents, usually the father, but not in all cases. The tenth house deals with desire for power and status, fall from position if power is misused, and administrative responsibilities and duties. The tenth house is related to the knees. It represents achievements and promotions.

Procedure for Delineating the Tenth House

Classify the sign pattern of the tenth house by:

1. The triplicity to which it belongs: Fire, Earth, Air, or Water pattern.
2. The quadruplicity to which it belongs: Cardinal, Fixed, or Mutable pattern.
3. Does the sign on the tenth house belong to the positive, masculine or receptive, feminine pattern?
4. Is the planetary ruler of the tenth-house sign in a positive, masculine or receptive, feminine sign?
5. Planets found in the tenth house and their aspects to other planets, if there are any.
6. The signs and houses in which the planets forming the aspects are found.
7. The signs and houses that the planets forming the aspects rule.
8. The signs and houses in which the exalted rulers of the planets involved in the aspects to the tenth-house planets are placed.
9. The aspects to the planetary ruler or rulers of the tenth house.

For further assistance in delineating the factors involved in this house, refer to the procedure outlined in detail in the second-house pattern.

The Eleventh-House Pattern

The eleventh house deals with the individual's goals, objectives, hopes and wishes, and the feeling of significance and fulfillment that these give to the individual. The sign on the eleventh house cusp, and the sign the planetary ruler is found in will describe the kind of friends and group associates the individual has and how these friendships and group asso-

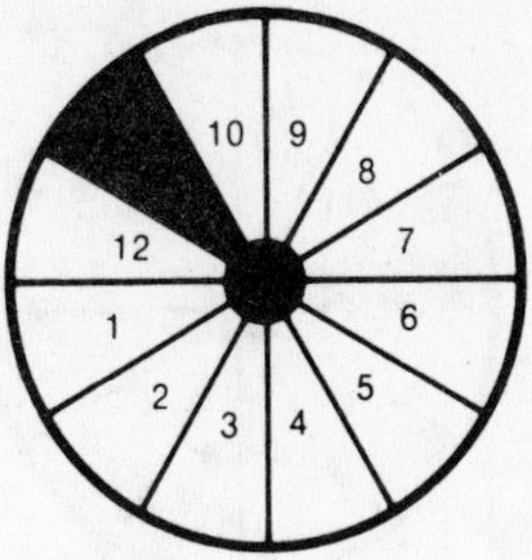

ciations are formed. Because Uranus is the ruler of the Natural eleventh house, it indicates the individual's openness to new ideas as revealed by Uranus. It deals with group creativity, occult, scientific, and humanitarian interests, universal brotherhood, a detached mental outlook, revolt against the abuse of power, and awareness of the universal laws and principles. It is related to the ankles.

Procedure for Delineating the Eleventh House

Classify the sign pattern of the eleventh house by:

1. The triplicity to which it belongs: Fire, Earth, Air, or Water pattern.
2. The quadruplicity to which it belongs: Cardinal, Fixed, or Mutable pattern.
3. Does the sign on the eleventh house belong to the positive, masculine or receptive, feminine pattern?
4. Is the planetary ruler of the eleventh-house sign in a positive, masculine or receptive, feminine sign?
5. Planets found in the eleventh house and their aspects to other planets, if there are any.
6. The signs and houses in which the planets forming the aspects are found.
7. The signs and houses that the planets forming the aspects rule.
8. The signs and houses in which the exalted rulers of the planets involved in the aspects to the eleventh-house planets are placed.
9. The aspects to the planetary ruler or rulers of the eleventh house.

For further assistance in delineating the factors involved in this house, refer to the procedure outlined in detail in the second-house pattern.

The Twelfth-House Pattern

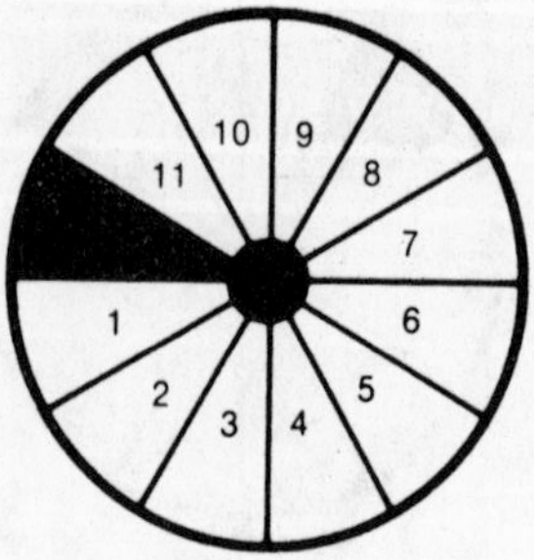

The twelfth house deals with the individual's psychological health; it is the house where the individual must work on making conscious the contents of the unconscious mind. This house deals with individuals' unconscious memories that are closely related to their karma or the law of cause and effect. The twelfth house deals with secret enemies and the result of past actions and relationships; thus it is the house of hidden support or self-undoing. The twelfth house deals with hospitals, mental institutions, religious retreats, places of solitude, jails, prisons, and other places of confinement. The twelfth house deals with the unconscious mind, private affairs of life, meditation, mysticism, intuitive awareness, imagination, the dream state, quiet appreciation of beauty, self-deception, unconscious distortions, neurotic tendencies, escapist tendencies, flights into fantasy, and wool gathering. It is related to the feet, limitations, restrictions, the accumulated results of the past which must be dealt with in the present, and it is what we bring into this life with us.

Procedure for Delineating the Twelfth House

Classify the sign pattern o fthe twelfth house by:

1. The triplicity to which it belongs: Fire, Earth, Air, or Water pattern.
2. The quadruplicity to which it belongs: Cardinal, Fixed, or Mutable pattern.
3. Does the sign on the twelfth house belong to the positive, masculine or receptive, feminine pattern?
4. Is the planetary ruler of the twelfth-house sign in a positive, masculine or receptive, feminine sign?
5. Planets found in the twelfth house and their aspects to other planets, if there are any.

6. The signs and houses in which the planets forming the aspects are found.
7. The signs and houses that the planets forming the aspects rule.
8. The signs and houses in which the exalted rulers of the planets involved in the aspects to the twelfth-house planets are placed.
9. The aspects to the planetary ruler or rulers of the twelfth house.

For further assistance in delineating the factors involved in this house, refer to the procedure outlined in detail in the second-house pattern.

As the planets in the heavens travel from one sign to the next, they activate the different areas of the horoscope. This activity of the planets in relation to the Natal Horoscope is called *transits*. The way the affairs of these houses will be stimulated or activated by the transiting planets is dependent upon the personal horoscope of the individual and the stage of growth that is to be mastered and the lessons that need to be learned. The transits activate inherent talents and skills that need to be unfolded and utilized. For information on the transits of the planets, see *Predictive Astrology* (Harper & Row).

7

Evaluating the Strength and Weakness of Planets

Every sign of the Zodiac has a planetary ruler, and some of the signs have their own primary ruler plus a co-ruler. Every sign of the Zodiac has an exalted ruler, and when a planet is found in the sign of its exaltation, it is in its most powerful sign position for volume or intensity of energy. This differs from a planet's rulership of its own sign, which provides the best possible conditions for the planet to most easily express itself. However, these conditions do not necessarily generate the planet's power. Much like a lamp that is plugged into a wall socket, the electricity that lights the lamp comes from a central power station. The wall, the wires, and the socket provide the conditions for the electricity to manifest itself. In this analogy the walls, wires, and socket represent a ruling planet found in its own sign. The power station represents the planet as the exalted ruler of a sign. When a planet is found in the sign of its exaltation, it is in its most powerful position for volume or intensity of energy.

If there is to be a proper evaluation of the strength and power of a planet in astrological interpretation, the signs and houses that are less conducive to the expression of the power of a planet should also be considered. This kind of positioning of planets is signified as a planet in its detriment or fall, indicating that the planet is limited in the expression of its basic characteristics.

A planet in its fall is always found in the sign opposite to the planet's exaltation. When a planet is in its fall it is weak and debilitated.

When a planet is in its detriment it is always found in the sign opposite its primary rulership. When a planet is in its detriment it is in a sign that limits expression, but it does not necessarily mean that it is weak. Thus a planet in its detriment is in a more favorable position than a planet in its fall because in the latter it is weak and debilitated.

The Sun is exalted in Aries, in its fall in the opposite sign Libra, in its rulership in Leo, and in its detriment in the opposite sign Aquarius.

The Moon is exalted in Taurus, in its fall in the opposite sign Scorpio, in its rulership in Cancer, and in its detriment in the opposite sign Capricorn.

Mercury is exalted in Aquarius, in its fall in the opposite sign Leo. Mercury is the primary ruler of Gemini and also Virgo. This combination must be taken into consideration when dealing with Mercury. Mercury is in its detriment in the opposite signs of Sagittarius and Pisces.

Venus is exalted in Pisces, in its fall in the opposite sign Virgo, in its rulership in Taurus and Libra. This combination must be taken into consideration when dealing with Venus. Venus is in its detriment in the opposite signs of Scorpio and Aries.

Mars is exalted in Capricorn, in its fall in the opposite sign Cancer. It is in its rulership in Aries and co-rules Scorpio. This combination must be taken into consideration when dealing with Mars. It is in its detriment in the opposite signs of Libra and Taurus.

Jupiter is exalted in Cancer, in its fall in the opposite sign Capricorn; it is in its rulership in Sagittarius and co-rules Pisces. It is in its detriment in the opposite signs Gemini and Virgo.

Saturn is exalted in Libra, in its fall in the opposite sign Aries; it rules Capricorn and co-rules Aquarius; it is in its detriment in the opposite signs Cancer and Leo.

Uranus is exalted in Scorpio, in its fall in the opposite sign Taurus; it rules Aquarius and co-rules Capricorn; and it is in its detriment in the opposite signs of Leo and Cancer.

Neptune is exalted in Cancer, in its fall in the opposite sign Capricorn. It rules Pisces and co-rules Sagittarius; it is in its detriment in the opposite signs of Virgo and Gemini.

Pluto is exalted in Leo, in its fall in the opposite sign Aquarius; it rules Scorpio and co-rules Aries; it is in its detriment in the opposite signs of Taurus and Libra.*

When dealing with planetary influences and planetary combinations, the planets in exaltation, detriment, fall, or their rulership signs give a valuable key in determining the impact and weight of the influence of

* See "Exaltation of the Planets," Chapter 8 of *The Astrologer's Handbook.*

the planet. Without this kind of scale, the determination and judgment of any planetary position or configuration lacks the preciseness and accuracy that are needed for proper interpretation.

In dealing with the planets in their signs of rulership, exaltation, detriment, and fall, there is an extension of the principle of this strength, weakness, ease, and debility of the planets that is carried on into the houses, determined by the Natural Zodiac, that serves as a basis for all astrological interpretation.

The term *dignity* when dealing with accidental placements is a term used in depicting a planet that is found in the house of its Natural rulership of the Natural Zodiac.

Example: The Moon rules the sign Cancer, which rules the Natural fourth house. When the Moon is found in the fourth house it is accidentally dignified, no matter what sign it is in, indicating that the Moon can function with ease in the fourth house of a horoscope.

To further clarify, when the Sun or any planet is found in the first house, which in the Natural Zodiac is the first house of Aries, the Sun or planets will take on the coloring of the sign Aries and its ruler Mars, which is the natural first house sign of Aries. Regardless of the sign that the Sun is in, when it is found in the first house it will take on the coloring of the sign Aries and the planet Mars its ruler. In addition to this basic coloring, the characteristics of the sign that the Sun is in will add to the original coloring of Aries and Mars.

When using accidental dignities or any other accidental house positions in interpretation, the planets in a sign must always correspond to the house that is delegated to that sign in the Natural Zodiac.

The Sun is accidentally exalted in the first house, it is in its accidental fall in the opposite seventh house. It is in its accidental dignity in the fifth house, which it rules in the Natural Zodiac, and in its accidental detriment in the opposite eleventh house.

The Moon is accidentally exalted in the second house, it is in its accidental fall in the opposite eighth house, it is in its accidental dignity in the fourth house, which it rules in the Natural Zodiac, and in its accidental detriment in the opposing tenth house.

Mercury is accidentally exalted in the eleventh house, and in its accidental fall in the opposing fifth house; it is in its accidental dignity in the third and sixth houses, which it rules in the Natural Zodiac. It is in its accidental detriment in the ninth and twelfth houses.

Venus is accidentally exalted in the twelfth house and in its accidental fall in the opposing sixth house. It is in its accidental dignity in the sec-

Planets	Exalt	Fall	Rulership	Detriment	Accidental Exalt	Accidental Fall	Accidental Dignity	Accidental Detriment
☉	♈	♎	♌	♒	1st	7th	5th	11th
☽	♉	♏	♋	♑	2d	8th	4th	10th
☿	♒	♌	♊ ♍	♐ ♓	11th	5th	3d–6th	9th–12th
♀	♓	♍	♉ ♎	♏ ♈	12th	6th	2d–7th	8th–1st
♂	♑	♋	♈ ♏	♎ ♉	10th	4th	1st–8th	7th–2d
♃	♋	♑	♐ ♓	♊ ♍	4th	10th	9th–12th	3d–6th
♄	♎	♈	♑ ♒	♋ ♌	7th	1st	10th–11th	4th–5th
♅	♏	♉	♒ ♑	♌ ♋	8th	2d	11th–10th	5th–4th
♆	♋	♑	♓ ♐	♍ ♊	4th	10th	12th–9th	6th–3d
⯓ or ♇	♌	♒	♏ ♈	♉ ♎	5th	11th	8th–1st	2d–7th

ond and seventh houses, which it rules in the Natural Zodiac. It is in its accidental detriment in the opposite eighth and first houses.

Mars is accidentally exalted in the tenth house, in its accidental fall in the opposing fourth house. It is accidentally dignified in the first and eighth houses and in its accidental detriment in the opposite seventh and second houses.

Jupiter is accidentally exalted when found in the fourth house. When it is found in the tenth house it is in its accidental fall. Jupiter is accidentally dignified when found in the ninth and twelfth houses and in its accidental detriment when found in the third and sixth houses.

Saturn is accidentally exalted when found in the seventh house. When found in the first house it is in its accidental fall. Saturn is in its accidental dignity when found in the tenth or eleventh houses; it is in its accidental detriment in the fourth or fifth house.

Uranus is accidentally exalted when found in the eighth house and in its accidental fall when in the second house. Uranus is in its accidental dignity when found in the tenth and eleventh houses and in its accidental detriment when found in the fourth or fifth house.

Neptune is accidentally exalted when found in the fourth house; it is in its accidental fall when found in the tenth house. Neptune is in its accidental dignity when found in the ninth or twelfth house and in its accidental detriment when found in the third or sixth house.

Pluto is accidentally exalted when found in the fifth house; it is in its accidental fall when found in the eleventh house. Pluto is in its accidental dignity when found in the first or eighth house and in its accidental detriment when found in the seventh and second houses.

In this order, a planet in the sign of its exaltation is in its most powerful position. Next in order is a planet found in the sign of its rulership. A planet in a house is most powerful when it is found in the house of its accidental exaltation. Next in order is the house of its accidental dignity.

Continuing with this order, a planet in its fall is in its weakest and most debilitated position. A planet in its detriment is limited in its expression of its basic characteristics, but not necessarily weak.

There can be various combinations of these strengths and weaknesses. *Example:* The Sun can be exalted in the sign Aries and placed in its accidental dignity in the fifth house. By the same logic the Sun could be exalted in Aries, which is powerfully placed by sign. However, it could be located in the seventh house of its accidental fall, thereby providing a debilitating environment in which the Sun must find the expression for its potential, making it difficult to shine.

8

Planet Patterns

The Mars Pattern

The principle represented by Mars is energy that is released by the Sun which is to be used in creative action and physical manifestation.

Mars as energy represents our contribution or effort in the creative manifestation of this release of energy.

Mars is the prime symbol of the sex impulse, the creative motivation of all life. This energy is often misused in sex for conquest or for pleasure instead of the healing and procreative role that it was destined for. Thus the planet Mars represents the energy that is expended for self-sustainment on all planes and levels of existence.

In Esoteric astrology, Mercury is the ruler of Aries, indicating that all action originates with thought or idea, followed by desire and action to obtain the desired object or goal.

There is a great deal of disorder in many lives due to the misdirection of the Mars energy in its projection into life. It affects our status in the world in which we live, indicated by the exaltation of Mars in Capricorn, the tenth-house sign of achievement, recognition, and honor or dishonor. Pluto as co-ruler indicates the ability of Mars to bring all activity to a higher level of expression with a new focus or direction.

Keywords and Phrases for Mars

Action motivated by desire—new beginnings—expenditure of energy—temper—physical exertion—business and professional ambition—competition—practical application of energy to perfect skills—how one starts things—attack on the problems of life—energy—initiative—impulsiveness—forcefulness—directness—courage—venturesomeness—aggressiveness—boldness—combativeness—violence—destructiveness—passion—sex—fire—accidents—cuts—bruises—and fevers.

Mars Aspects

Mars conjunctions indicate a personal tendency to direct action in the affairs ruled by Mars and the planet or planets making the conjunction. Conjunctions of Mars give ample energy for work or action. A Mars conjunction can be the basis for constructive accomplishment because it is accompanied by initiative and courage.

If the Mars conjunction receives stress aspects, that is, a square, opposition, or quincunx from other planets, there can be a tendency to rash, ill-considered action. Planets in stress aspect to a Mars conjunction indicate a need for individuals to cultivate an attitude of peace and love and think carefully before taking action.

The conjunction affects the departments of life ruled by the signs and houses which Mars and the planets forming the conjunction rule, also the house and signs of their exaltation.*

Sextiles to Mars

The sextile indicates an opportunity for constructive action which leads to experience that is the basis of all wisdom. Mars gives the courage and initiative to overcome obstacles and thus make progress. The nature of the sextile aspect bestows intelligent direction of Mars energy.

The house in which Mars is found, the houses where Aries, Scorpio, and Capricorn are found, and the planet or planets, with their rulers, sign, and house positions represent the departments of life that will somehow be affected by the sextile aspect.

Squares to Mars

Square aspects to Mars indicate that individuals need to learn the lesson of patience. If this is not done, these individuals will feel frustrated in their desire for action. If individuals are to channel their energy in an intelligent way, they must organize and utilize this energy to produce

* See aspects of Mars to planets in *The Astrologer's Handbook.*

useful results, since driving ambition usually accompanies a Mars square. The Mars square demands that these individuals also consider the needs and rights of others as well as their own. The areas of life affected by the Mars square will be the affairs ruled by the signs and houses in which the square is found, including their exalted rulers and their position in the horoscope.

Trines of Mars

Mars trines indicate an easy flow of the Mars energy into constructive channels. The Mars trine, if utilized, endows individuals with a passionate love of life with great growth-producing potential. These individuals can use this energy for creative and practical accomplishment that will enable them to fulfill their high or spiritual ideals. This trine will find its constructive expression through the planets forming the trine, the houses in which the planets are placed, the houses which the planets rule, and the houses that contain the planets forming the trine.

Oppositions to Mars

Mars oppositions indicate relationship problems arising out of the individuals' tendencies to rash or aggressive actions. This opposition indicates an inclination to competitiveness, strain, and anger. This expression can manifest in verbal bickering or something more serious. Used properly, it can indicate firm and energetic action in partnerships.

The Mars opposition demands an awareness of the other person. There is a need for these individuals to learn to love and to view issues from the other person's point of view as well as their own. A refusal to cooperate can lead to violent conflicts with others. These characteristics will manifest in the signs and houses in which planets involved in oppositions are placed and the houses they rule, also in the signs and houses of the exalted rulers of the planets involved in the opposition.*

Mars is the primary ruler of the sign Aries and the co-ruler of the sign Scorpio. Wherever Aries is found in the horoscope, regardless of the house, Mars will rule that department of the life. The department of life that carries Aries is where the individual will be involved with direct action and concerned with the immediate now requiring decision-making. The initial impact that is received from any type of stimulation in the

* See "Part II: Interpreting the Aspects" in *The Astrologer's Handbook.*

house carrying Aries will be responded to with aggressive, decisive, and often impulsive action. Whether this type of response is carried through to the conclusion of any action taken is dependent on whether the planet Mars, which rules Aries, is in an aggressive, masculine sign. Further amplification is dependent upon whether Mars is found in a Fire, Earth, Air, or Water sign, and whether it is in a Cardinal, Fixed, or Mutable sign.

The Mars action has an inherent desire for change, represented by the Cardinal sign Aries which initiates new activities and is co-ruled by Pluto, that eventually refines these activities and raises them to a higher level of expression.

If Mars is found in a positive, masculine Fire or Air sign the individual will carry on with the initial impulse with energy and leadership and will take positive action whenever it is necessary.

If Mars is found in a receptive, feminine sign, the individual will respond to the initial impulse by taking action when prodded to do so by others or by outside influence, or the individual may wait for suitable circumstances to carry on with the original impulse or action. Either the aggressive, positive or feminine, receptive response will prevail regardless of the triplicity or quadruplicity that Mars is found in.

Example: If Mars is found in the sign Libra, an aggressive, masculine, Cardinal sign, the action of Mars will dictate that the dynamic will and leadership qualities will manifest through positive action.

If Mars is found in a Cardinal, receptive, feminine sign such as Cancer, the initial impulse to action and decision-making will be continued only if prodded into further action by an outside influence or by waiting for suitable circumstances to carry on the action. Under the positive, masculine, Cardinal sign the impulse is carried on in the way it began. Under the receptive, feminine, Cardinal pattern the action will be stimulated by factors outside of the individual. If this kind of stimulation or response is not forthcoming, the whole initial action can be dropped. The insight into these response patterns is one of the most important factors in astrological interpretation. This does not mean that one kind of response pattern is superior to the other. It means that the responses are different, and that a positive, masculine response cannot be expected when the pattern is receptive, feminine or vice versa. This kind of expectation is like going to a dry well for water.

The principles of this Mars response pattern deal with the affairs of the house that has Aries on the cusp or intercepted. These affairs are linked with the affairs of the house where Mars is found.

Example: If Aries is on the fourth-house cusp and Mars is in Scorpio in the tenth house, it indicates that these individuals will initiate activities in the home in an aggressive, enterprising manner. However, because Mars is in Scorpio, a Fixed, goal-oriented, Water, receptive, feminine sign, these individuals are liable to abandon these initial activities with a deep emotional feeling that this energy should be expended in a profession instead of the home. These individuals will feel that they attract enough work in their professions. This pattern can cause conflict between domestic duties and professional responsibilities. With this type of pattern response, it must be taken into consideration that Mars also co-rules Scorpio; therefore, these individuals would be preoccupied with improving their professional performance and professional reputation. This is because of the co-rulership of Pluto which elevates the action of Mars to a higher form of expression.

In dealing with these response patterns the following order should be followed.

1. Mars rules the house where Aries is found, and in this house the individual will initiate action.
2. The house or department in which Mars is found will be linked to the affairs of the house where Aries is found.
3. The house that carries the sign Scorpio will also be linked in some way to these activities.
4. The house that carries Capricorn where Mars is exalted will also be linked to the Mars pattern.

Without a thorough knowledge and understanding of the basic concepts of astrology any interpretation would be superficial at best.

Mars is the key to action and desire and represents the individual's capacity for direct action which is based on a desire of some sort. The Mars influence, more than any other planet, needs guidance, tempering, and alloying with other factors. The best intentions of ideas are useless without action.

Mars is exalted in the practical, Cardinal, Earth sign of Capricorn, indicating the essential relationship between action and practical results. If this energy is properly channeled, it brings practical accomplishment, but if the action is misguided it can bring destruction.

If Mars is in a Cardinal sign there is a need for continual activity or change, and if action and changes are not forthcoming, these individuals become bored. They will act decisively and sometimes impulsively to make the most of existing circumstances and motivation, for the action will be based on the present circumstances rather than on the past or future goals.

If Mars is found in a Fixed sign these individuals will be motivated by future goals. They will be determined and even stubborn, and they will adhere to a course of action that will eventually give them what they desire.

If Mars is found in a Mutable sign, the motivation to action is based on past memories or experience, rather than future goals or present circumstances. These individuals will want to repeat the pleasant actions and avoid painful ones, and they will be adaptable and changeable in their actions. However, if the actions are motivated by neurotic tendencies, the irrational behavior can propel them into trouble. On the other hand, if the energy has been wisely focused, Mars in a Mutable sign can indicate an adaptable, highly-skilled individual with a versatile capacity for action, enabling the individual to get around difficulties by periodically changing tactics.

If Mars is found in a creative, inspirational Fire sign, the individual will have a dynamic will, abundant energy, and leadership qualities, and will take positive action.

If Mars is found in a practical Earth sign, the individual's desires will be motivated by practical considerations. The individual is not likely to take action unless there is an opportunity for material benefit or to acquire wealth or property.

If Mars is found in an intellectual Air sign, the individual will be vehement about ideas and concepts with a tendency to identify the ego with a personal point of view and personal opinions. The desire and action of Mars will be based on intellectual considerations and guided by reason and intelligence.

If Mars is found in an emotional Water sign, the desires and actions will be based on emotional considerations. If the Mars energy is used constructively, the individual will be motivated by love and empathy for others. However, if the emotional considerations are based on a distorted subconscious mechanism, the individual can act in a destructive way.

Mars in a sign indicates through what kind of expression the individual will take action. Mars will be colored by the characteristics of the sign it is found in. It gives information about the individual's ambitions and work. This is because desire leads to ambition, as shown by Mars' exaltation in the sign Capricorn.

Because impulsive action and expression of forceful energy often lead to danger, the position of Mars will show how violence and danger can enter into an individual's life.

Mars in the houses indicates the areas of the life in which the individual expresses actions and desires. It indicates the area where the individual must exert energy and initiative to achieve results. It also indicates the area that could be connected with conflict.

The constructive or destructive use of the Mars energy will be in the area of experience where Mars is found in the horoscope. It will affect the houses or departments of life that carry Aries, Scorpio, and Capricorn.

The aspects made to Mars by other planets indicate the degree of harmony or inharmony and the positive or negative results from the action of Mars.

The planets that are involved in any aspect with Mars must follow the same procedure in delineation as Mars.

1. The house cusp carrying the sign Aries.
2. The house or area of life Mars occupies.
3. The type of sign Mars is in, positive or negative.
4. The triplicity or quadruplicity to which it belongs.
5. The house that carries the sign Scorpio.
6. The house that carries the sign Capricorn.
7. The planets that aspect Mars, their signs, houses, and exaltation rulers must be considered in the overall interpretation of how the Mars energy and the desire principle is directed.*

The Venus Pattern

Venus is the primary ruler of two signs, Taurus and Libra. Wherever Taurus and Libra are found in the horoscope, regardless of the house, Venus will rule over that department of the life. The house that carries Taurus, which is a receptive, feminine, Earth sign, is where individuals will be determined in their attitude toward money-making and their emotional and material comfort. Taurus is a goal-oriented sign with an eye toward future security on all levels of being. The values of this house will be Fixed and form an attitude that does not change easily. Taurus is the natural second-house sign representing values, indicating that the house carrying Taurus will represent a great part of the individual's value system. Any impact or stimulation to the house that carries the sign Taurus will be judged for its practical value and what effect it will have on the individual's material and emotional security. Because Taurus is a receptive, feminine sign it attracts whatever it needs for its expres-

* See the chapter "Planets in the Signs and Houses" in *The Astrologer's Handbook.*

sion, or the individual will wait for the proper circumstances to develop before taking action. Venus as the ruler is also feminine and exerts a magnetic energy that attracts people and possessions to the individual. Venus as ruler of this Earth sign attracts possessions of refinement, practicality, and lasting beauty. It is also the key to the individual's financial, social, romantic, artistic, and musical talents and activities.

Venus also rules Libra, exerting this magnetic energy to attract a partner or companion to share life's experiences. Venus rules the principle of love in romantic relationships or close personal relationships. It indicates the capacity or opportunity to create beauty and refinement. The sign and house in which Venus is found will indicate these individuals' approach to art and beauty and their ability to empathize with others emotionally. Venus describes the woman's attraction for the opposite sex.

Example: If Venus is in Gemini in a woman's chart, the woman will want to attract a man who will be intelligent, will exchange ideas, communicate with her, and will also enjoy traveling about with her. She would also want him to enjoy her brothers, sisters, and neighbors as she does. If Venus in Gemini receives stress aspects from other planets there would be this emotional need; however, there would be problems with it. Venus also indicates what she is able to give to a man. Venus in Gemini, being in a Mutable sign, would indicate that she offers all her skills and gathered information to be shared in the relationship in an intellectual, versatile way.

Venus in a man's horoscope indicates the type of woman he would like to attract, but this does not necessarily mean that Venus represents the type he will marry.* Venus is exalted in the sign of Pisces, which deals with the law of cause and effect, and the Eternal has a way of intervening and providing the partner who will supply the experience that is needed to round out lessons in love and cooperation.

The energy of Venus gives individuals an opportunity to make life beautiful and to develop a sense of the beautiful. This can be done by disciplining emotional responses in a way that will be inspiring and harmonious in the relationship exchange. Venus indicates that there is a constant need to feed the fires of love if the bonds of affection with life partners, friends, and relatives are to be kept. This is demanded from individuals no matter how well Venus is placed in their horoscope. This constant need is because Taurus, which Venus rules, is a Fixed sign which deals with the emotional and material needs of individuals and

* The seventh house, planets in the seventh, its sign, and its ruler and exalted ruler will describe the marriage partner for either sex.

because Libra, which is also ruled by Venus, is a Cardinal sign, which indicates constant activity in this exchange.

Wherever Libra is located in the horoscope is where individuals should initiate the kind of cooperation that is called for in bringing a balanced situation that will create the necessary conditions for balance, peace, love, and harmony.

The very nature of Venus wants to smooth out difficulties and maintain a sense of harmony and rhythm. If the principles of Venus are not used, individuals will be incapable of recognizing or feeling true love. Individuals will lack the proper respect for others and can become slothful, coarse, and disorderly, showing a lack of refinement and sensitivity to others.

The lack of awareness of this principle of love and cooperation represented by Venus can cause individuals to be their own worst enemy by causing their own self-undoing, which is indicated by Venus exalted in the sign Pisces, which is the sign of our hidden support or self-undoing. Pisces deals with confinement of all kinds, and if individuals lack the ability to love and cooperate in the expression of the Venus principle, they make a jailor of themselves by alienating themselves from others.

Venus, the ruler of Taurus, gives us data concerning the individual's attitude toward money, personal possessions, and creature comforts. Venus as ruler of Taurus represents the urge of individuals to draw to themselves the means of material sustenance. This must be done on an ethical level with a just exchange with the other person. If individuals attempt to gain materially without the proper kind of exchange of values, they can end up by being in prison for their unlawful activities. This is indicated by Libra which represents the scales of justice and Pisces the sign of confinement. Many individuals who are confined in mental institutions are there mostly because they cannot respond to or give love. Every individual will some day learn that love is the most transcendent and exalted product of the evolutionary process.

Taurus is a receptive, feminine sign, indicating that the house that carries Taurus will be the area where individuals will be receptive and passive concerning the affairs of that house. They will be goal-oriented, determined, and persevering in that area of life. If Venus, the ruler of Taurus, is placed in a receptive, feminine sign, they will proceed with the same type of receptivity and perseverance. If Venus is found in a positive, aggressive sign, these individuals will initiate activities that will help them in acquiring money, possessions, social activities, and romantic relationships.

Libra is a positive, aggressive sign, and wherever it is located in the horoscope will be the area that individuals will be active and take the initiative in forming new friendships, romantic relationships, and social and partnership activity. This is because Libra is a Cardinal sign dealing with the here and now of the present moment. If Venus, the ruler, is posited in a positive, aggressive sign, these individuals will actively seek ways to promote these relationships and the acquisition of money, possessions, and emotional satisfaction. If Venus is posited in a receptive, feminine sign, after the initial action is taken, represented by the positive sign Libra, then these individuals wait for further developments before taking any further action, or they wait for the proper opportunity to develop before taking action.

Keywords and Phrases for Venus

Marriage–partnerships–close personal relationships–relationships with women or the opposite sex–romantic attractions–social sensitivity–art–music–luxury items–money–valuable personal possessions–power to attract that which you need–acquisitiveness–nature of appreciation–how things are finished–beauty–refinement–values–harmony–vanity–ostentation–retention–indulgence–indolence.

Venus in the signs indicates how individuals express their emotions in personal relationships, especially in love and marriage. It also indicates their attitude toward money, personal possessions, creature comforts, and social and aesthetic values.

Venus in the houses indicates areas in which individuals express themselves socially, romantically, and artistically.

Example: If Venus is found in the tenth house, these individuals would find an artistic outlet of some kind through their career or they would form a close relationship with people connected with their career. They could engage in social or money-making activities through their work or profession. The house or department of life in which Venus is found indicates the type of people with whom individuals will establish close relationships, friendships, or romances.

If Venus is found in a Cardinal sign, these individuals will take an active approach to money-making, social activities, and romantic relationships, and the present circumstances of these activities will be of immediate concern to the individual.

If Venus is found in a Fixed sign, these individuals will have a determined attitude toward money-making. They will be thorough in handling their artistic and social endeavors and will see them through to completion. Venus in a Fixed sign indicates that once a relationship has been established the individual will be steadfast and loyal. However, if the relationship has been seriously betrayed the individual will never reinstate it on the same basis, there will always be certain reservations.

If Venus is in a Mutable sign, these individuals will be adaptable in handling their social, artistic, and romantic affairs. These individuals will draw on past experience to adjust to all types of circumstances. In their artistic endeavors they will have a keen imagination coupled with ingenuity. They will also have diverse ways of making money. If this Mutable tendency is not used in a positive manner, the individual can be inconstant and fickle in relationships; however, this is less so in the Mutable sign of Pisces.*

If Venus is found in a Fire sign, these individuals will actively seek romantic and social fulfillment. They will have a sense of color and drama in their artistic expressions. They will display initiative and leadership in money-making endeavors.

If Venus is found in an Earth sign, these individuals will be practical and sensuous in their artistic, financial, social, and romantic affairs. They will demand quality and durability in their personal possessions. Because the Earth signs are receptive and feminine, they will wait for romantic and social opportunities to present themselves instead of actively seeking them out.

If Venus is found in an Air sign, these individuals will have a strong sense of social relationships with an interest in the feelings and psychology of others. They will establish friendships with intellectually stimulating people, and their romantic partners will display a great deal of social charm.

If Venus is found in a Water sign, these individuals will have an emotional approach to art, music, social activity, and romantic and business partnerships. They will exhibit deep feelings of empathy and sympathy for others. They can be easily hurt by social mistreatment or neglect.

Conjunctions of Venus

Venus conjunctions indicate a dynamic personal expression of the individual's social, romantic, and aesthetic proclivities. These individuals will be gentle and graceful when expressing emotions. This kind of expression attracts others to them, especially those of the opposite sex.

* See Venus in the signs and houses in *The Astrologer's Handbook*.

This ease and sensitivity extends to the signs and houses in which the conjunction is found. The signs and houses that the planets forming the conjunction rule, also the signs and houses in which the exalted rulers are found, will all be interrelated in some way.

Sextiles of Venus

Sextiles of Venus indicate an opportunity to develop social qualities related to the planets involved in the sextile and the houses they rule. This sextile gives individuals an opportunity to develop and refine aesthetic and emotional expression. This development and refinement will come through and affect the areas that the planets involved in the sextile are found in, plus the sign and houses they rule and the sign and houses that hold their exalted rulers. These areas will be affected by the opportunities presented by the sextile aspect.

Squares of Venus

Venus squares indicate that these individuals will experience difficulties in social relationships and in emotional fulfillment. There can be unhappy experiences in love and romance, or the individual can be indulgent and sensual. There can be an emotional blockage or some social difficulties. The areas involved are indicated by the signs and houses occupied and ruled by Venus and the planets forming the square. The exalted rulers and the houses they are in are all involved somehow in the problems generated by the square.

Trines of Venus

Trines of Venus favor a general popularity, love, and romance. These individuals will have a soothing and pacifying effect on others because of their gracious manner. These individuals will attract people who will benefit them in some way. Trines to Venus are indicative of musical or artistic talent or the appreciation of these arts. The areas involved are indicated by the signs and houses ruled by Venus and the planets forming the trine aspect. The exalted rulers and the houses they are in will be involved somehow in the good fortune and expansion that are indicated by the trine aspect.

Oppositions of Venus

Oppositions of Venus indicate that these individuals will have relationship problems in emotional, marital, and romantic life. These individuals are liable to be oversensitive or can demand too much emotional gratification and yet deny it to others. There is a need for these individuals to be aware of the needs of others and to act accordingly.

When dealing with Venus, the houses carrying Taurus and Libra and the house carrying Pisces must be considered; the houses in which the planets are placed that make the aspect and the houses that they rule must be included in the final determination of the Venus qualities and the way they are expressed by the individual.*

The Mercury Pattern

Mercury is the primary ruler of the signs Gemini and Virgo, and Mercury is exalted in the sign Aquarius. Cosmic consciousness is related to the sign Aquarius. The individual reasoning power which is ruled by Mercury is one of the creations of the superconscious mind which functions in and through individual intelligence. This is done by the reflection of universal ideas through the individual mind of each of us. The sudden action of the planetary exaltation ruler Uranus gives answers to problems in sudden flashes of insight. Therefore, the house with Aquarius on its cusp is the power house of Mercury.

Because Mercury rules two Mutable signs, and because it is exalted in a Fixed sign, information and ideas are disseminated and circulated in the intellectual Air sign of Gemini and given concrete manifestation by skills and work in the Mutable-Earth sign of Virgo. The end product should have a universal application if used constructively, represented by Aquarius, the sign of humanity (the universal law of supply being that nothing exists in the universe that does not have its right use). Thus Mercury, which rules ideas, communication, and skills, is the instrument that helps us realize our goals and objectives while we are functioning on this physical plane and consequently raises us above the animal kingdom.

Mercury, ruler of Gemini and Virgo, gives individuals the power to use their hands in skills. Mercury also opens up lines of communication

* See aspects made to Venus by other planets in "Part II: Interpreting Aspects" of *The Astrologer's Handbook.*

with other human beings. Mercury's exaltation in Aquarius helps to transcend the limitations of time and space through radio, television, and supersonic aircraft, all involving the Air element. Mercury, a Mutable-Earth sign, brings all of this into practical physical manifestation.

Mercury deals with all communicative action through the spoken or written word. The principle of this planet Mercury has a lot to do with tone as it moves through the air waves, and it is well to know that we must become aware of the tones or words that can be grating, jarring, or healing. It is also through the power of Mercury that words that need to be spoken are withheld. Under Mercury individuals need to learn the POWER of the spoken word as a vehicle for expressing clear, unbiased thinking, encouragement, and truth. Under the Mercury pattern individuals should open their minds with a willingness to learn and understand truth. Destructive criticism, prejudice, and falsehoods will distort the thinking process, and individuals are usually unaware that the thoughts that they harbor affect their health, both mentally and physically, and also their work performance.

If individuals wish to realize a higher degree of mental and physical health, the power of thought and the spoken word must be used to express that which is true and loving. In using the power of Mercury individuals should train the mind to recognize and realize truth and to be constantly aware of the kind of thoughts that are invited into the mind. When this is done, individuals will come to the realization that thoughts are things, and that the power of thought is to be used to evaluate truthfully and to use constructive judgment when dealing with others. The individual will be willing to consider helpful suggestions and to respond to opportunities to learn and understand, instead of closing the mind to all new ideas and thoughts that will lift humanity to a higher form of expression, represented by Mercury's exaltation in the sign Aquarius.

The Mercury pattern in the horoscope indicates individuals' degree of intelligence, mental attitudes, and the ability to think and communicate. The closest major aspect made to Mercury indicates the predominant mental interest and intellectual focus of individuals.

Mercury in the signs indicates the way in which individuals think and their ability to communicate. Mercury in the signs represents the focusing lens through which the creative powers are directed. Mercury in the signs indicates the concerns that occupy individuals' minds, the kind of information and facts that individuals regard as important, and what they choose to ignore.

Mercury in the houses represents the area of activity that will be influenced by individuals' thoughts and communication. Mercury in the houses indicates the type of environment and activities from which individuals draw their ideas.

Example: If Mercury is in the seventh house, individuals collect information and are concerned with information through marriage, partnerships, close interpersonal relations, and communication with the public.

Keywords and Phrases of Mercury

Ideas—formulation of ideas—conscious mind—communication—decision-making—sensory perception—the thinking processes—short trips—siblings—neighbors—co-workers—health—diet—medicine—work—employment—specialized skills—transportation—mind—awareness of the immediate environment—rationalization—intellectual mediation—attitudes formed from early environment—neutral planet—youths—all blood relatives—adaptability—skepticism—worry—criticalness—inquisitiveness—nervousness—verbosity—and restlessness.*

If Mercury is in a positive, masculine sign, the mind will be curious and aggressive.

If Mercury is in a receptive, feminine sign, the mind will attract and deal with that which confronts it rather than reaching out aggressively as does Mercury when found in a positive sign.

Even if this Mercury pattern receives stress aspects from other planets indicating conflicts and problems, these factors will activate the intelligence.

If Mercury is found in a Cardinal sign, the individual will be decisive in following a course of action. However, if Mercury is in a receptive, feminine, Cardinal sign, the individual will wait for the opportune time to decide upon a course of action. The danger of Mercury in Cardinal signs is the making of impulsive decisions.

If Mercury is found in Fixed signs, the individual will be cautious and deliberate in decision-making; however, once the decision is made the individual is usually unwilling to change his or her mind. Thus if this Mercury pattern receives stress aspects, there can be irrational fixed attitudes that could be unbending.

If Mercury is found in a Fixed, positive sign, the individual will be aggressive in promoting his own ideas and decisions.

* See "Mercury in the Signs and Houses" in Chapter 6 of *The Astrologer's Handbook.*

If Mercury is in a Fixed, receptive sign, the individual will wait for the proper opportunity to present his or her already fixed and formed ideas.

If Mercury is found in a Mutable sign, the individual will be adaptable and flexible in making decisions and will draw on past experience for guidance. However, if this Mercury pattern receives stress aspects from other planets, the individual could make irrational decisions in terms of present circumstances.

If Mercury is found in a Mutable, positive sign, the individual will be aggressive in ideas and decision-making, but also flexible in making adjustments.

If Mercury is found in a Mutable, receptive sign, before taking action the individual will wait to deal with ideas and decisions until confronted with them, and action will be based on past experience. If this Mercury pattern receives stress aspects from other planets, the decisions can be irrational in terms of present circumstances.

If Mercury is found in a Fire sign, the individual will display mental leadership and will tackle intellectual or mental problems with energy and self-confidence. If this Mercury pattern receives stress aspects from other planets, there is the danger of egocentric mental attitudes.

If Mercury is in an Earth sign, the individual will evaluate ideas and information on the basis of their practical use and application. If this Mercury pattern receives stress aspects from other planets, there is the danger of an excessively materialistic outlook.

If Mercury is found in an Air sign, the individual's communications will be concerned with social relationships, psychology, and group endeavors, indicated by Mercury's exaltation in the sign Aquarius. Mercury in an intellectual Air sign is interested in the pursuit of intellectual ideas in and of themselves. If this Mercury pattern receives stress aspects, there is the danger of the overtheoretical, impractical mental outlook. The individual does not understand that the best ideas are of no use unless they can be put into action.

If Mercury is found in a Water sign, the individual's thinking is colored by emotional factors. The individual's decisions are often based on emotional feelings, and he or she is able to communicate emotions and is receptive to the feelings of others. If this Mercury pattern receives stress aspects from other planets, there is the danger of emotional biases, distorted reason, and an inaccurate perception of reality.*

* See Mercury in the signs in *The Astrologer's Handbook*.

Conjunctions of Mercury

Conjunctions of Mercury indicate that the individual's mind is given power and understanding in reasoning and communicating ability. This ability will be found in the areas in which the planets making the conjunction are placed, the houses these planets rule, and the houses that carry the exaltation signs of the planets involved in the conjunction. The planet Mercury, which is part of this pattern, rules Gemini and Virgo and is exalted in Aquarius; therefore, the houses with Gemini, Virgo, and Aquarius are the houses that represent the houses that are involved in the Mercury part of the conjunction. The same procedure follows for the planet or planets that are making the conjunction to Mercury.

Example: If Mercury is conjunct Mars, the above is applied, plus the house and sign that Mars is found in, and the houses carrying Aries and Scorpio which Mars rules, and the house carrying Capricorn where Mars is exalted. This same procedure holds true for any type of aspect.

Sextiles to Mercury

Sextiles to Mercury indicate that the individual has an opportunity for mental growth and developing skill in writing and communicating. This sextile also gives the opportunity to form new friendships and to express ideas through groups and associations. The sextile indicates that the individual has good thinking in the areas in which the planets forming the sextile are found, the houses that they rule, and the houses that contain the signs of their exalted rulers.

Squares to Mercury

Squares to Mercury indicate that the individual will have problems, difficulties, and mental blocks in learning and communication. This does not mean that these individuals are not intelligent and mentally active; it means that they are inclined to be opinionated and one-sided in their viewpoints, or they use their abilities fruitlessly or destructively. Often there is an overemphasis on skepticism, argumentativeness, or mental pride. These difficulties will be in evidence in the houses occupied by the planets making the square aspect, also the signs and houses that the planets involved in the square rule. Included are the houses and signs that carry the exalted rulers of the planets involved in the square.

Trines of Mercury

Trines of Mercury indicate the ability for the individual to think and communicate rapidly and harmoniously. This aspect indicates a creative and inspired use of the mind. This proper use of the mind brings success in life and acceptance of ideas. The individual will benefit from an education that will make possible social and professional advancement. The individual will do well and comprehend clearly in the areas of experience that involve the planets making the trine, also the areas in which the ruling planets are found, and the areas that are occupied by the exalted rulers of the planets forming the trine.

Oppositions to Mercury

Oppositions to Mercury indicate that the individual will have difficulties in relationships that stem from differences of opinion and outlook. The individual has trouble in communicating with others and a tendency to argue and confuse. It is important that these individuals try to see the other person's point of view as easily as they see their own. These differences will be in the areas in which the two planets forming this opposition are found and the signs and houses which the planets forming the opposition rule. Also included will be the houses in which the exalted rulers of planets forming the opposition are found.*

The Moon Pattern

Man and all Nature are affected by the Moon as it waxes and wanes. The Moon exerts a considerable influence over the general or ordinary common daily affairs of life. It exerts an influence over the everyday business, domestic, and practical affairs. It deals with the public and women and the part they play in the individual's life. The Moon has no basic nature of its own but serves to reflect and focus the qualities of the signs and other planets upon the human mind. The Moon is the planet of the mother; it represents the ability to nurture a child or to take care of a business. It is an attribute of the maternal, nurturing principle.

The Moon represents our automatic reactions to outside stimuli. It indicates our likes, dislikes, feelings, and emotions. It represents the sum total of our makeup which includes memory, reason, and reflection. The Moon represents the consciousness of the self. The Moon is a mental factor symbolizing the subconscious mind of feeling. The Moon repre-

* See "Part II: Interpreting Aspects" in *The Astrologer's Handbook.*

sents the mechanism of the instinctual mind as the storehouse of the memories of the past. This storehouse is often filled with fears, hatreds, and tensions that can be stimulated by reactions to domestic, parental, national, and racial relationships.

The Moon is exalted in Taurus which is ruled by Venus. Venus also rules Libra which represents the principle of balance through exchange, and Libra is also the sign of relationships through which this exchange takes place. The Moon is responsible for conveying form and physical manifestation, which Taurus deals with. Taurus deals with money and possessions and represents the avenue, reservoir, or storehouse through which these material things can be gained. Therefore the Moon's exaltation in the sign Taurus is the key to acquiring the material needs necessary for individuals to live their lives in comfort and to give them emotional and material security that are conducive to right reactions.

When there is the proper exchange between the Libra, Taurus, Venus, and Moon factors, individuals will display a loving, friendly, appreciative attitude without any expression of fear or tension in relationships. It is only through this balanced exchange that the subconscious, represented by the Moon, can be emptied of wrong reactions and replaced with loving reactions, bringing in a new value system for individuals. When individuals come to the realization that money, possessions, or the lack of these things along with the relationship problems engendered by the family and other factors evoke all kinds of emotions within them, they will take an honest look at the causative factors behind their reactions and make a conscious evaluation of their unconscious reactions.

It is money, possessions, and relationships or the lack of a true understanding of these factors that hold both the rich and the poor to the lessons engendered by the Moon's exaltation in the sign Taurus.

The Moon rules Cancer, and wherever Cancer is found in the horoscope is where the individual's nurturing instincts will manifest. The sign the Moon is in indicates the kind of attitudes that were instilled in the individual by the family in childhood. The sign position also shows how early experiences have colored the individual's emotional outlook. It indicates the way individuals will react to external influences and the actions of others. The Moon in the sign shows how individuals will conduct the home life.

If the Moon receives stress aspects, there can be emotional difficulties with the family. Domestic problems can interfere with professional responsibilities. The individual could be moody, lazy, and suffer from digestive problems of some kind because the Moon rules the stomach. There can also be problems where women and money are concerned.

The Moon rules the subconscious mind, indicating that any stress aspects made to the Moon point out a need for emotional discipline and control. There is a need to transmute the feelings and develop personal detachment.

Keywords and Phrases of the Moon

Motherhood–women–domestic affairs–family matters–habit patterns –creature comforts–everyday business transactions–moods–feelings–money–home–dealings with the public–real estate–farming–food–domestic products and services–memory bank–clannishness–sensitivity–instinct–changeable–receptive–emotional–women's health–women's menses cycle–indicator of marriage partner for a man–the way one sees one's mother–Moon as minute hand indicating when things are likely to culminate in action. The moon represents an indiivdual's automatic response to outside stimuli based on early conditioning and maturation.

Conjunctions to the Moon

Conjunctions to the Moon indicate intense feelings with a dominant emotional influence in the affairs of the planets involved in the conjunction. Domestic affairs, food, and parental considerations will also influence the affairs of the planets involved in the conjunction. In these matters the individual is inclined to act out of unconscious impulses, hereditary patterns and early conditioning. Women often play an important part in these matters. The areas that are affected by the conjunction are the signs and houses occupied by the Moon and the planets making the conjunction, the houses the planets rule, the houses that carry the signs Cancer and Taurus, and the exaltation signs and houses of the planets making the conjunction to the Moon.

Sextiles to the Moon

Sextiles to the Moon indicate an opportunity for emotional growth and general development. Women will play an important part in furthering the individual's progress. The mother or a home relationship can be of considerable help. The sextile indicates harmonious emotional communication with women, and it aids in the development of friendships. These opportunities for growth will be in the areas in which the Moon and the planets forming the sextile are found, the signs and houses that the Moon and these planets rule, and the signs and houses of their exalted rulers.

Squares to the Moon

The squares to the Moon indicate that the individual will experience emotional blockage and frustrations that arise out of early childhood conditioning. This often takes the form of social and racial prejudices. This kind of conditioning hampers the ability of the individual to act as an emotionally free agent. There can be an unconscious resentment toward women as a result of conflicts with the mother. If these emotional habit patterns are allowed to crystallize, they will become an obstacle to general happiness. The areas affected will be in the signs and houses that the Moon and the planets are placed in, and the signs and houses that they rule, and the signs and houses of their exalted rulers.

Trines of the Moon

Trines of the Moon usually indicate a happy childhood and a successful family life, and indicate habit patterns and unconscious conditioning that are conducive to individuals' social progress and relationships with women. Thus they can make use of their creative imagination and the automatic responses that stem from the unconscious. These individuals react with sensitivity to the moods of others.

The benefits of this trine will come through the houses in which the planets are found, the signs and houses they rule, and the signs and houses of the exalted rulers of the Moon and the planets involved in the trine.

Oppositions of the Moon

Oppositions of the Moon indicate emotional problems in relationships. There can be a psychological mirroring effect whereby individuals will project their own emotional problem onto others and blame them for their own unrecognized faults. There is a need for these individuals to learn emotional detachment and objectivity especially in the affairs of the signs and houses in which the Moon and the planets forming the opposition are found, the houses they rule, and the signs and houses carrying their exalted rulers.

If the Moon is found in a Cardinal sign, the individual will have an emotionally impulsive nature. There can be flareups of temper, and the individual can be changeable in emotional expression. If the Moon is in a Cardinal, positive sign, there can be a great deal of activity with women, and the individual will take the initiative in matters concerning the home, financial dealings, and dealings with the public.

If the Moon is in a Cardinal, receptive sign, the individual will attract family, domestic, financial, and public activities; however, the individual is apt to wait for the right circumstances for these activities to take place.*

If the Moon is found in a Fixed, receptive sign, individuals will attract tional need for financial and domestic security. They will be goal-oriented in handling financial and domestic affairs. These individuals are unwilling to change their established emotional attitudes. There is a need for a stable home and family condition, also an emotional need to love and be loved.

If the Moon is found in a Fixed, positive sign, individuals will initiate goals in their family, financial, and domestic affairs that will serve for the security and well-being of the self and family.

If the Moon is found in a Fixed sign, individuals will have the emo-financial and emotional security through their romantic partner, friends, joint monies, and goods of the dead. These individuals are also unwilling to change their emotional attitudes. These individuals may not be overt in displaying their fixed emotional attitudes; however, if they are pressed they can be just as forceful in maintaining their fixed opinions and attitudes.

If the Moon is found in a Mutable sign, individuals will vacillate in their emotional responses. They will have a restless nature, using their skills and past experience to achieve domestic, financial, and emotional security.

If the Moon is found in a Mutable, positive sign, individuals will use their initiative and intellectual ability and foresight in attracting this kind of security.

If the Moon is found in a Mutable, receptive sign, individuals will wait for the opportunity or proper circumstances to present themselves to work and use their skills in perfecting their services and their own health and the health of others either in the home or in their work area. Thus they derive a great deal of emotional satisfaction and fulfillment.

* See planets in aspect in *The Astrologer's Handbook*.

If the Moon is in a Fire sign, individuals' emotions will serve as a creative outlet of some kind. There is less emotional dependency on others; they want to follow their own path, right or wrong, and make their own decisions as to when to withhold or express their emotional feelings. The will is strong in these matters.

If the Moon is in an Earth sign, there is an emotional need to serve others, also to attract the good things in life, such as good food and material comfort. Because the Earth signs are receptive, feminine signs, women play an important role in their lives.

If the Moon is in an Air sign, there is an emotional need for freedom to circulate as they please. They can be emotional about all close ties, those that are too close and those that are not close enough. The emotions are manifested through the intellect.

If the Moon is in a Water sign, individuals will be emotional, sensitive, and personal concerning family and family affairs. There will be intense, sensitive reactions to the moods and feelings of others.*

The Sun Pattern

The Sun is the principal life giver in this universe, and its power has a special significance in the horoscope. If individuals do not develop the potential of the Sun, they will have an obscure place in the world in which they move. The Sun represents the will of individuals, and the influence of the planets is superior to everything but our free will that is represented by the power of the Sun. Therefore, we and everything in the universe depend on the Sun, the giver of life. In dealing with our will and the life-giving energy of the Sun, individuals are opening themselves up to a power that is not seen, much like a seed that is hidden in March but produces a blossom in May.

Inherent in the expression of the Sun are the will, drive, purpose, and vitality to go ahead. The conscious use and application of the Sun power must be constructive.

The Sun rules the sign Leo which is a Fixed, Fire, positive sign, expressing the creativity inherent in the Sun. Leo individuals have a flair for the dramatic, and the Sun, ruler of Leo, the house and sign it is placed in, the house that carries Leo on its cusp, the house with Aries (the exalted ruler of the Sun) on its cusp, and the fifth house are the areas where the creative ideas of the Sun are dramatized.

* See planets in the signs and houses in *The Astrologer's Handbook*.

If the individual is to be a trustworthy manager of this life energy, this power must not be used for ego gratification, and this urge to survive should not be used in a competitive manner with other human beings. This is often the tendency because the Sun is exalted in the sign of Aries which can be egocentric and competitive. If individuals are continually competing with the world in which they move, they cannot constructively use this power in a dynamic self-expression, which is the purpose of their lives. Accomplishment rather than competition should be the criterion used in the inspirational use of the Sun power.

The house in which the Sun is found is where individuals should shine; this they must do if they are to avoid frustration. The Sun rules Leo, a Fire sign that is learning the lesson of love. These individuals can express this love by helping others to shine and express their Sun potential. This is a constructive substitute for competition.

If individuals are to unfold the power of the Sun, they must go about the business of living with strength of will, dignity, and courage to face any opposition, just as the seed is confident that the Sun which warms the Earth will help it in its push to the direct rays of the Sun.

When dealing with the Sun power, individuals must know that the limelight that is represented by the Sun cannot be focused on them unless they use the will represented by the Sun to initiate new starts in their creative endeavors, represented by the Sun exalted in Aries. Mercury is the Esoteric ruler of Aries, dealing with the idea that all action has its origin in thought. If thoughts are scattered on worthless trifles, and life is frittered away with individuals living only for pleasure and amusement, or if individuals do not think and have opinions that do not constitute knowledge, especially about the business of living, they can not direct this Sun power in a constructive way.

If we are to be conscious of health and self-mastery, the will represented by the Sun, when used constructively, will help to unfold this power inherent in the giver of life.

The house in which the Sun is placed is a place of power, the house with Leo on its cusp is an added place of power, and the house with Aries, the exalted sign of the Sun, is where loving, creative thoughts will lighten the dark recesses of the heart and mind, giving individuals a new start where they can initiate action that will open up new avenues for the expression of the potential of the Sun.*

* See Sun in the houses in Chapter 6 of *The Astrologer's Handbook.*

Keywords for the Sun

Drive for significance—will power—creative self-expression—personal leadership—authority figures—personal authority—ego identity—social relationships with important people—pleasure—children—education of children—sex for pleasure and conquest—romantic activity—love affairs—theater—entertainment—speculation—enterprise—vitality—unconditioned self—individuality—where we shine—desire for recognition—one of the significators of the marriage partner in a woman's chart—indicator of one's health—Sun being masculine is also an indicator of the men in your life—where one can apply the will.

Conjunctions to the Sun

Conjunctions emphasize the individual's will power, creative ability, and initiative. Whether this expression is constructive or destructive will depend upon other aspects made to the conjunction and whether the conjunction involves malefic or benefic planets. The areas affected will be the house in which the conjunction is found, the signs and houses ruled by the planets involved in the conjunction, and the signs and houses containing their exalted rulers.

Sextiles of the Sun

Sextiles of the Sun indicate opportunities for self-expression, mental development, and the unfolding of the creative potential of the individual. These opportunities will come through the houses in which the planets forming the sextile are placed, the houses and signs they rule, and the houses and signs in which their exalted rulers are found.

Squares to the Sun

Squares to the Sun indicate that the individual will experience difficulty in using the will and the power potential of the Sun in a harmonious and wise manner. This square can be indicative of the past misuse of power, which in turn affects even the health and vitality of the individual. The difficulties and frustrations of this square will come from the planets and houses in which the square is found, the signs and houses that the planets rule, and the signs and houses of their exalted rulers. These will be the areas where a great effort of the will is needed in order to overcome the obstacles that stand in the way of the constructive use of the power of the Sun and the planets involved in the square.

Trines of the Sun

Trines of the Sun indicate an easy flow of the creative self-expression that indicates leadership and good fortune and favors good relationships and the creative arts. The individual will be favored with good health if the rest of the horoscope permits it. The individual can benefit from education, working with children, and the sports or entertainment world. The good fortune indicated by trines to the Sun will be found in the signs and houses in which the planets making the trine are found, the signs and houses these planets rule, and the signs and houses that contain the exalted rulers.

Oppositions of the Sun

Oppositions of the Sun indicate that the individual will experience a conflict of will between the energy of the Sun and the energy of the planet forming the opposition. There can be a tendency to egotism and to dominate relationships which could cause resentment in others and frustration for the individual. Sun oppositions indicate that there is a need for the individual to consider all viewpoints impartially. If individuals are faced with strife, they should not take a partisan point of view; this will help them to maintain harmonious relationships that the opposition demands if these individuals are to function with others in a cooperative manner. The nature and the areas of these conflicts will be determined by the signs and houses in which the planets forming the opposition are placed, the signs and houses which the planets rule, and the signs and houses of their exaltations.*

For the Sun in Cardinal, Fixed, and Mutable signs, in Fire, Earth, Air, and Water signs, also in the positive, masculine and receptive, feminine signs see the chapter on Sun signs in this book.

The Pluto Pattern

Pluto is the primary ruler of the sign Scorpio, the co-ruler of Aries, and is exalted in the sign Leo. Pluto, like the Sun, deals with the power of the will. As the co-ruler of Aries it demands that individuals regenerate

* See aspects to the Sun and planets in Part II, "Interpreting Aspects" of *The Astrologer's Handbook.*

their self-image. The exaltation ruler Leo demands that individuals regenerate their attitudes toward pleasure and bring to a higher level of expression the children of their mind and body. Under Pluto individuals gain experience through the handling of collective resources which Scorpio rules. Scorpio being the sign of sex indicates that the will is to be used in finding a balance in the sexual expression. This expression is tied to Leo dealing with sex for pleasure.

Pluto, ruler of Scorpio, deals with concentrated power. As ruler of this Fixed, Water sign, the silent inner workings of this concentrated power will eventually give a new start to the individual in the house and sign in which Pluto is found, and in the houses containing Scorpio, Aries, and Leo. Scorpio, a Fixed, Water sign, does not work in the open; it works in secret, indicated by its rulership of the Natural secret eighth house.

Pluto deals with the power of the will, and because memory and mental habits follow in the same pattern, a conscious effort of the will is required to change these patterns and give the individual a new start, promised by Pluto's co-rulership of Aries. Mercury is the Esoteric ruler of Aries and deals with thought; therefore, the power of the will must be exerted so that individuals can consciously choose their focus of attention, selecting the thoughts to be entertained by their conscious mind. To the extent that individuals can consciously choose their thoughts do they have free will, and at this point it is good to remember that all action originates in thought and individuals are bound by the consequences of action.

Some schools of psychology advance the idea that individuals should give vent to their emotions, be disagreeable if they want to, be themselves whether the self is something other people can live with or not. However, Pluto, which rules Scorpio, which rules the emotions that are sometimes too deep for tears, demands that the desires represented by Mars the co-ruler of Scorpio be lifted up to a higher expression and transmuted into holy desires. Anyone can be disagreeable, anyone can hate and resent, but to love, to understand, and to raise the status of the consciousness takes a definite conscious exercise of the power of the will which Pluto deals with in the horoscope. Reserve and self-control of the outer expression are only the beginning. Pluto also deals with the recycling process, the recycling of waste products. Pluto in the horoscope indicates where individuals must clean up and recycle the residues of their physical, emotional, and mental bodies as well as of their environment. The residue of old conditions must not be allowed to poison the ongoing process of life. Unresolved thoughts, indicated by Mercury's

Esoteric rulership of Aries, where Pluto co-rules, and emotions of the past can poison the psyche, thus interfering with perception and distorting reason. This principle applies to worldwide recycling if we are to survive this technological age with its pollutants.

Pluto represents the stage in life when actions or activities that have been going on more or less subconsciously suddenly become a basis of active consideration. Mars, the co-ruler of Scorpio, represents the great ocean of desire from which the confusions and frustrations of the sex impulse originate. Pluto, the primary ruler of Scorpio, the sign of sex, and co-ruler of Aries representing the principle of desire, exalted in Leo the sign of love, gives the power to transform such conditions to a higher form of expression.

Pluto rules the eighth house of collective resources, joint monies, corporate money, inheritance, and goods of the dead. If Pluto receives stress aspects from the other planets these collective resources can be used for self-aggrandizement or to coerce others. The misuse of these resources is a tactic often employed by underworld or large corporate structures which Pluto also rules; however, these same tactics can be used within the individual's life.

The sign and house in which Pluto is placed, the house carrying Scorpio which Pluto rules, the house carrying Aries which Pluto co-rules, and the house carrying Leo where Pluto is exalted are the departments of life where the individual can make use of the power to transform the activities of life to a higher level of expression. In these departments the admonition from on high is regenerate, climb, cooperate, believe in My justice and My promise of heaven on Earth.*

Keywords and Phrases of Pluto

Need for regeneration of existing conditions—death of old conditions and initiation of new changes—irrevocable change—the need to accept change and transformation—increased resourcefulness and creativity—desire to understand the fundamental causes and motivation behind events—stimulation of the intuitive clairvoyant faculties—involvement with occult activities and practices—involvement in advanced science and technology, especially atomic energy—corporate business enterprises—matters relating to joint finances—insurance—taxes—alimony—goods of the dead—secrecy and intrigues—death and involvement with the affairs

* See Pluto in the signs and houses in *The Astrologer's Handbook.*

of the dead—transformer—obsession—dictator—transcendence—rejuvenation—fanaticism—elimination—control—the masses—power—intensification—reorganization—alchemy—regimentation—underworld.

Conjunctions of Pluto

Pluto conjunctions indicate that individuals have the power to transform their own nature and their mode of self-expression; this transformation can be for better or for worse. Conjunctions of Pluto endow individuals with a powerful will and a penetrating insight into the underlying forces of life. This power of concentration often leads to clairvoyant and occult abilities. It gives an interest in science, especially in the field of atomic energy or any type of energy that deals with transformation. The use of this willpower will be demonstrated in the signs and houses in which the conjunction is found, the signs and houses which the planets involved in this conjunction rule, and also the signs and houses that contain their exalted rulers.

Sextiles to Pluto

Sextiles to Pluto indicate that individuals have an opportunity for self-transformation and mental growth through the dynamic use of their willpower. Often these individuals affect the world in which they move through writing, communication, friendships, and group endeavors. They often travel for reasons that others cannot fathom. There can be an interest in the occult. These interests and opportunities will come through the signs and houses which form the sextile, the signs and houses which the planets involved in the sextile rule, and the signs and houses in which the exalted rulers involved in the sextile are found.

Squares to Pluto

Squares to Pluto indicate that individuals often attempt the impossible. There can be problems with impatience and overbearing dictatorial attitudes that only serve to defeat their purpose. These attitudes will affect the houses that carry the two planets making the square, the signs and houses they rule, and the signs and houses where their exalted rulers are found.

Trines to Pluto

Pluto trines indicate that good fortune and spiritual development can be realized through concentration and the creative use of the will. These individuals have the ability to improve, reform, and transform their environments. They make good spiritual leaders, healers, and clairvoyants. They also have prophetic ability. This good fortune will manifest itself in the houses that contain the two planets in the trine, the signs and houses that they rule, and the signs and houses that contain the exalted rulers of the planets that form the trine.

Oppositions to Pluto

Oppositions to Pluto indicate relationship problems that stem from demanding, dictatorial, or domineering attitudes. Attempts at reforming others without their consent or wishes generate resentment, thus alienating these individuals from warm human contacts. This kind of attitude can also lead to arguments and impasses that affect the individual's relationships. Individuals with this opposition should heed the first astrological rule that one does not try to change the other person, just change the self. If the change is constructive, others will try to emulate you through contagion. The areas affected by this opposition will be the houses carrying Pluto, and the planets that form the opposition, the houses that Pluto and the planets rule, and the houses that contain the exalted rulers of the planets in opposition.

If Pluto is in a Cardinal sign, the individual will feel a need for constant change, improvement, and new activity. The individual will be inclined to activity and will constantly pursue social change with major emphasis on immediate crises affecting humanity. This is because the Cardinal signs are decision-making signs and deal with the here and now. The danger lies in an overreaction to situations as they arise, and this type of situation can lead to long-range consequences.

If Pluto is in a Fixed sign, individuals will be goal-oriented and determined, even relentless in their efforts to bring about what they consider large-scale changes in civilization. There can also be a fanatical adherence to fixed ideologies with this Fixed position of Pluto.

Pluto in a Mutable sign will be concerned with cleaning up and regenerating the mental and emotional residues of past experience. Pluto in a Mutable sign enables individuals to draw upon past knowledge and experience for this cleaning-up process. The danger of this placement is that individuals can be trapped by their past habit patterns and vacillate in their purpose to change them.

If Pluto is found in a positive, masculine sign, individuals will have the ability to bring about major changes and transformations through their own initiative.

If Pluto is found in a receptive, feminine sign, individuals bring about changes and transformation in response to necessity which is dictated by existing conditions.

If Pluto is found in a Fire sign, individuals are likely to bring about dramatic, revolutionary changes in their life-style affecting the sexual mores, economic, and educational conditions that are part of their lives. The negative expression of the Fire sign placement is egotism, revolutionary attitudes that lack constructive improvement, and automatic rejection of old conditions and adhering to that which is pleasurable.

If Pluto is found in an Earth sign, there will be important transformations in individuals' work, business, financial, professional, and political activities. Their medical and dietary practices will undergo a major change. The negative expression of Pluto in an Earth sign is a materialistic trend in social values and customs.

If Pluto is found in an Air sign, individuals will have penetrating insights into literary, scientific, and sociological fields. The negative expression of Pluto in an Air sign is a fanatical adherence to intellectual dogmas.

If Pluto is found in a Water sign, individuals will be concerned with emotional, psychological, and psychic issues. They will experience a need to clean up and regenerate emotional habit patterns that are individual and social. The negative expression of this Pluto position can be undue vehemence of the personal emotions or a destructive use of psychic powers.

The Jupiter Pattern

Jupiter is the ruler of Sagittarius and in the Natural Zodiac rules the ninth house, which is the house of the higher inspirational mind. Jupiter is the co-ruler of the sign Pisces and is exalted in the nurturing sign of Cancer. Jupiter is the preserver of all things in time and space. It represents the growth and expansion of the creative powers. Its mission is to preserve the essence of the seed of the individual (the seed represents that which we will eventually become as spiritual beings) until the individual can express the life contained within the seed. This seed is preserved until it finds a proper environment that will be conducive to its unfoldment and that will assist in producing the blossom and eventually the fruit. Thus Jupiter contains the seed and promise of what the individual can become.

Jupiter indicates the way individuals can grow and expand and expect greater enrichment in their lives. This expansion is conditioned by the aspects that are made to Jupiter by other planets. Jupiter co-rules Pisces, which is the sign of hidden support or self-undoing; therefore this enrichment is circumscribed by individuals' past actions and motivation.

As the ruler of the Natural ninth house, Jupiter represents insights, illumination, and all higher education. Jupiter represents true judgment and understanding which is distilled from experience. As the ruler of the Natural ninth house, Jupiter stands for the abstract mind, justice, law, aspiration, wealth, and expansion.

Jupiter as the planet of the judge and lawmaker inquires into our motives and purposes, and under Jupiter the moral qualities within us begin to develop. Jupiter stands for soul growth, expansion, and magnanimity, and its power expands and sustains, especially where constructive progress is taking place. If the action is destructive, then Saturn with its admonition of "Thou shalt not" takes over. Traditionally the principles of both Jupiter and Saturn must be taken into consideration when dealing with one or the other. Jupiter deals with growth and expansion and Saturn deals with form, the structure-building of the form, and the contracting and crystallizing of the form. The principle of growth and expansion represented by Jupiter must always work through form, and Jupiter amplifies whatever Jupiter touches. It represents the individual's capacity for free interchange with life and the feeler that the individual puts out for opportunity.

Jupiter's placement is where the individual expands and sustains and where the individual can make constructive progress in life. Jupiter rules institutions and professions concerned with cultural rules and traditions. It deals with educational, philosophic, religious, and cultural institutions. It deals with the codification of thought and conduct.

The house that carries Jupiter, the house that Jupiter rules, and the house that carries Cancer, the exalted ruler, are the areas of good luck, health, growth, and expansion for the individual. Jupiter like Mars stands for a type of energy that needs control and discipline. If the Jupiter urge to improve and expand is perverted there can be false pride, untruthfulness, false superiority, arrogance, and condescension. Jupiter represents wealth and abundance, and if Jupiter is perverted the individual will give money and wealth a power that it does not possess. The expansion principle of Jupiter should be based on ethical behavior and is linked to the individual's relation to the prevailing social order that is ruled by Jupiter.

Jupiter, the sign and house in which it is placed, the sign and house it rules, and the sign and house of its exalted ruler represent the areas where individuals can improve their own conditions and put into action ideas that will make growth and expansion possible for another.

Jupiter is the symbol of the teacher and represents the paternal instinct that can be used in guiding another person along the lines of unfoldment.

Jupiter rules Sagittarius, a Mutable sign that deals with skills and the utilization of past experience. Jupiter as the great benefic represents that storehouse of abundance which should be shared with others, and where the individual should express a sincere, joyous, positive attitude of gratitude to the spiritual parent represented by Jupiter. The position of Jupiter indicates the department of life that individuals need to discipline and train themselves as moral leaders, and where they need to develop the capacity to give generously but wisely.

Jupiter in the signs indicates individuals' ethical, religious, and philosophic standards and beliefs. It indicates how they express growth and expansion, how they do things on a large scale, and how they are likely to receive financial benefits. Jupiter in the signs indicates how they have earned the goodwill of others and is indicative of their right to receive spiritual protection.

Jupiter in the houses represents the area where individuals receive the flow of the good things of life. It represents the department of life through which individuals will express religious, philosophic, and educational ideas. In this area they can work with the larger social order in sharing their material and spiritual abundance.

Keywords and Phrases of Jupiter

Benevolence—good luck—expansion—growth—optimism—enthusiasm—willingness to enter into new experience—faith—religion—philosophy—higher education—cultural awareness—personal ethics—sense of justice—churches, universities, and other cultural institutions—legal affairs—long journeys—foreigners—foreign countries—higher mind—reward of karma—jovial—wisdom—understanding—the prevailing social order—eternal values—overconfidence—overoptimism—excessiveness—bigotry—conceit—arrogance—false pride—hypocritical—dissipation—indulgence—excess.*

* See Jupiter in the signs and houses in *The Astrologer's Handbook.*

Conjunctions to Jupiter

Jupiter conjunctions indicate that the individual has a general attitude of optimism, goodwill, and awareness of constructive possibilities. These individuals are generous and benevolent, and because of this they gain the confidence and willing cooperation of others. The house in which Jupiter and the planets making the conjunction are found, the house and sign they rule, and the signs and houses of their exalted rulers are the areas where good fortune, growth, and expansion are possible in the individual's life.

Sextiles to Jupiter

Sextiles to Jupiter indicate an opportunity for rapid mental growth and that the individual will have many friends. The individual can profit through education, writing, travel, and communication. The sextile indicates that the individual will work well with groups and get along well with brothers, sisters, and neighbors. These opportunities will come through the houses in which the planets involved in the sextile are found, the signs and houses they rule, and the signs and houses of their exalted rulers.

Squares to Jupiter

Jupiter squares indicate that individuals are liable to be overly ambitious, overly optimistic, and attempt and promise more than they can accomplish. Although the optimism is good, these individuals must make certain that they have a solid foundation on which they can build and expand. They should learn to use moderation and careful forethought where ambitions are concerned; otherwise, when they fall short of their goals, their careers and reputations can suffer. These problems arise in the areas of life that contain Jupiter and the planets involved in the square aspect, the signs and houses they rule, and the signs and houses in which their exalted rulers are found.

Trines of Jupiter

Trines of Jupiter indicate that good fortune and easy progress can be made in this life. This indicates that individuals have talents and resources that they can call upon if they choose. This trine signifies that past actions are being rewarded. The resources, talent, and fortune which individuals can use will be found in the houses containing the planets that are involved in the trine aspect, the signs and houses they rule, and the signs and houses that contain their exalted rulers.

Oppositions of Jupiter

Jupiter oppositions indicate that individuals will have relationship problems because of a tendency to demand too much from others or to take too much for granted. They lack a sense of gratitude, and there is a tendency to promote grandiose schemes at the expense of others. Their hail-fellow-well-met attitude is not always appreciated or accepted by others. These difficulties will emerge in the houses that carry Jupiter and the planets involved in the opposition, the houses these planets rule, and the signs and houses that contain their exalted rulers.*

If Jupiter is found in a Cardinal sign, individuals will seek to grow and expand through some kind of social or cultural activity. Moral and ethical judgments will be based on present circumstances rather than past or future expectations.

If Jupiter is found in a positive, masculine sign, individuals will take the initiative in these activities.

If Jupiter is found in a receptive, feminine sign, individuals are apt to rely on outside influences or people to instigate them to action and expansion along these lines.

If Jupiter is found in a Fixed sign, individuals will aspire to a definite and fixed educational and cultural goal. They are not likely to compromise principles, and they are liable to have rigid ideas about religion, philosophy, education, ethics, and correct social behavior. On the negative side, this can result in an inflexibility and a refusal to see the other person's point of view.

If Jupiter is found in a positive, masculine sign, individuals will initiate the actions that will help them realize their educational and cultural roles.

If Jupiter is found in a receptive, feminine sign, individuals will be stirred to take action in these matters by other people or by an opportunity that presents itself that can result in this type of expansion.

If Jupiter is found in a Mutable sign, individuals' ethical, religious, educational, and social values will be based on past experience and con-

* See planets and aspects in "Part II: Interpreting Aspects" of *The Astrologer's Handbook*.

ditioning. These individuals have the ability to adapt themselves to the ever-changing social order. The danger is that past conditioning may interfere with the accurate perception of present and future cultural and social possibilities.

If Jupiter is found in a positive, masculine sign, individuals will take the initiative in religious, educational, social, or cultural activities or in arranging for long-distance travel.

If Jupiter is found in a receptive, feminine sign, individuals are likely to accept and follow the prevailing religious, educational, social, or cultural views or values, or they will rely on other people or influences to get them involved in these activities.

If Jupiter is found in a Fire sign, individuals will possess an abundance of self-confidence that will enable them to attempt large-scale endeavors. They can become a leader in educational, cultural, or religious affairs. These individuals can inspire enthusiasm and confidence in others. Should their endeavors fail, they always manage to find new fields for growth and expansion. The optimism signified by Jupiter does not allow these individuals to be daunted or disappointed by defeat. The danger is that their egos can prevent them from taking an objective and unbiased view of reality and could blind them to the whole truth of a situation.

If Jupiter is found in an Earth sign, individuals will judge matters by their practical results. There must be a measurable benefit or they will lose interest. They take a practical approach to religion, education, philosophy, and social tradition. The danger is that material things can become an end in themselves rather than a means to an end, and thus thwart the spiritual purpose of the individual's life.

If Jupiter is in an Air sign, individuals have an intellectual approach to philosophy, education, and social traditions. They are generally well informed and knowledgeable about these matters. They are fond of philosophical discussion and debate. They like to circulate in order to experience as many life-styles, traditions, and cultural ideas as possible. They feel they will know more if they circulate and intermingle. The danger is that if these intellectual tendencies are carried to extremes, these individuals are liable to have an impractical, theoretical approach to life. These individuals may pay lip service to exalted ideals but neglect to put them into practice.

If Jupiter is found in a Water sign, individuals' moral and social values are liable to be biased in favor of familiar and emotionally comfortable family traditions and values of the culture in which they were raised. These individuals are likely to have strong emotional ties to the family.

They also have deep feelings, compassion, and understanding for others. The danger is that they must be careful not to let their feelings interfere in any moral or social issue.

The Saturn Pattern

Saturn represents the individual's capacity for self-discipline, organization, and perseverance in the pursuit of long-range goals. Saturn rules the Cardinal, receptive, feminine Earth sign of Capricorn, and is exalted in the Cardinal, intellectual Air sign Libra. Saturn is the planet of fate in regard to time and space; it signifies restraint and responsibility and the power to fulfill and utilize that which will bring the individual security. Under Saturn individuals perfect their innate skills and establish a reputation and public standing. Saturn is the ambassador of the Eternal and symbolizes the father principle, unlike Jupiter which represents the nurturing principle. Saturn, much like the earthly father, will sometimes be forced to apply the lash of necessity which will compel the individual to tread the narrow way of attainment. Saturn gives us only what we earn through our own efforts and deals with the serious purpose of life and the ability to pursue a discipline over a long period of time.

The action of Saturn is slow, persistent, cold, and calculated. It allows no flaws in any undertaking; therefore Saturn frustrates and checks so that the progress is true and the expression perfected. Patience is the keyword if one is to fulfill the requirements of Saturn. Saturn symbolizes Father Time with his hourglass and scythe in hand. The area where Saturn is found in the horoscope, the house Saturn rules, and the signs and houses containing the exalted ruler are the areas where individuals must build structure into their lives through organization, patience, and perseverance. Saturn will not permit individuals to leave the school of life until the course has been run and finished. Saturn's curriculum embodies the lessons of tact, diplomacy, method and system, justice, honor, industry, mechanical ability, fair-mindedness, and most of all a joyous and loving fulfillment of legitimate responsibilities. If this is not done, there can be lack in the life, loneliness, and depression. If individuals do not measure up under Saturn they are liable to become depressed and in turn impose harsh restrictions or regimentation on others. However, at times restrictions under Saturn can be useful if they are tempered with compassion and wisdom and a desire to do what is best for all. Saturn always demands that individuals do what is right with a healthy and reasonable attitude.

Saturn is the cosmic timekeeper; thus individuals must cope with their own creation. The vibrations that are set up under Saturn act as a boomerang on their own creator, and under it one reaps what one sows. It represents the immutable justice of the spiritual and evolutionary law.

Because of the demands of Saturn, the obstructing influence of this planet can be a blessing in disguise, and pain or pleasure can prod individuals to their ultimate goal. As Shakespeare said, "There is nothing good nor bad but thinking makes it so."

Under Saturn individuals develop patience and persistence and well-doing in the facing of responsibilities. Saturn represents the law but does not punish because individuals were tempted but because they yielded and failed to discriminate between good and evil. The aphorism "Whom the Lord loveth, he chasteneth" truly applies to Saturn, demanding that individuals take up the responsibilities of life and develop capacities in such a way that they will reap the rewards and honors which Saturn bestows on the children who obey the law of responsibility and fulfillment. The sign and house that hold Saturn and the houses that carry the signs Capricorn, Aquarius, which Saturn co-rules, and Libra are the departments of life where individuals must fulfill themselves if they are to avoid frustration. This can be done only by obeying the laws of Saturn, thus gaining the freedom promised by Aquarius.

In these areas of life Saturn demands that individuals climb one more hill, but not on someone else's back.

Saturn in the sign indicates the kinds of responsibilities individuals are obliged to face and the type of lessons they must learn. Saturn is also an important factor in determining individuals' careers; it gives important clues to the type of work that individuals will be suited for and the kind of career they will eventually pursue. It is usually through hard work and discipline and coping with many difficulties that individuals find order and security. Saturn in the sign shows how persons seek status and recognition and where they will try to accomplish something of lasting value in the eyes of the world.

Saturn in the houses indicates the area where the practical circumstances of life require that individuals act with discipline and responsibility, thus forcing individuals to mature. It shows where they must build structure into their lives and where they will express their practical ambitions. This is revealed by the house that holds Saturn and the houses where Capricorn, Aquarius, and Libra are placed.*

* See Saturn in the signs and houses in *The Astrologer's Handbook*.

Keywords and Phases for Saturn

Capacity for discipline—unavoidable responsibilities—things that take time and discipline to bring to fruition—relationships that involve long-term responsibilities—relationships with established authority—long-range career plans—established people—old people—friendships, groups, and organizations with a serious purpose—political and professional ambitions—public reputation—profession—government—legal affairs—skeletal structure—mathematics—sense of responsibility—celestial school master—difficult lessons—time—separation—fear—defensive mechanism—self-discipline—constriction—crystallization—exacting—caution—produces wisdom—suspicion—cold—seriousness—stability—obstruction—suppression—pessimism—selfishness—limitation.

Conjunctions of Saturn

Conjunctions of Saturn indicate that individuals are generally conservative, serious, and respected for self-discipline. These individuals are ambitious and hard-working; however, they will be confronted with many obstacles and limitations which they must overcome. There is a certain austerity about these individuals that often discourages warm relationships. The characteristics will manifest in the houses in which the planets involved in the conjunction are found, the signs and houses that these planets rule, and the signs and houses of their exalted rulers.

Sextiles of Saturn

Sextiles of Saturn indicate that individuals have opportunities for progress and mental development through serious hard work and good organization. These individuals will be loyal to their friends, brothers and sisters, neighbors, and organizations. This stabilizing influence will be noticeable in the areas where the planets forming the sextile are found, the signs and houses which they rule, and the signs and houses of their exalted rulers.

Squares of Saturn

Squares of Saturn indicate that individuals must overcome severe obstacles and limitations that frustrate their ambitions and desire for happiness. These individuals must work twice as hard to obtain the same results that others may obtain with ease. Saturn squares indicate major life problems that must be overcome, and because they are major problems they spur individuals to greater achievements. The difficulties encountered under Saturn squares tend to affect individuals' careers and homes. These difficulties will affect the houses in which Saturn and the planets forming the square are found, the signs and houses which these planets rule, and the signs and houses of their exalted rulers.

Trines of Saturn

Trines of Saturn indicate that individuals will have good fortune and lasting success because of disciplined creativity and serious philosophic outlook. Their high moral conduct inspires confidence and trust in others and because of this they are often given positions of responsibility. Trines of Saturn give these individuals organizing and managerial abilities. They also make good teachers. These abilities will be reflected in the houses in which the planets forming the trine are found, the signs and houses they rule, and the signs and houses of their exalted rulers.

Oppositions of Saturn

Oppositions of Saturn indicate that individuals will appear much too serious and austere, and they will seem unfriendly and unapproachable to others. This can make these individuals feel lonely and frustrated, and Saturn demands that they do not become embittered and isolated, for otherwise they will aggravate the situation more. Others will look upon these individuals as having problems that arise from their own negative, restrictive attitudes and lack of cooperation. These difficulties will arise in the areas in which the oppositions are found, the signs and houses which these planets rule, and the signs and houses in which their exalted rulers are found.*

If Saturn is found in a Cardinal sign, individuals will be decisive in handling business and professional affairs. They will organize and act on the opportunities as they are presented to them, especially those that will help career advancement.

If Saturn is found in a positive, masculine sign, individuals will take the initiative in organizing business and professional affairs and they will make immediate use of every advantage to further their careers.

* See Saturn in aspect to other planets in "Part II: Interpreting Aspects" of *The Astrologer's Handbook.*

If Saturn is found in a receptive, feminine sign, individuals will be liable to organize and manage existing enterprises rather than establish and initiate new ones.

If Saturn is found in a Fixed sign, individuals will organize business and career efforts in a way that will help them to achieve long-range goals. Saturn in a Fixed sign gives great staying power; however, if Saturn receives stress aspects from other planets, these individuals can be stubborn, fixed, and unyielding in their attitudes.

If Saturn is found in a positive, masculine sign, individuals will take the initiative toward organizing and achieving long-range goals.

If Saturn is found in a receptive, feminine sign, individuals will wait for opportunities or the proper time to organize and advance business goals.

If Saturn is found in a Mutable sign, individuals will rely on past experience, accumulated knowledge, and their own inherent skills to organize business and professional affairs. However, if Saturn receives stress aspects, individuals can be fearful and their self-confidence is often inhibited by painful memories of the past. These can stand in the way of individuals' success.

If Saturn is found in a positive, masculine sign, individuals will initiate and organize their accumulated experience and skills and use them to further business and professional affairs.

If Saturn is found in a receptive, feminine sign, individuals will attract or wait for the proper opportunity to present itself. Then they can use the skills and knowledge that they have acquired from past experiences in a way that will further profession and career.

If Saturn is found in a Fire sign, individuals will have a natural capacity for leadership and the ability to initiate new projects in professional and business spheres of activity. However, they should avoid egotistical, authoritarian attitudes that could stand in the way of long-range goals.

If Saturn is found in an Earth sign, individuals will display practical business, professional, and organizational abilities. These individuals will have a natural knack for organizing practical work and responsibilities. However, if Saturn receives stress aspects, these individuals can develop a materialistic outlook that brooks no interference with the job that needs to be done.

If Saturn is found in an Air sign, individuals have a natural intellectual organizing ability and the capacity to give concrete expression to abstract concepts. These individuals will be capable of mental discipline and organization in literary, educational, and scientific fields. They also have mathematical ability. If this intellectuality is carried too far, these individuals can appear cold, aloof, detached, even insensitive to others.

If Saturn is found in a Water sign, individuals are likely to show a great depth of feeling and at other times can become emotionally depressed and morose. Therefore, a cheerful environment and a positive, optimistic attitude are essential for this position of Saturn.

The Uranus Pattern

Uranus indicates the way in which individuals go about seeking freedom and new experiences. The house containing Uranus is where individuals will want freedom and eventually get it. If they do not get this freedom, they will rebel at every restraint. In this area of their life individuals will become independent, intuitive, and inventive. Uranus rules the sign Aquarius which is a Fixed, goal-oriented, and intellectual Air sign and co-rules Saturn. It rules the eleventh house in the Natural Zodiac, which deals with the individual's goals and objectives, friends, groups, and organizational associates. The house and sign Uranus is found in, the house that carries Aquarius and Capricorn, and the house that carries Scorpio where Uranus is exalted will be the areas through which the individual will seek new friends and group associates.

Uranus is the planet of altruism and brotherly love and deals with the motivation behind the individual's goals and objectives. Altruism does not require the return of love that is bestowed on others; the love of Uranus extends beyond home, kin, and country, it is a universal love. Uranus is exalted in Scorpio which is the sign of sex, but Uranus does not concern itself with sex in its highest application; it is the agent of change and transformation. Uranus represents a universal love, which does not mean that the love for family will lessen, but that it will be fulfilled in a greater degree, giving the individual freedom and allowing the same freedom for others. Uranian love is like the love that binds a student to a teacher.

Uranus is a higher octave of Venus, in that it transcends personal love and is the Esoteric ruler of Libra. Venus gives to its mate and blood relations, but Uranus, which is the higher octave ruler, goes beyond sex and family love to cosmic proportions that go beyond desire or the Mars or Venus love.

This Uranian energy is often used in clandestine love affairs. The misuse of the Uranian energy has an adverse affect on the morals of many.

There is a disregard for all conventional codes and at times a perversion of the use of sex. The misuse of the Uranian energy in any form indicates that the individual has not fulfilled the requirements of Saturn, which is the planet that demands fulfillment of responsibility and of building structure into the life. Until this building can be done in a joyous and fulfilling way, the ring-pass-me-not of Saturn will keep the individual chained to this kind of responsibility. When this responsibility is not taken on joyfully, the individual can use the Uranian energy to act rashly and spill out this energy in sex or fruitless rebellion. However, in the twinkling of an eye the lightning-like vibration of Uranus will eventually break this kind of pattern and alter the individual's life. When this happens, the individual will start fulfilling the requirements of Saturn with regard to relationships, responsibilities, and utilization of skills and resources, and automatically begin to function in a progressive and impersonal way. The Uranus urge to liberation will eventually free the individual from constricting conditions and in turn the individual will contribute lovingly to the liberation of others. When this happens, Saturn will not impose any more chains on the individual; however, the individual will take the chains and don them and become a leader in some unusual way.

If Uranus is found in a positive, masculine sign, individuals will be aggressive in their action and desire for independence and freedom and will persist in this type of pursuit for as long as they live.

If Uranus is found in a receptive, feminine sign, individuals will initiate ways to acquire freedom; however, they will be inclined to wait for and be receptive to the opportunities that will eventually lead to freedom.

Uranus is the habit breaker and the opener of doors. It symbolizes the alchemist, the scientist, the magician-priest, the creative artist, and the astrologer with impersonal wisdom that comes as a result of alchemical experiences.

Individuals who are set apart by the Eternal in this work of liberation on all levels of experience always have Uranus prominent in the chart, and even though it receives stress aspects from other planets (because Saturn which rules time is linked with Uranus), Saturn is the last planet in the order of the original Sacred Seven Planets indicating that the lessons of Saturn are mandatory regardless of any freedom offered by Uranus. Individuals eventually learn that Uranus stands for the responses that are new within them and that Uranus does not cause chaos unless lessons are needed. The punishments of Uranus are catastrophic and alert individuals to a need for controlled direction in life. The loves of Uranus are volcanoes of the heart, that can send the lover into a new world of physical, emotional, and mental expression.

Uranus is the higher octave of Venus, the ruler of an intellectual Air sign, and exalted in the sign Scorpio which is an occult sign and houses the secret of electricity which Uranus rules. Electricity has become our willing servant spanning the space of this planet, breaking down the caste system by making knowledge available to all humanity. Through the agency of electricity which Uranus rules, music, science, literature, and the cultural activities of people all over the Earth can be exchanged.

Uranus is the Esoteric ruler of Libra, and when Uranus has transformed personal love into the love that truly personifies brotherhood, there will be a tremendous charge of renewing life that will enable us to consciously take on the twelve labors of Hercules that will help us to give the genius in ourselves, represented by Uranus, its highest expression.* These labors symbolize our journey from the "clod to God" as we travel the spirals of our evolutionary life.†

Keywords and Phrases of Uranus

Friends, groups, and organizations–scientific research and development–sudden events and changes–breakthroughs–unusual happenings–electronics–advanced technology–astrology–occult pursuits–large-scale corporate finances–disruptive events–independence–originality–inventiveness–freedom–eccentricity–rebelliousness–unconventionality–scientific urge–flashes of intuition–humanistic–impersonal–groups–nonconformists–reformers–idealistic–altruistic–genius–ingenuity–life contribution to the race–isolation–magnetism–electricity. Because Uranus is the Esoteric ruler of Libra, it also deals with psychology.

Conjunctions of Uranus

Conjunctions of Uranus indicate that individuals will have dynamic tendencies that are original and creative. They will have strong willpower and the capacity for dynamic action. These individuals will not be bound by tradition because of their strong need for independence. These individuals will be friendly and humanitarian with an interest in the occult or new areas of scientific discoveries. These individuals often have

* See *The Twelve Labors of Hercules* by Corinne Heline.
† See Uranus in the signs and houses in *The Astrologer's Handbook.*

sudden, unexpected changes come into their lives. These tendencies will manifest in the signs and houses in which the conjunction is found, the signs and houses of the planets involved in the conjunction, and the signs and houses of their exalted rulers.

Sextiles of Uranus

Sextiles of Uranus indicate that individuals will have sudden opportunities for mental growth and progress due to their receptivity and interest in new ideas. These individuals can communicate well, make friends easily, and often show an interest in groups and organizations, especially of an occult nature. These individuals are intuitive and clever and often scientifically inclined. These abilities will manifest in the houses occupied by the two planets forming the sextile, the signs and houses they rule, and the signs and houses of their exalted rulers.

Squares of Uranus

Squares of Uranus indicate that individuals are likely to block their own progress and success by instability, impulsiveness, and rash action. The square indicates that the Uranian energies need controlling and direction, and because these individuals will have the tendency to change their minds often, refuse good advice, and tend to be unreasonable, willful, and obstinate, a great deal of work can be brought to naught through some foolish action. That which has taken these individuals a long time to build can be destroyed with one stubborn, rebellious act. These difficulties will manifest in the houses in which the planets forming the square are found, the signs and houses they rule, and the signs and houses that contain their exalted rulers.

Trines of Uranus

Trines of Uranus indicate that individuals are intuitively creative and have an original way of doing things. These individuals are usually in advance of their time and place of background. They often experience sudden and unexpected good fortune which is utilized in a creative and expansive way. These individuals are generally happy and have many friends and exciting adventures. These benefits will come through the houses in which the planets forming the trine are found, the signs and houses these planets rule, and the signs and houses which contain the exalted rulers of the planets making the trine.

Oppositions of Uranus

Oppositions of Uranus indicate relationship problems that arise out of unpredictable, demanding, unreasonable attitudes toward others. These individuals are liable to be undependable, erratic, willful, and rebellious against any kind of restraint and therefore difficult to deal with. These individuals are likely to damage their relationships through their unwillingness to sacrifice their personal desires and freedoms. These difficulties and problems will manifest in the houses in which the planets forming the opposition are found, the signs and houses these planets rule, and the signs and houses of their exalted rulers.*

If Uranus is found in a Cardinal sign, there is a strong need for constant new activity. These individuals will be quick and decisive in adjusting to new circumstances and changing conditions. These individuals have a knack for turning seemingly chaotic conditions to their immediate advantage because of the Cardinal ability of decision-making and dealing with present circumstances. If Uranus receives stress aspects, these individuals will tend to be impatient with routine and because of this impatience will find it difficult to bring their projects to a conclusion.

If Uranus is found in a Cardinal, positive sign, individuals will initiate unusual ideas, projects, friendships, and group associations.

If Uranus is found in a Cardinal, receptive sign, individuals will want these same changes; however, they are liable to wait until outside stimuli necessitate sudden change and wait for the proper time to utilize or put into action these ideas.

If Uranus is found in a Fixed sign, individuals will be determined to express their creative independence and will not be deterred in their course of action. There will be great energy and determination in following through on their original ideas and concepts. If Uranus receives stress aspects in a Fixed sign, these individuals can be obstinate in pursuing their objectives even if their ideas are impractical.

If Uranus is found in a Fixed, positive sign, individuals will initiate and become leaders in bringing their creative ideas to fruition, and they will keep their eye on the goal until it has been fulfilled.

If Uranus is found in a Fixed, receptive sign, individuals will also be goal-oriented; however, they will wait for the right time to put these original ideas and concepts into practice, enabling them to realize goals through proper timing.

* See planets in aspect to Uranus in "Part II: Interpreting Aspects" of *The Astrologer's Handbook.*

If Uranus is found in a Mutable sign, individuals will accomplish much from the utilization of past experience. These individuals will be adaptable and versatile in adjusting to changing conditions. They will have the ability to break away from old attitudes and habit patterns, which is not true of other planets in Mutable signs. Uranus in a Mutable sign gives individuals the ability to bring to light old ideas and concepts and blend them with the new in a harmonious and workable manner. If Uranus receives stress aspects in a Mutable sign, painful memories can suddenly surface and can cause the individual to act in an irrational and unpredictable manner.

If Uranus is found in a Mutable, positive sign, individuals will be aggressive in their attempts to break away from old habit patterns; they will be aggressive in utilizing past experience; and they will also be aggressive in adapting and adjusting to changing conditions.

If Uranus is found in a Mutable, receptive sign, individuals will wait until some kind of outside stimuli necessitate the sudden change and demand that they adjust to changing conditions. They will wait until they are stimulated to make use of and utilize past experiences in responding to that which is new.

If Uranus is found in a Fire sign, individuals will initiate new enterprises and will have vision and insight in finding new ways of doing things. This kind of leadership will inspire others and gain their support. These individuals will be strong-willed and independent in their expression of the creative drive. If Uranus should receive stress aspects, these individuals can be headstrong and egotistical, which can make cooperation difficult.

If Uranus is found in an Earth sign, individuals will put their original and creative ideas into practical use. These individuals will have the ability to find new and more efficient ways of handling business, financial, and professional affairs. If Uranus receives stress aspects, these individuals could be overly materialistic in their attitudes toward friends and group associations. Their attitudes toward business affairs could be erratic, eccentric, and impractical at times.

If Uranus is found in an intellectual Air sign, individuals will demonstrate an ease in establishing new friends and group associates, and these individuals will have inspired and unusual intellectual abilities. Many unique ideas will come to them through sudden flashes of illumination. If Uranus receives stress aspects, there can be a lack of mental concentration. The ideas can be scattered or these individuals can be easily distracted by new ideas and experience.

If Uranus is found in a Water sign, individuals will have strong intuitive abilities. They will have the ability to understand and empathize with people from all walks of life. However, if Uranus receives stress aspects, their sudden changes of mood can confuse and upset those with whom they are dealing.

The Neptune Pattern

Neptune is the planet that deals with the aesthetic and intuitive faculties of the individual. It has to do with the imagination and the picture-making faculty of the mind. It deals with the storehouse of memory where the past history of the individual is recorded in detail. Although the individual does not have conscious access to this information, this does not mean that it does not exist in a deeper level of awareness. Neptune is like the tip of an iceberg, the major portion is submerged in the deep levels of the mind called the unconscious or subconscious. These memories predispose the likes, dislikes, abilities, and personal limitations of the individual. It is the key to irrational and inexplicable behavior.

Neptune also confers creative, musical, and artistic talent. Its energy is representative of gifted photographers, actors, designers, architects, or any profession that requires creative imagination. The magic art of Neptune gives individuals their highest impulse through poetry, art, drama, dance, music, and sculpture. The energy of Neptune if used constructively will depict beauty or express beauty in some way. Neptune in its artistic expression of beauty needs the techniques of timing, reading, and movement.

Neptune rules the sign Pisces, co-rules the sign Sagittarius, and is exalted in Cancer, the sign of the mother and the nurturing instinct. Neptune represents the mother in a universal sense, and in its highest aspect it represents compassion, understanding, and love that reaches everyone and everything. It represents us reacting and responding to the inspiration of our higher intuitive self. It is the instrument through which individuals choose to make themselves an instrument of the Eternal on the stage of life. The part that they play should be ennobling, inspiring, and triumphant. The vibrations of Neptune should be used in the service of beauty, healing, and realignment in all phases of life. Neptune is the transmitter of galactic energies to our solar system,* and the house containing Neptune holds the secret of how the individual expresses cosmic consciousness. Where Neptune is found is the area that is the source of

* See *The Secret Doctrine* by Madame H. P. Blavatsky.

the individual's inspiration. It is the point that transcends all separateness and the point that represents heaven or hell on Earth and opens the way for the individual to experience cosmic consciousness. This takes place through prayer and devotion to high ideals and through purification of the body which brings into play Pisces' polar opposite sign of Virgo. Virgo is ruled by Mercury and deals with the conscious mind whose function it is to direct the contents of the unconscious mind in a positive and constructive manner. This is why the placement of Neptune and the sign Pisces represents the areas of hidden support or self-undoing. The exaltation sign of Neptune is Cancer, which like Pisces is a Water sign and mirrors all the emotions and activities of its environment. Much like Neptune, the Moon as ruler of Cancer represents conditioning by the family and also deals with the unconscious and is another area that affects the Neptunian response of the individual. The ultimate perversion of Neptune occurs when an individual under the pretense of an ideal exerts dominion over the mind and body of another for self-glorification. In this category is the religious fanatic who abuses, tortures, and enslaves others for the glory of his or her own religious beliefs, which can happen even though the person may be sincere in his or her beliefs.

If individuals respond in a negative way to the energy of Neptune, there can be a tendency to lose themselves in drink and drugs which rob them of the energy to fulfill their ambition. Or they can become indolent loafers full of dreams that have no reality in substance. Neptune's flights from reality can also indicate cheats, or dishonest persons, or individuals can become prey of others who rob or defraud them. Neptune in its negative phase also indicates individuals whose flight from reality can bring them into the world of the delinquent, neurotic, or psychotic. The sick and disorganized people who are swayed completely by the emotions that are lodged in the subconscious mind must learn to deal with the present reality.

Neptune as ruler of the Mutable sign Pisces indicates the area where individuals are able to express their imaginative and intuitive faculties. Pisces deals with skills and the utilization of past experience; therefore, the houses carrying Pisces and its ruler Neptune and its exalted ruler Cancer enable individuals to draw on their past experience and conditioning, be it favorable or unfavorable, to solve present problems. These individuals are always making choices, and if past conditioning has been painful, they should know that every moment is new and that old responses need not be repeated. These individuals should utilize the attributes of the polar opposite sign of Virgo and develop their skills and perfect their work methodology in the practical material world. This in turn will aid them in the realization of emotional, mental, and physical health.

Keywords and Phrases of Neptune

Intuition—imagination—psychic sensitivity—artistic creativity—long journeys, especially by water—obligation—ideals and idealism—memories of the past—self-sacrifice—sympathetic—fantasy—illusion—dreams—subconscious mind—past—euphoria—subliminal—hidden compulsions—escape—hypnotism—hallucination—mysticism—mediumship—slavery—confinement—alcohol—neurotic and psychotic tendencies—places of seclusion—hospitals—jails—prisons—drugs—chemicals—daydreaming—wool gathering—photography—cinematography—petroleum—water—impressionable—subtle.*

Conjunctions of Neptune

Conjunctions of Neptune indicate that individuals are being influenced by the unconscious or the intuitive superconscious aspect of the mind, which is indicated by Neptune being co-ruler of the sign Sagittarius. Either way, these individuals' actions will be difficult or impossible to understand by others. These individuals appear mystical or other-worldly to the average person. If the conjunction receives harmonious aspects from other planets, these individuals will display emotional understanding and spiritual compassion. If the conjunction receives stress aspects from other planets, these individuals will have a tendency to ignore reality and delude themselves. The conjunction will affect the areas where the planets forming the conjunction are found, the signs and houses that these planets rule, and the signs and houses of their exalted rulers.

Sextiles of Neptune

Sextiles of Neptune indicate that individuals will have opportunities for spiritual and mental growth through the use of their imagination and intuitive faculties. They are likely to direct some of their energy in working for idealistic causes. Their creative ability can be expressed through writing, friendships, and group associations. These opportuni-

* See Neptune in the signs and houses in *The Astrologer's Handbook.*

ties will come through the houses in which the planets forming the sextile are found, the signs and houses that carry the rulers of the planets forming the conjunction, and the signs and houses of their exalted rulers. Thus many areas of the horoscope are affected and influence most individuals' life activities.

Squares of Neptune

Squares of Neptune indicate that individuals experience a great deal of confusion and disorganization that arise out of their unconscious negative conditioning. Often these individuals will evade responsibilities and refuse to face up to reality. When they decide to confront their unrealistic notions, they are pulled into situations that are impossible to control. It is almost as if the ideal keeps eluding the suffering individual. Creative expressions are frustrated at every turn. These individuals are usually endowed with magnetic physical attractions, yet they never seem to find the complete fulfillment of love which they are forever seeking to attain. The ambition of this square often manifests itself in artistic illumination and intuitive inspiration and exaltation, or it can result in cynicism, rage, or hopeless fury against life. Or the individual can resort to drink or drugs. At times this square indicates that these individuals are subject to negative psychic influences which will further confuse and disorganize their lives. These dangers and aspirations will be manifested in the houses containing Neptune and the planets forming the square, the signs and houses that Neptune and these planets rule, and the signs and houses of their exalted rulers.

Trines of Neptune

Trines of Neptune indicate that individuals will experience good fortune through the creative use of their intuitive and imaginative faculties. These individuals will have heightened artistic taste. They will have a sensitive response to music and art. They will be idealistic, often possessing clairvoyant, intuitive, and telepathic abilities. They may have a marked degree of spiritual insight and display creative abilities in the fields of art, religion, and education. These abilities will be found in the areas where Neptune and the planets forming the trine are found, the signs and houses they rule, and the signs and houses of their exalted rulers.

Oppositions of Neptune

Oppositions of Neptune indicate relationship problems through which strange and disturbing emotions are aroused. These individuals confuse others because of their unconscious emotional reactions that make them appear undependable in their relationships. Because of this reaction they can be misunderstood, and those involved in the relationship can be confused because they do not know where they stand with the individual. These individuals with the Neptune opposition can have a tendency to project their own psychological difficulties on other people or they can assume the psychic problems of others. There can be deception and unreliability in relationships. If individuals are to handle this opposition in a harmonious manner, they must focus the Neptune energy into the areas where planets make good aspects to the planets involved in the opposition. These difficulties will manifest in the houses in which the planets forming the opposition are found, the signs and houses they rule, and the signs and houses of their exalted rulers.

If Neptune is found in a Cardinal sign, individuals have an intuitive awareness of what is needed in any situation as it occurs. This is because the individuals are intuitively sensitive to their immediate environment. If Neptune receives stress aspects, these individuals can easily be thrown off balance by the psychic and emotional impact in daily crisis.

If Neptune is found in a Cardinal, positive sign, these individuals will initiate creative, imaginative, and artistic activities. This also applies to religious, educational, and cultural activities.

If Neptune is found in a Cardinal, receptive sign, these individuals will use their imaginative and intuitive faculties in response to the influence of the people and conditions in their immediate environment.

If Neptune is found in a Fixed sign, individuals will be intuitively drawn to the possibilities of the future. They will exercise determination and perseverance in the pursuit of their visionary goals. If Neptune receives stress aspects in a Fixed sign, these individuals can be stubborn in adhering to distorted religious and cultural beliefs.

If Neptune is found in a Fixed, positive sign, individuals will express their leadership qualities in the pursuit of their goals. They will be inspired by the possibilities that are inherent in these goals.

If Neptune is found in a Fixed, receptive sign, individuals will be drawn into a creative, imaginative expression of their goals by others. Their intuitive faculties will be stimulated by a feeling that the time is ripe for the expression of their creative imagination.

If Neptune is found in a Mutable sign, these individuals' intuitive and creative imagination will be strongly influenced and stimulated by their past experiences. These individuals will have the ability to tap the resources of their subconscious mind and use skills that were acquired in the past. These skills will be a means for the expression of their creative imagination in the present. If Neptune receives stress aspects from other planets, these individuals can become easily trapped in painful subconscious memories which can cause neurotic or psychotic behavior and interfere with these individuals' creative effort.

If Neptune is found in a Mutable, positive sign, individuals will initiate imaginative and creative projects by using their skills and past experience in their creative, artistic, religious, or cultural endeavors.

If Neptune is found in a Mutable, receptive sign, individuals will exercise their imaginative, creative, and intuitive faculties, using their skills and past experience by responding to some outside stimuli. By this kind of response they make use of these faculties.

If Neptune is found in a Fire sign, individuals will express their intuitive and imaginative abilities in a dramatic and forceful way. If Neptune receives favorable aspects from other planets, these individuals have the ability to become cultural, educational, or religious leaders in some way. If Neptune receives stress aspects, these individuals must be careful that their egotistical tendencies will not lead them to delusions of grandeur.

If Neptune is found in an Earth sign, individuals will use their inspiration, creative, and intuitive faculties in the solving of practical problems. If Neptune receives stress aspects, there is the danger of prostituting spiritual and intuitive abilities for financial gain.

If Neptune is found in an Air sign, individuals will express their intuitive and imaginative abilities through an intellectual outlet of some kind. Neptune in an Air sign favors those who are in the profession of creative writing or any work that demands the use of the intellect in a creative and imaginative expression. If Neptune receives stress aspects, the undisciplined imagination and mental wanderings can lead to the neglect of practical responsibilities.

If Neptune is found in a Water sign, where it is at home, the intuitive abilities and creative imagination are intensified, and these individuals have the ability to empathize with and intuitively sense other people's moods and feelings. If Neptune receives stress aspects from other planets, this acute sensitivity can indicate that these individuals can be emotionally drawn into the problems of others. They can be overly susceptible to negative psychic conditions and subliminal suggestions in their environment.

9

Divisions of the Horoscope—Hemispheric Emphasis

There are four divisions of the horoscope and its houses. These divisions are called *Hemispheric Divisions.* There is the Eastern Hemisphere, Western Hemisphere, Northern Hemisphere, and Southern Hemisphere. See example below.

When dealing with Hemispheric Emphasis only the planets and the lights in the houses are considered. Other things such as the Nodes and Arabic Parts, or anything else found in some charts, are not considered in this delineation.

Eastern Hemisphere

WHEN THE MAJORITY OF THE PLANETS ARE FOUND IN THE EASTERN HEMISPHERE—houses ten, eleven, twelve, one, two, and three—it indicates that these individuals tend to choose their own life-style and set of social and business conditions in which they move. These individuals are in a phase of initiating new endeavors and entering into new experiences. They will experience freedom in making decisions and choices rather than feeling bound by obligations to others. However, they often experience a sense of loneliness or isolation. They tend to feel that nothing worthwhile happens unless they make it happen. They must reach out to establish relationships and create conditions which would automatically be provided for one with a Western Emphasis.

When the preponderance of the planets is found in Fire or Air signs,

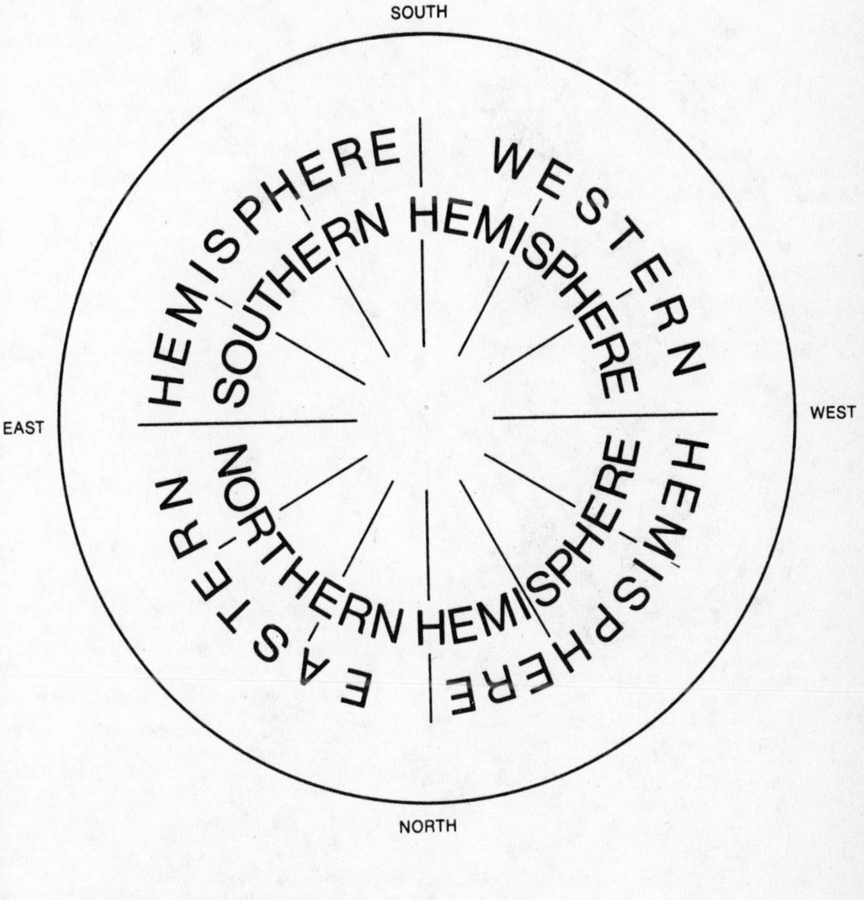
SOUTH
EAST
WEST
NORTH
SOUTHERN HEMISPHERE
NORTHERN HEMISPHERE
EASTERN HEMISPHERE
WESTERN HEMISPHERE

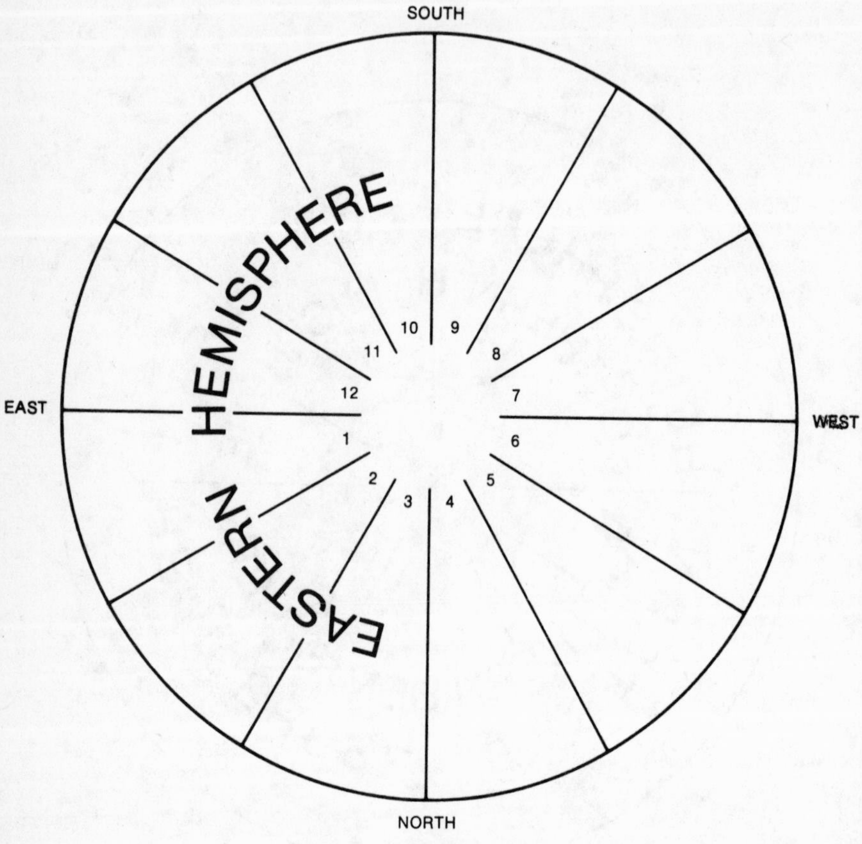

Eastern Hemisphere

The Eastern Hemisphere includes houses ten, eleven, twelve, one, two, and three.

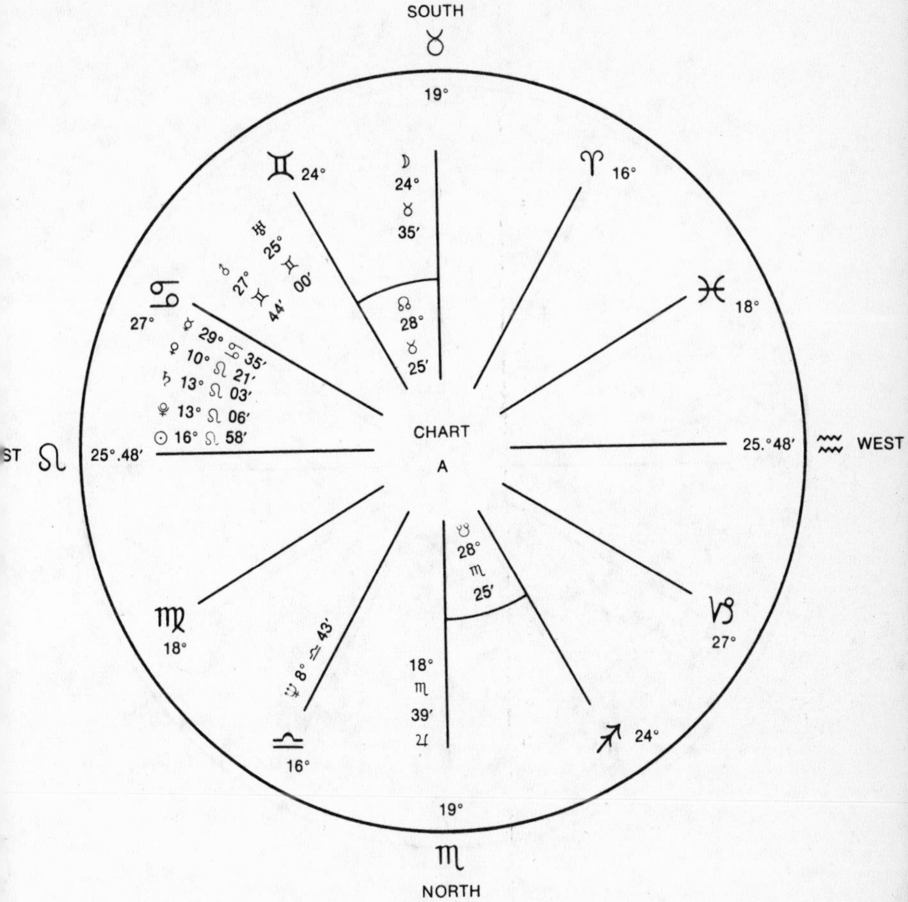

Example of Eastern Hemispheric Emphasis with the Majority of the Planets in Positive, Masculine Signs

Note: All of the planets are in the eastern sector of the chart—that is, the tenth, eleventh, twelfth, first, second, and the third houses.

This chart is an example of all planets east; however, the majority of the planets are in Fire and Air signs, known as the positive, masculine signs. Uranus and Mars are in Gemini; Venus, Saturn, Pluto, and the Sun in Leo; and Neptune is in Libra.

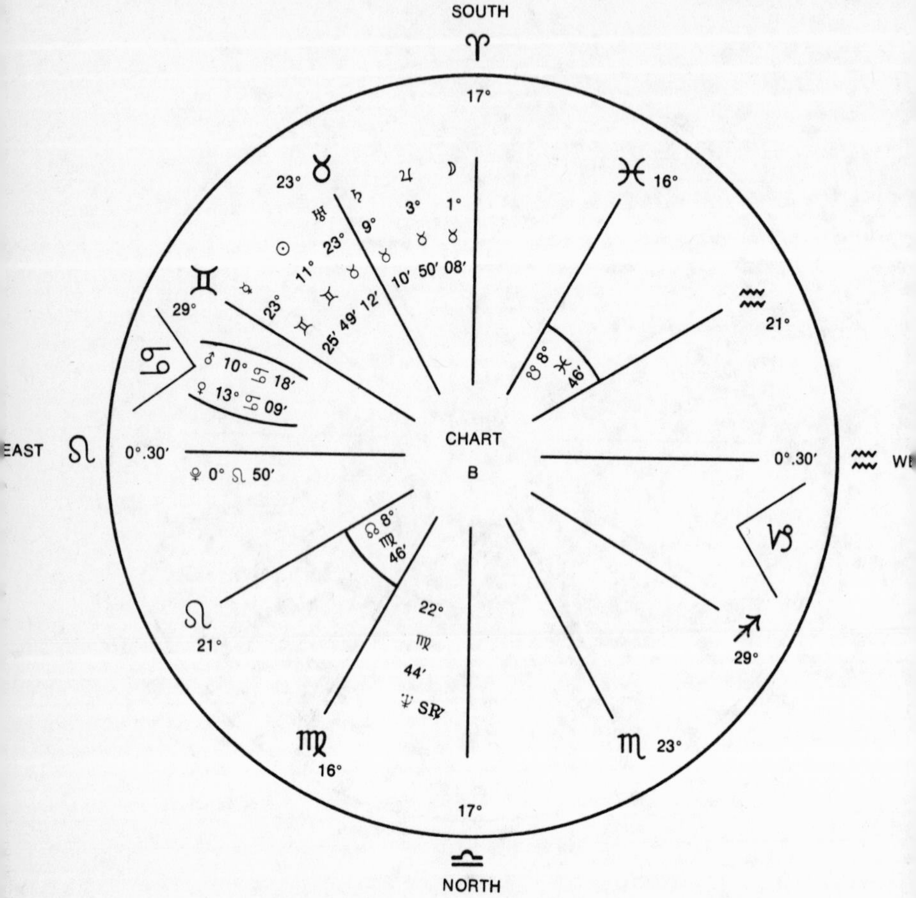

Example of Eastern Hemispheric Emphasis
with the Majority of the Planets in Receptive, Feminine Signs

Note: All of the planets are in the eastern sector of the chart—that is the tenth, eleventh, twelfth, first, second, and the third houses.

This chart is an example of all planets east; however, the majority of the planets are in the Earth and Water signs, known as the receptive, feminine signs. The Moon, Jupiter, Saturn, and Uranus are in Taurus; Venus and Mars are in Cancer; and Neptune is in Virgo.

known as the positive, masculine signs, individuals can be so aggressive in promoting their ideas that they dominate immediate situations, much to the annoyance of others. If individuals lack enthusiasm for the subject under discussion, they will display an exasperating indifference and will try to introduce a subject that will bring the focus of attention back to them or their interests. This kind of projection is comfortable for the individual; however, others are overwhelmed and experience a sense of frustration in any cooperative activities in which the individual is involved.

When the preponderance of the planets is found in the receptive signs of Earth and Water, known as the negative, feminine signs, in the Eastern Hemisphere individuals are often caught up in a psychological dichotomy. These individuals experience an ambivalence: One part of the character is aggressive and wants to initiate all kinds of activities; however, they feel they should wait until they are confronted with opportunities that they could grasp to show their initiative and enterprise. There is a certain amount of frustration that this particular planetary setup engenders. The positive quality of confidence and optimism is lacking. However, this does not mean that these individuals do not have the ability for initiative and enterprise, but that they do not project this ability and therefore do not attract those who would be receptive to their ideas. In other words, they must take themselves in hand, outline what they have to offer, and actively seek those who would be receptive to what they have to give. This is not an easy thing for these individuals to do. However, this is required of them. Otherwise, there will be a feeling of frustration, lack of fulfillment, and lack of appreciation. Therefore, this obstacle must be overcome if these individuals are to realize their potential. This pattern represents a frustration for these individuals.

Western Hemisphere

When the majority of the planets are found in the Western Hemisphere—houses four, five, six, seven, eight, and nine—it indicates that the needs and wishes of others play an important part in determining how these individuals function. This does not mean that these individuals do not have free will; however, they must find an outlet for their personal creativity amid the activity of others. It can best be expressed by handling or utilizing the circumstances and conditions in which they find themselves. Often the activities are conditioned by obligations to others. Opportunities for experience will arise through activities and circumstances related to other people.

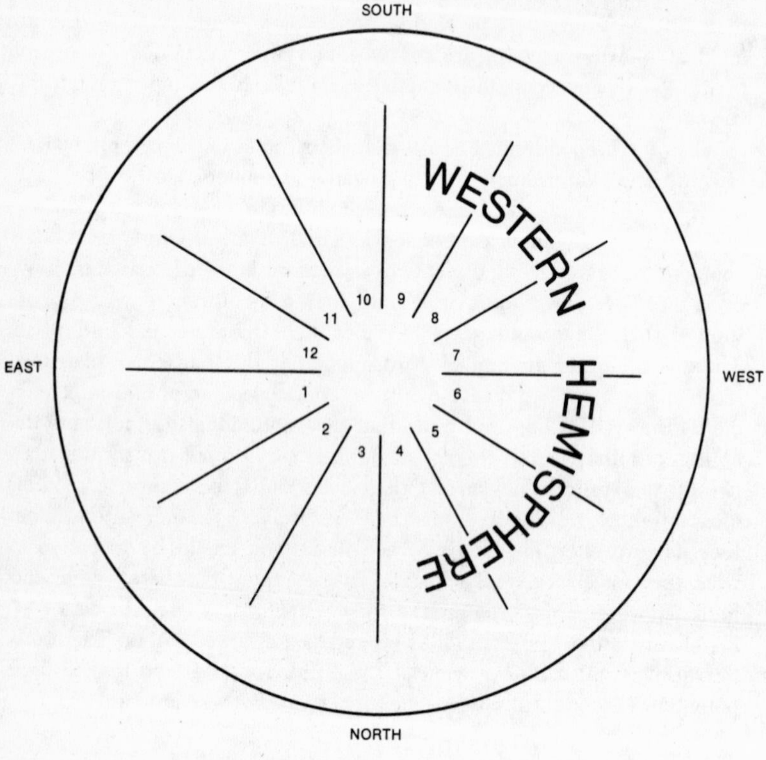

Western Hemisphere

The Western Hemisphere includes houses four, five, six, seven, eight, and nine.

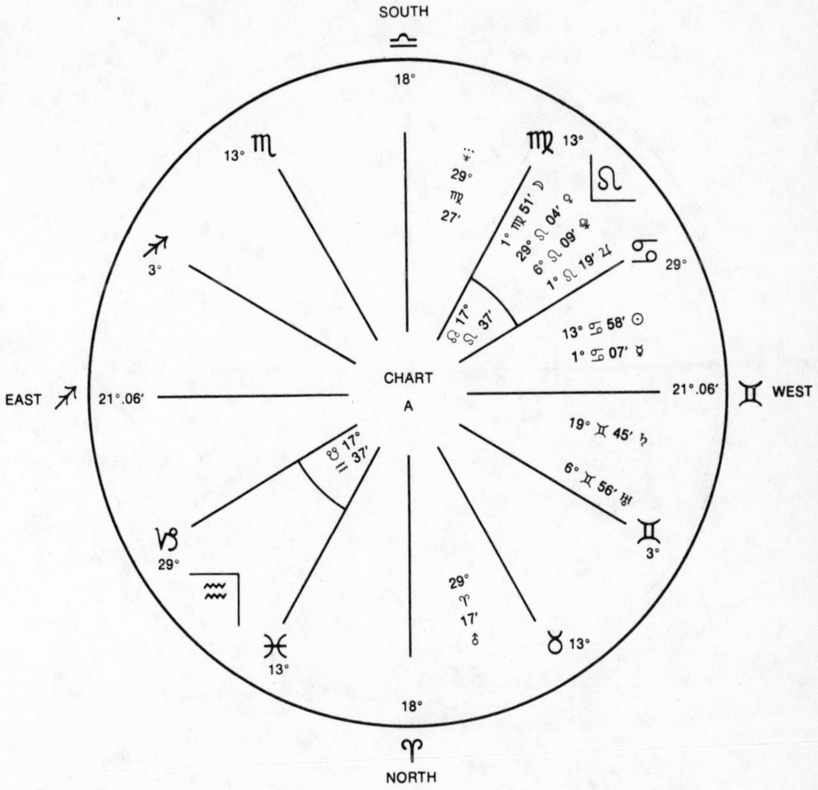

Example of Western Hemispheric Emphasis
with the Majority of the Planets in Positive, Masculine Signs

Note: All of the planets are in the western sector of the chart—that is the fourth, fifth, sixth, seventh, eighth, and ninth houses.

This chart is an example of all planets west; however, the majority of the planets are in Air and Fire signs, known as the positive, masculine signs. Mars is in Aries; Uranus and Saturn are in Gemini; and Jupiter, Pluto, and Venus are in Leo.

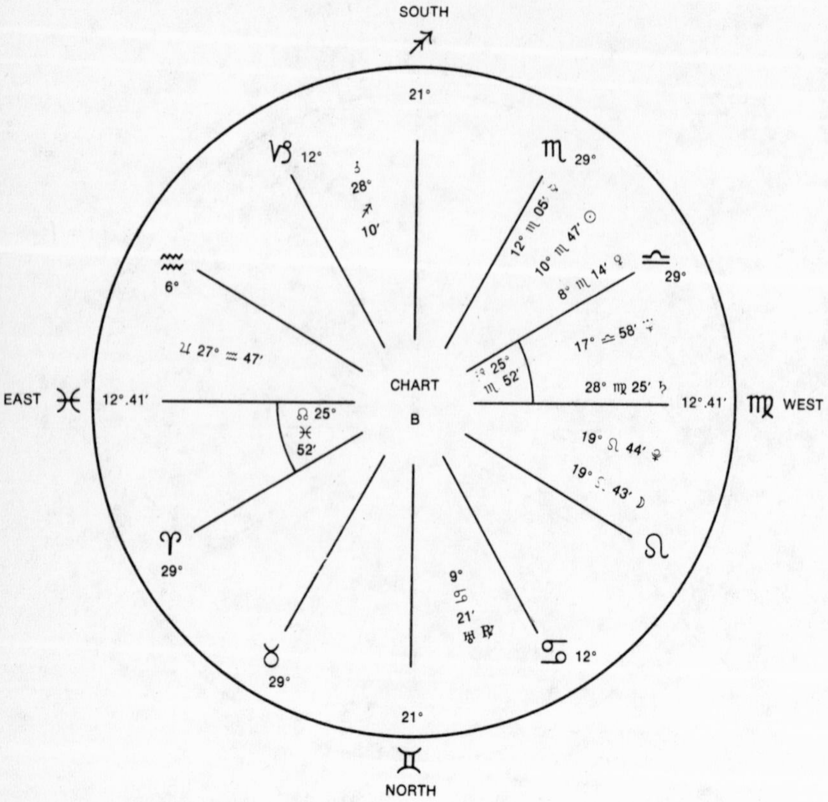

Example of Western Hemispheric Emphasis
with the Majority of the Planets in Receptive, Feminine Signs

Note: The majority of the planets are in the western sector of the chart—that is, in the fourth, fifth, sixth, seventh, eighth, and ninth houses.

This is an example of most planets west; however, the majority of the planets are in Earth and Water signs, known as the receptive, feminine signs. The Sun, Venus, and Mercury are in the sign Scorpio; Saturn is in Virgo; and Uranus is in Cancer.

When the preponderance of planets in the Western Hemisphere is found in the Fire and Air signs, which are the positive, masculine, aggressive signs, as in Chart A, these individuals will have a sense of frustration because their positive, optimistic, and self-confident natures find it difficult to have other people influencing their destiny. These individuals must wait for the proper time and opportunity to present their ideas, and they must be presented in such a manner as not to overwhelm those with whom they are dealing. These individuals feel positive and vital within themselves; however, the frustration comes as the result of having to consider other points of view and then discern how to integrate their thoughts and ideas so that the interaction with others can be harmonious. With this kind of emphasis, these individuals have an inner frustration because of their personal projection—they want to impress others and have them adhere to their ideas; however, the circumstances of their life experience demand that they cooperate with others and their ideas in order for them to achieve success. To function under this set of circumstances, they must learn to listen first, to cooperate, and to bring forth their ideas unobtrusively. This must be done in a diplomatic manner in such a way that the creative ideas of others are taken into consideration.

When the preponderance of the planets west are found in the Earth or Water signs, which are the negative, feminine receptive signs, these individuals are easily influenced by the thoughts and actions of others. The natural tendency for these individuals is to acquiesce to the initiatory activities of others. In order to avoid total conformity to the wishes and desires of others, these individuals must define what their wishes are in the matter and how they would go about implementing them. In this manner they could fulfill themselves and avoid frustration by interacting with others in a positive way. If these individuals handle this pattern in such a manner, they will have a sense of fulfillment and well-being.

The chart with negative, feminine planets in the Western Hemisphere poses no problems within the individual; however, the challenge is in assembling the faculties of courage in presenting ideas in an explicit, practical, and diplomatic way to command a hearing.

Southern Hemisphere

When the majority of the planets are found in the Southern Hemisphere, above the horizon—houses seven, eight, nine, ten, eleven,

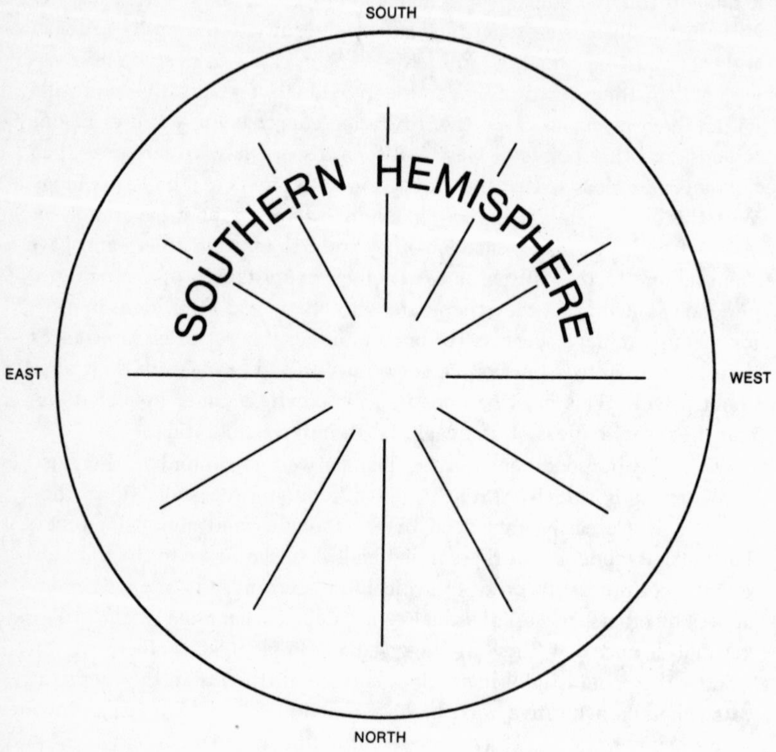

Southern Hemisphere

The Southern Hemisphere includes houses seven, eight, nine, ten, eleven, and twelve.

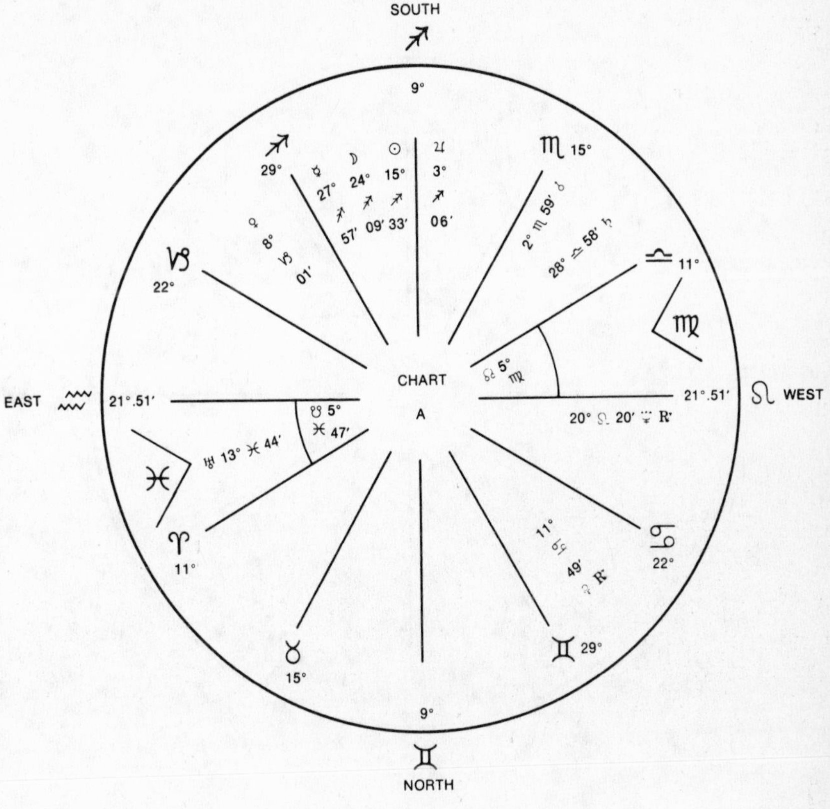

Example of Southern Hemispheric Emphasis with the Majority of the Planets in Positive, Masculine Signs

Note: The majority of the planets are in the southern sector of the chart—that is in the seventh, eighth, ninth, tenth, eleventh, and twelfth houses.

This chart is an example of most planets south; however, the majority of the planets are in Air and Fire signs, known as the positive, masculine signs. Saturn is in Libra; and Jupiter, Sun, Moon, and Mercury are in Sagittarius.

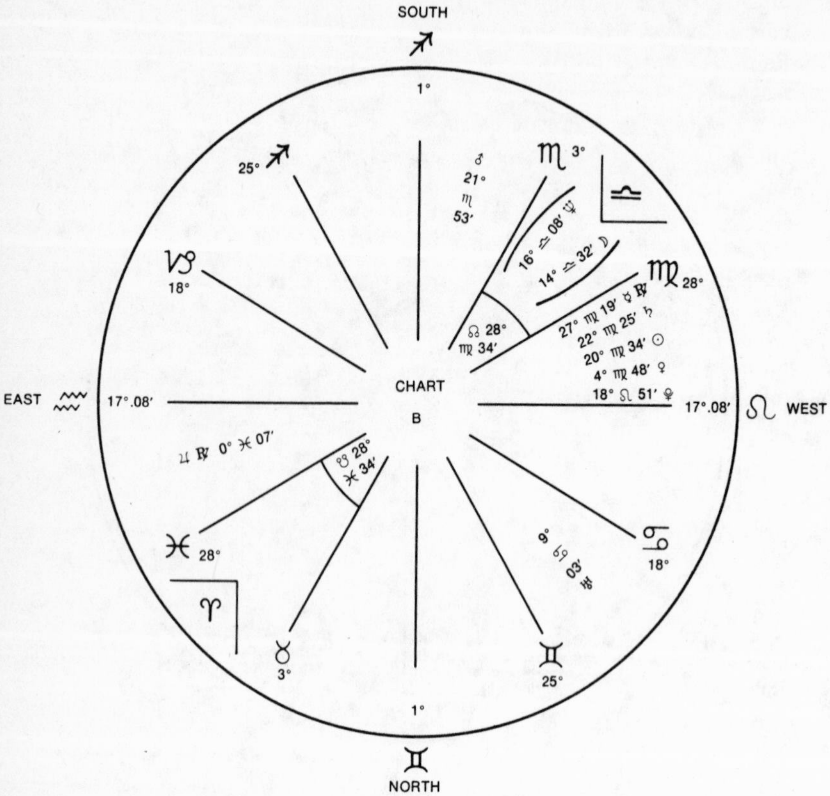

Example of Southern Hemispheric Emphasis with the Majority of the Plahets in Receptive, Feminine Signs

Note: The majority of the planets are in the southern sector of the chart—that is in the seventh, eighth, ninth, tenth, eleventh, and twelfth houses.

This is an example of most planets south; however, the majority of the planets are in Earth and Water signs, known as the receptive, feminine signs. The Sun, Venus, Saturn, and Mercury are in Virgo; and Mars is in Scorpio.

and twelve—it indicates that these individuals have an objective, impersonal interest in life, especially in regard to what is happening around them on a large scale—whether it affects them or not. These individuals' activities and concerns will be apparent and they will get involved with practical activities that go beyond personal consideration. Because of these concerns, they are apt to achieve some kind of public recognition during some phase of their life.

When the preponderance of the planets is found in Fire and Air signs, known as the masculine, positive signs, these individuals feel at home and very comfortable in the aggressive, competitive atmosphere in which they find themselves. These individuals display the natural powers of leadership, self-confidence, and optimism necessary to maintain their place in the sun.

With this kind of emphasis, these individuals feel very comfortable where their abilities and talents are publicly recognized. However, they must guard against sacrificing all other values for their profession. Another pitfall is having an aggressive, autocratic attitude that makes others uncomfortable if they do not have the same self-assurance.

When the preponderance of planets in the Southern Hemisphere are found in the receptive signs of Earth and Water, known as the negative, feminine signs, these individuals have to function in the outer world where they meet positive, aggressive types, all involved in seeking a place in the sun. This presents a psychological dilemma to these individuals because they lack the aggressive attributes necessary to function comfortably in such circumstances. Therefore, in order for these individuals to feel that they are effective, they must formulate and organize their ideas in such a manner that they will demand a hearing. In this way, they can avoid some of the frustration and feelings of inadequacy imposed by such circumstances.

These individuals with the preponderance of negative, feminine signs in the Southern Hemisphere experience a sense of discomfort and frustration amid the positive, aggressive circumstances in which they find themselves. These conditions can cause a psychological trauma with which these individuals must deal. For example, a man who achieves a position of authority because of work well done in the shadow of a prominent person can fail when he must take the reins of authority himself. The sensitivity of water and the practicality of earth cannot withstand the pressure of decision-making and criticism.

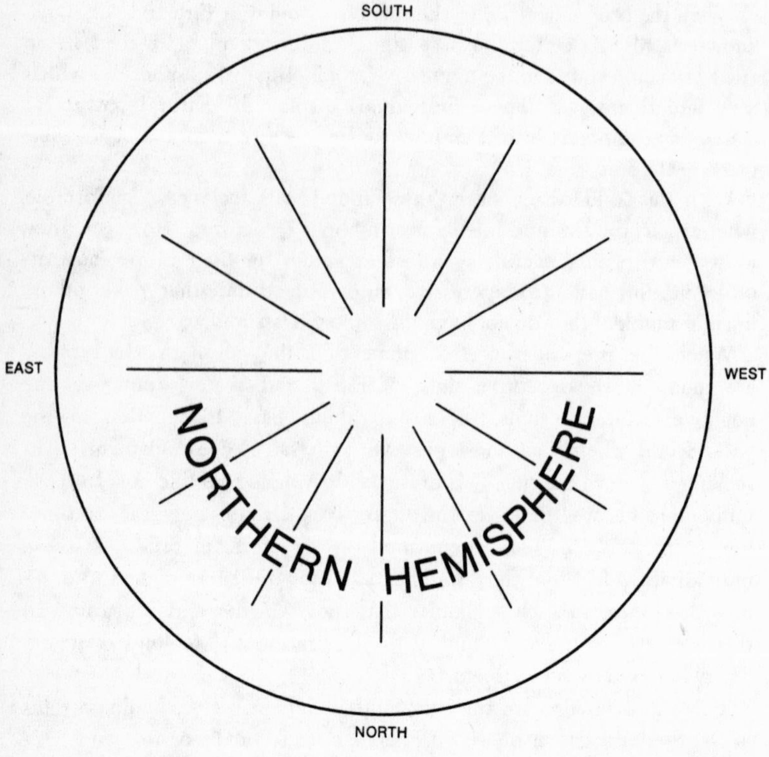

Northern Hemisphere

The Northern Hemisphere includes houses one, two, three, four, five, and six.

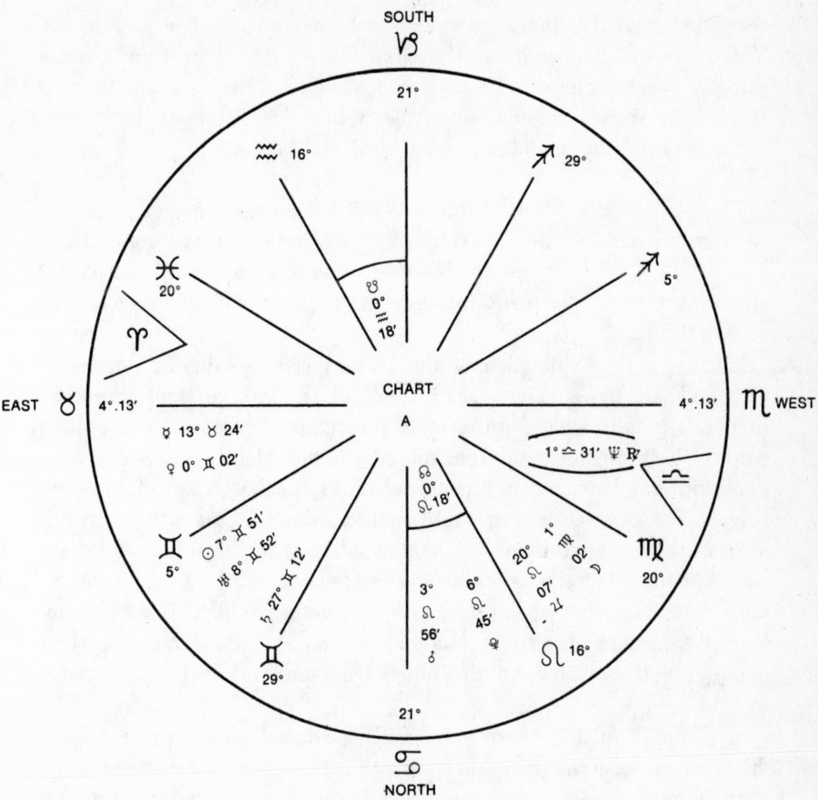

Example of Northern Hemispheric Emphasis with the Majority of the Planets in Positive, Masculine Signs

Note: The majority of the planets are in the northern sector of the chart—that is in the first, second, third, fourth, fifth, and sixth houses.

This is an example of all planets north; however, the majority of the planets are in Air and Fire signs, known as the positive, masculine signs. The Sun, Venus, Uranus, and Saturn are in Gemini; Mars, Pluto, and Jupiter are in Leo; and Neptune is in Libra.

Northern Hemisphere

When the majority of the planets are found in the Northern Hemisphere, below the horizon—houses one, two, three, four, five, and six—it indicates that these individuals will have a subjective view of life. This view will be based on a visceral response to those things which directly affect these individuals' personal affairs. They are apt to work behind the scenes rather than in the public eye. Although their work could concern public affairs, a great deal will be done in private, in the background.

There are modifications of this outlook. A preponderance of planets in Air signs or planets ruled by Mercury would indicate that these individuals would have a somewhat objective viewpoint; however, they would still tend to be intellectually interested in that which is of personal concern to them.

When the preponderance of the planets is found in the aggressive Fire and Air signs, known as the masculine, positive signs, these individuals usually have a problem in projecting their ideas in the outer world. The problem stems from the ease with which they dominate the domestic and home environment, which is familiar, comfortable, and private. However, they must guard against a domineering attitude in this area, as those around them see them as a lion at home and a mouse outside. The habit patterns and attitudes established in the home are viewed with a jaundiced eye when projected in the outer world. This is a psychological drawback, for these individuals cannot understand why their dominance is accepted on the home front and rejected in the outer world.

With this emphasis, these individuals are faced with a psychological dilemma, because the domestic sphere of action does not provide a large enough arena to merit the attention and approbation which they desire. Therefore, they are liable to feel confined and unappreciated.

When the preponderance of planets in the Northern Hemisphere are found in the signs of Earth and Water, known as the receptive, feminine signs, these individuals need to work in the seclusion of an environment which provides an arena in which they feel secure and comfortable in their way of doing things. This innate need for psychological security is the drive that is instrumental in giving them a solid foundation to carry on their work, thus providing them with the ability to give physical and spiritual comfort to others.

If the need for this kind of security is not understood by these indi-

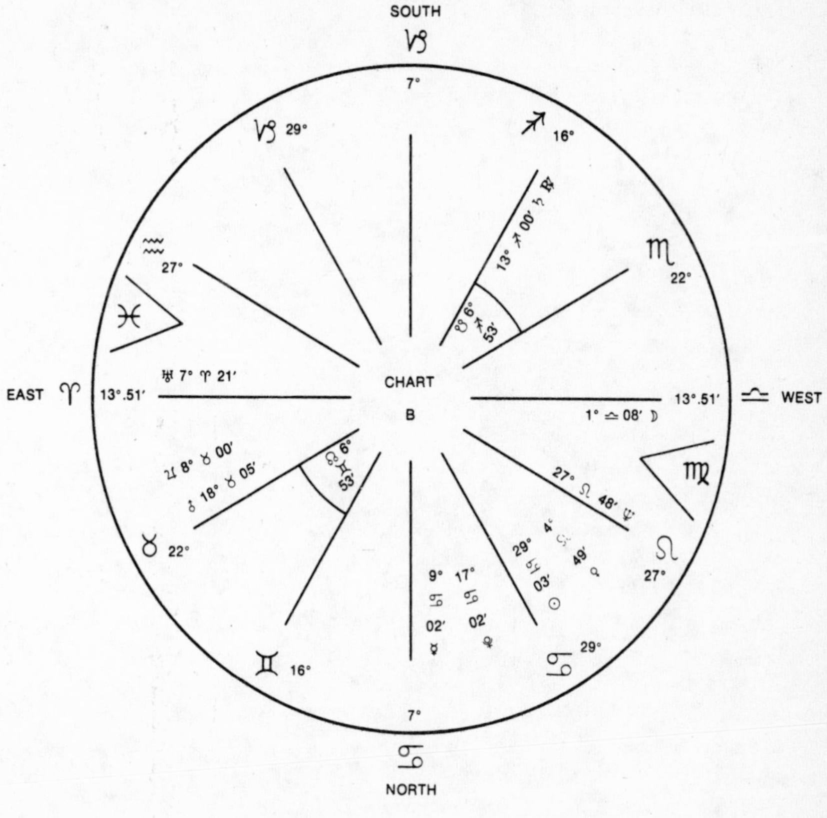

Example of Northern Hemispheric Emphasis with the Majority of the Planets in Receptive, Feminine Signs

Note: The majority of the planets are in the northern sector of the chart—that is in the first, second, third, fourth, fifth, and sixth houses.

This is an example of most planets north; however, the majority of the planets are in Earth and Water signs, known as the receptive, feminine signs. Jupiter and Mars are in Taurus; Mercury, Pluto, and the Sun are in Cancer.

viduals, they can become psychologically ill-aligned by continually directing their focus toward being in the public eye. This kind of focus will pose problems for these individuals unless they have those around them who will protect them from overcommitting themselves because of their receptive nature.

10

The Seven Basic Planetary Patterns

There are seven patterns which are used to give an overall view of the nature of individuals and the way they approach life. These are based on the grouping and spacing of the planets in the Natal Horoscope. These patterns were originally researched and developed by Dr. Marc Edmund Jones.

In dealing with these patterns, the orbs for aspects are wider than those used in aspect interpretation. Nodes, Arabic Parts, and so forth are not included in these patterns.

If the Sun is involved in a pattern aspect, an orb of 17 degrees is allowed for the pattern aspect. If the Moon is involved in a pattern aspect, an orb of 12 degrees and 30 minutes is allowed. For planets involved in pattern aspects, an orb of 10 degrees is allowed.

The seven basic pattern types include the Splash, which deals with the whole chart; the Bundle, which deals with one-third of the chart; the Bowl, which deals with one-half of the chart; the Bucket, which deals with one-half of the chart with one planet outside of the half which acts as a handle on the Bucket; the Locomotive, which deals with two-thirds of the chart; the Seesaw, which deals with two sections of the chart with empty spaces opposite each other; and the Splay, somewhat like the Splash, which covers the whole chart, with the difference being that the planets tend to collect in three separate groups.

When the time of birth is unknown, these patterns can still be used in delineation because the Moon rarely travels far enough in twenty-four hours to offset a pattern.

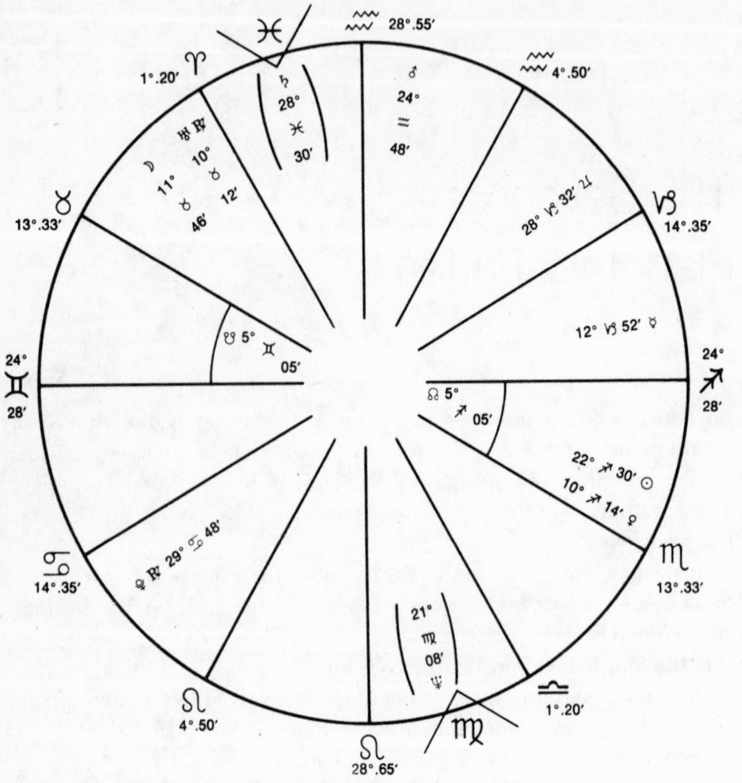

Example of a Splash Pattern

The Splash Pattern must have one or more planets in each quadrant of the chart.

The Splash Pattern

In the perfect Splash Pattern there would be five oppositions; however, such a pattern is extremely rare. Usually the planets are scattered more or less evenly throughout the whole chart with a planet or planets in every quadrant. Some oppositions are generally found in this type of grouping. This type of pattern would indicate a capacity for wide interests. These individuals can involve themselves in many activities, thus expanding their experience into many different arenas and giving a universal approach to life. If these individuals fail in the constructive use of such a pattern, they can scatter their energies, waste opportunities, and become "jacks-of-all-trades-and-masters-of-none." There should be a concentrated effort on the part of these individuals, in matters of career or profession, to learn all the ramifications of their chosen work, for by knowing all the different facets of a business they will feel a sense of satisfaction in performing their appointed tasks. This will provide the diversification that is essential for this pattern. If this is not done these individuals are apt to change their profession or job periodically.

If the majority of the planets are found in positive, aggressive, masculine signs, these individuals are apt to indulge in an abnormal number of activities. Along with this action is the refusal to listen to the objective advice of others to concentrate their energy in one area.

Should these planets be found in Cardinal signs, these individuals will have the potential for instant action that deals with the here and now. At best, they can deal with crisis situations; at worst, they scatter their energies.

If the preponderance of planets is found in the receptive, feminine signs, these activities have less impact on others. However, the activity is still evident.

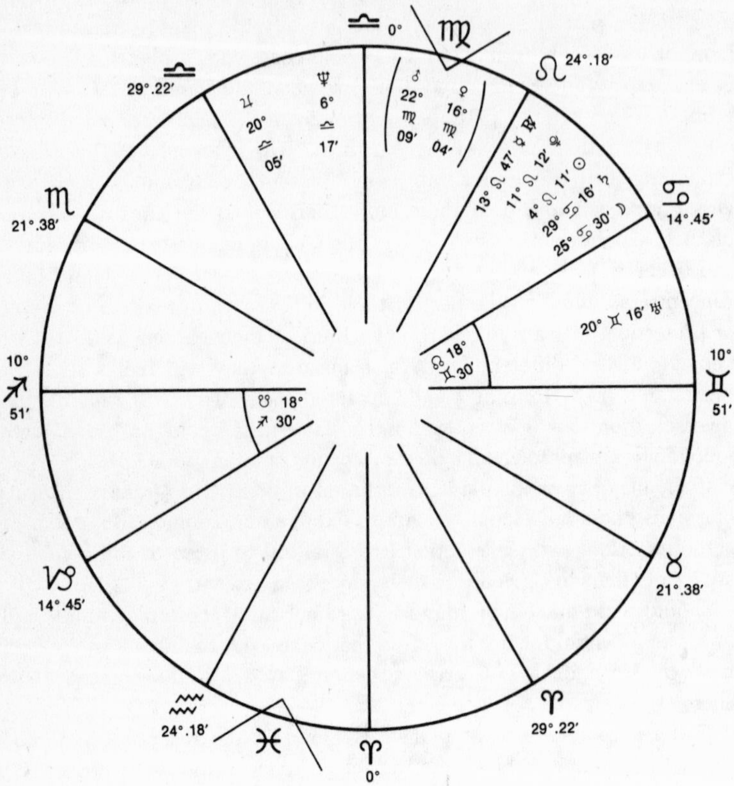

Example of a Bundle Pattern

In a Bundle Pattern all the planets and lights are bundled together within a trine aspect. In the chart above the planet Uranus in Gemini in the seventh house forms a trine with Jupiter in Libra in the tenth house. All the planets in the chart are found enclosed within these two planets.

The Bundle Pattern

In the Bundle Pattern all the planets and lights are concentrated in one-third of the chart. In other words all the planets are confined within a trine. The perfect Bundle would contain a stellium. This does not always happen, however. The houses occupied by the planets would be the focus of the concentrated interests of these individuals.

These individuals' lives are directed in a concentrated sphere of activity; this concentration does not allow for a wide variety of interests. They are wrapped up in their own personal, limited interests and activities regardless of how they affect those in their immediate environment, domestic or otherwise. Because of this concentrated focus, these individuals have the ability to build a powerful business or a professional reputation in their particular field. The conjunctions involved in this pattern give them the dynamic power needed to build their enterprise, whatever it may be.

To refine this pattern, note in which hemisphere the Bundle is located and apply the interpretation of the Hemispheric Emphasis to the Bundle interpretation.

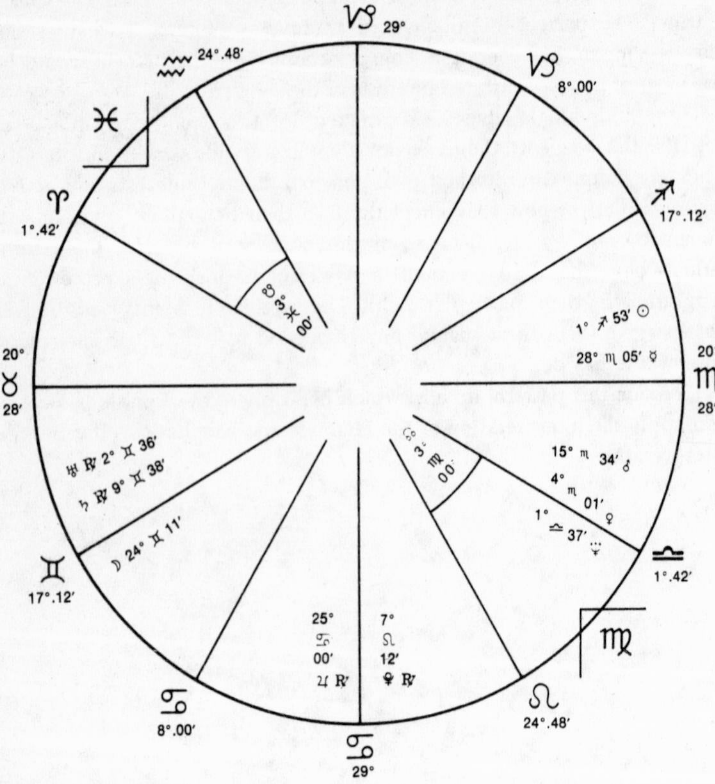

Example of a Bowl Pattern

All the planets occupy one-half of the chart. The occupied half of the chart is separated from the empty half of the chart by the opposition of Uranus in Gemini in the first house and the Sun in Sagittarius in the seventh house.

The Bowl Pattern

In this pattern all the planets are concentrated in one-half of the chart. They are separated from the empty half by the two planets in opposition to each other.

The perfect Bowl chart always has the opposition. This separation can make individuals feel that something is lacking or missing in their life experience. It is as though these individuals are always at work trying to orient themselves and find some kind of balance that will give them a sense of completeness. This imbalance causes them to direct their attention toward self-improvement. This pattern makes these individuals feel that they have something of consequence to contribute to their fellow man.

The more even the distribution of planets in the occupied half of the chart, the more these individuals adhere to this type of expression.

If the Bowl Pattern does not contain the rim opposition, these individuals lack the awareness that is inherent in the opposition. Thus there is an intense yearning to arrive at some kind of sustained direction in life.

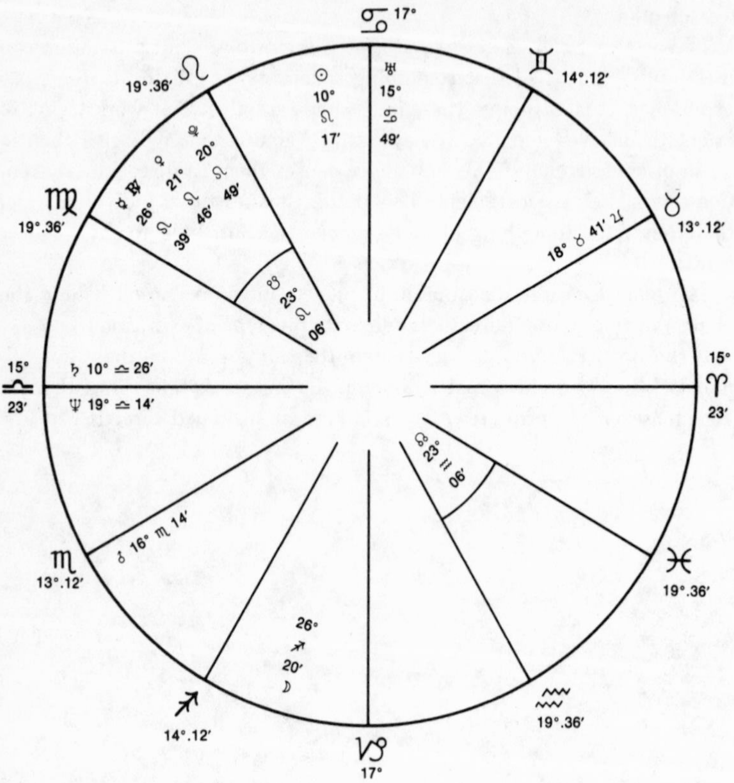

Example of a Bucket Pattern

The Bucket Pattern is similar to the Bowl Pattern in that one-half of the chart is occupied, the difference being that one planet is found outside the opposition that forms the rim of the Bucket. In this example the planet Mars in Scorpio in the second house is in opposition to Jupiter in Taurus in the eighth house. The Moon in Sagittarius is in the third house outside the rim opposition and represents the handle.

The Bucket Pattern

In this pattern all the planets but one are in one-half of the chart. The single planet plays an important part in this patterning. The Bowl part retains the same meaning as the Bowl chart—that is, individuals feel they have something to contribute to others.

The handle planet acts as a focusing agent and indicates the way individuals will offer their contribution. The position of the handle is important in this pattern. If the handle is located before the midpoint of the opposition, these individuals have a cautious, self-conscious approach to life. If the handle is exactly on the midpoint of the opposition, these individuals can be overbearing and at times cruel in their expression. If the handle planet is located past the midpoint of the opposition, these individuals can respond in a rash, impulsive manner.

The handle indicates that the individual is caught up in some kind of expression that must have an outlet. This outpouring is so intense at times that these individuals fail to have the proper concern for themselves, their resources, or the effect that their actions may have on others.

At best, this Bucket Pattern indicates the teacher or person who inspires and directs others. At its worst, this pattern can produce an individual with aggravating propensities. In all cases these individuals live life with a great deal of zest.

Occasionally a Bucket Pattern is found with a handle containing two planets. For the handle to be valid the planets in conjunction should be within one degree orb. In this type of Bucket handle, the individual alternates between two expressions based on the principles involved in this type of conjunction. Alternating expression is activated by the transiting planets.

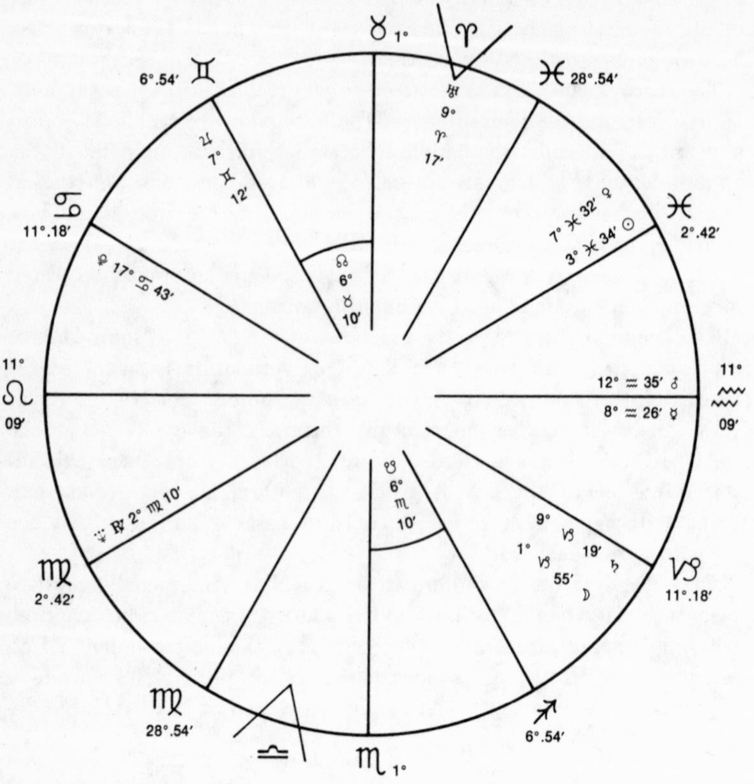

Example of a Locomotive Pattern

In this pattern two-thirds of the chart must be occupied, and the remaining third must be empty and spanned by a trine aspect between the two planets facing the empty space. The Moon in Capricorn is in the fifth house in trine aspect to Neptune in Virgo in the first house.

The Locomotive Pattern

In this pattern the planets are spread over two-thirds of the chart. The empty area of the chart must be spanned by a trine, that is, the two planets facing the empty area at either end must be in trine aspect.

Locomotive Pattern individuals are endowed with a great amount of power. This power is the result of the distribution of the planets and the urge to fill the empty gap in the chart. There is a psychological need to get on the right track to express the creative potential of the chart. These individuals have an inherent feeling that there is always a big job that needs to be done or a gap that needs to be filled. They are actively involved in the social and intellectual world in which they move. They enter into new experiences with great faith in their ability to succeed in this undertaking. When goals are reached, Locomotive Pattern individuals expect some kind of recognition or appreciation. If this is not forthcoming, these individuals can become bitter and rebellious.

This pattern indicates that these individuals have the ability to apply themselves to their projects in a practical manner, thus enabling them to be extremely successful in life. This steady, organized, and practical application of the will enables them to achieve great heights. However, there is the danger of an autocratic attitude once these individuals are on their way to the top.

The planet traveling in a clockwise direction and facing the open trine is the lead planet or "engine" of this Locomotive Pattern. It plays an important part in analyzing the character.

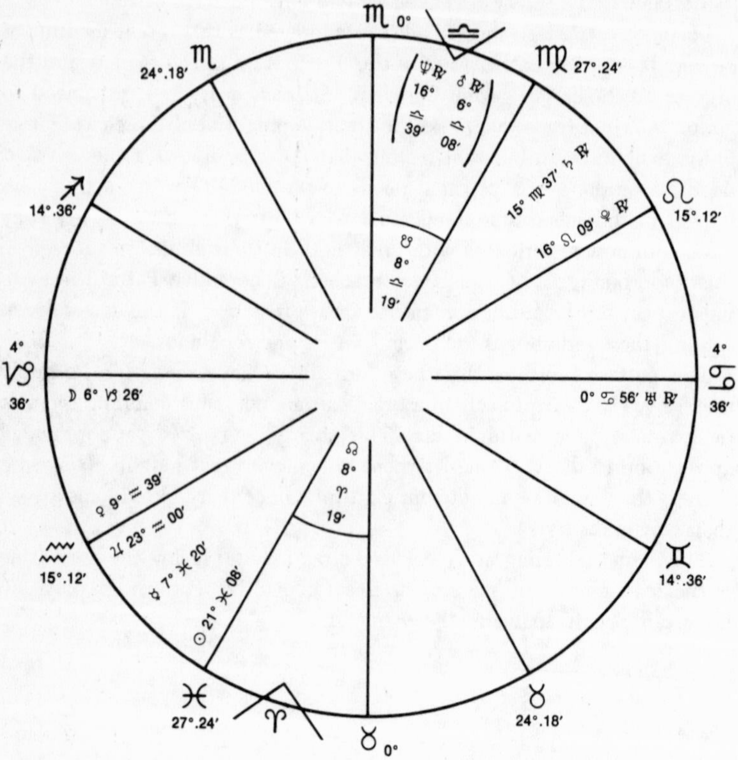

Example of a Seesaw Pattern

In this pattern the planets are divided into two groups. The two groups are approximately in opposition to each other. Each group is flanked by empty spaces of at least a 60-degree span. In the example the empty spaces are signified by the Moon in Capricorn in the first house and Neptune in Libra in the ninth house; on the other side by the Sun in Pisces in the second house and Uranus in Cancer in the sixth house.

The Seesaw Pattern

In this pattern the planets are placed in two groups roughly opposed to each other. However, the empty houses must be in exact opposition to each other. A span of at least a sextile in both the unoccupied sections is required for this pattern. These individuals are constantly confronted with opposing views, giving them an unusual awareness of other factors in any given situation. Thus these individuals have unusual ability in finding solutions to problems that would baffle others.

There is a capacity for intellectual exchange and for the "give and take" of ideas. There is a constant weighing and balancing of issues, which gives these individuals the ability to adjust very quickly to any situation.

These individuals will lose power if they do not recognize and use the fluid exchange that is inherent in this pattern.

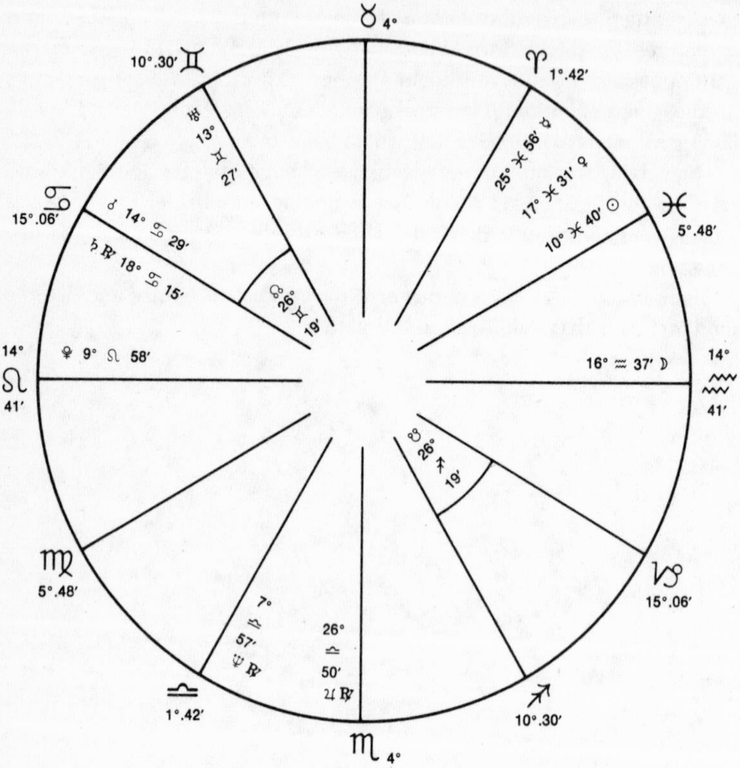

Example of a Splay Pattern

In the Splay Pattern the planets are generally found in three groups, usually involving a major configuration such as a T square or Grand Trine. These configurations are not always present, and at times a planet may be found outside the three groups. In the example all the quadrants are not occupied as in the Splash Pattern, the quadrant between the fourth house and the sixth house being empty.

The Splay Pattern

In this pattern the planets are clustered in spokelike groupings throughout the chart. The perfect Splay Pattern would contain three distinct groups of multiple conjunctions, but this is rare. This pattern has a common denominator with the Bundle and Locomotive patterns in that the trine is the major basis of the pattern. Individuals with this kind of pattern are unforgettable in that they have a unique way of building experience into their lives.

Splay Pattern individuals cannot be classified in the same category as other people. They are extremely individualistic either in life-style or in that which is important to them. They have their own special tastes and style. Others may consider them eccentric in some respects; however, Splay Pattern individuals have a certain naïveté which makes them oblivious to the kind of impression they are creating. This pattern produces the intense but impersonal individual with special interests.

Planets in High Focus

From the seven basic patterns three emerge with a planet in High Focus, indicating that the particular planet dominates the self-expression of the individual in some special manner.

The three patterns that have planets in High Focus are the Bowl Pattern, the Bucket Pattern, and the Locomotive Pattern.

The High Focus planet in the Bowl Pattern is the planet that faces the open space traveling in a clockwise direction. This is called the Cutting Planet. The High Focus planet in the Bucket Pattern is the Handle planet. The High Focus planet in the Locomotive Pattern is the planet facing the open space traveling in a clockwise direction and it is also labeled the Cutting Planet.

Any of the eight planets or the lights (Sun and Moon) can be the High Focus planet for these patterns. Dr. Marc Edmund Jones uses special keywords indicating how these planets affect the character.

Sun–masterly; Moon–intense; Mercury–inquisitive; Venus–intimate; Mars–indomitable; Jupiter–paternal; Saturn–shrewd; Uranus–experimentative; Neptune–authoritative; Pluto–transcendent.

If the Sun is in High Focus (masterly), these individuals enter into new experience through a show of personal power and creativity. If the Sun's power is used constructively, they shine benevolently with masterful control. If the Sun receives stress aspects from other planets, such as a square, opposition, or inconjunct, these individuals have an exaggerated opinion of their own importance or worth.

If the Moon is the planet in High Focus (intense), individuals enter into new experiences by attempting to be a nurturing factor in the activities in which they are engaged. This is an unconscious mothering response, that is, individuals feel that a maternal response is required of them. This intense desire to help and to nurture can be of great comfort to others. However, the emotional response to others is geared toward playing whatever role is thought to be required at the moment. In time, this can prove to be psychologically debilitating for the individual.

If Mercury is the planet in High Focus (inquisitive), individuals are drawn into experience through curiosity. Intellectual pursuits tend to introduce them to new experience. Used constructively this can result in research work in a given field because of the instinctive curiosity and communication of ideas connected with Mercury. If Mercury receives stress aspects, such as the square, opposition, or inconjunct, individuals can become busybodies, wanting to know all about the affairs of others, or there can be a difference in mental outlook.

If Venus is the planet in High Focus (intimate), individuals become involved in new experiences through business, social, and artistic contacts that will provide them with opportunities for involvement with important people, who in turn will enhance their standing in some way in these matters. Used constructively, this kind of selective involvement can produce the opportunity for enrichment in any of these activities. If Venus receives stress aspects from other planets, such as a square, opposition, or inconjunct, these individuals can be looked upon as social climbers or as opportunists.

If Mars is the planet in High Focus (indomitable), individuals enter into new experiences through their initiative, courage, and a desire and drive to get involved in new activities. This kind of stimulus for new adventures prevails throughout the entire life. Used constructively, this gives individuals the courage and energy to initiate new ways of doing things or initiate activities that are beneficial to others. If Mars receives stress aspects from other planets, such as the square, opposition, or inconjunct, individuals can get involved in activities impulsively without proper consideration of the outcome. In extreme cases individuals can become involved in dangerous or undesirable activities. Often there is considerable strife associated with these new experiences.

If Jupiter is the planet in High Focus (paternal), individuals enter into new experience through educational, religious, and cultural activities, guiding others with confidence. This confidence has its base in the individuals' experience or educational background which was developed in order to be of help to others. Used in a constructive manner, this makes these individuals enthusiastic and optimistic, thus inspiring confidence in others. If Jupiter receives stress aspects from other planets, such as a square, opposition, or inconjunct, unrealistic optimism can get these individuals into trouble or they may take on more than they can handle. Jupiter in High Focus often indicates the educator in some field.

If Saturn is the planet in High Focus (shrewd), individuals enter into new experiences through a systematic, organized approach. These individuals will be shrewd and cautious, sizing up the possibilities inherent in the new situation. Used constructively, this High Focus planet indicates an individual with high aims and ambitions which are realized through discipline and organization. If Saturn receives stress aspects from other planets, such as a square, opposition, or inconjunct, the individual is liable to take on too much responsibility and work.

If Uranus is the planet in High Focus (experimentative), individuals enter into new experiences related to scientific, occult, or humanitarian activities. The opportunity for new experience often comes through friends, organizations, or corporate affairs. If handled in a constructive way, this planet in High Focus can bring the realization of personal goals and objectives. If Uranus receives stress aspects from other planets, such as a square, opposition, or inconjunct, these individuals must have freedom at all costs. This desire for freedom can be detrimental to their well-being. They must learn to live within traditional structures with some modicum of cooperation. If this is not done the talent and originality indicated by Uranus will be wasted.

If Neptune is the planet in High Focus (authoritarian), individuals enter into new experience through a subtle kind of authority that is acquired through activities carried on behind the scenes. These activities could involve educational, religious, medical, or philosophic institutions. Often karmic circumstances involve these individuals in these activities. Used constructively, this can bring the desired ends to fruition. If Neptune receives stress aspects from other planets, such as a square, opposition, or inconjunct, the individuals can be confused or deceived in their involvement with new experiences.

If Pluto is the planet in High Focus (transcendent), individuals enter into new experience because of their ability or efforts to improve current conditions. Used constructively, this makes the individual resourceful and innovative in regenerating the circumstances and conditions in which they find themselves. If Pluto receives stress aspects from other planets, such as a square, opposition, or inconjunct, they can assume an autocratic attitude in their attempts to influence or remake others.

11

Natural Disposition

The Natural Disposition of a horoscope, which is represented by the oppositions in the individual's chart, indicates a psychological slanting that must be dealt with in a pertinent way throughout the entire life.

Although the individual may not be aware of this slanting on a conscious level, this undercurrent or slanting is always present and must be dealt with in a harmonious manner; otherwise there is a continuous conflict and unrest.

If the chart contains one opposition or if several planets are involved in the same opposition by conjunction, in this type of interpretation it is considered one opposition.

If all the planets involved in this opposition are found in Cardinal signs, that is, Aries, Libra, Cancer, or Capricorn, individuals are continually caught up in crisis situations. These individuals are action-oriented, ambitious, and egocentric. In other words, the action that takes place around them was initially pioneered by these individuals as a result of ambition, boredom, or inactivity.

When the opposing planets involved in the opposition are found in Fixed signs, that is, Taurus, Scorpio, Leo, or Aquarius, individuals are continually caught up in conflicts that deal with their principles or ideals. In the final consideration the individual's own set of values, principles, and ideals will always have top priority regardless of the issue at hand.

When the opposing planets involved in the opposition are found in

Mutable signs, that is, Gemini, Sagittarius, Virgo, or Pisces, individuals have a psychological drive to interact and communicate with others. The Mutable signs deal with skills; however, individuals with this Natural Disposition must use their skills for and with others.

When there are two oppositions in a chart involving two of the quadruplicities—for example, Sun in Cancer opposition to Mars in Capricorn and Saturn in Aquarius in opposition to Moon in Leo—the missing quadruplicity in this case would be the Mutable quadruplicity. By the absence of an opposition in the Mutable quadruplicity, the Mutable quadruplicity would emerge as the Natural Disposition. This is indicative of a very subtle psychological slanting—these individuals would adhere to their ideals, goals, and principles; also, the need for activity on some level would be present. However, the final slanting of such a planetary setup would be toward the Mutable quadruplicity, indicating interest in and interaction with others.

When there are three oppositions in a chart involving all three quadruplicities—or if there are *no* oppositions in the chart—these individuals are free agents to determine their actions and slantings.

This rule does not apply if the opposition should fall in a hidden aspect, such as when planets involved in the opposition are in two different quadruplicities.

Example: Saturn in three degrees of Gemini in opposition to Jupiter in twenty-seven degrees of Scorpio. This is an opposition by orb; however, it could not apply as the Natural Disposition because the planets are in different quadruplicities.

For special details on the Natural Disposition, see *The Essentials of Astrological Analysis* by Marc Edmund Jones.

The Dynamic Focus of the Personality

The Dynamic Focus of the personality deals with the closest square or opposition in the birth horoscope, a Marc Edmund Jones tool.

If individuals are to avoid frustration and work with the challenges that this focus presents, they must have an understanding of the positive potential of such a challenge.

First, determine whether the Dynamic Focus is a square or an opposition. Second, if there are several close squares and oppositions, determine which is the closest by degrees, minutes, and seconds. The closest in orb will be the Dynamic Focus of the personality. The planets involved will give sharp clues to the individual's assets and handicaps.

Next, determine which planet in the square (or opposition) dominates. There are two factors that determine the strength of the planets: (1) Is one or both planets a part of an aspect pattern or High Focus planet in such configurations as a Grand Square, T square, Yod, and so on? (2) Determine the strength of the planet by exaltation, detriment, or accidental dignity, also by the quadrant placement.

If the Dynamic Focus is a square it indicates that adjustments must be made and energy must be expended if individuals are to realize gain. The square has a fourth and tenth house connotation, Saturn and Moon influence, indicating that individuals must take advantage of the challenge offered in the world around them. The square indicates that these individuals must willingly build in new experiences and abilities that will round out the undeveloped areas of their experience.

If the Dynamic Focus is an opposition, individuals are confronted with a situation of either cooperation or conflict between the psychological drives represented by the two planets in point focus.

The opposition has a first house, Aries and Mars connotation and a seventh house, Libra and Venus connotation.

The planets are divided into several departments; however, for purposes of simplification we will divide them into two groups. The Sun, Moon, Jupiter, and Saturn represent the planets of inner experience. Mars, Venus, Mercury, Uranus, Neptune, and Pluto are the planets of outer experience. If the two planets involved in Dynamic Focus are found in departments of inner experience or outer experience—that is, both planets in the same department—individuals are inclined to work in harmony and cooperation with what interests them.

If the point focus is made up of one planet from the inner experience department and the other from the outer experience department, these individuals will be apostles of change—nonconformists. They cannot get all wrapped up in self-interests, neither can they lose themselves through some social necessity.

If the Sun is involved in a point focus square, individuals must make a special effort to use the will and power potential represented by the Sun in a harmonious and wise manner. If these individuals will do this, it will spur them to greater achievement; otherwise they are liable to get discouraged, and frustration and lack of fulfillment will be the result.

If the Moon is involved in a point focus square, individuals must let go of all racial and social prejudices, and all frustrations and emotional blockages that probably stem from early childhood. They must let go of any unconscious resentment toward women; otherwise they will find it difficult to act as emotionally free agents.

If Mercury is involved in a point focus square, individuals can be intelligent and mentally active; however, their viewpoint is liable to be one-sided. If they are to use their abilities in a constructive and fruitful manner, they must guard against intellectual pride, argumentativeness, and skepticism.

If Venus is involved in a point focus square, individuals must develop appreciation and right response in social relationships. They must avoid self-indulgent tendencies and develop a consideration for the other person if emotional and social difficulties are to be avoided. These individuals must work at developing their own resources if they are to have emotional and material equilibrium.

If Mars is involved in a point focus square, individuals must consider the needs and rights of others. They need to exercise patience. There is a need to channel the energy in an intelligent manner, organizing the energy to produce useful results; otherwise, the desire for action that this square represents can cause individuals to lash out in rash ways, creating problems. The reason for this is that a driving ambition usually accompanies a Mars square. These individuals must learn to finish that which they begin; otherwise they will eventually lose confidence in themselves.

If Jupiter is involved in a point focus square, individuals must use moderation and careful forethought and not attempt more than they can adequately handle. There should be a solid foundation that is realistic on which to build and expand; otherwise they will be viewed as foolish optimists and their careers and reputations will suffer.

If Saturn is involved in a point focus square, individuals must work very hard in order to overcome obstacles and limitations that could frustrate their ambitions. They must overcome a tendency to negative thinking and acquire a positive attitude.

If Uranus is involved in a point focus square, individuals must guard against unpredictable, impulsive, rash actions. Much good work can be brought to naught through some foolish action. These individuals can change their minds and plans often, and because of this tendency serious mistakes can be made. They should guard against a tendency to be unreasonable, willful, and obstinate.

If Neptune is involved in a point focus square, individuals must accept responsibility and face up to reality. They must learn organization in order to avoid confusion and destructiveness. They should guard against unconscious, negative conditioning which could lead them to emotional excesses and impracticality.

If Pluto is involved in a point focus square, individuals should avoid a ruthless, overbearing attitude and not attempt the impossible. Dictatorial attitudes and a lack of patience can defeat their purpose.

The opposition involved in a point focus would indicate a need for cooperation and an awareness of the other person.

If the Sun is involved in a point focus opposition, individuals should consider all viewpoints impartially; when faced with strife they should avoid a partisan point of view or a tendency to pick sides. There can be a conflict of wills which could lead to frustration. These individuals should resist the temptation to dominate, as this attempt to dominate will cause resentment in others.

If the Moon is involved in a point focus opposition, individuals will have to learn and practice emotional detachment and objectivity. Emotional problems in relationships are often caused by individuals projecting their emotional problems on others and blaming others for their own unrecognized faults. There can be a psychological mirror effect in which the individuals' lack of awareness of the need for cooperation at any given moment is blamed on the other person.

If Mercury is involved in a point focus opposition, individuals must take into consideration the other person's point of view. If this is not done, communication problems are certain. Relationship problems could arise out of differences of opinion and mental outlook.

If Venus is involved in a point focus opposition, individuals are likely to be overly sensitive and demand emotional gratification while neglecting to give others the same consideration. There is a great need to consider others if disappointment and unhappiness are to be avoided. This lack of awareness of the needs of others would suggest problems in the emotional, marital, and romantic sphere.

If Mars is involved in a point focus opposition, individuals are forced to become aware of the other person and of the necessity for cooperation. There can be an unfortunate inclination toward competitiveness, fighting, and anger. This could manifest itself as verbal bickering or rash, aggressive action toward others. These individuals must learn to view any issue from the other person's point of view. If these factors are handled properly there can be firm, energetic action in partnerships or close personal relationships.

If Jupiter is involved in a point focus opposition, individuals must avoid taking too much for granted. There can also be a tendency to promote grandiose schemes at the expense of others or to demand too much from them. These individuals should also remember that familiarity breeds contempt, and in this case could cause relationship problems where the hail-fellow-well-met attitude would not be appreciated.

If Saturn is involved in a point focus opposition, individuals should avoid negative, restrictive and selfish attitudes. These individuals could appear to be unfriendly and unapproachable because of a serious and austere projection. These characteristics must be corrected if isolation, loneliness, and frustration are to be avoided.

If Uranus is involved in a point focus opposition, individuals must guard against unpredictable, unreasonable, and demanding attitudes toward others. The individual is likely to damage relationships through an unwillingness to sacrifice personal desires and freedom. Others are liable to see them as undependable, erratic, and willful, and therefore as difficult to deal and work with.

If Neptune is involved in a point focus opposition, individuals should guard against unconscious emotional problems. Relationship problems often develop because of deceptiveness and unreliability. These individuals can have a tendency to project their psychological difficulties on others or assume the burden of the psychic problems of others, thus causing confusion and misunderstanding.

If Pluto is involved in a point focus opposition, individuals are liable to generate relationship problems by indulging in demanding, dictatorial, or domineering attitudes. Relationship problems can also arise if individuals try to reform others according to their own design without consideration for the wishes, desires, and rights of others. Such attitudes often lead to arguments and impasses, generating resentment and alienating individuals from warm human contacts.

12

Mental Chemistry

One of the astrological tools introduced by Dr. Marc Edmund Jones is called Mental Chemistry. The term *Mental Chemistry* does not deal with an individual's intelligence or lack of it. It deals rather with the impressions received from any outside stimuli and how people rationalize what is going on around them.

There are four different combinations that determine Mental Chemistry. All individuals have one of them in their chart. The groups are as follows:

Group A: The Moon traveling fast the day of birth and Mercury trailing the Sun. (Balanced)
Group B: The Moon traveling slow the day of birth and Mercury preceding the Sun. (Balanced)
Group C: The Moon traveling fast the day of birth and Mercury preceding the Sun. (Anxious)
Group D: The Moon traveling slow the day of birth and Mercury trailing the Sun. (Deliberate)

Group A: Moon Fast, Mercury Trailing the Sun, Balanced

This combination indicates that these individuals adjust to circumstances as they are. Their perception is keen and sharp and the mind evaluates circumstances in a rational, organized way. This type of Mental Chemistry poses no problem for these individuals.

Group B: Moon Slow, Mercury Preceding the Sun, Balanced

This combination gives individuals a slow, deliberate perception of what is going on, followed by a rapid mental response. This type of Mental Chemistry poses no problem for these individuals.

Group C: Moon Fast, Mercury Preceding the Sun, Anxious

With this combination, individuals usually jump to conclusions without considering all the circumstances involved. There is a sense of urgency whereby these individuals react impulsively to the information received without waiting for details or for the whole picture to unfold. Thus, these individuals interject their own conclusions in any given situation, much to the annoyance of the individual relating the event. There is much impatience in conversing with others and in listening to what they have to say. This impatience is an outstanding characteristic of the personality which needs to be tempered with understanding of self and others. The information received is not always recalled, thus preventing the individual from making proper judgments.

Group D: Moon Slow, Mercury Trailing the Sun, Deliberate

With this combination individuals deliberate over every impression and detail involved in a situation. These individuals want to make certain when judging or appraising a situation that they have all the facts and details. This caution and thoroughness and mulling over all the details is often exasperating to others. These individuals somehow do not comprehend that life does not allow for such extreme deliberations. When this need for deliberation is blocked, these individuals withdraw into their own private world. The plus side of this combination is that once these individuals have collected all the information and details, they become a fountain of information regarding a subject that has attracted their interest.

To determine Mental Chemistry, one must ascertain the speed of the Moon's travel during the twenty-four-hour period of the day the individual was born. This twenty-four-hour period can be determined from an ephemeris which has the individual's year and date of birth. (This information can be found in either a noon or midnight ephemeris.)

The Moon's average rate of travel is 13 degrees 10 minutes per day. However, it can travel as fast as 15 degrees per day or as slow as 11 degrees plus per day. Before this information can be used, the Greenwich Mean Time must be calculated. The directions are given at the end of this chapter.

The books needed to compute the Moon's travel are:

Time Changes in the USA by Doris Chase Doane.

Time Changes in the World (if the birth is in a foreign country) by the same author.

Longitudes and Latitudes in the USA by Eugene Dernay.

Longitudes and Latitudes in the World (if the birth is in a foreign country) by the same author.

An ephemeris for the year, month, and date of birth is also necessary. When using a noontime ephemeris, proceed as follows:

If the Greenwich Mean Time of birth is A.M., subtract the Moon's position the day previous to the birth from the Moon's position the day of birth. This will give the twenty-four-hour travel of the Moon for an A.M. birth (Greenwich Mean Time).

If the Greenwich Mean Time of birth is P.M., subtract the Moon's position the day of birth from the Moon's position the following day. This determines the Moon's travel for the twenty-four-hour period within which the individual was born.

When using an ephemeris calculated for midnight at Greenwich, there are three possibilities:

In the majority of cases the Greenwich Mean Time will be on the same day as the day of birth. Therefore, find the difference in the Moon's position on the day of birth and the day after.

In some instances the Greenwich Mean Time goes back before the midnight of the day of birth. In this case use the day before the birth and the day of the birth to find the twenty-four-hour travel.

When the Greenwich Mean Time goes beyond the midnight at the end of the day of birth, find the difference in the Moon's position the day of birth and the day after.

If the Moon's travel is 13 degrees 10 minutes or more, then it is considered a Fast Moon.

If the Moon's travel is less than 13 degrees 10 minutes, it is considered a Slow Moon.

The next step involves the position of Mercury relative to the Sun. All planets travel in a clockwise direction (retrogradation is not a factor). Therefore, it must be determined whether Mercury precedes or trails the Sun.

The combination of the twenty-four-hour travel of the Moon and the position of Mercury relative to the Sun gives the four types of Mental Chemistry, Groups A, B, C, and D, as previously described. Groups A and B are labeled Balanced Mental Chemistry, Group C is called Anxious Mental Chemistry, and Group D is called Deliberate Mental Chemistry.

Method for Calculating the Twenty-four-Hour Travel of the Moon

In order to calculate Greenwich Mean Time, obtain an ephemeris that contains the data for the year of birth. Turn to the page containing the year, month, and day of birth. The exact time of birth must be ascertained, because some birth dates need to be corrected for daylight savings time, war time, or power shortage time. This information is given in the *Time Changes* book. If any of these time changes was in effect at the time of birth, one hour should be subtracted from the given time of birth. This is because births are recorded by local clock time during such times. (Exceptions to this rule in the United States are certain cities in the states of Pennsylvania and Illinois; therefore, a birth in this state must be checked carefully in order to ascertain what kind of time was used in recording the birth of the individual.) During the war years in England in the summer months, both daylight savings time and war time were used, making it necessary to subtract two hours from the birth in the summertime and one hour during the winter months. The exact time these time changes take place is listed in the *Time Changes* book.

After the corrections for daylight savings time, war time, or power shortage time have been made, the next step is to find the true local time of birth.

In the book of *Longitudes and Latitudes,* find the page listing the state and city of birth. There will be four columns of figures.

The first column gives the longitude of a given city.

The second column gives the latitude of a city.

The third column lists in minutes and seconds the correction for the local mean time of the city. In this column there will be either a plus or minus sign just before the listing of the minutes and seconds. This plus or minus sign instructs one either to add or subtract these minutes and seconds to or from the local time. If it is a plus sign (+), then add these minutes and seconds to the birth hour. If it is a minus sign (−), then subtract the correction.

Example: Female born June 24, 1923, 4:20 P.M., Somerville, Massachusetts.

The first step is to check the *Time Changes* book for daylight savings time, war time, or power shortage time. This birth took place during daylight savings time. Therefore, one hour is automatically subtracted from the birth hour, making the birth time 3:20 P.M.

From now on the birth will be referred to as 3:20 P.M.

Next look in the book giving the longitudes and latitudes in the United States.

In this book, in the first column, the longitude for Somerville is listed as 71 degrees west 06 minutes. In the second column the latitude is listed as 42 degrees north 22 minutes. The next column lists the local time variation, which is used in finding true local time. In the book it is listed in this manner: L.T. Var. The local time variation for Somerville is fifteen minutes and forty-four seconds with a plus sign before it, indicating that fifteen minutes and forty-four seconds must be added to the birth time (which has been corrected for DST).

	Birth Hour	Minutes	Seconds
Add the local	3	20′	00″ P.M.
time variation	+	15′	44″
	3	35′	44″ P.M. true local time

The next step is to find the Greenwich Mean Time of birth. (The reason for this is that all time is measured from Greenwich, England.) In order to do this, it is necessary to add the Greenwich Mean Time variation listed in the fourth column of the *Longitudes and Latitudes* book to the true local time.

	Hours	Minutes	Seconds
Correction for	3	35′	44″ P.M. true local time
GMT variation;	+4	44′	16″
because there is a plus sign, ADD	7	79′	60″ P.M.

This sum is the Greenwich Mean Time; however, this must be written in the correct form for hours, minutes, and seconds, because the minute and second column must not exceed 59. When these columns add up to 60 or more, subtract 60 and add one whole unit to the next column on the left. This is done because:

60 seconds equal 1 whole minute,
60 minutes equal 1 whole hour.

Proceed to reduce this sum as follows: Subtract 60 seconds from the second column and add 1 minute to the minute column; do the same in the minute column–subtract 60 minutes and add 1 hour to the hour column.

Hours	Minutes	Seconds
7	79′	60″
	+ 1′	−60″
	80′	00″
+1	−60′	
8	20′	00″ P.M. Greenwich Mean Time

In order to find the twenty-four-hour travel of the Moon, it is necessary to determine whether the Greenwich Mean Time is before noon (A.M.) or afternoon (P.M.).

In this example the Greenwich Mean Time has gone past noon. Therefore the position of the Moon on the day of birth must be subtracted from the position of the Moon on the day after the birth. This information is found in the ephemeris for the year and date of birth.

Position of the Moon day after birth:	June 25, 1923	21°	36′
Position of the Moon day of birth:	June 24, 1923	−7°	02′
Twenty-four hour travel of the Moon		14°	34′

As was stated, any rate of travel 13 degrees 10 minutes or more in the twenty-four-hour period of birth is considered a Fast Moon. Any travel slower than 13 degrees 10 minutes is considered a Slow Moon.

Example of an A.M. Birth

Male born October 8, 1912:	4	40′		A.M. Cleveland, Ohio
Local time variation:	+	33′	12″	
	4	73′	12″	
Subtract 60′:	+1	−60′		
	5	13′	12″	A.M.
Greenwich Mean Time variation:	+5	26′	48″	
	10	39′	60″	A.M.
Subtract 60″:		+ 1′	−60″	
	10	40′	00″	A.M. Greenwich Mean Time

		16	64
Position of the Moon day of birth:	October 8, 1912	~~17°~~	~~04′~~
Position of the Moon day before birth:	October 7, 1912	−2°	30′
Twenty-four-hour travel of the Moon		14°	34′

As explained before, there are 60 seconds in each minute and 60 minutes in each hour. In the example above, the second column is impossible to subtract; therefore, one whole unit must be borrowed from the minute column and changed into seconds and added to the second column. One whole unit equals 60 seconds; therefore 60 seconds must be added to the 4 seconds already there, making a total of 64 seconds. Now it can be subtracted.

Both examples have the Moon fast in motion and therefore labeled Fast-moving Moons.

Balanced Mental Chemistry

Moon Fast—Mercury behind the Sun	Birth Data: June 10, 1948, 11:30 A.M., Boston, Massachusetts

Time Changes: Daylight savings time in effect — 11:30 A.M.
Subtract one hour from birth time: — −1

10:30 A.M.

Longitude	Latitude	Local time variation	Greenwich Mean Time variation
71W04	42N22	+00:15:44	+04:44:16

10: 30: 00 A.M.	10: 45: 44	A.M. true local time
+ 15: 44	+ 4: 44: 16	G.M.T. variation
10: 45: 44 A.M.	14: 89: 60	Reduce this answer to the proper
	+ 1: −60	hours, minutes, and seconds.
	14: 90: 00	
	+ 1: −60	
	15: 30: 00	P.M. Greenwich Mean Time

The Greenwich Mean Time is after Noon. Therefore, the dates used to find the twenty-four-hour travel of the Moon are the day of the birth and the day after the birth:

	43	
June 11:	13°	50′
June 10:	−29	16
	14°	34′

Because the Moon is moving faster than the mean average which is 13 degrees 10 minutes, it is said to be a fast-moving Moon.

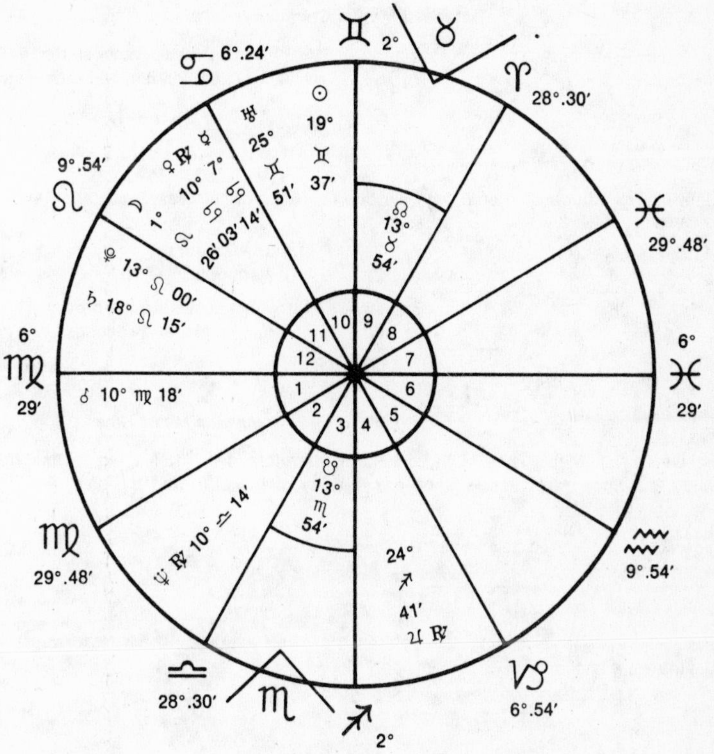
♊ 2°
♉
♈ 28°.30′
♋ 6°.24′
♌ 9°.54′
♓ 29°.48′
6° ♍ 29′
6° ♓ 29′
♍ 29°.48′
♒ 9°.54′
♎ 28°.30′
♏
♐ 2°
♑ 6°.54′
☉ 19° ♊ 37′
♅ 25° ♊ 51′
♀ ℞ ☿
10° 7°
☽ 1°
♌ ♋ ♋
26′ 03′ 14′
♇ 13° ♌ 00′
♄ 18° ♌ 15′
♂ 10° ♍ 18′
♆ ℞ 10° ♎ 14′
24° ♐ 41′ ♃ ℞
☊ 13° ♉ 54′
☋ 13° ♏ 54′
1 2 3 4 5 6 7 8 9 10 11 12

Balanced Mental Chemistry

Moon Slow—Mercury
ahead of the Sun

Birth Data: December 13, 1947,
1:27 P.M., Somerville, Massachusetts

Time Changes: No daylight, war, or power shortage time.

Longitude	Latitude	Local time variation	Greenwich Mean Time variation
71W06	42N23	+00:15:38	+04:44:22

1: 27: 00 P.M.	1: 42: 38	P.M. true local time
+ : 15: 38	+4: 44: 22	G.M.T. variation
1: 42: 38 P.M.	5: 86: 60	Reduce this answer to the proper
	+ 1: −60	hours, minutes, and seconds.
	5: 87: 00	
	+1: −60	
	6: 27: 00	P.M. Greenwich Mean Time

The Greenwich Mean Time is before Noon; therefore, the dates used to find the twenty-four-hour travel of the Moon are the day of the birth and the day after the birth:

December 14:	13°	27′
December 13:	− 1	24
	12°	03′

Because the Moon is moving slower than the mean average, which is 13 degrees 10 minutes, it is said to be a slow-moving Moon.

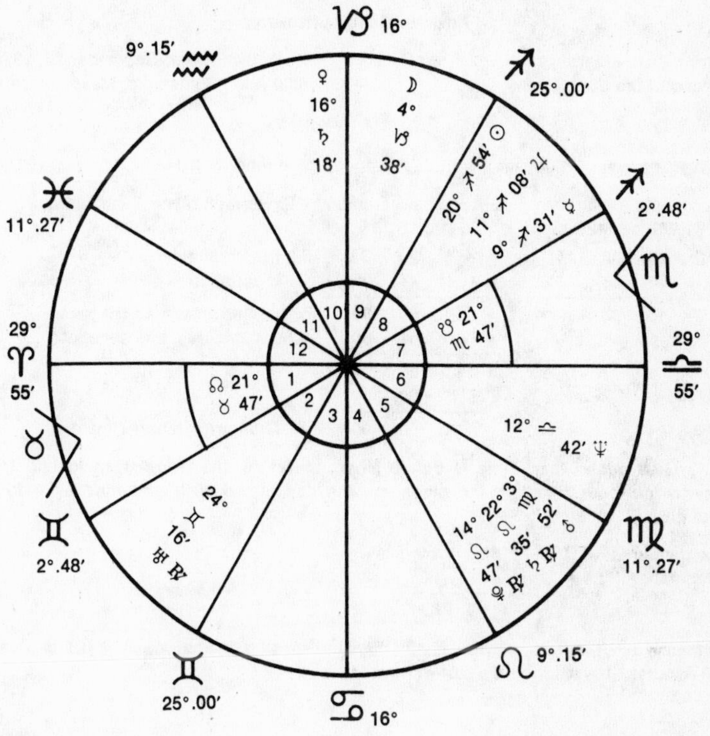

♑ 16°
9°.15′ ♒
♐ 25°.00′
♓ 11°.27′
♐ 2°.48′
♏
29° ♈ 55′
29° ♎ 55′
♉
♊ 2°.48′
♍ 11°.27′
♊ 25°.00′
♌ 9°.15′
♋ 16°
♀ 16° ♄ 18′
☽ 4° ♑ 38′
20° ♐ 54′ ☉
11° ♐ 08′ ♃
9° ♐ 31′ ☿
☋ 21° ♏ 47′
☊ 21° ♉ 47′
12° ♎ 42′ ♆
24° ♊ 16′ ♅ ℞
14° ♌ 47′ ♇ ℞
22° ♌ 35′ ♄ ℞
3° ♍ 52′ ♂
10 9 8 7 6 5 4 3 2 1 12 11

Anxious Mental Chemistry

Moon Fast—Mercury
ahead of the Sun

Birth Data: December 22, 1920,
6:00 A.M., Somerville, Massachusetts

Time Changes: No daylight, war, or power shortage time.

Longitude	Latitude	Local time variation	Greenwich Mean Time variation
71W06	42N23	+00:15:38	+04:44:22

6: 00: 00 A.M.	6: 15: 38	A.M. true local time
+ : 15: 38	+ 4: 44: 22	G.M.T. variation
6: 15: 38 A.M.	10: 59: 60	Reduce this answer to the proper
	+ 1: −60	hours, minutes, and seconds.
	10: 60: 00	
	+ 1 −60:	
	11: 00: 00	A.M. Greenwich Mean Time

The Greenwich Mean Time is before Noon, therefore, the dates used to find the twenty-four-hour travel of the Moon are the day of the birth and the day before the birth.

December 22:	18°	24′
December 21:	− 4	22
	14°	02′

Because the Moon is moving faster than the mean average which is 13 degrees 10 minutes, it is said to be a fast-moving Moon.

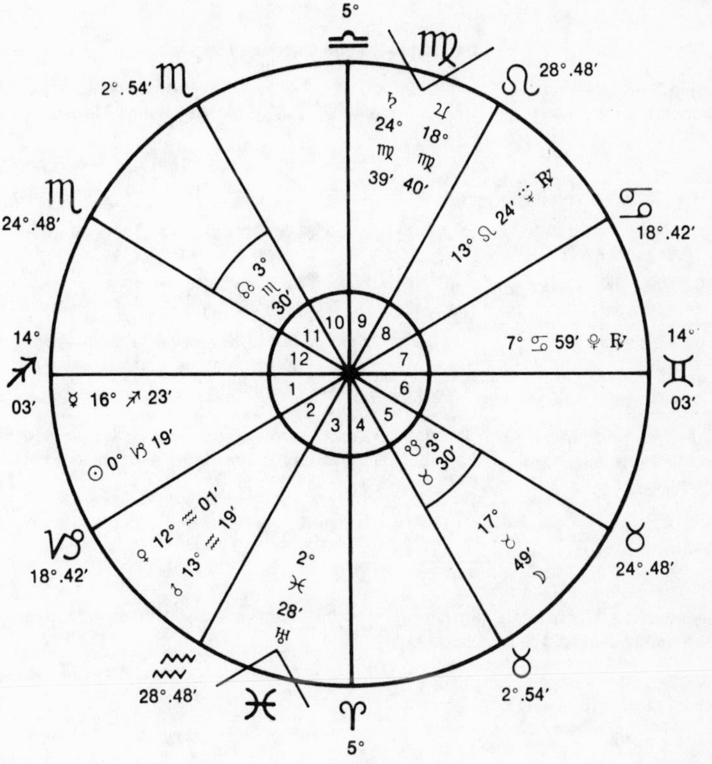
5° ♎
♍
2°. 54′ ♏
♌ 28°.48′
♄ 24° ♍ 39′
♃ 18° ♍ 40′
♏ 24°.48′
13° ♌ 24′ ♇ ℞
♋ 18°.42′
☊ 3° ♏ 30′
14° ♐ 03′
7° ♋ 59′ ♆ ℞
14° ♊ 03′
10 9 8 7 6 5 4 3 2 1 12 11
☿ 16° ♐ 23′
☉ 0° ♑ 19′
☋ 3° ♉ 30′
♑ 18°.42′
♀ 12° ♒ 01′
♂ 13° ♒ 19′
2° ♓ 28′ ♅
17° ♉ 49′ ☽
♉ 24°.48′
♒ 28°.48′
♓
♈ 5°
♉ 2°.54′

Deliberate Mental Chemistry

Moon Slow—Mercury behind the Sun	Birth Data: April 8, 1951, 3:59 A.M., Weymouth, Massachusetts

Time Changes: No daylight, war, or power shortage time.

Longitude	Latitude	Local time variation	Greenwich Mean Time variation
70W58	42N13	+00:16:09	+04:43:51

3: 59: 00 A.M.	4: 15: 09	A.M. true local time
+ 16: 09	+4: 43: 51	G.M.T. variation
3: 75: 09 A.M.	8: 58: 60	Reduce this answer to the proper
+1: −60	+ 1: −60	hours, minutes, and seconds.
4: 15: 09 A.M.	8: 59: 00	A.M. Greenwich Mean Time

The Greenwich Mean Time is before Noon. Therefore, the dates used to find the twenty-four-hour travel of the Moon are the day of the birth and the day before the birth.

April 8:	41°	25′
April 7:	−29	02
	12°	23′

Because the Moon is moving slower than the mean average which is 13 degrees 10 minutes, it is said to be a slow-moving Moon.

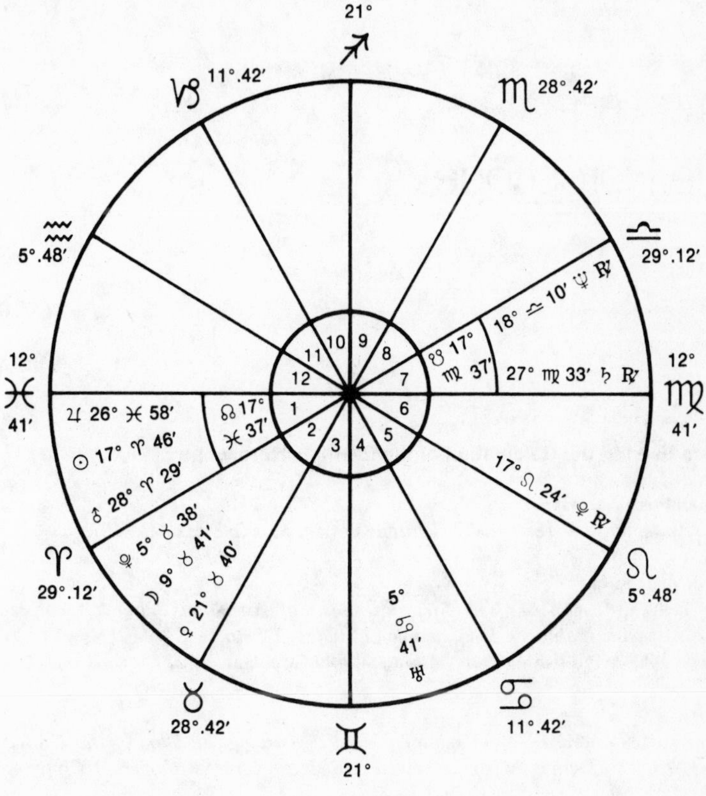
21° ♐
♑ 11°.42′
♏ 28°.42′
♒ 5°.48′
♎ 29°.12′
12° ♓ 41′
12° ♍ 41′
♈ 29°.12′
♌ 5°.48′
♉ 28°.42′
♋ 11°.42′
♊ 21°
18° ♎ 10′ ♆ ℞
☋ 17° ♍ 37′
27° ♍ 33′ ♄ ℞
☊ 17° ♓ 37′
♃ 26° ♓ 58′
☉ 17° ♈ 46′
♂ 28° ♈ 29′
♀ 5° ♉ 38′
☽ 9° ♉ 41′
☿ 21° ♉ 40′
17° ♌ 24′ ♇ ℞
5° ♋ 41′ ♅
1 2 3 4 5 6 7 8 9 10 11 12

13

Erecting the Horoscope

Texts Used in the Calculation of the Example Horoscope

Ephemeris (Noon):
Ephemeriden: 1890–1950 (Zurich: Verlag, Max S. Metz AG., 1971).

Table of Houses:
Dalton, Joseph G., *The Spherical Basis of Astrology Being a Comprehensive Table of Houses for Latitudes 22° to 56° . . .* (New York: Macoy Publishing and Masonic Supply Company, 1927).

Atlas:
Astro Numeric Service (compiler), *AFA Astrological Atlas of the United States* (Tempe, Arizona: American Federation of Astrologers, 1975).

Time Adjustment Books:
Doane, Doris Chase, *Time Changes in the USA* (revised edition) (San Francisco: Quarto Productions, 1973, 1966).
———, *Time Changes in Canada and Mexico* (San Francisco: Quarto Productions, 1968).
———, *Time Changes in the World (except Canada, Mexico, USA)* (San Francisco: Quarto Productions, 1971).

Note: The last three publications are *now* published by the American Federation of Astrologers, P.O. Box 22040, Tempe, Arizona 85282.

Erecting the Wheel

A. Write the name and birth data across the top of the page.

Example: Female born July 24, 1942, 2:58 A.M. Eastern War Time, Syracuse, New York.

B. Refer to *Time Changes in the USA, Times Changes in Canada and Mexico,* or *Time Changes in the World* (whichever is appropriate for the birth location) to determine the form of time in effect at the time of birth. If Daylight Saving Time, War Time, or any other form of "advanced" time was in effect (because of a power shortage or any other reason), cross out the birth time and record it as being one hour earlier—that is, in *Standard* time. (Be careful of Pennsylvania and Illinois births, as in these states births were recorded strictly in Standard Time on birth certificates for certain years. See pages 186 to 191 of *Time Changes in the USA* in these cases.) If the birth was recorded in Standard Time, DO *NOT* deduct the hour for time correction.

Example: This individual was born at 2:58 A.M. *Eastern War Time.* War Time was a nationally observed form of "advanced" time (like year-round Daylight Saving Time) that was in effect from 2:00 A.M. February 9, 1942, to 2:00 A.M. September 30, 1945. The state of New York observed War Time *and* recorded all births occurring during this period in this "advanced" time. Hence, we deduct one hour from the time given for birth, making it 1:58 A.M. Eastern *Standard* Time. (This information was found in *Time Changes in the USA,* published by the American Federation of Astrologers, P.O. Box 22040, Tempe, Arizona 85282, page 102.)

C. Refer to the *AFA Astrological Atlas of the United States* for the latitudes and longitudes of American births or *Longitudes and Latitudes Throughout the World,* by Eugene Dernay, for births outside the United States. In our example, we are dealing with a United States birth. Copy this information and place it under the data at the top of the page; this will consist of the longitude and latitude of the birth location, the Local Mean Time variation and the Greenwich Mean Time variation.

Example: From the *AFA Astrological Atlas of the United States,* page 199, in the left-hand column under "Syracuse, New York":

Longitude	Latitude	EST (Local Mean Time variation)	Longitude (GMT variation)
76W09.0	43N3.1	−4:36	5:04:36

Determining the Sidereal Time of Birth	**Explanatory Calculations**	**Sidereal Time Calculation**

Step 1

Take the *Standard Time* of birth and add the Local Mean Time variation to it. (Note that if the Local Mean Time variation is minus, *subtract* it from the Standard Time of birth.)

Explanatory Calculations:

	h	m	s	
	1	58	00	A.M. EST
–		4	36	
	1	53	24	A.M. LMT

Step 2

Using a Noon ephemeris, find the year, month, and day of birth. Copy from the ephemeris the Sidereal Time—in hours, minutes, and seconds (h m s)—as listed under "Sternzeit" for the Noon *preceding* the time of birth (in this case, the value of Noon, July 23, 1942, as this is the Noon immediately preceding the time of birth).

Sidereal Time Calculation:

h	m	s
8	02	22

Step 3

There is a necessary adjustment for universal time (clock time) to ephemeris time—based on the year of birth—that must be added to the Sidereal Time found in Step 2. This value varies from year to year. A table for this correction is found on page XV of the *AFA Astrological Atlas of the United States.* Turn to this table, find the year of birth and *add* (or subtract, if birth occurred before 1903) the amount given for the year of birth to the Sidereal Time found in Step 2. In this case, the correction is 25 seconds of time.

Sidereal Time Calculation:

	h	m	s
+			25
	8	02	47

Step 4

This step requires the determination of the elapsed time interval since the previous noon to the time of birth in Local Mean Time. In this case, the birth occurred at 1:53:24 A.M. Local Mean Time (LMT). The elapsed time would be: (a) 12 hours from the previous noon to the midnight preceding birth, *plus* (b) 1 hour 53 minutes and 24 seconds from midnight to the time of birth, or a total of 13 hours 53 minutes and 24 seconds. Graphic illustration of this can be found on the "time line" drawn below.

Explanatory Calculations:

	h	m	s
	12	00	00
+	1	53	24
	13	53	24

Sidereal Time Calculation:

h	m	s
8	02	47

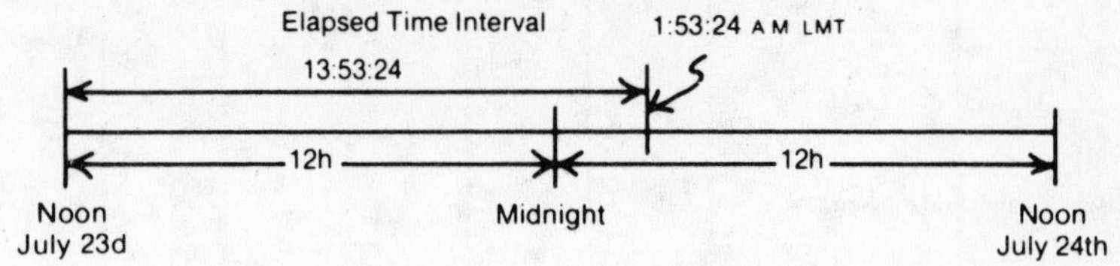

Step 5

It takes one year of solar time for the Earth to travel around the Sun. Due to this revolution, one day of "star" time must be made up.

This one day or 24-hour period must be divided by the average number of days in a year (365¼ days). This equals a correction of 3 minutes and 56 seconds for each day or 9.86 seconds for each hour. A table for this correction factor is located in Dalton's *Table of Houses* on page V (Table A), "Correction of Mean to Sidereal Time."

To complete this step, Greenwich Mean Time must be determined by using the Standard Time Meridian for the recorded birth time; this was done at the beginning of this example and determined to be 1:58 A.M. *Eastern Standard Time.* Eastern Standard Time is based on the 75° Meridian, which is 5 hours west of Greenwich Mean Time. (This is based on the fact that the world is divided into twenty-four time zones—every 15° of longitude away from Greenwich, which is 0° Longitude, equals one hour of solar time off of Greenwich Mean Time. Therefore, the Eastern Standard Time zone is 5 hours from Greenwich Mean Time.)

Explanatory Calculations

24 hrs. per yr.
×60 min. per hr.

1440 min. per yr.
×60 sec. per min.

86400 sec. per yr.

86400 sec. per yr.
÷
365¼ days per yr.
equals:
3 min. 56 sec. per day (appr.)
÷
24 hrs. per day
equals:
9.86 sec. per hr. (appr.)

75°W—EST Meridian
÷
15° per hr. of solar time
equals:
5 hrs. from Greenwich

Sidereal Time Calculation

	h	m	s
	8	02	47
+	13	53	24
	21	55	71
+		1	−60
	21	56	11

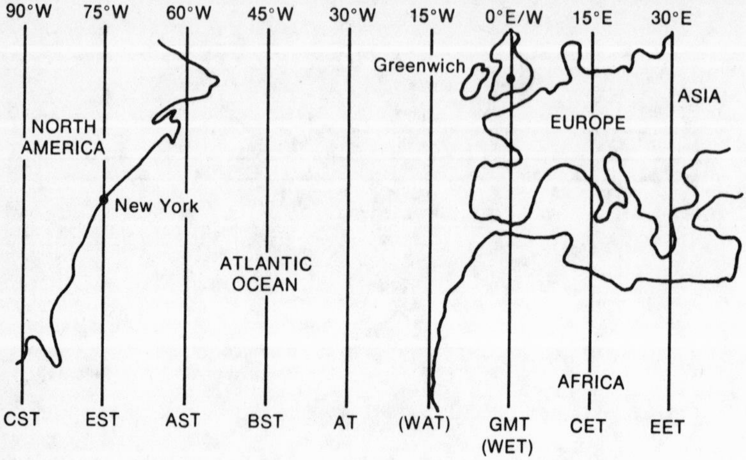

	Explanatory Calculations	**Sidereal Time Calculation**
Therefore, the birth time—which is 1:58 A.M. EST—*plus* 5 hours for the Greenwich Mean Time variation to the Eastern Standard Time Meridian, makes the total 6:58 A.M. GMT at birth.	1 58 A.M. EST +5 00 GMT to EST variation 6:58 A.M. GMT	h m s 21 56 11
Because a Noon ephemeris is used in this example and it is an A.M. birth in Greenwich Mean Time, the elapsed time since the *previous* noon to the birth time in Greenwich Mean Time is 6 hours 58 minutes, *plus* the 12-hour noon-to-midnight interval of the day before birth (refer again to the "time line," if necessary), giving a total of 18 hours 58 minutes 00 seconds.		
Now, go to Table A in Dalton's *Table of Houses,* page V, and find "18" hours under the "hour" column to the extreme left of the table. The "correction" column beside the "18" in the "hour" column specifies a correction of 2 minutes 57.42 seconds.	m s 2 57.42	
Then, go to the "minute" columns in the same table and find the column containing "58" minutes; note the correction in the "correction" column immediately		

	Explanatory Calculations	**Sidereal Time Calculation**
to its right, which is 9.53 seconds.	+ 9.53	
Next, add the two values found as the corrections for 18 hours and 58 minutes; that is, add 2 minutes 57.42 seconds to 9.53 seconds, round this result to the nearest second, and add it to the Sidereal Time Calculation so far computed.	7 3 0~~6~~.~~95~~ m s (remember there are 60 seconds to a minute)	+ 3 07 21 59 18 h m s
The result is the Sidereal Time of Birth.		

Determining the Approximate Natal House Cusps

The Sidereal Time of Birth, as found in the previous section, is used to locate the Midheaven degree (or degree on the tenth-house cusp) and the approximate degrees of respective signs for the balance of the house cusps. This is done by ascertaining the *closest* sidereal time found in the *Table of Houses* to that of birth. Having located the Midheaven (tenth-house cusp) degree and copied it onto the wheel, it is necessary to locate the nearest degree of latitude to that of birth in the extreme left-hand column of each page in the *Table of Houses.* Where the row to the right of this latitude intersects the column already found for the Midheaven (MC), copy the figures and signs given for the eleventh, twelfth, Ascending first-, second-, and third-house cusps onto the respective houses of the wheel. Then, put the *same* degree of the *opposite* sign on each of the remaining house cusps opposing those already filled in.

Example: Turn to page 61 in Dalton's *Table of Houses* and find the nearest sidereal time to that of birth as listed across the top of the page; in this case, the nearest sidereal time to that of the birth is 22 hours 00 minutes 42 seconds, giving 28° ♒ for the Midheaven (MC) or tenth-house cusp. Next, move down this column to where it intersects the line of latitude (listed in the extreme left-hand column of the page) closest to that of birth; in this case, the nearest degree of latitude is 43°. Copy out the house cusps as given in the *Tables* at this intersection point: 28°♒ on the tenth-house cusp or Midheaven; 0.2° ♈ on the eleventh-house cusp; 12.8° ♉ on the twelfth-house cusp; 24°24′♊ on the Ascendant or first-house cusp; 14.3°♋ on the second-house cusp; and 4.2°♌ on the third-house cusp. Next, fill in the opposing house cusps with the *same* degrees, but the *opposite* signs, to those already determined. (Libra opposes

Aries, Scorpio opposes Taurus, Sagittarius opposes Gemini, Capricorn opposes Cancer, Aquarius opposes Leo, and Pisces opposes Virgo.)

Note: The positions for the eleventh-, twelfth-, second-, and third-house cusps as given in these tables are in degrees and *tenths* of a degree. *Do not* confuse these *tenths of a degree* with *minutes of arc,* as they are not the same. Each *tenth of a degree* represents *six minutes of arc,* as will be explained later in these instructions.

After completing the wheel from the *Table of Houses,* note that, in this case, the sign Leo is found on the cusps of the third and fourth houses (and, conversely, the sign Aquarius is found on the ninth- and tenth-house cusps).

In contrast to the Natural Zodiac, which has exactly 30° in each sign, the houses of the horoscope in all cases north or south of the Equator contain either more or less than 30° of the Zodiac (this is due to the tilt of the Earth in the plane of its rotation—the Ecliptic).

In this example, there are slightly more than 32° in the Zodiacal arc contained in the tenth and fourth houses. There are the last 2° of Aquarius, the entire 30° of the sign Pisces, and two-tenths of the first degree of the sign Aries in the tenth house. Conversely, the same situation arises in the fourth house, where we find the last 2° of the sign Leo, the entire 30° of the sign Virgo, and two-tenths of the first degree of the sign Libra.

All of the signs of the Zodiac are found somewhere in any horoscope, and are always found in their natural sequential order. In a case similar to our example, where the entire 30° of a Zodiacal sign are found contained within a single house, it is a special case and the sign contained therein is called an "intercepted sign."

Traveling the Planets

The next step is to travel the planets to their actual natal positions at the time of birth. These will be placed in the wheel that was set up in the previous section.

The planetary positions as given in any ephemeris are listed for Greenwich Mean Time (GMT).

There are two types of ephemerides in common use today, those based on midnight, and those based on noon. The example horoscope computed in this text uses a noon ephemeris, and the following instructions are based upon the use of such an ephemeris.

To determine the actual positions of the planets at birth, the following procedure is used:

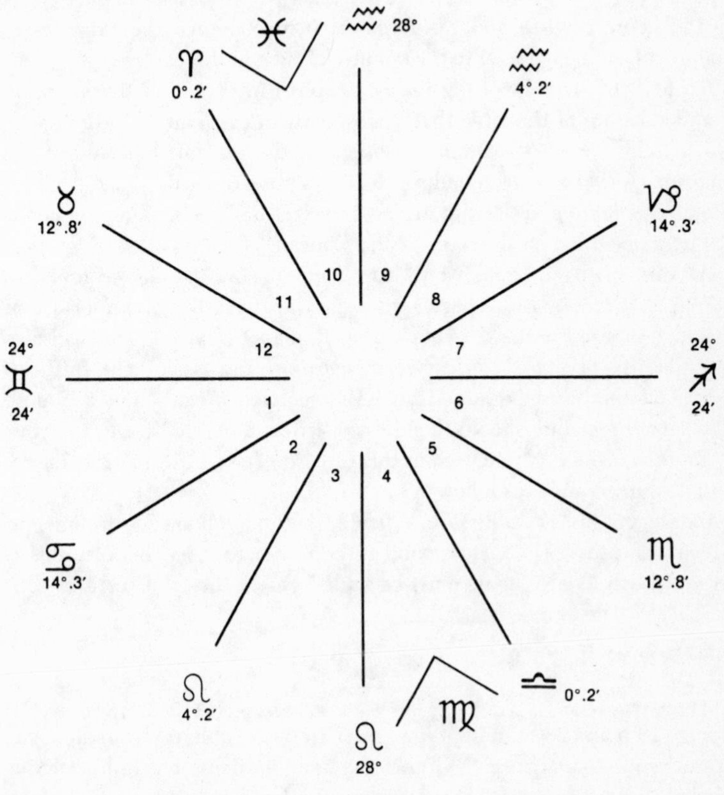

House Cusps as Transcribed Directly from Dalton's *Table of Houses*

All P.M. births in Greenwich Mean Time (that is, the answer found in Step 5 in "Erecting the Wheel") must be converted into a logarithm that will be used in the correction of each planet traveled. This is called the *permanent* or *constant logarithm.* To determine this permanent "log," it is necessary to refer to a "Table of Diurnal Logarithms" located in the back of the ephemeris (in this case on pages 378 through 379 of the noon ephemeris *Ephemeriden: 1890–1950,* also known as the *Swiss Zurich Ephemeris*). The numbers 00 to 23 listed across the top of the pages refer to the hours of time and the numbers 0 to 59 down the extreme-left column of each page refer to the minutes of time in this case.

To find the permanent log for a P.M. birth in GMT, find the hour column at the top of the table that corresponds to the hour of birth (GMT). Next, follow down the minute column on the extreme-left side of the page to the value corresponding to the minute of birth (GMT). Where the hour column and the minute row intersect will be the figure which is the *permanent log* for the travel of the planets.

All A.M. births in Greenwich Mean Time (again, the answer found in Step 5 in "Erecting the Wheel") must also be converted into a logarithm that will be used in the correction of each planet traveled. This will also be called the *permanent* or *constant logarithm.* In cases of A.M. births in GMT, 12 hours must be added to the Greenwich Mean Time as found. The same procedure should then be applied as described for P.M. births.

Example: The example used in this text is an A.M. birth in GMT. Therefore, the procedure is as follows:

In Step 5 in "Erecting the Wheel," the individual's birth time, in Greenwich Mean Time, was found to be 6:58 A.M. GMT. Because this is an A.M. birth, twelve hours must be added before the permanent or constant log can be found. Thus:

$$\begin{array}{r} 6{:}58 \\ +12{:}00 \\ \hline 18{:}58 \end{array}$$

that is, 18 hours 58 minutes. Now, refer to the "Table of Diurnal Logarithms" and search across the top of the table until you reach the column labeled "18"; then, search the extreme left-hand column on that page until you locate the row labeled "58." Where this row intersects the column labeled "18" is where the permanent or constant log will be found. The permanent log in this case is *0.1022.*

Next, refer back to the ephemeris under the month and year of birth—in this case, July, 1942. Look down the far-left column on this monthly table, labeled "TAG," and find the date of birth—the twenty-fourth. As this is an A.M. birth in GMT, the day of birth and the day *before* birth must be used in traveling the planets. (If it were a P.M. birth in Greenwich Mean Time, you would refer to the day of and the day *after* birth to travel the planets.) Next, subtract each planetary position given for the day before birth from that position given for the day of birth. The answers thus obtained represent the twenty-four-hour travel of each of the planets. These answers must all be converted into logarithms so that they may be properly traveled.

This is done by again referring to the "Table of Diurnal Logarithms." The numbers across the top of the table now correspond to the *degrees* of travel found in the twenty-four-hour motion of the planets, and the *minutes* of motion will again be found in the extreme left-hand column of each page. The intersection point of the minutes row and the degree column will give the log of the twenty-four-hour travel. The figure thus obtained for each planet must be *added* to the permanent or constant log. The resultant answers will be the logs of the actual travel of each of the planets since the previous noon in GMT. These logarithms (logs) must be converted back into degrees and minutes of travel for each planet. This is done by finding the *nearest* printed logarithm in the table corresponding to the sum just found for each planet and noting the row and column in which this log is found. Referring to the top of the column will give the number of degrees of travel, and referring to the extreme left-hand row will give the minutes of travel. These two values (that is, degrees and minutes) must be added to the position of the planet on the day *before* birth *because this is an* A.M. *birth* (in GMT). (If it were a P.M. birth in GMT, these degree and minute values would be added to the GMT position on the day *of* birth.) The answer will be the correct position of the planet for the time, day, and place of birth. This procedure should be repeated for each planet traveled.

The last step is to place the traveled planets in the wheel. It must be noted that, unlike the natural wheel that has 0° of each sign on the respective house cusps, the personal horoscope contains an uneven number of degrees in each house, and the degrees on these house cusps are determined by the time as computed in "Erecting the Wheel." When placing the planets in the wheel, first find the house cusp carrying the sign in which the planet is found. Next, note the degree and minute of the sign found on that cusp. If the degree and minute position of the traveled planet is less than that found on the house cusp, the planet must be placed in the house immediately clockwise to that house cusp. If the degree and minute position of the planet is greater than that found on the house cusp, then the planet must be placed in the house immediately counterclockwise to that house cusp.

"Joan Stables"	July 24, 1942	2:58 A.M. EWT	Syracuse, New York
Local Mean Time Variation: -4:36 Greenwich Mean Time Variation: +5:04:36		1:58 A.M. EST	43N03.1; 76W09.0

h m s	
1:58:00 A.M.	Time of Birth (EST)
- 4:36	Local Mean Time (LMT) Variation
1:53:24 A.M.	Local Mean Time of Birth
+12:00:00	Noon (7/23) to Midnight (7/24)
13:53:24	Elapsed Time (in LMT) since previous Noon to LMT of Birth

h m s	
1:58:00 A.M.	Time of Birth (EST)
+ 5:00:00	EST Variation from Greenwich Mean Time (GMT)
6:58:00 A.M.	Time of Birth in GMT
+12:00:00	Noon (7/23) to Midnight (7/24)
18:58:00	Elapsed Time (in GMT) since previous noon to GMT of Birth

	h m s
Sidereal Time (S.T.) for Noon (GMT) on 7/23/42 --	8:02:22
Sidereal Time Correction for the year 1942 --	25
Elapsed Time (in LMT) since previous Noon to LMT of Birth --	13 53 24
Correction for Elapsed Time (in GMT) since previous Noon to GMT of Birth ---------- (18 hours)	2 57.42
(18 hours & 58 minutes) (58 minutes)	9.53
SIDEREAL TIME OF BIRTH	21:59:17.95
	21:59:18

0.1022 Log--PERMANENT LOG for travelling the planets (see log table under "18" column, "58" row)

"Travelling" the planets by using the 24-hour motion of the planets for July 23-24, 1942:

Sun ☉

	29° ♋ 116'
7/24/42 Noon Position	~~0°~~ ♌ ~~56'~~ 59"
7/23/42 Noon Position	-29° ♋ 59'41"
24-hour motion	0° 57'18"

Log of 24-hour motion = 1.4025

PERMANENT LOG	0.1022
Log of 24-hour motion	+1.4025
Log of actual "travel"	1.5047

1.5047 ≅ log of 0°45' = Sun's "travel"

7/23/42 Noon Position	29° ♋ 59'41"
Sun's "travel"	+ 0° 45'00"
	29° ♋ 104'41"
	+ 1° -60'
	30° ♋ 44'41"
	-30°
Actual Sun Position at Birth	0° ♌ 44'41"

Moon ☽

7/24/42 Noon Position	14° ♐ 41'
7/23/42 Noon Position	- 0° ♐ 01'
24-hour motion	14° ♐ 40'

Log of 24-hour motion = 0.2139

PERMANENT LOG	0.1022
Log of 24-hour motion	+0.2139
Log of actual "travel"	0.3161

0.3161 ≅ log of 11°35' = Moon's "travel"

7/23/42 Noon Position	0° ♐ 01'
Moon's "travel"	+11° 35'
Actual Moon Position at Birth	11° ♐ 36'

Mercury ☿

7/24/42 Noon Position	20° ♋ 19'
7/23/42 Noon Position	-18° ♋ 19'
24-hour motion	2° 00'

Log of 24-hour motion = 1.0792

PERMANENT LOG	0.1022
Log of 24-hour motion	+1.0792
Log of actual "travel"	1.1814

1.1814 ≅ log of <u>1°35'</u> = Mercury's "travel"

7/23/42 Noon Position	18° ♋ 19'
Mercury's "travel"	+ 1° 35'
Actual Mercury Position at Birth	19° ♋ 54'

Venus ♀

7/24/42 Noon Position	1° ♋ 30'
7/23/42 Noon Position	- 0° ♋ 18'
24-hour motion	1° 12'

Log of 24-hour motion = 1.3010

PERMANENT LOG	0.1022
Log of 24-hour motion	+1.3010
Log of actual "travel"	1.4032

1.4032 ≅ log of <u>0°57'</u> = Venus's "travel"

7/23/42 Noon Position	0° ♋ 18'
Venus's "travel"	+ 0° 57'
	0° ♋ 75'
	+ 1° -60'
Actual Venus Position at Birth	1° ♋ 15'

Mars ♂

7/24/42 Noon Position	25° ♌ 05'
7/23/42 Noon Position	-24° ♌ 27'
24-hour motion	0° 38'

Log of 24-hour motion - 1.5786

Jupiter ♃

7/24/42 Noon Position	9° ♋ 58'
7/23/42 Noon Position	- 9° ♋ 45'
24-hour motion	0° 13'

Log of 24-hour motion - 2.0444

PERMANENT LOG	0.1022
Log of 24-hour motion	+1.5786
Log of actual "travel"	1.6808

1.6808 ≅ log of 0°30' = Mars's "travel"

7/23/42 Noon Position	24° ♌ 27'
Mars's "travel"	+ 0° 30'
Actual Mars Position at Birth	24° ♌ 57'

Saturn ♄

7/24/42 Noon Position	9° ♊ 15'
7/23/42 Noon Position	- 9° ♊ 09'
24-hour motion	0° 06'

Log of 24-hour motion = 2.3802

PERMANENT LOG	0.1022
Log of 24-hour motion	+2.3802
Log of actual "travel"	2.4824

2.4824 ≅ log of 0°05' = Saturn's "travel"

7/23/42 Noon Position	9° ♊ 09'
Saturn's "travel"	+ 0° 05'
Actual Saturn Position at Birth	9° ♊ 14'

PERMANENT LOG	0.1022
Log of 24-hour motion	+2.0444
Log of actual "travel"	2.1466

2.1466 ≅ log of 0°10' = Jupiter's "travel"

7/23/42 Noon Position	9° ♋ 45'
Jupiter's "travel"	+ 0° 10'
Actual Jupiter Position at Birth	9° ♋ 55'

Uranus ♅

7/24/42 Noon Position	3° ♊ 39'
7/23/42 Noon Position	- 3° ♊ 37'
24-hour motion	0° 02'

Log of 24-hour motion = 2.8573

PERMANENT LOG	0.1022
Log of 24-hour motion	+2.8573
Log of actual "travel"	2.9595

2.9595 ≅ log of 0°02' = Uranus's "travel"

7/23/42 Noon Position	3° ♊ 37'
Uranus's "travel"	+ 0° 02'
Actual Uranus Position at Birth	3° ♊ 39'

Neptune ♆

7/24/42 Noon Position	27° ♍ 39'
7/23/42 Noon Position	-27° ♍ 38'
24-hour motion	0° 01'

Log of 24-hour motion = 3.1584

PERMANENT LOG	0.1022
Log of 24-hour motion	+3.1584
Log of actual "travel"	3.2606

3.2606 ≅ log of 0°01' = Neptune's "travel"

7/23/42 Noon Position	27° ♍ 38'
Neptune's "travel"	+ 0° 01'
Actual Neptune Position at Birth	27° ♍ 39'

Pluto ♇

Using Noon, July 24, 1942, as the GMT of Birth (Pluto moves so slowly that it permits this approximation)

7/25/42 Noon Position	5° ♌ 15'
7/17/42 Noon Position	- 5° ♌ 01'
8-day motion	0° 14'

$\frac{7}{8} \times 14' = \frac{98'}{8} \cong \underline{12'}$ = Pluto's "travel"

7/17/42 Noon Position	5° ♌ 01'
Pluto's "travel"	+ 12'
Actual Pluto Position at Birth	5° ♌ 13'

North Node of the Moon ☊

Using Noon, July 24, 1942, as the GMT of birth (the Moon's North Node moves so slowly that it permits this approximation)

7/25/42 Noon Position	5° ♍ 58'
7/22/42 Noon Position	- 6° ♍ 07'
3-day motion	- 0° 09'

7/22/42 Noon Position	6° ♍ 07'
Node's "travel"	- 0° 06'
Actual Node Position at Birth	6° ♍ 01'

$\frac{2}{3} \times -9' = \frac{-18'}{3} = \underline{-6'}$ - Node's "travel"

Interpolating the House Cusps

Interpolating the house cusps utilizes a similar procedure to that of traveling the planets to the birth positions. Because the cusp positions, as given in Dalton's *Table of Houses,* are approximate for a specific sidereal time and latitude, they, too, need to be "traveled" or interpolated for the exact sidereal time and location of birth.

For those who might aspire to take the eight-hour certification examination given by the American Federation of Astrologers (P.O. Box 22040, Tempe, Arizona 85282), the ability to interpolate is mandatory.

Step 1

Proceeding with this explanation by using the example horoscope, the first step in this interpolation is to locate, in the *Table of Houses,* the two Midheaven (MC) positions between which the Sidereal Time of Birth falls. Take these two Midheaven (MC) positions and find the time difference between them (in minutes and seconds of time); in this case, the Sidereal Time of Birth falls between 27°♒ (S.T. 21:56:52) and 28°♒ (S.T. 22:00:42) on the Midheaven. The difference thus obtained is 3 minutes, 50 seconds.

h	m	s	
22	00	42	S.T.—28°♒ MC
−21	56	52	S.T.—27°♒ MC
	3	50	Difference

(remember that there are 60 seconds to each minute and 60 minutes to each hour of time)

Next, find the logarithm for this difference by turning to the "Table of Diurnal Logarithms." Find the "03" column at the top of the page, and then locate the intersection point of this column with the "52" second row (from the column at the extreme left of each page). Copy the figure found there; in this case, the value or figure is *0.7966.*

0.7966 = logarithm for 3 min. 50 sec.

Step 2

Then, take the Sidereal Time of Birth, subtract the lesser sidereal time figure from it and obtain the answer in minutes and seconds of time. The Sidereal Time of Birth (as determined in "Erecting the Wheel") is 21 hours 59 minutes 18 seconds. The lesser sidereal time figure for a Midheaven degree—that for 27°♒ MC—is 21 hours 56 minutes 52 seconds. Subtracting this figure from the Sidereal Time of Birth gives an answer of 2 minutes 26 seconds. Due to the Sidereal Time of Birth falling between these two Midheaven points—

h	m	s	
21	59	18	S.T. of birth
−21	56	52	S.T.—27°♒ MC
	2	26	Difference

27° ♒ and 28° ♒—the next step is to find the permanent or constant log for this "travel" between these two points. To do this, refer to the "Table of Diurnal Logarithms" and, again, using the row of numbers across the top of the page for minutes and the extreme left-hand column for seconds of time, locate the logarithm corresponding to the number of minutes and seconds found earlier in this step, in this case for 2 minutes, 26 seconds. To do this, find the "02" column at the top of the page and the "26" row in the second column on the extreme left of the page. Where this row and column intersect is the figure *0.9940.*

0.9940 = logarithm for 2 min. 26 sec.

Step 3

Subtract the logarithm found in Step 1 of this section from the logarithm found in Step 2. The result is the permanent or constant logarithm for "traveling" the house cusps *for sidereal time.* In this case, the permanent log is *0.1974.* The log thus found will be used in *each* of the calculations for interpolating the house cusps.

0.9940	log—2m 26s
−0.7966	log—3m 50s
0.1974	PERMANENT LOG for Sidereal Time

Step 4

All tenth-house cusp or Midheaven (MC) calculations are unique because there is *no* change in the position of this cusp due to the latitude of the birth location. However, there is still a correction to be made for the Sidereal Time of Birth.

In the example, take the travel of the Midheaven—which, using Dalton's *Table of Houses,* is *always* 1°—and turn to the "Table of Diurnal Logarithms." Locate the column and row corresponding to the degrees and minutes of this "travel"—1°. Go to the column "01" at the top of the table and find where this column intersects the "0" second row at the extreme left of the page. Copy this number from the table and add it to the permanent log. In this case, the number is *1.3802,* to which we add *0.1974* (from Step 3) and obtain the result *1.5776.* This last figure is the logarithm of "travel" of the house cusp for sidereal time. This must now be converted

1.3802	log—1° MC "travel"
+ .1974	log—PERMANENT LOG for S.T.
1.5776	"Travel" of MC for S.T. of Birth

back into degrees and minutes of arc so that we may find the true Midheaven (MC) of the horoscope. Referring again to the "Table of Diurnal Logarithms," locate the nearest printed log to this result (1.5776); in this case, the closest logarithm is 1.5786 located in the "00" column at the "38" row. Thus, the "travel" for the Midheaven or tenth-house cusp is 00°38′ of arc. *Adding* this 38′ increment to the lower—or *base*—Midheaven (MC) value of 27°♒ gives the result of 27″♒38′. This is the true MC for the Sidereal Time of Birth as calculated.

′	° 00	
38	1.5786	< 1.5776
39	1.5673	

1.5776 ≅ log—0°38′
27°♒00′ *Base* MC
+ 0° 38′
27°♒38′ True Midheaven for S.T. of Birth

Step 5

Proceeding to calculate the other house cusps, we note in the *Table of Houses* that there is no change in the eleventh-house cusp for the latitude of birth; therefore, in this particular example, there is no correction needed for latitude. However, there is still a correction for sidereal time that is needed. Thus, the same procedure that was applied to the tenth-house cusp or Midheaven (MC) should be used here (see calculation page).

The procedure for interpolating the twelfth-house cusp in this example is the *general procedure* to be used in interpolating all of the house cusps, with the exception of the Midheaven (MC) or tenth-house cusp.

We have already determined the permanent or constant log for sidereal time in Step 3. This step must be applied to the calculation of *all* house cusps. There is an added step which must be applied in calculating the eleventh-, twelfth-, first- (Ascendant), second-, and third-house cusps. In addition to the permanent log for sidereal time, we must find a permanent log for the change due to latitude of birth so that the house cusps can be "traveled" for the latitude of the birth location.

First, we must correct the geographical latitude of birth by using "Table B—Correction for Latitude" as found on page V of Dalton's *Table of Houses*. The values given in this table for the respective degrees of latitude must *always* be *subtracted* from the geographical latitude of the place of birth—in this case, as given in the *AFA Atlas*. The birth example occurred at 43°03.1′ north latitude. Referring to "Table B" and locating latitude 43°, we find the correction value immediately to the right of the latitude degree to be 11′42″. Deducting this value from the geographical latitude of birth—43°N03.1′ or 43°N03′06″—we arrive at the result: 42°N51′25″. To the nearest minute of arc, it would be 42°N51′. This result is the *geocentric latitude of the birth location.*

42°03.1′ North Latitude = Birth Latitude

Convert .1′ to ″ of arc:

	.1′
	×60″/′
	6″
42°N03′06″	Geographical Birth Lat. in ° ′ ″
− 11′42″	Correction for lat.
42°N51′25″	Geocentric Birth Lat. in ° ′ ″

Step 6

Because the *Table of Houses* gives the house cusps for every *degree* of latitude, we must interpolate or "travel" these cusps (except the Midheaven) for the actual latitude of birth (geocentric). To do so, we must find a permanent log for latitude that will be applied to each of the house cusps. First, we must determine the latitudinal difference between the positions given in the *Tables*—1° in all cases—and find the logarithm for this value. Then, we must determine the difference between the actual geocentric latitude of birth and the lesser latitude listed. In this case, the difference is 51′ of arc, which we must convert into its proper logarithm. Turning to the "Table of Diurnal Logarithms," find the values for 1° of arc and 0°51′ of arc and subtract the former from the latter; that is, subtract the logarithm for 1°—*1.3802*—from that for 0°51′—*1.4508*. The result is the permanent logarithm for latitude and must be applied to find the house-cusp change due to the latitude of the birth location for each of the subsequent house cusps; in this case, the permanent logarithm is *0.0706*.

42°N51′	Geocentric Birth Lat. to nearest ° ′
43°	North latitude
−42°	North latitude
1°	Difference
42°N51′	Geocentric Birth Lat.
−42°N00′	Lesser of the two above latitudes
51′	Difference
1.4508	log—0°51′ latitude
−1.3802	log—1° latitude
0.0706	PERMANENT LOG for Lat.

Step 7

Next, refer to the *Table of Houses* under the lesser Midheaven (MC) value (as found in Step 2 of this section)—27°♒ in this example—and locate the "12 H.," or house column, in the "42° Lat." row. Copy the value printed there. In this case, 11.1°♉ is found. Also, copy the value in the same column for "43° Lat."—in this case 11.5°♉. Subtract the *first* value from the *second.* The result is .4°. This represents four-tenths of one degree. There are 60 minutes in a degree; therefore, multiplying 60 minutes/degree by .4 degrees produces the result of 24′ of arc. This is the total change of the twelfth-house cusp between 42° and 43° of north latitude. Now, convert this figure into a logarithm by referring to the "Table of Diurnal Logarithms"; the result is *1.7781.* Add to this the permanent log for latitude (found in Step 6 above); the result is *1.8487.* This logarithm represents the "travel" of the twelfth-house cusp for latitude in this example, and must be converted back into degrees and minutes of arc by referring once again to the "Table of Diurnal Logarithms" and finding the nearest printed log to this value—in this case, *1.8573* in the "00" degree column and the "20" minute row. The "travel" for the twelfth-house cusp in this example would therefore be 0°20′ due to the latitude of birth.

This 0°20′ must be recorded and kept for further use in this house's cusp calculation.

11.5°♉	12th-house cusp at 27°♒ MC, 43°N Lat.
−11.1°♉	12th-house cusp at 27°♒ MC, 42°N. Lat.
.4°	Difference

.4°
×60′/°
24′

1.7781	log—0°24′ 12-house cusp "travel"
+0.0706	log, PERMANENT LOG for lat.
1.8487	log—"Travel" of 12th-house cusp for Birth lat.

′	° 00	
20	1.8573	< 1.8487
21	1.8361	

1.8487 = log—0°20′

Step 8

Next, refer once again to the *Table of Houses* and locate the values printed for the 12th House cusp at 42° latitude with 27°♒ on the Midheaven (11.1°♉) and with 28° ♒ on the Midheaven (12.3° ♉). Copy these values and subtract the lesser from the greater. The result is the total house-cusp "travel" for the 12th House cusp as the Midheaven changes from 27° to 28° of Aquarius—1.2° of arc. Again, we must convert the "tenths of a degree" figure into degrees and minutes of arc; hence, .2° multiplied by 60′/° gives the result: 12′. There-

12.3°♉	12th House cusp at 28° MC, 42°N. Lat.
−11.1°♉	12th House cusp at 27° MC, 42°N. Lat.
1.2°	difference

1° + .2°
× 60′/°
1° 12′

fore, the total "travel" of the 12th House cusp in this case is 1°12′.

To determine the actual "travel" for the Sidereal Time of Birth in this example, we must find the logarithm of this motion (1°12′) and add it to the permanent log (already found in Step 3 of this section), then reconvert the resulting figure back into degrees and minutes of actual "travel." To do this, refer to the "Table of Diurnal Logarithms" and locate the log for 1°12′—in this case *1.3010.* Add to this the permanent log for sidereal time (found in Step 3 of this section); the result is *1.4984.* Return to the "Table of Diurnal Logarithms" and find the printed log nearest to this value; in this case, it is *1.4956* located in the "00" degree column in the "46" minute row. Therefore, the "travel" of this house cusp for sidereal time in the example is 0°46′ of arc.

1.3010 log	1°12′ 12th House cusp "travel"
+ 0.1974 log	PERMANENT LOG for S.T.
1.4984 log	"Travel" of 12th house cusp for Sidereal Time of Birth

	° 00	
45	1.5051	
46	1.4956	< 1.4984

$1.4984 \cong \log = 0°46'$

Step 9

Take this figure and add it to the "travel" for latitude found in Step 7 (0°20′); the result is 0°66′—converted (remember that there are 60′ in each °) to 1°06′. Thus the total "travel" or interpolation for the twelfth-house cusp in this example is *1°06′ of arc.*

Refer again to the *Table of Houses* in the "12th-House" column under 27°♒ on the Midheaven, 42° lat., and copy the value printed there—11.1°♉. This must be converted into degrees and minutes of the sign Taurus by multiplying the "tenths of a degree" figure—.1°—by 60′/° and adding it to the 11° of the Taurus figure. The result is 11°06′♉. Next, add the total "travel" figure as determined in Step 9 of this section—1°06′—to this figure. *The result is 12°12′♉ which is the twelfth-house cusp for this example.*

0°20′	"Travel" of 12th-house cusp for lat.
+0°46′	"Travel" of 12th-house cusp for S.T.
0°66′	
+1−60	
1°06′	Total "travel" of 12th house cusp
11.1°♉	12th-house cusp at 27°♒ MC, 42°N Lat.
11′°+.1°	
× 60′/°	
11° 06′	
11°06′♉	12th-house cusp above
+ 1°06′	Total "travel" of 12th-house cusp
12°♉12′	12th-house cusp for the date, time and location of the example chart

Step 10

Repeat this procedure for the remaining houses of the wheel and check and compare with the example horoscope.

From the Table of Houses:

	h m s			h m s	
Midheaven (MC)--28° ♒ =	22:00:42	Sidereal Time	Sidereal Time of Birth =	21:59:18	Sidereal Time
Midheaven (MC)--27° ♒ =	-21:56:52	Sidereal Time	Midheaven (MC)--27° ♒ =	-21:56:52	Sidereal Time
	3:50	Difference		2:26	Difference

0.9940 Log of Sidereal Time change from MC 27° ♒ to Sidereal Time of Birth
-0.7966 Log of Sidereal Time change from MC 27° ♒ to MC 28° ♒

0.1974 PERMANENT LOG for Sidereal Time

Latitude Correction:

Geographic Latitude of Birth Location = 43°N.03.1' = 43°N.03'06"
Correction for Latitude, Geographic to Geocentric, for 43°N. = 11'42"

43°N.03'06" Geographic Latitude
- 11'42" Correction: Geographic to Geocentric

42°N.51'24" = 42°N.51' Geocentric Latitude of Birth Location

Listings for House Cusps given for each Degree of Latitude in Table of Houses, hence:

43°N. Latitudes between which Geocentric
-42°N. Birth Location falls

1° Difference

42°N.51' Geocentric Latitude of Birth Location
-42°N.00' Nearest Latitude less than above listed

0° 51' Difference

1.4508 Log of 0°51'
-1.3802 Log of 1°00'

0.0706 PERMANENT LOG for Latitude

10th House Cusp (Midheaven--MC)

NOTE: There is no variation of the Midheaven or 10th House Cusp due to the Latitude of the Birth Location; the Midheaven position is independent of Latitude.

28° ♒ 00'	Midheaven Degrees between which the
-27° ♒ 00'	Sidereal Time of Birth falls
1° 00'	Difference

Log of difference = 1.3802

PERMANENT LOG for S.T.	0.1974
Log of MC "travel" - $1^{\circ}00'$	+1.3802
Log of actual MC "travel" for S.T.	1.5776

1.5776 $\cong$ Log of $0^{\circ}38'$ = MC "travel"

Base MC position	27° ♒ 00'
MC "travel"	+ 0° 38'
Actual MC (10th House Cusp) Position at Birth	27° 38'

11th House Cusp

30° ♓
~~0~~.2° ♈ 11th House Cusp @ 28° ♒ MC, 42°N. Lat.
-29.0° ♓ 11th House Cusp @ 27° ♒ MC, 42°N. Lat.
1.2° Difference

1.2° = 1° + .2°
× 60'/o
1° 12'

Log of difference (1°12') = 1.3010

PERMANENT LOG for S.T.	0.1974
Log of cusp "travel" - 1°12'	+1.3010
Log of actual cusp "travel" for S.T.	1.4984

1.4984 ≅ Log of 0°46' = 11th House Cusp "travel"

Base 11th House Cusp Position - 29.0° ♓ =	29° ♓ 00'
11th House Cusp "travel" for S.T.	+ 0° 46'
11th House Cusp "travel" for Lat.	+ 0° 00'
Actual 11th House Cusp Position at Birth	29° ♓ 46'

29.0° ♓ 11th House Cusp @ 27° ♒ MC, 43°N. Lat.
-29.0° ♓ 11th House Cusp @ 27° ♒ MC, 42°N. Lat.
0.0°

NO CORRECTION OR "TRAVEL"
FOR LATITUDE

12th House Cusp

12.3° ♉ 12th House Cusp @ 28° ♒ MC, 42°N. Lat.
-11.1° ♉ 12th House Cusp @ 27° ♒ MC, 42°N. Lat.
1.2° Difference

1.2° = 1° + .2°
× 60'/o
1° 12'

11.5° ♉ 12th House Cusp @ 27° ♒ MC, 43°N. Lat.
-11.1° ♉ 12th House Cusp @ 27° ♒ MC, 42°N. Lat.
0.4° Difference

0.4° = .4°
× 60'/o
0°24'

Log of difference ($1^\circ 12'$) = 1.3010

PERMANENT LOG for S.T.	0.1974
Log of cusp "travel"	+1.3010
Log of actual cusp "travel" for S.T.	1.4984

1.4984 $\cong$ Log of $\underline{0^\circ 46'}$ = 12th House Cusp "travel" for S.T.

Log of difference ($0^\circ 24'$) = 1.7781

PERMANENT LOG for Lat.	0.0706
Log of cusp "travel"	+1.7781
Log of actual cusp "travel" for Lat.	1.8487

1.8487 $\cong$ Log of $\underline{0^\circ 20'}$ = 12th House Cusp "travel" for Lat.

Base 12th House Cusp Position - 11.1° ♉ =	11° ♉ 06'
12th House Cusp "travel" for S.T.	$+ 0^\circ$ 46'
12th House Cusp "travel" for Lat.	$+ 0^\circ$ 20'
	11° ♉ 72'
	$+ 1^\circ$ -60'
Actual 12th House Cusp Position at Birth	12° ♉ 12'

1st House Cusp (Ascendant--ASC)

$2\overset{2}{\not 3}^\circ$ ♊ $\overset{9}{\not 3}4'$	1st House Cusp @ 28° ♒ MC, 42°N. Lat.
-22° ♊ 38'	1st House Cusp @ 27° ♒ MC, 42°N. Lat.
0° 56'	Difference

Log of difference ($0^\circ 56'$) = 1.4102

PERMANENT Log for S.T.	0.1974
Log of cusp "travel"	+1.4102
Log of actual cusp "travel" for S.T.	1.6076

1.6076 $\cong$ Log of $\underline{0^\circ 36'}$ = 1st House Cusp (ASC) "travel" for S.T.

$2\overset{2}{\not 3}^\circ$ ♊ $\overset{8}{\not 1}8'$	1st House Cusp @ 27° ♒ MC, 43°N. Lat.
-22° ♊ 38'	1st House Cusp @ 27° ♒ MC, 42°N. Lat.
0° 50'	Difference

Log of difference ($0^\circ 50'$) = 1.4594

PERMANENT LOG for Lat.	0.0706
Log of cusp "travel"	+1.4594
Log of actual cusp "travel" for Lat.	1.5300

1.5300 $\cong$ Log of $\underline{0^\circ 42'}$ = 1st House Cusp (ASC) "travel" for Lat.

Base 1st House Cusp (ASC) Position	22° ♊ 38'
1st House Cusp (ASC) "travel" for S.T.	+ 0° 36'
1st House Cusp (ASC) "travel" for Lat.	+ 0° 42'
	22° ♊ 116'
	+ 1° - 60'
Actual 1st House Cusp (ASC) Position at Birth	23° ♊ 56'

2nd House Cusp

13.8° ♋ 2nd House Cusp @ 28° ♒ MC, 42°N. Lat.
-13.0° ♋ 2nd House Cusp @ 27° ♒ MC, 42°N. Lat.
0.8°

0.8° = .8°
x 60'/o
0°48'

Log of difference (0°48') = 1.4771

PERMANENT LOG for S.T.	0.1974
Log of cusp "travel"	+1.4771
Log of actual cusp "travel" for S.T.	1.6745

1.6745 ≅ Log of 0°30' = 2nd House Cusp "travel" for S.T.

13.5° ♋ 2nd House Cusp @ 27° ♒ MC, 43°N. Lat.
-13.0° ♋ 2nd House Cusp @ 27° ♒ MC, 42°N. Lat.
0.5° Difference

0.5 = .5°
x 60'/o
0°30'

Log of difference (0°30') = 1.6812

PERMANENT Log for Lat.	0.0706
Log of cusp "travel"	+1.6812
Log of actual cusp "travel" for Lat.	1.7518

1.7518 ≅ Log of 0°26' = 2nd House Cusp "travel" for Lat.

Base 2nd House Cusp Position - 13.0° ♋ =	13° ♋ 00'
2nd House Cusp "travel" for S.T.	+ 0° 30'
2nd House Cusp "travel" for Lat.	+ 0° 26'
Actual 2nd House Cusp Position at Birth	13° ♋ 56'

3rd House Cusp

3 10
~~4.0~~° ♌ 3rd House Cusp @ 28° ♒ MC, 42°N. Lat.
\- 3.1° ♌ 3rd House Cusp @ 27° ♒ MC, 42°N. Lat.
0.9° Difference

0.9° = .9°
× 60'/o
0°54'

Log of difference (0°54') = 1.4260

PERMANENT LOG for S.T.	0.1974
Log of cusp "travel"	+1.4260
Log of actual cusp "travel" for S.T.	1.6234

1.6234 ≅ Log of 0°34' = 3rd House Cusp "travel" for S.T.

3.3° ♌ 3rd House Cusp @ 27° ♒ MC, 43°N. Lat.
\- 3.1° ♌ 3rd House Cusp @ 27° ♒ MC, 42°N. Lat.
0.2° Difference

0.2° = .2°
× 60'/o
0°12'

Log of difference (0°12') = 2.0792

PERMANENT LOG for Lat.	0.0706
Log of cusp "travel"	+2.0792
Log of actual cusp "travel" for Lat.	2.1498

2.1498 ≅ Log of 0°10' = 3rd House Cusp "travel" for Lat.

Base 3rd House Cusp Position - 3.1° ♌ =	3° ♌ 06'
3rd House Cusp "travel" for S.T.	+ 0° 34'
3rd House Cusp "travel" for Lat.	0° 10'
Actual 3rd House Cusp Position at Birth	3° ♌ 50'

14

An Example of a Professional Delineation with Rules and References

For purposes of identification, the individual whose horoscope is used in the example interpretation will be called Joan. She is a living person, and she has given the authors her permission to use her chart as an example. This horoscope was delineated in a class at the New England School of Astrology, and both she and her husband were astounded at the accuracy of the interpretation, especially since she was new to astrology and to everyone in the class. She has verified the accuracy of the delineation.

The first part deals with astrological patterns that supply insights into the general overall characteristics of the individual which reinforce the more intricate details that are supplied by the planetary positions and aspects. This general view must be considered all through the fine points of interpretation if the delineation is to be accurate.

The first part is to divide the hemispheres of the chart and interpret them as in the chapter on Hemispheric Emphasis in this text.

Joan has eight out of the ten bodies in the eastern hemisphere. Five of the planets are in positive, masculine signs and three in receptive, feminine signs. Uranus, Saturn, Sun, Pluto, and Mars are in positive, masculine signs, and Venus, Jupiter, and Mercury are in receptive, feminine signs, indicating that Joan tends to choose her own life-style and set of social and business conditions in which she moves. This pattern indicates that she is in a phase of initiating new endeavors and entering into new

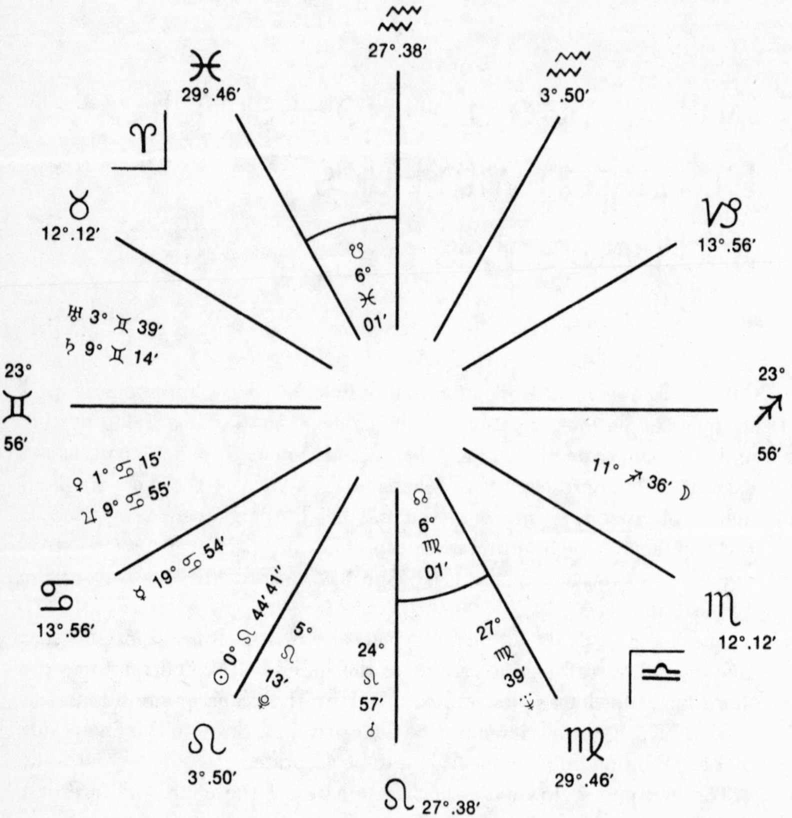

Fully Interpolated Natal Horoscope for "Joan Stables"
July 24, 1942; 2:58 A.M. EWT; Syracuse, New York

experiences. She will have freedom in making decisions and choices rather than feeling bound by obligations to others. This pattern often gives her a sense of loneliness or isolation. At times she feels that nothing worthwhile happens unless she makes it happen. She must reach out to establish relationships and create conditions which would automatically be provided for one with a Western Emphasis. Five of the planets are found in Fire and Air signs which are positive, masculine signs, indicating that she is aggressive in promoting her ideas and dominates immediate situations. If she lacks enthusiasm for the subject under discussion she will display an exasperating indifference or will try to introduce a subject that will bring the focus of attention back to her or her own interests. This kind of projection is comfortable for her; however, at times it can overwhelm others and they can experience a sense of frustration.

The next pattern divides the horoscope north from south (see text on Northern Hemisphere emphasis). Note that eight of the planets are below the horizon in the Northern Hemisphere; this indicates that she has a subjective view of life based on a visceral response to those things which directly affect her interests and personal affairs. She is apt to work behind the scenes rather than in the public eye.

Although her work could concern public affairs, a great deal of her work will be done in private or in the background. Six of these planets are found in receptive, feminine signs, indicating that she needs to work in the seclusion of an environment which provides an arena in which she can feel secure and comfortable. This innate need for psychological security is the basis that is instrumental in giving her a solid foundation to carry on her work, and in turn this provides her with the ability to give physical and spiritual comfort to others. This kind of security is a definite need for her because of this pattern. Half of the planets are in receptive, feminine signs, indicating that she attracts those who are in need of understanding; the other half are in positive, masculine Fire signs which provide her with creative leadership to help and inspire others in their decisions.

The next step in interpretation is to define the temperament-type pattern (see chapter "The Seven Basic Planetary Patterns" in this text).

Joan's horoscope falls into the Bowl Pattern. The Uranus-Moon opposition divides the occupied half of the horoscope from the unoccupied half (Nodes are not included in these patterns). This division of the planets gives Joan a psychological feeling that something is lacking or missing in her life experience; thus she is always working or trying to orient herself to find some kind of balance that will give her a sense of completeness. This psychological void causes her to direct her energies toward self-improvement. This pattern makes her feel that she has something of consequence to contribute to others.

The next step is to find the Natural Disposition in her horoscope, which indicates her psychological slanting (see chapter on Natural Disposition in this text). Joan's Natural Disposition is found in Mutable signs, Uranus in Gemini in the twelfth house opposing the Moon in Sagittarius in the sixth. This indicates that Joan has a psychological drive to interact and communicate with others. The Mutable signs deal with skills and the utilization of experience; therefore Joan will use her skills with and for others.

The next step in interpretation is the Mental Chemistry of the individual (see chapter on Mental Chemistry). Joan has a fast-moving Moon with Mercury preceding the Sun. This is called Anxious Mental Chemistry. This gives her a sense of urgency whereby she reacts impulsively to the information she receives without always waiting for the details to unfold. She also is liable to inject her own conclusions in a given situation; if a conclusion is verbalized, it can bewilder or annoy the individual relating the event. She can be unnecessarily impatient, and this trait needs to be tempered with an understanding of herself and others.

The next step in interpretation is to ascertain her Scout Planet. This is the first planet ahead of the Sun traveling in a clockwise direction (see the psychology of the Scout Planet in *Predictive Astrology*). The Scout Planet indicates the affairs of life that are constantly brought to the fore and demand some kind of response, and it must be dealt with and handled effectively before the power potential of the Sun can be expressed. In Joan's horoscope Mercury is the Scout Planet, indicating that she will base her course of action on information gathered from books, communications media, conversations with friends, and those in her immediate environment, especially brothers, sisters, and neighbors. She is likely to plan her actions rationally and ahead of time. Work, health, clothes, personal appearance, friendships, and communications demand attention as do comings and goings and short trips. Mercury rules her first and fifth house, indicating that her children, her pleasures, her social life, and her creative efforts are included in the activity of the Scout Planet. The exaltation sign of Mercury is on the ninth- and tenth-house cusps, indicating that philosophy, law, religion, higher education, foreigners, and foreign travel as well as her status in the world in which she moves are related to this action of Mercury as her Scout Planet.

The next step is to find the Cutting Planet, which is the planet that is facing the largest open space traveling in a clockwise direction. It is the planet that sets the tone for new cycles of experience (see Cutting Planet in *Predictive Astrology* and planets in High Focus in this text). Uranus as her Cutting Planet indicates that she will enter into new experience through unexpected events and sudden occurrences. These are brought about through the agency of friends, groups, organizations, corporate affairs, or through the pursuit of her personal goals and objectives. These new experiences may be related to scientific, occult, or humanitarian activities and endeavors.

The next planet to be considered is the trailing planet, which is at the other end of the open space, this time facing in a counterclockwise direction. The Moon as her trailing planet indicates that she concludes her cycles of experience with a changed sense of values about the seemingly unimportant daily activities of her life. Taurus, which is the exaltation sign of the Moon, is on the twelfth-house cusp of her horoscope, indicating that these values can be her hidden support or her self-undoing.

The next step is to ascertain the closest square or opposition in the horoscope, which is called the Point Focus of the personality and represents one of the outstanding characteristics of the individual. This aspect must be delineated in detail. (See chapter on the Point Focus of the personality in this text.) Joan's Point Focus is the Moon in opposition to Saturn. In this opposition the Moon is also her trailing planet. This opposition indicates that Joan will be confronted with situations of either cooperation or conflict between the psychological drives represented by the two planets in Point Focus. Both planets, the Moon and Saturn, are from the inner department, indicating that she will be inclined to work in harmony and cooperation with what is of interest to her, emphasizing her Northern Hemisphere Emphasis. The Moon in opposition indicates that she will have to learn and practice emotional detachment and objectivity. She has to be careful that her emotional problems are not projected on others and that she does not blame them for her own unrecognized faults (see Moon patterns in this text). In other words, this opposition indicates that there could be a psychological mirror effect in which her own lack of awareness or the need for cooperation at any given moment is blamed on the other person. This is very subtle and hidden from her conscious mind because of her highly developed intellectual traits. Saturn in this opposition indicates that she should avoid negative, restrictive, and selfish attitudes. Both planets involved in the opposition are involved in the inner department, indicating that she can work to improve the conditions brought about by this opposition. However, at times she would appear unapproachable and unfriendly because of a serious, austere projection. Although the class did not see her that way, she admitted that some people do see her this way. This kind of projection must be corrected if isolation and loneliness are to be avoided. This is reinforced by the Eastern Emphasis of her chart, indicating that she must reach out in her relationships. The Moon opposition Saturn could indicate that her parents are responsible for instilling rigid attitudes during childhood. It also indicates a tendency toward emotional depression and a danger of developing an unsympathetic attitude in her later years. This opposition can indicate unfruitful relationships and family ties. It also indicates a formal manner that makes others feel either ill at ease, indifferent, or bored. There can be a lack of emotional flexibility or optimism in relationships with others. She would have an inclination to judge her relationships and respond to them on the basis of past experiences, especially since the opposition is found in Mutable signs and houses. Past unpleasant experiences are liable to block her ability to respond to others in a free and natural way. Saturn as part of this opposition is conjunct her natal Uranus, indicating that she is liable to alternate between a Saturn type of response and then at times an open, friendly, Uranus response. This could be very confusing to others. It could also mean that she would have difficulty making friends, or her family could disapprove of her friends. This opposition could also indicate that her life could be thwarted by parental and domestic responsibilities which could be real or imagined. There could be conflict between her domestic and professional responsibilities. Employers or superiors could unconsciously remind her of her parents, and there could be some difficulties with older established people. However, because both the Moon and Saturn are from the inner department, she will try to cooperate and work in a harmonious manner.

The Moon represents that aspect of behavior that depends on automatic responses; it indicates responses that are instinctual and based on past experiences which cannot be remembered. Therefore, a conscious effort of the will is required if there is to be a change in the stressful effects of these patterns. Because Saturn is in the hidden twelfth, it will be difficult for her to keep a conscious awareness for choosing a particular path of expression. Her Moon in Sagittarius indicates that she will aspire to high goals; it also indicates an idealistic emotional nature. However, at times she would lack a realistic sense of life. The Moon in Sagittarius would make her fond of foreign travel and even taking up residence in a foreign country (which she has done). Because the Moon is in a Fire sign, this position would alleviate some of the emotional depression represented by this opposition. Her Moon in a Fire sign would help to make her a little more optimistic and cheerful than would ordinarily be the case with this opposition. Because of the rate of the progression of the Moon, she can never get out from under this opposition because the Moon progresses at the same rate that Saturn travels. Her Moon is in the Aries decanate of Sagittarius and in the fifth duad, which gives a connotation of Sagittarius-Aries or Jupiter-Neptune-Mars-Pluto.* This indicates that she would be a crusader for her personal, social, religious, and cultural beliefs and that she would try to apply these beliefs to her daily living. She would want to refine and improve on existing conditions. She would also try to spearhead religious and social reforms to help overcome corruption, indifference, and lethargy. The combined Pluto-Neptune influence of this duad would indicate an awareness of and deep insights into the causes of existing social ills and the actions that would be needed to remedy the situation. She would have a tendency to identify with certain social values, and because the Moon deals with instinctual responses, these responses would stem from personal, emotional, unconsciously motivated reasons. Because of this her objectivity is often clouded.

The Moon is in the sixth house, indicating that her health could fluctuate and be influenced by her emotions and could affect her work. Diet will be a major determining factor in her health. The Moon in the sixth would also indicate that she would like small animals (Virgo as Natural ruler of the sixth house rules small animals) and also large animals, which are ruled by Sagittarius (she rides horses).

Saturn, the other planet involved in the opposition, indicates the capacity for self-discipline and organization. Saturn's influence would give her the ability to pursue a discipline over an extended period of time. It enables her to perfect gradually her innate skills and establish a reputation and professional standing, especially since Saturn is in a Mutable sign which deals with skills. Saturn gives us what we earn through our own efforts. This opposition of the Moon and Saturn also indicates that if she does not measure up to her own expectations or those of her parents, she can become depressed. When this happens there can be a tendency to impose hard restriction or regimentation on others. Such restrictions can be useful if they are tempered with compassion and wisdom to do what is best for all concerned.† Saturn in the intellectual sign Gemini indicates that she has a practical, well-disciplined, systematic

* See *The Zodiac Within Each Sign* by Frances Sakoian and Louis Acker.

† See Saturn in the signs and houses and Saturn opposing the Moon in *The Astrologer's Handbook.*

mind, that she has a capacity for discipline in thinking, reasoning, writing, and solving problems of all sorts. Any ideas she might entertain would be judged on their practical usefulness and whether they have been proven out to be successful or useful through direct experience. She would be particular about clarity in working out the details of contracts and agreements. She would want honesty in communication and dependability in dealing with others. Saturn in Gemini also gives her the ability to give concrete expression to abstract concepts. Saturn is the planetary ruler of the eighth house dealing with other people's money, joint money, and inherited money, and is in opposition to the Moon ruling the second house of money. Both of these planets are in Mutable signs and would give her the ability to hold onto money or have it tied up in some legal way. This is because of Saturn co-ruling her ninth house. Saturn is in the first decanate of Gemini and in the fourth duad, making this the Gemini-Virgo or Mercury-Mercury duad. This would indicate that she would be concerned with a practical application of her knowledge and she would be adaptable with a tendency to scatter her energies.

This Point Focus opposition affects her second house of money, moveable possessions, her values, and her earning capacity because of the Moon ruling the second house. It includes her secret twelfth house where Taurus, the sign of the Moon's exaltation, is placed, and it is placed in the sixth house affecting her work and health. Saturn is in Gemini in the twelfth, and it rules the eighth of inherited money, joint finances, corporate money, and other people's values. The fifth house carries the intercepted sign of Libra in which Saturn is exalted, bringing her children, creative expression, social life, and pleasures into play. Saturn also co-rules the ninth and tenth houses, indicating that her religious, educational, philosophic, and cultural beliefs and her status in the world are all involved in this Point Focus opposition of Saturn and the Moon.

Aspect configurations are the next step when looking at a horoscope.* Joan has a double sextile aspect which is made up of a hidden trine between Neptune and Uranus and the Sun in the position of the midpoint, making a sextile aspect to Neptune on one side and Uranus on the other. The intellectual energy of the Sun due to the Sun being the body forming the sextile making the double sextile to the trining planets, indicates that Joan has the knowledge and awareness to release the creative, expansive energy of the trine aspect. However, the double sextile indicates that she must be willing to put this creative awareness into action and make use of the opportunities that this double sextile promises. The

* See chapter on the role of aspects in *Predictive Astrology*.

energy of the double-sextile aspect flows freely and easily if she is willing to utilize it; otherwise it will clog the open avenue which leads to this creative expression. This double sextile will be referred to again later on in the delineation.

She also has a double semisextile between Uranus, Venus, Sun, and Pluto. Uranus, Sun, and Pluto are sextile to each other and they are all semisextile to Venus. The intellectual nature of the sextile is focused through Venus as the central planet making the sextile. This configuration gives her the ability to understand and communicate whatever she needs in order to utilize and amass the resources that will enable her to use her skills and past experiences to achieve her goals and objectives. The sextile aspect per se involves the Mutable sign Gemini, dealing with skills, and Uranus, dealing with goals and the perseverance needed to attain them. The semisextile partakes of the nature of Pisces and the twelfth house, which indicates past experience. The sign Taurus is the second house sign which is the other half of the semisextile connotation, which indicates the resources. These connotations are all based on the Natural Zodiac. Because Venus is exalted in Pisces, the Natural twelfth-house sign, and because it rules Taurus, it indicates that this has a Venus connotation and Venus is the Focus Planet. Venus represents the principle of attraction (see "The Venus Pattern" in this text); therefore this configuration gives Joan the ability to attract wealth, social contacts, and romantic opportunities. This configuration often indicates unusual artistic talents (which she has), business ability (which she has), and social refinement, especially in communication. The Mercury nature of the sextile combined with the Venus nature of the semisextile indicate that she would have literary ability (she is also a writer) and a precise manner of communication. This configuration provides the opportunity for her to realize her goals of self-expression and the rewards and values connected with them; however, this configuration also demands that she systematically take advantage of every opportunity. There will be more on this configuration later.

Joan has Gemini on the Ascendant. The Ascendant indicates the way she views reality, and it indicates her fundamental capacity from which her self-expression springs.* The Ascendant is associated with awareness or consciousness itself. Communication is very important to her, serving as a framework for her activities. This is also indicated by her Natural Disposition in a Mutable sign, Mercury as her Scout Planet, and the

* See the sign Gemini and "The Mercury Pattern" in this text.

Mutable signs serving as the rim opposition of her Bowl Pattern. This would indicate a curiosity and thirst for knowledge. Education would be a necessity for her. She would need more than one interest and she would rarely lose control because her ingenuity would provide solutions to any challenge. She would search for personal intellectual security amid her constantly changing experiences. She would need changes of atmosphere and would like to travel. She would be a nonconformist, and she would feel that she must maintain her separateness, because she feels she is different from those around her.

She has the Gemini-Pisces, Mercury-Neptune duad of Gemini rising,* which gives her an image-making ability enabling her to see things in her mind's eye as if they were actual realities.† This ability would indicate talent in art, writing, photography, film-making, and design engineering. This would give her a desire to read occult literature and investigate psychic mysteries. This would also give her an interest in psychology, alternate states of consciousness, and sociological matters related to hospitals and institutions (these interests have all been confirmed by Joan).

Her Ascendant is positive, indicating that she has leadership qualities and that she is self-initiating, and that she can start out aggressively. However, because the ruler of her Ascendant is in the receptive sign of Cancer, she will take ideas and thoughts home to digest and evaluate them to see if they can be used in her creative efforts. This is because Mercury is in the second house of values and its exaltation sign is on the ninth and tenth houses, making her very aware of how these values will affect her status.

Mercury is in a Cardinal, Water sign and rules her first and fifth houses, indicating that her mind is influenced by emotional patterns which would cause her to look at the facts that are important to her and ignore others. This position of Mercury would give her a good memory because of the emotional intensity that would be associated with her thoughts. She would also absorb information subliminally or learn by osmosis, and much of her mental processes occur on an unconscious level, although they would manifest as conscious intent.

Mercury in Cancer in the second house would give her good business ability, especially in dealing with food, domestic and consumer products, and real estate. Mercury in the second house indicates that she would think a lot about money and business affairs. Her value system would be

* See *The Zodiac Within Each Sign.*
† See "The Neptune Pattern" and the "Mercury Pattern" in this text.

based on that which would produce concrete, practical results. She would pursue her education in order to improve her earning power. Inherited money would be kept as a nest egg. Mercury is in the eighth duad of Cancer, which is the Cancer-Aquarius, Moon-Uranus-Saturn duad, indicating that her home would be used as a meeting place for friends and group activities, and her close friends would be treated like family members. This duad would indicate that her home would be equipped with electric gadgets and have unusual home furnishings, and the architecture of the home itself would be unusual. Because of the Uranus influence she would demand freedom in her family relationships in order to be free to pursue her own interests and to be able to come and go as she pleased. Mercury rules her fifth house, and this duad of Cancer with its Uranus influence would indicate that she would experiment in applying the latest theories of child psychology in her relationship with her children. She would be interested in their intellectual development and want her children to develop in a free and unique way.

The Sun rules the dynamic expression of energy in the process of creation. Joan's Sun is in Leo in the second house, and wherever the Sun is found in the horoscope is where the individual must shine. Her Sun is in the creative, Fixed, Fire sign of Leo. It rules her third and fourth houses. Wherever the sign Leo is found in the chart it gives the individual a managerial capacity for acting as a central dramatic figure around which others gather. Therefore, with the Sun in the second house she would manage money and resources, information, and children, because Leo rules children. With the Sun in Leo she would have a lot of confidence and could tackle large or difficult projects. Because of her creative powers and optimism derived from the Fire sign Leo and because it is a Fixed sign, once she chooses her goal she will not be deterred by opposition, difficulty, or frustration. The creativity of Leo, a Fire sign, on her third- and fourth-house cusps indicates that she could shine through writing, communication, drama, the arts, children and their education, and creative activities in the home. She would be magnanimous, creative, and authoritative. She would pursue both work and play with complete dedication to the moment. Pluto is conjunct the Sun, giving her much magnetism, power, and vitality. Providence helps her when she needs it most,* for new fields of action will open at times when there does not seem to be a visible solution to problems. She would dislike repetition. Once she sees the point, she could become quite impa-

* See "The Sun Pattern" and also the sign Leo in this text.

tient with any further rhetoric. Because her Sun is so strong in her horoscope, having seven aspects to it plus being the focal planet in her double sextile and involved in the double semisextile, the creative and performing arts and her children would have a significant place in her life. Because Leo is the natural ruler of the fifth house of children, she would not condone any adverse criticism of her children by others.

The Sun is sextile to Uranus and Saturn, indicating that she would have many opportunities to achieve her ambitions and that she would shoulder her responsibilities and work to secure anything she has gained, especially where inheritance or joint money are concerned. This is further confirmed by Saturn ruling the eighth house of joint monies and legacies and being posited in the twelfth house, indicating that it would represent her hidden support. Because Uranus is part of the double sextile configuration, it indicates that she has much willpower and a perceptive mentality that allows her to accomplish things that others only dream about. She could be a leader of movements and a reformer. She would inspire confidence in others and portray a sense of the dramatic that would make her accepted and obeyed, an asset considering that she has five children. Uranus in Gemini in the twelfth house indicates that she would want to search into her unconscious. She would go on a quest for a higher spiritual identity in the inner reaches of her mind, and because Uranus is exalted in the sign Scorpio she would have great intuition that borders on clairvoyance. Her friends would confide their secrets to her. She would also work behind the scenes for humanitarian or scientific goals. This would also give her an interest in astrology.

With her Uranus in Gemini she was born into a generation of people who are destined to a new way of thinking, with pioneering concepts in science, literature, education, electronics, and communication. Uranus being conjunct Saturn would make her restless, and she would alternate between this restlessness and disciplined organization. She would have a need to be exposed to new ideas and social contacts. This conjunction of Uranus and Saturn would indicate she understands the underlying law that we create our destiny with our minds, and this conjunction would give her the ability to break habitual living patterns as a result of her awareness of alternate modes of activity. Uranus is in the fourth duad of Gemini, which is the Gemini-Virgo, Mercury-Mercury duad indicating that she would be concerned with a practical application of her knowledge, and yet she would scatter her energies at times.

Although she does not have any aspects to Mercury other than the semisextile to her Ascendant, Mercury is in parallel position to Venus and Jupiter, giving her the power to attract and expand, using the power of the lesser benefic Venus and the greater benefic Jupiter.* These parallels have the connotation of conjunctions.

Joan's Sun is sextile Neptune, adding to her image-making power and adding to her ability to translate it into reality or concrete manifestation, indicated by Neptune in the practical sign Virgo. She could even focus on areas such as empire-building and acquiring wealth and power. This sextile also gives her a keen sensitivity to the joys and sufferings of others, which would be combined with mystical insights and a humanitarian outlook. Her Neptune is in the Virgo-Leo, Mercury-Sun duad, indicating vitality and staying power with the ability to be an excellent teacher and worker with young people. This duad would indicate that she would assume a position of leadership and authority and would not remain in a subordinate position for long. She would be authoritative about details and see that others did not neglect small but important matters. She would dramatize her work or her profession and have the ability to inspire others with greater enthusiasm in the performance of their tasks. Thus she would have the ability to influence the attitudes of others in a subtle way. Her Neptune is in Virgo, the sign of health, and placed in the fourth house, indicating that she was born at a time when the ghosts of the Depression were still influencing the thoughts and actions of the people and the materialistic value of the dollar. Neptune in this fourth house would indicate strong unconscious ties with the family of a karmic origin.† One of her parents would be a source of concern to her, probably the mother, because of the mother's psychological problems. Or there could be secrets about the family or home life. The Sun is also conjunct Pluto, indicating tremendous energy at her disposal and giving her the ability to regenerate and change herself as well as her surroundings (Pluto in the third house). This would come about by the proper use of her vitality, creative ability, and resources, represented by the Sun in the second house.

It is important that her will be brought into harmony with the Divine Will, for if she fails to do this her efforts could backfire and cause her self-undoing. Pluto is in her third house, indicating higher forms of energy affecting the destiny of all mankind; therefore this conjunction could develop into a power complex. At this point, it is well for her to remember that her will and power come from the universal source of

* See "The Jupiter Pattern" and "The Venus Pattern" in this text.

† See Neptune in the signs and houses in *The Astrologer's Handbook*.

energy and she must maintain harmony with it. Pluto in her third house gives her a penetrating mind and strong opinions, and she will not compromise her beliefs unless factual evidence proves her wrong. Her original creative ideas will attract friends and partners who will help her utilize and improve her ideas. Pluto in the third indicates that she will travel for secret or mysterious reasons, encountering strange experiences in her travel. Her Pluto is in the third duad of Leo which is the Leo-Libra, Sun-Venus duad, again indicating her artistic abilities and that she is very romantic and attractive to the opposite sex because of her charm, grace, magnetism, and self-confidence. This also indicates that she would be kind and firmly just in the handling of her children.

The next aspect is a minor aspect,* the Moon inconjunct Jupiter. Both of these planets are involved with the last half of life (the Moon is the ruler of the Natural fourth-house sign Cancer and Jupiter is exalted there). This would indicate that she would have to watch her weight. She could make difficulties for herself by taking on more than she could handle, or she could become involved with someone who overextended his total resources at some time and made demands on her that could upset her equilibrium. She could also take over work that was left unfinished or improperly executed, and this could also cause emotional upset from time to time. Legal complications and religious attitudes in the family environment could interfere with her happiness. There could be legal problems over property, joint finances, and inheritance. This aspect would indicate a need to do something of major consequence, and because of this she would find it difficult to take care of all the tasks that she assigns to herself. The Moon and Jupiter are the two planets involved in this aspect. Jupiter is in the first house in Cancer, affecting her personality; the Moon rules Cancer which is on the second house cusp, affecting her earning ability, possessions, and values. Jupiter rules the seventh house of marriage and partnerships. The Moon is in the sixth, indicating that these conditions affect her work and her health.

The Moon opposition Uranus indicates that any kind of psychic involvement which does not serve a useful purpose in her spiritual unfoldment should be avoided; however, this aspect could be used in the study of astrology, giving her unusual insights. Because Uranus is part of the double semisextile and the double sextile configuration and involved in the opposition of the Moon, she could change her residence frequently. She could also change her moods and attitudes, which would

* See *That Inconjunct Quincunx: The Not So Minor Aspect.*

confuse others. This also indicates that she would acquire sudden new acquaintances.

The Moon is also trine to Pluto, giving her the ability to know just when and where to act with the most efficient use of her energy and resources. Pluto rules the sign Scorpio which is on her sixth-house cusp of health and work, indicating almost supernatural energy, powers of concentration, and a strong will. This would also indicate an interest in systems of self-development and health-building, such as yoga, diet, and nutrition. Pluto co-rules the sign Aries, which is intercepted in the eleventh house involving her friends, groups, goals, and objectives, and because Aries is a Cardinal sign and also a Fire sign, and because Pluto is placed in a Fire sign, she could become an inspired leader. Pluto is exalted in the sign Leo, which is on her third- and fourth-house cusps, indicating that her ideas, communications, comings and goings, and her home would be involved in these interests and expressions.

The next major aspect is the Venus square to Neptune. Venus in Cancer is involved in a hidden square to Neptune in Virgo.* Venus is also involved in a hidden trine to the Midheaven and is sextile to the north Node. Venus is in the sensitive, receptive, Water sign of Cancer, indicating that her feelings can be easily hurt; therefore, she would hide her vulnerability behind a dignified exterior. This would also indicate that her moods would fluctuate and be unpredictable. Venus is in the first house indicating that there would be an important need for financial and domestic security. Venus rules marriage, and the second and seventh houses in the Natural Zodiac, indicating that marriage would be the means by which she would have a stable domestic life where she could cherish her family and own her own home. Because Venus is square to Neptune, she would need a demonstration of affection in order to feel secure and loved. Venus in Cancer would indicate that she would want her home to be a place of beauty and comfort and a focus for special activities (Venus rules the fifth where Libra is intercepted). Venus in Cancer gives her a delicate femininity which eventually expresses itself in a maternal way. She likes to keep house for those she loves and give love and affection to her children.

Venus is in a Cardinal sign and in the first house, indicating that she will initiate action when she is bored and lonely; however, because Venus is in a receptive, feminine Water sign there is a definite power of attraction which through her ability to empathize with others brings

* See hidden aspects in triplicities and quadruplicities in this text.

about the action she needs. This position is very sensitive, indicating that she could be easily hurt by social mistreatment or neglect. This first-house position gives her personal grace, a pleasing manner, physical beauty, a friendly demeanor, and a manner which is socially outgoing and active in her efforts to develop friendship and romance. She would like beautiful clothes and things that would enhance her personal appearance. Her ability to mix socially would result in business, romantic, and marital opportunities. The Venus-Neptune square would indicate emotional problems connected with the unconscious mind and the imagination; this is also indicated by Venus ruling her twelfth house. This could be indicative of a desire to live in a fantasy world in order to avoid some of the harsher realities of life. This is also reinforced by Neptune being square to her Ascendant and Descendant and inconjunct her Midheaven, indicating that at times she would want to escape from domestic and professional duties through daydreaming, friends, or group activities. Both of these planets are placed in angular houses, making this a strong aspect, and when set off by a transit can bring about difficult events with which she must deal. This square also indicates that there is danger of a scandal through dubious relationships, romantic or otherwise, or a scandal through a financial involvement of some kind. Venus as well as Mars deals with sex, and sex could be the grounds for an attack. Her marital happiness could be in danger by lack of honesty and directness. These emotional complexes could be indicative of sexual fantasies which could cause self-undoing because Venus rules the twelfth.

At times she could be lazy and disorderly, yet this state would be accompanied by a feeling that she should get busy and get things in order. However, because of Venus trining her Midheaven and her fourth-house cusp (hidden aspect), she would have harmony in the home. This trine of Venus to the Midheaven would indicate that her ambitions would be continuous, and also that her beauty, charm, and social grace would win her the favor of people in important places. This harmony in the home, which creates a favorable social atmosphere, gives her status. Venus trine the Midheaven and sextile the fourth-house cusp would affect the first house, rules the twelfth house, and it also rules Libra intercepted in the fifth house, and is exalted in the eleventh house. The tenth house and fourth are also affected.

The next aspect is Mars sextile the Ascendant. Mars is in the Leo-Taurus, Sun-Venus duad, which indicates that she could express herself dramatically. This also indicates her leadership ability and self-confidence, which in turn inspire confidence in others. She would be competitive in whatever activities are important to her, and she would want to be in the forefront of what interests her in her environment. She would have strong opinions and beliefs, and she could assert herself aggressively when she wants to obtain and deliver information. This could make her a good newspaper reporter, except that Mars in the third house is in opposition to the Midheaven, indicating conflict with authority figures.

Jupiter is in Cancer in her first house and is very strong because it is in its sign of exaltation.* It is posited in an angular house, and rules the angular seventh house, indicating that Joan came from a good family background, that she would be taught religious and moral principles at an early age, that she would want a secure, friendly, comfortable home environment, that she would have a strong maternal instinct with an inclination to mother the world, and that she could inherit money from her family. This Jupiter in the first also indicates that she would like eventually to be regarded as an authority in some field of religion, philosophy, or education. This is because Jupiter is disposited by the Moon in Sagittarius, a positive, masculine sign.† She would pursue higher studies in these fields as a means to outfit herself in her search for her role in life. Because Jupiter is in her first house she would have a Divine protection as if Providence were always looking out for her.

Referring back to the Point Focus opposition in her horoscope of the Moon in opposition to Saturn, it must be pointed out that the transiting Moon activates this opposition several times in the month. This opposition is set off when the Moon enters 9 degrees of Gemini and 9 degrees of Sagittarius and the influence lasts until the Moon has passed 11 degrees and 35 minutes, also when the Moon transits the midpoint of this opposition on either side when in the signs Virgo and Pisces. The other factor that needs special attention is that Mercury being her Scout Planet (the planet ahead of the Sun in a clockwise direction) and the Sun being the planet of lowest degree, 0° Leo 44′ 54″, and Leo ruling the third house of Mercury's domain, plus the fourth house, indicate that the information she gathers and the work she has chosen to do have a tendency to overwhelm her whenever a transiting planet enters into a new sign and makes its first aspect to the Sun. These transits should all be itemized so that she can plan her work schedule in a way that will be productive, thus using astrology in a positive manner.‡

* See strength and weaknesses of the planets in this text.
† See the chapter on dispositors of the planets in *The Astrologer's Handbook*.
‡ For transits see *Predictive Astrology*.

Because Venus is the planet of next lowest degree and because Venus and the Sun have more aspects than any of her other natal planets, the periods when transiting planets enter into new signs and the type of aspects they make to the Sun and Venus should be carefully worked out and applied.

Because a human being has many facets to his character and many ways of handling his life, a whole book could be written on the details of these experiences. What was given here covered the outstanding traits and characteristics of the individual, Joan Stable. When these characteristics are brought out in an astrological analysis, some of the statements can appear to be contradictory. However, there are many facets to a human being; hidden violence can exist within individuals while they are displaying a peaceful demeanor. Or individuals can be warm and friendly at one time and cold and aloof at another time. All of these characteristics can be contained within one individual and interact in his or her self-expression at different times.

This is to acknowledge to the readers of this text that my husband and I have found my first astrological reading to be profoundly accurate and stimulating.

JOAN STABLE

Bibliography

American Federation of Astrologers, Inc. *AFA Astrological Atlas of the United States*. Tempe, Arizona: American Federation of Astrologers, 1975.

Bailey, Alice A. *Esoteric Astrology*. New York: Lucis Publishing Co., 1951.

Blavatsky, H. P. *The Secret Doctrine*. Pasadena, California: Theosophical University Press, 1893.

Dalton, Joseph G. *The Spherical Basis of Astrology*. Richmond: Macoy Publishing and Masonic Supply Company, 1927.

Doane, Doris Chase. *Time Changes in the USA*. Downey, California: Graphic Arts Press, 1966, revised 1973.

Heindel, Max. *The Message of the Stars*. Oceanside, California: Rosicrucian Fellowship.

Jones, Marc Edmund. *The Essentials of Astrological Analysis*. New York: Sabian Publishing Society, 1960.

Ephemeriden 1890–1950. Zurich: Verlag, Max S. Metz AG., 1971.

Sakoian, Frances and Acker, Louis. *The Astrologer's Handbook*. New York: Harper & Row, 1973.

———. *The Astrology of Human Relations*. New York: Harper & Row, 1976.

———. *Predictive Astrology*. New York: Harper & Row, 1977.

———. *The Zodiac Within Each Sign, Interpreting the Horoscope with Decanates and Duads*. Arlington, Massachusetts: N.E.S.A. Publishing Company.

Suggested Reading

The Astrologer's Handbook by Frances Sakoian and Louis Acker. Published 1973 by Harper & Row, New York.

Astrology, Mundane and Spiritual by S. R. Parchment. Published 1933 by American Federation of Astrologers, P.O. Box 22040, Tempe, Arizona 85282.

The Astrology of Human Relationships by Frances Sakoian and Louis Acker. Published 1976 by Harper & Row, New York.

The Astrology of Personality by Dane Rudhyar. Published 1936 by Lucis Publishing Co., New York.

Esoteric Astrology by Alice Bailey. Published 1951 by Lucis Publishing Co., New York.

The Essentials of Astrological Analysis by Marc Edmund Jones. Published 1946 by Sabian Publishing Society, Theosophical Publishing House, Wheaton, Illinois.

The Guide to Horoscope Interpretation by Marc Edmund Jones. Published 1946 by Sabian Publishing Society, Theosophical Publishing House, Wheaton, Illinois.

The Lunation Cycle by Dane Rudhyar. Published 1967, distributed by Llewellyn Publications, St. Paul, Minnesota.

Meditations on the Signs of the Zodiac by John Jocelyn. Published 1966 by Multimedia Press, The Naylor Company, San Antonio, Texas.

Phases of the Moon by Marilyn Busteed, Richard Tiffany, and Dorothy Wergin. Published 1974 by Shambhala Publications, Inc., 2045 Francisco Street, Berkeley, California 94709.

Predictive Astrology by Frances Sakoian and Louis Acker. Published 1977 by Harper & Row, New York.

The Pulse of Life by Dane Rudhyar. Published 1963 by Service, The Hague, Netherlands, distributed by Llewellyn Publications, St. Paul, Minnesota.

Saturn by Alan Leo. Published 1970 by Samuel Weiser, Inc., 734 Broadway, New York, New York 10003.

The Secret Doctrine by H. P. Blavatsky. Published 1893 by Theosophical Publishing House, London.

Studies in Astrology by Elman Bacher. Published 1962 by The Rosicrucian Fellowship, Oceanside, California.

The Twelve Labors of Hercules by Alice A. Bailey. Published 1974 by New Age Press, Inc., Lucis Press Limited, 235 Finchley Road, Hampstead, London NW36LS, England.

The Zodiac Within Each Sign by Frances Sakoian and Louis Acker. Distributed by N.E.S.A., 1 Monadnock Road, Arlington, Massachusetts 02174.

Glossary

Air Signs Gemini, Libra, and Aquarius.

Angle Houses The first, fourth, seventh, and tenth houses.

Arabic Part An imaginary point in a horoscope, the "Part of Fortune" being the most popular, that denotes the focused concentration of certain energies, for example, good fortune, illness, marriage, etc.

Ascendant Most clearly defined as that degree of the Zodiac coming over the Eastern horizon at the particular time and location of a birth or event (that is, at the True Local Time and Geocentric Latitude of the occurrence).

Aspect A condition in the Zodiacal relationship (Angle) between two heavenly bodies, or between one such body and an Angle, house cusp, or imaginary point, where there arises an implied astrological significance.

Cardinal Signs Aries, Cancer, Libra, and Capricorn.

Conjunction An aspect of 0°; it is achieved when two heavenly bodies, or one such body and an Angle, house cusp, or imaginary point, are found at precisely the same degree of Zodiacal longitude.

Cusp That imaginary point or line which separates two distinct signs of the Zodiac or two distinct houses of a horoscope.

Cutting Planet That planet in a horoscope that is found facing the largest open Zodiacal space in a clockwise direction.

Decanate One of three divisions—0° to 10°, 10° to 20°, 20° to 30°—of a Zodiacal sign.

Descendant In contrast to the Ascendant, most clearly defined as that degree of the Zodiac setting on the Western horizon at the particular time and location of a birth or event (that is, at the True Local Time and Geocentric Latitude of the occurrence).

Duad One of twelve divisions, each 2½° (that is, 0° to 2½°, 2½° to 5°, etc.), of a Zodiacal sign. There are twelve signs in the Zodiac; hence, there are 144 duads, twelve to each sign.

Dynamic Focus The closest (in orb) or nearest-to-exact square or opposition in a horoscope.

Earth Signs Taurus, Virgo, and Capricorn.

Ecliptic That plane formed by the Earth, in its orbit, as it sweeps its path around the Sun.

Ephemeris An astrological compilation (usually a book) that lists *at least* the Zodiacal longitudes of the Sun, Moon, and planets, at Noon or Midnight Greenwich Mean Time, for each day of the solar or Earth year.

Esoteric Astrology Knowledge and understanding of the secrets or metaphysics of the astrological discipline.

Exaltation That sign of the Zodiac from which a planet derives its power, meaning, and significance in expression; in essence, the meaning behind a planet's expression, "why" it behaves the way it does.

Feminine-Receptive Signs Taurus, Cancer, Virgo, Scorpio, Capricorn, and Pisces.

Fire Signs Aries, Leo, and Sagittarius.

Fixed Signs Taurus, Leo, Scorpio, and Aquarius.

Grand Trine A configuration composed of three planets where two of these bodies are each trine a third *and* each other.

Grand Square A configuration composed of four planets where one of these bodies both opposes a second *and* squares a third and fourth that, too, are in opposition.

Greenwich Mean Time A world-accepted standard of reference with regard to time and longitudinal distances (measured in degrees). All time meridians or zones are measured from the degree of longitude passing through the Royal Observatory located at Greenwich, England—labelled 0° Longitude.

Hemispheric Divisions The half-circles of the horoscope defined when the wheel is divided by either the Meridian or the Horizon—that is, the Midheaven/Nadir axis or the Ascendant/Descendant axis.

Hemispheric Emphasis Occurs when there are more planets located in one hemisphere than in its opposite–that is, Northern vs. Southern and Eastern vs. Western.

Horoscope From the Greek *horoskopos–hora,* "hour," and *skopeo,* "to view." A scheme or figure of the heavens at a given time and place.

House A division of the horoscope that concerns itself with specific areas of activity in an individual's life.

Local Mean Time A time calculation based upon the moment that the Sun crossed the Midheaven at a given location.

Logarithms (log) Proportional parts of a quadrant, expressed numerically, that permit the mathematical computation of astrological positions by addition and subtraction, rather than by multiplication and division.

Mental Chemistry A tool used by astrologers to understand mental responses.

Meridian An imaginary line or circle on the Earth that passes through both poles and is used to denote longitudes of locations on its surface. Also, in astrology, an imaginary line in the heavens passing through its poles and the zenith at any location.

Midheaven The Zodiacal point at which the meridian falls at a particular time and location on a particular day.

Mutable Signs Gemini, Virgo, Sagittarius, and Pisces.

Nadir The Zodiacal point found precisely opposite the Midheaven.

Natural Disposition Refers to the psychological slanting inferred by the number and quality of oppositions occurring in a horoscope.

Natural Zodiac The traditional or natural order of signs of the Zodiac, beginning with 0° of Aries.

Node The line formed by the intersection of a planet's plane or orbit and the Ecliptic; placements in the Zodiac are usually referred to as "Nodal Points."

Orb The space within which an aspect is judged to be effective.

Planetary Patterns Astrological tools that depict important characteristics of an individual.

Point Focus A planet that is part of a configuration and has special emphasis.

Positive-Masculine Signs Aries, Gemini, Leo, Libra, Sagittarius, and Aquarius.

Quadruplicity A grouping of four signs that displays a particular quality of expression–Cardinal/initiatory, Fixed/stable and Mutable/adaptable.

Scout Planet The planet that immediately precedes the Sun in a clockwise direction.

Sextile An aspect of 60°; it is achieved when two heavenly bodies, or one such body and an Angle, house cusp, or imaginary point, are found precisely 60° from one another in Zodiacal longitude.

Sidereal Time Literally, "star time." A method of reckoning time based on two successive passes of the *same* star to a point in the heavens.

Square An aspect of 90°; it is achieved when two heavenly bodies, or one such body and an Angle, house cusp, or imaginary point, are found precisely 90° from one another in Zodiacal longitude.

Stellium Four or more planets which, together, constitute a cluster.

Sun Signs Those portions of the year–about 30 days each–in which the Sun is said to be passing through each particular sign of the Zodiac.

Trailing Planet That planet in a horoscope that is found facing the largest open Zodiacal space in a counter-clockwise direction.

Traveling the Planets Determining, by use of an ephemeris, the correct Zodiacal positions of the planets for a particular time, date, and place.

Trine An aspect of 120°; it is achieved when two heavenly bodies, or one such body and an Angle, house cusp, or imaginary point, are found precisely 120° from one another in Zodiacal longitude.

Triplicity A grouping of three signs that displays a particular temperament in expression–Fire/creative, Earth/practical, Air/intellectual, and Water/emotional.

Tropical Placidean A method of determining house cusps based on an Earth-centered view of the heavens.

Vernal Equinox That point in the Zodiac each solar year when the Sun's apparent position in relation to the Earth falls at precisely 0° of the Zodiacal sign Aries.

Water Signs Cancer, Scorpio, and Pisces.

Zenith That point in the heavens that is directly overhead at a particular location on the Earth's surface.

Zodiac The astrological division of the heavens into twelve signs, or individual quality-temperaments, each comprising exactly one-twelfth of a sweep of the heavens or 30° and totalling 360°.

Index